Culture

in a

Diverse

America

THE HISTORY OF COMMUNICATION
Robert W. McChesney and John C. Nerone, editors

A list of books in the series appears at the back of this book.

Print
Culture
in a
Diverse
America

Edited by
James P. Danky
and
Wayne A. Wiegand

UNIVERSITY OF ILLINOIS PRESS
URBANA AND CHICAGO

UNIVERSITY OF ILLINOIS PRESS
1325 SOUTH OAK STREET
CHAMPAIGN, ILLINOIS 61820-6903
WWW.PRESS.UILLINOIS.EDU

This book is printed on acid-free paper.

Library of Congress Cataloging-in-Publication Data
Print culture in a diverse America / edited by
James P. Danky and Wayne A. Wiegand.
p.   cm. — (The history of communication)
Includes bibliographical references (p.   ) and index.
ISBN 0-252-02398-6 (acid-free paper).
ISBN 0-252-06699-5 (pbk. : acid-free paper).
1. Ethnic press—United States.
2. American newspapers—Foreign language press.
3. American periodicals—Foreign language press.
I. Danky, James Philip, 1947-   .
II. Wiegand, Wayne A., 1946-   .
III. Series.
PN4882.P75   1998
302.2'244'0973—dc21
97-33935
CIP

Digitally reprinted from the first paperback printing

For John Cole,

friend,

supporter,

inspiration

CONTENTS

ACKNOWLEDGMENTS

At the annual meeting of the Advisory Board of the Center for the History of Print Culture in Modern America (1993), the chairman, Carl Kaestle, proposed that the Center sponsor a national conference that would highlight new scholarship in print culture. During that autumn, the codirectors worked with colleagues on the University of Wisconsin–Madison campus as well as around the United States and even Europe to draft a call for papers for "Print Culture in a Diverse America." In late 1994 the conference proposals were carefully evaluated by a committee consisting of Advisory Board members Rima Apple, Steve Vaughn, and Sue Searing, codirectors Wayne Wiegand of the University of Wisconsin–Madison and James Danky of the State Historical Society of Wisconsin, and Maureen Hady, the Center's assistant director. The diligence of this group remains a warm memory and useful example of collective intelligence and cooperation.

In May 1995, Maureen organized a flawless conference. Over two days a most diverse group of scholars—from graduate students to senior faculty—shared their work and created new bonds. Maureen was ably assisted in her organizing efforts by a number of Society staff members, including Carol Crossan, Amy Castle, John Cherney, Traci Regis, Maridelys Detres, and Nathan Greer.

The editors of this volume gladly dedicate it to John Cole, Director of the Center for the Book in the Library of Congress, who has been a good friend of the Center for the History of Print Culture in Modern America since its founding. The two grants from his office were instrumental in the Center's early work; his wise counsel and advice over the years since the Center for the History of Print Culture in Modern America was established in 1992 has helped to define its mission in the emerging world of print culture studies.

We greatly appreciate the support of Robert McChesney, of the University of Wisconsin–Madison, and John Nerone, of the University of Illinois at Urbana–Champaign, who edit the History of Communication series for the University of Illinois Press. At the Press, Karen Hewitt and her assistant, Madeleine Marchaterre, kept us on track and helped to produce a much better book than we first envisioned. In Madison, Paul Hass, a longtime friend and colleague, brought his editorial talents to bear and also much improved the final manuscript. The enthusiastic support of Kevin Graffagnino, Library Director of the State Historical Society of Wisconsin, was critical to the success of the enterprise. The Center's "home" is in the School of Library and Information Studies, where it has benefited from the advice of Jane Robbins, Jim Krikelas, and from Louise Robbins, the current director.

To all these friends and colleagues who generously gave of their time, our thanks.

Print
Culture
in a
Diverse
America

Introduction: Theoretical Foundations for Analyzing Print Culture as Agency and Practice in a Diverse Modern America

WAYNE A. WIEGAND

For the past five hundred years, most of humankind has been informed by print. In the United States, for example, all people in America's multicultural and multiclass society have for two centuries used or been influenced by print, sometimes for common purposes, sometimes for divisive purposes. In the early nineteenth century, theologians frequently cited a single text—the Bible—both to support and oppose slavery. In the late nineteenth century, advocates of public libraries, on the other hand, argued that making many texts (the "best reading," they called it) freely available to most citizens would strengthen democracy and serve the common good. In recent years, scholars from a variety of academic disciplines interested in studying this complex phenomenon have begun calling it "book history," "print culture history," or even "print culture studies." Some have argued that this new interdisciplinary area will become as important as the history of art and the history of science. Others have argued that it has the potential to close a perplexing division in the humanities between theory and empiricism.[1]

But such predictions are probably exaggerated. At this writing, print culture history might be better characterized as one manifestation of a rapidly emerging scholarship on reading within a much broader shift in the focus of humanities research "from culture as text to culture as agency and practice."[2] This scholarship on reading has also evolved close contacts with cultural studies; and, like cultural studies, it has benefited from the recent developments of a series of theoretical frames—including postmodernism, neo-Marxism, feminist theory, Foucauldian archaeology, and New Historicism—all of which suggest that the realities we have come to know are at least in part a product of our own making.[3] Janice Radway divides this scholarship on reading into four categories:[4] (1) literacy studies, (2) reader-response theory, (3) ethnographies of reading, and (4) a social history of books that I am here calling "print culture history."[5]

Literacy studies were largely inaugurated by two books published in 1979. In *The Literacy Myth: Literacy and Social Structure in the Nineteenth Century City,* Harvey Graff examines the evolution of literacy in nineteenth-century urban America through multiple lenses, including social class, the relationship of power among groups, and the efforts of some to use literacy to control others. In *The Printing Press as an Agent of Change: Communications and Cultural Transformation in Early Modern Europe,* Elizabeth Eisenstein argues that the West was transformed not so much by its ability to read and write as by the capacity of a recently invented printing process to reproduce and thereby diffuse that writing. Technical work was much more rapidly duplicated, Eisenstein notes, and research more readily preserved and circulated. The vernacular became celebrated and homogenized, modern criticism was introduced, and a set of market circumstances evolved in which authors became celebrities. Graff's and Eisenstein's scholarship demonstrates that identifying the context in which literacy was (and is) practiced is vitally important to understanding print culture history.[6]

Much of reader-response theory grows out of the works of Wolfgang Iser and Hans Robert Jauss.[7] They argue against the conventional approach to reading. At one time or another in the past, they might point out, almost everyone reading this essay probably had completed a set of literature courses in secondary and higher education that required them to ask the question, "What did the author mean in the text?" Much in-class discussion of the texts centered around that question; frequently, students realized, their grades depended upon their ability to parrot the textual interpretation of their instructor. But for Iser, Jauss, and other reader-response theorists, meaning in the text is not an object to be described but an effect to be experienced. Basic to this approach is a conviction that a universally valid interpretation of any text is untenable. Readers search for meaning in the text, and the search is heavily influenced by their own contemporary situations, contemporary and historical norms, all of which vary from one socioeconomic group to another and over time. Readers cannot detach themselves from the texts; the act of reading links them to the texts and at the same time induces them to create conditions necessary for the effectiveness of that text.

Part of this creative process involves what Iser and Jauss call the "moving" or "wandering" viewpoint. They argue that the meaning of a text is heavily influenced by the consistency of attention to reading. The object of the text is imagined through different consecutive phases of reading that require a participant to situate herself inside the text. The act of reading thus becomes a continual interplay between modified expectations and transferred memories, and construction of the connections between these expectations and memories is almost entirely the province of the reader. So what does this "wandering viewpoint" produce? The mind, in its never-ending quest to make sense of the world around it, builds a consistency out of the process of selection that then forms a basis for comprehension. The text, in part, becomes an event in which the reader reacts to what she herself has produced. Involvement is a condition of the experience. But the interaction between the text and the reader is asymmetrical, forced by the necessary conditions of interaction. Because there is no face-to-face contact between author and reader, there is no check on the reader to test the accuracy of author intention. As a result, for the reader, texts contain blanks and negations that she must fill in or resolve. These uncertain and indefinite qualities of a text then serve to stimulate. Blanks function as potential connections because they designate vacancies in the overall system of the text. They force the need to combine, to connect, and in connecting blanks the reader's mind is triggered into acts of ideation—a highly creative activity with potential for high satisfaction.

In the United States, reader-response theory has been taken up most persuasively by Stanley Fish, author of the widely influential book *Is There a Text in This Class?*[8] Fish argues that readers do not read like literary critics; instead, they "poach"—meaning they raid a text for their own purposes. Much of this poaching is driven by an individual's needs. Texts are actually sites at which readers activate particular signifiers and follow strategic patterns that are not necessarily intentionally or consciously manipulated. In fact, readers function as members of particular interpretive communities—groups of people connected along demographic lines such as gender, race, creed, age, class, or sexual orientation—and thus their poaching follows patterns common to the group. Taken together, Iser, Jauss, and Fish have shown that in the reading process the reader is an active agent who exercises a great deal of creativity in making sense of a text.

The category "ethnographies of reading" is probably best illustrated in a recently published collection of essays entitled *The Ethnography of Reading*. The essays variously address subjects that range from ancient rabbinical readings of Hebrew scriptures to the scribes and storytellers of pre-modern Japan. What binds them all together are attempts to define the contexts of the actual reading practices exercised by particular groups at particular times. Especially useful for the present essay is Elizabeth

Long's "Textual Interpretation as Collective Action," in which she argues that the modern construction of the solitary reader ignores a thoroughly social base for reading. Long combines historical research into turn-of-the-century literary societies and reading clubs with an analysis of sixty groups of readers in Houston, Texas, during the 1980s to discover among them a "social infrastructure." She suggests that this infrastructure includes shared interpretive frameworks, shared participation in a set of institutions, shared social relations, and shared economic activities. She demonstrates how group members negotiate their readings with each other, with their cultures, and with their society. Along with other ethnographers of reading, Long shows that reading is a communal activity based in a social infrastructure grounded on shared interpretive frameworks and practiced in shared institutions.[9]

That brings us to our fourth category of the scholarship on reading: "book" (or what I am here calling "print culture") history. According to Robert Darnton, one of its foremost practitioners, book history constitutes "the social and cultural history of communication by print," the purpose of which is "to understand how ideas were transmitted through print and how exposure to the printed word affected the thought and behavior of mankind during the last five hundred years."[10] Print culture historians draw not only upon cultural and literacy studies, reader-response theory, and ethnographies of reading, they also harness a variety of theoretical frames that facilitated the shift in humanities research from culture as text to culture as agency and practice. "Basic to the history of the book is an understanding that literature is a human institution, part of a matrix of social and cultural forces from which it emerges, rather than a pure or abstract idea, independent of history," argues Michael Winship. Any publication, he says, "represents the state of technology and economic organization of its time. It both acts on and is acted upon by the social work and cultural environment of these historical collaborators and forces."[11]

Researchers working in print culture history ask questions such as: How have relations between authors, publishers, literary agents, booksellers, and distributors—and ultimately readers—changed in the five hundred years since the invention of movable type? What, how, and how much did people read? How did government legislation, censorship, or new print technologies affect authors and readers? How did print culture shape history and society? Generally, scholars in this branch of inquiry address issues related to the book as economic commodity, the political uses of print culture, and the historical sociology of the circulation and readership of print culture materials. They also unite several fields and in the United States have inspired numerous conferences and programs, many of which have been sponsored by the American Antiquarian Society's Program in the History of the Book in American Culture, established in 1983.

Interest in the subject has been building since the French cultural historians Lucien Febvre and Henri-Jean Martin developed a very influential *histoire du livre* in the 1950s. In effect, Febvre and Martin lifted book history from the domain of historians of printing by applying the techniques of social and economic history to the study of the impact of printed matter on human relations. In the process, they began to ask questions about why printed material was produced and read; they also began to analyze the cultural forces surrounding the use of printed materials as a lens to explore the social lives and *"mentalités"* of common people.[12] Then, in the 1970s, German book historians began to incorporate the reception theories of Iser and Jauss into their analyses in an attempt to gauge the extent and nature of the interpretation of texts. Many detected a shift in reading practices in the mid-eighteenth century from "intensive" (i.e., the reading of a few texts, such as the Bible, again and again to fathom deep and complex meanings) to "extensive" (i.e., the reading of many texts for broader understanding).[13]

American and British literary scholars harnessed the work of these German pioneers and began to look at the history of print culture through a variety of lenses. Some used theories of how readers respond to texts. Others tapped Marxist analysis to explore the relationship between literary production and social class. Some took up deconstruction's challenge to examine author intentions and the neutrality of texts. Yet others saw in the history of print culture new ways to analyze how texts become canonized. In recent years, literary scholars working these angles have begun to explore such diverse topics as working-class ideologies in nineteenth-century dime novels, the emergence of African-American periodicals, and the nature of women authors and their readers.[14]

Signs of growth in the field of print culture history abound. In 1991 the Society for the History of Authorship, Reading, and Publishing (SHARP) was founded. Since then SHARP has hosted an annual summer conference (with the locations alternating between the United States and abroad), and in 1998 SHARP published its first issue of *Book History,* a new serial intended for print culture scholars of all historical periods and countries. In 1992, the Pennsylvania State University established an interdisciplinary Center for the History of the Book. That same year the University of Wisconsin at Madison and the State Historical Society of Wisconsin joined forces to establish a Center for the History of Print Culture in Modern America. In 1994, two more initiatives occurred. In September, the Center for Southern Studies at the University of North Carolina at Chapel Hill established a study group on the history of the book in order to focus attention on print culture history in the Southeast; in October, scholars from English, history, journalism, and library and information studies and professional staff members from the library system at the University of Texas at Austin started a study group on the history of print culture in the Southwest. In 1995, Drew University established its Center for the History of the Book. All of these efforts have been assisted by the Library of Congress's Center for the Book, authorized by Congress in 1978 to promote reading. John Y. Cole, director of the center since 1979, maintains close ties to all organizational developments in print culture history scholarship.

In 1993, the National Endowment for the Humanities approved a $250,000 grant to the American Antiquarian Society (AAS) to produce a five-volume history of the book in the United States designed to examine the influence of print on the development of literacy, the formation of democracy, and the transmission of culture. Cambridge University Press will publish this project, as well as a multivolume "History of the Book in Great Britain" that is simultaneously underway. Both will attempt to do for the United States and Great Britain what a four-volume series that traces the history of French publishing and reading practices—*Histoire de l'édition française*[15]—has already done for that country. Work is well underway on multivolume book history projects for Germany, Italy, and Australia as well.

In 1992, the English department at the University of South Carolina instituted a Ph.D. minor in book history. In 1994, the University of London established a School of Advanced Study whose Centre for English Studies offers an interdisciplinary master's degree in the history of the book. The latter combines research and teaching expertise on the university's faculty with bibliographical and textual expertise on the professional staffs of institutions such as the British Library, the British Museum, and the Public Records Office. In 1998, the University of Wisconsin–Madison's Center for the History of Print Culture in Modern America initiated an interdisciplinary Ph.D. minor in print culture history unrestricted by geography or chronology.

All of these efforts have led to a substantial literature, first in Europe, then (since about 1980) in the United States. Print culture history was initially imported to the United States by influential American scholars studying European history, such as Elizabeth Eisenstein and Robert Darnton, who has contributed such well-received titles as *The Business of Enlightenment* and *The Great Cat Massacre and Other Episodes in French Cultural History*.[16] In the United States, much of the published literature in print culture history traces its origins to the American Antiquarian Society's Program in the History of the Book in American Culture. Because the society's library of 650,000 volumes and thousands of newspapers represents the major archives of the printed word in America before 1876, the AAS has been the principal center for bibliographical scholarship on American printing for more than a century. Since 1983 the AAS program has also facilitated and encouraged research by print culture scholars into its collections.[17] As a result, much of the research in Cathy Davidson, *Revolution and the Word* (1986), William J. Gilmore, *Reading Becomes a Necessity of Life* (1989), David Hall, *Worlds of Wonder, Days of Judgment* (1989), Michael Warner, *Letters of the Republic* (1990), Frankie Hutton, *Early Black Press in America* (1993), Ronald J. Zboray, *A Fictive People* (1993), Richard H. Brodhead, *Cultures of Letters* (1993), and Michael Winship, *American Literary Publishing in the Mid-Nineteenth Century* (1995) was done in AAS collections.[18]

But while the AAS program has pioneered in American print culture history scholarship, published research emanating from it has naturally and inevitably been limited by the nature of AAS collections, whose scope is limited to pre-1876 materials. As a result, primary sources that document the vastly more socioculturally diverse print culture history of the United States since 1876 are seriously understudied. Moreover, the field is significantly fragmented by geography. Much of this is evident in an article on the newly emerging history of print culture published in a 1993 issue of the *Chronicle of Higher Education*. Among the twenty-five titles Karen Winkler included in the selected list of recent works she compiled, eighteen relate to works on American print culture history. Of those eighteen, only three extend their scope of analysis into twentieth-century America, and only seven encompass people living west of the Appalachian Mountains. None cover important twentieth-century cultural institutions such as the American public library or print's role in the experiences of twentieth-century African Americans, women, labor groups, Native Americans, immigrants, Asian Americans, and gays, lesbians, and bisexuals.[19]

Primarily to address this gap, the Center for the History of Print Culture in Modern America was established in 1992 as a joint program of the University of Wisconsin at Madison and the State Historical Society of Wisconsin. The center's goal is to help determine the historical sociology of print in modern America (c. 1876 to the present) in all its culturally diverse manifestations. Its objectives include:

—encouraging the multidisciplinary study of print culture history on campus and serving as a multidisciplinary focus for research in print culture by scholars of modern American history throughout the country from such diverse fields as literature, sociology, political science, journalism, publishing, education, reading and library history, the history of science, and gender and ethnic studies;

—facilitating research into the rich print culture research collections owned by both library systems that focus on newspapers, periodicals, advertising, printed ephemera, and books (including school and college texts, children's literature, trade and scholarly monographs, and mass-market paperbacks);

—stimulating research into the print culture collections of groups whose gender, race, occupation, ethnicity, and sexual orientation (among other factors) have historically placed them on the periphery of power but who used print sources as one of the few means of expression available to them;

—aiding in the development of an international perspective on print culture in modern America, including the reception of American publishing abroad and foreign publishing in the United States, in English and other languages;

—and building upon the initiatives of the AAS program and working with the Center for the Book at the Library of Congress (and with the various state centers for the book) on joint programs, exhibits, colloquia, symposia, and publications.

◩

In May 1995, the Center for the History of Print Culture in Modern America hosted its first conference, "Print Culture in a Diverse America," in Madison, Wisconsin. The contents of the present volume were selected from among the presentations at that conference. Although they all take unique perspectives, the authors of the included essays have in some way drawn from cultural and literacy studies, reader-response theory, and/or ethnographies of reading. Each has, in turn, benefited in some way from one or more of the theoretical frames that helped foster the broader shift in the focus of humanities research from culture as text to culture as agency and practice.

In the first section, four authors focus on forgotten serials. Rudolph J. Vecoli analyzes how the Italian immigrant press helped construct a social reality for Italian Americans in the late nineteenth and early twentieth centuries. He examines the contents of titles published in major metropolitan centers, as well as in small towns, and covers centrist newspapers with large circulations as well as radical journals with limited readership. He concludes by suggesting that although print culture was important, it was not the only means used by immigrants to create their new world.

Norma Fay Green's study of *StreetWise*, one of the most significant newspapers produced by homeless people, peers inside the editorial, production, and distribution challenges of transforming a group of disenfranchised and inexperienced citizens into a functioning staff. The meaning of the empowering experience Green describes is a decisive counter to some of the most cherished beliefs many hold about writing and poverty.

In her essay on the *Boston Chronicle,* Violet Johnson calls attention to the diversity of African-American newspapers published in this century. By casting her analysis against the early twentieth-century ideology of Pan-Africanism, Johnson illuminates the separate world of blackness in Boston, identifies its Caribbean immigrant strains and the role of radical politics and nationalism, and establishes a rich social context for a new kind of press history.

Yumei Sun acknowledges that the vast literature on immigrants and their presses has been a significant source of knowledge and insight, but she argues that its East Coast and European focus has led print culture historians to overlook the experiences of immigrants from Asia and their publications. In the pages of San Francisco's major Chinese-language newspaper, *Chung Sai Yat Po,* during the first two decades of the twentieth century, she finds indicators of how San Francisco's Chinese community viewed itself. The newspaper, she argues, functioned as an agent for change and facilitated Chinese assimilation into the larger culture.

The "iron triangle" of race, class, and gender has often been criticized by academics seeking to recapture a history that depended upon white males' cultural production. In the world of print culture history, this view has created an approach that defines importance in economic terms and creates a field of vision too narrow to explain the world of texts and readers from more marginalized groups whose existences are evident in print culture primary sources such as newspapers, periodicals, poetry, and locally produced fiction. In their investigations, the four authors in the second section of this collection focus on texts that challenge the limited world of publishing that has long assumed center stage. In so doing, they uncover readers whose historical presence has often been ignored. Lynne M. Adrian has excavated one of the most idiosyncratic periodicals in American history: *"Hobo" News.* The pages of this publication offer a window into the world of rootless men and their self-portraits of life at the margins of society.

Education has long been viewed as an essential tool for those who want to enter the middle class. In his study of black magazines, such as the *Colored American Magazine, Crisis, Opportunity,* and *Alexander's,* Michael Fultz insists that such insight was not limited to whites. Fultz sets the political context for these journals and identifies how the long-term educational goals figured into the social context that African Americans sought to define in the 1920s.

Elizabeth McHenry resurrects the lives of a group of black female readers whose existence confronted two barriers: gender and race. In her investigation of African-American literary societies in the late nineteenth and early twentieth centuries, McHenry argues that they were created to serve part of the common goals of social progress and that they ultimately provided a necessary set of experiences that helped ground writers who later contributed to the Harlem Renaissance.

Osage, Iowa, may be a long way from Harlem, but the importance of this small northern Iowa community for print culture historians, Christine Pawley argues, in fact lies in its very common, small-town, American features. By making inventive use of local public library records over a five-year period at the end of the nineteenth century, Pawley goes inside readers' worlds and their chosen texts. She links gender, class, and ethnicity to specific titles read by individual members of all these groups and discovers clear patterns of use. Thus, she brings to life in a new way these "common readers" of the late nineteenth century—a group of people hitherto unknown to print culture historians.

The third section examines print materials' reconstruction of events. The relationship of memory to the phenomena being reconstructed is an essential part of the human experience. Written and spoken words provide the basis for human knowledge as well as a source for human disagreement. In his elegant discussion of how print addressed and explained the sinking of the *Titanic* in 1912, Steven Biel has consulted a wide variety of newspapers and periodicals, exploring the uses editors and correspondents made of the disaster in their pages. He uncovers gender, class, and race perspectives in a contest among serial publishers to craft the event's "true" meaning for their different audiences.

Although Langston Hughes is part of the contemporary American canon, Elizabeth Davey demonstrates that this was not always the case. In the 1930s, Hughes became so frustrated with the limits of commercial publishing and its ignorance of and/or ambivalence about African Americans that he began to market his own poetry through public performances. Davey's research reminds students of print culture history that there are many roads to generate—and document—a readership.

When *The Autobiography of an Ex-Colored Man* first appeared in 1912, James Weldon Johnson was shielded by "the secret of authorship." In her analysis of why Johnson sought anonymity before Knopf published the "classic" edition of his book in 1927, Jacqueline Goldsby goes far beyond racial explanations. Instead, she explores the world of black politics and, especially, the dominant role played by Booker T. Washington. Recognizing that Johnson wanted a diplomatic career and perceiving that he was an intellectual with creative musical ideas, Goldsby explores Johnson's deeply conflicted identity as author and, more than eighty years after the book's initial publication, locates his autobiographical voice more accurately in its narrative frame.

Each of the eleven essays in this book represents a foray into the multicultural world of readers and reading in America over the last century and a half. That is appropriate for a conference sponsored by the Center for the History of Print Culture in Modern America, whose directors and board members believe that the history of print culture must be a cooperative enterprise involving and drawing from the widest array of disciplines. The center hopes that the publication of this volume will not only answer some major questions about and fill some major gaps in the diverse post-1876 history of print in the United States, but that it will also serve to encourage others to explore the vast potential of this understudied yet promisingly rich new area of scholarship.

NOTES

1. Karen Winkler, "In Electronic Age, Scholars Are Drawn to Study of Print," *Chronicle of Higher Education*, July 14, 1993, A6–A8. See also Julie Bates Dock, ed., *The Press of Ideas: Readings for Writers on Print Culture and the Information Age* (Boston: Bedford Books of St. Martin's Press, 1996), 1–20.

2. I am indebted to Sarah Maza for this useful phrase. See her "Stories in History: Cultural Narratives in Recent Works in European History," *American Historical Review* 101 (1996): 1503.

3. Titles typically cited include Michel Foucault, *The Archaeology of Knowledge and the Discourse on Language* (New York: Pantheon Books, 1972); Jürgen Habermas, *The Theory of Communication Action*, vol. 1: *Reason and the Rationalization of Society* (Boston: Beacon Press, 1984); Antonio Gramsci, *Prison Notebooks*, vol. 1, trans. Joseph A. Buttigieg and Antonio Callari (New York: Columbia University Press, 1992); Elizabeth Kamarck Minnich, *Transforming Knowledge* (Philadelphia: Temple University Press, 1990); Sandra Harding, *Whose Science? Whose Knowledge? Thinking from Women's Lives* (Ithaca, N.Y.: Cornell University Press, 1991); Pierre Bourdieu, *Distinction:*

A Social Critique of the Judgement of Taste, trans. Richard Nice (London: Routledge, 1986); Michel de Certeau, *The Practice of Everyday Life,* trans. Steven Rendall (Berkeley: University of California Press, 1984); and Stephen Greenblatt, *Renaissance Self-Fashioning: From More to Shakespeare* (Chicago: University of Chicago Press, 1980). For useful summaries of cultural studies, see John Storey, *Cultural Studies and the Study of Popular Culture: Theories and Methods* (Athens: University of Georgia Press, 1996); and John Fiske, *Understanding Popular Culture* (New York: Routledge, 1989).

4. Janice Radway, "Beyond Mary Bailey and Old Maid Librarians: Reimaging Readers and Rethinking Reading," *Journal of Education in Library and Information Science* 35 (Fall 1994): 275–96. See also David Hall, "Readers and Reading in America: Historical and Critical Perspectives," *Proceedings of the American Antiquarian Society* 103, pt. 2 (1993): 337–57; and Carl Kaestle, "The History of Readers," in *Literacy in the United States: Readers and Reading since 1880,* ed. Carl F. Kaestle, Helen Damon-Moore, Lawrence C. Stedman, Katherine Tinsley, and William Vance Trollinger Jr. (New Haven, Conn.: Yale University Press, 1991), 33–72.

5. I prefer the term "print culture history" to "book history" because it more accurately addresses the history of all printed materials and the realities in which they functioned. For purposes of this essay, I also prefer it to "print culture studies" because of its temporal focus.

6. Harvey Graff, *The Literacy Myth: Literacy and Social Structure in the Nineteenth-Century City* (New York: Academic Press, 1979); Elizabeth Eisenstein, *The Printing Press as an Agent of Change: Communications and Cultural Transformation in Early Modern Europe,* 2 vols. (Cambridge: Cambridge University Press, 1979). For a more recent assessment, see Kaestle et al., *Literacy in the United States,* esp. chaps. 1, 5, and 10.

7. See, for example, Wolfgang Iser, *The Act of Reading: A Theory of Aesthetic Response* (Baltimore: Johns Hopkins University Press, 1978); and Hans Robert Jauss, *Experiences and Literary Hermeneutics,* trans. Michael Shaw (Minneapolis: University of Minnesota Press, 1982). See also Susan R. Suleiman and Inge Crossman, eds., *The Reader in the Text: Essays on Audience and Interpretation* (Princeton, N.J.: Princeton University Press, 1980); and Jane Tompkins, ed., *Reader-Response Criticism: From Formalism to Post-Structuralism* (Baltimore: Johns Hopkins University Press, 1980).

8. Stanley Fish, *Is There a Text in This Class? The Authority of Interpretive Communities* (Cambridge, Mass.: Harvard University Press, 1980).

9. Jonathan Boyarin, ed., *The Ethnography of Reading* (Berkeley: University of California Press, 1993). Long's essay is on 180–211.

10. Robert Darnton, "What Is the History of Books?," in *The Kiss of Lamourette: Reflections in Cultural History,* by Robert Darnton (New York: W. W. Norton, 1990), 107. This influential essay appeared first in *Daedalus* 111 (Summer 1982): 65–83 and has been reprinted in Kenneth E. Carpenter, ed., *Books and Society in History: Papers of the Association of College and Research Libraries, Rare Books and Manuscripts Preconference, 24–28 June, 1980, Boston, Massachusetts* (New York: R. R. Bowker, 1983), 3–26; and Cathy Davidson, ed., *Reading in America: Literature and Social History* (Baltimore: Johns Hopkins University Press, 1989), 27–52.

11. Michael Winship, "Afterword," in *Literary Publishing in America, 1790–1850,* by William Charvat (Amherst: University of Massachusetts Press, 1993), 95–96. This is a reprint of Charvat's book, which was first published in 1959. See also Roger Chartier, *Forms and Meanings: Texts, Performances, and Audiences from Codex to Computer* (Philadelphia: University of Pennsylvania Press, 1995).

12. See especially Lucien Febvre and Henri-Jean Martin, *The Coming of the Book: The Impact of Printing, 1450–1800,* trans. David Gerard (London: Verso, 1984), a translation of their *L'Apparition du livre* (Paris: Albin Michel, 1958).

13. See, for example, Rolf Engelsing, *Analphabetentum und Lektüre. Zur Sozialgeschichte des Lesens in Deutschland zwischen feudaler und industrieller Gesellschaft* (Stuttgart: Metzler, 1973); and his *Der Burger als Leser. Lesergeschichte in Deutschland, 1500–1800* (Stuttgart: Metzler, 1974).

14. See, for example, Kathryn Shevelow, *Women and Print Culture: The Construction of Femininity in the Early Periodical* (London: Routledge, 1989); Donald Franklin Joyce, *Gatekeepers of Black Culture: Black-Owned Book Publishing in the United States, 1817–1981* (Westport, Conn.: Greenwood, 1983); Michael Denning, *Mechanic Accents: Dime Novels and Working-Class Culture in America* (London: Verso, 1987); and Jane Tompkins, *Sensational Designs: The Cultural Work of American Fiction, 1790–1860* (New York: Oxford University Press, 1985).

15. Henri-Jean Martin, Roger Chartier, and Jean-Pierre Vivet, eds., *Histoire de l'édition française,* 4 vols. (Paris: Promodis, 1982–86).

16. Robert Darnton, *The Business of Enlightenment: A Publishing History of the Encyclopédie, 1775–1800* (Cambridge, Mass.: Harvard University Press, 1979); id., *The Great Cat Massacre and Other Episodes in French Cultural History* (New York: Basic Books, 1984).

17. See, for example, David D. Hall and John B. Hench, eds., *Needs and Opportunities in the History of the Book: America, 1639–1876* (Worcester, Mass.: American Antiquarian Society, 1987).

18. Cathy Davidson, *Revolution and the Word: The Rise of the Novel in America* (New York: Oxford University Press, 1986); William J. Gilmore, *Reading Becomes a Necessity of Life: Material and Cultural Life in Rural New England, 1780–1835* (Knoxville: University of Tennessee Press, 1989); David D. Hall, *Worlds of Wonder, Days of Judgment: Popular Religious Belief in Early New England* (New York: Alfred A. Knopf, 1989); Michael Warner, *The Letters of the Republic: Publication and the Public Sphere in Eighteenth-Century America* (Cambridge, Mass.: Harvard University Press, 1990); Frankie Hutton, *The Early Black Press in America, 1827 to 1860* (Westport, Conn.: Greenwood Press, 1993); Ronald J. Zboray, *A Fictive People: Antebellum Economic Development and the American Reading Public* (New York: Oxford University Press, 1993); Richard H. Brodhead, *Cultures of Letters: Scenes of Reading and Writing in Nineteenth-Century America* (Chicago: University of Chicago Press, 1993); and Michael Winship, *American Literary Publishing in the Mid-Nineteenth Century: The Business of Ticknor and Fields* (Cambridge: Cambridge University Press, 1995). See also Mary Kelly, *Private Women, Public Stage: Literary Domesticity in Nineteenth-Century America* (New York: Oxford University Press, 1984); Richard H. Brodhead, *The School of Hawthorne* (New York: Oxford University Press, 1986); Lawrence Buell, *New England Literary Culture from Revolution through Renaissance* (Cambridge: Cambridge University Press, 1986); Richard D. Brown, *Knowledge Is Power: The Diffusion of Information in Early America, 1700–1865* (New York: Oxford University Press, 1989); and Susan Coultrap-McQuin, *Doing Literary Business: American Women Writers in the Nineteenth Century* (Chapel Hill: University of North Carolina Press, 1990).

19. Winkler, "Electronic Age," A7.

PART I

Deconstructing Forgotten Serials

1 The Italian Immigrant Press and the Construction of Social Reality, 1850–1920

RUDOLPH J. VECOLI

Print culture increasingly gained importance among American immigrants at the turn of the century, becoming a major resource and an instrument with which they fashioned ethnic identities and ethnic communities. Print culture, however, presumes literacy—and were not immigrants, and Italians in particular, semiliterate at best? Illiteracy rates varied greatly among immigrant nationalities. In the period 1900–1910, the percentage of illiterates among immigrants ranged from 1 percent for Scandinavians to 65 percent for Portuguese. Indeed Italians, the largest immigrant group of the period, had one of the highest rates of illiteracy. Northern Italians were 11 percent illiterate; among southern Italians, representing the majority, the figure was 52 percent.

Sharp increases in literacy, however, were a concomitant of mass emigration in European countries. Italy, for example, experienced a dramatic decrease in illiteracy during the years of the most intense emigration (from 69 percent to 38 percent between 1871 and 1911). This was particularly true for the Mezzogiorno (southern Italy): illustrative was the decline in illiteracy from 80 percent to 54 percent in the region of Campania. While other forces were at work (e.g., compulsory military service), emigration provided a major stimulus for the acquisition of literacy.[1]

In areas of intense emigration, the ability to read gained an importance that it had not previously had. While information about travel, work opportunities, and much else was often gained by word of mouth, those who could read the letters from America, steamship posters, broadsides, and immigrant manuals had a significant advantage. From the 1890s onward, the threat of a literacy test for admission to the United States created a heightened demand for schooling. In various districts of southern Italy, literacy classes were established specifically to prepare people to pass such a test.[2]

No one was more aware of the importance of literacy than those immigrants who had, to their sorrow, experienced the price of illiteracy. They urged their *paesani* to learn to read, to establish schools for their children, and even sent money home for educating the young. During the peak years of emigration, enrollments rose rapidly in the elementary schools of southern Italy. Once in America, customary knowledge that had sufficed in the village was often inadequate to provide guidance as to appropriate behavior. The ability to read street signs, train schedules, safety warnings in mines and mills, employment notices, and commercial advertisements became essential for everyday living. But even more than such factual information, immigrants required an orientation to the social reality of this new country—and a definition of its meaning in their lives. Newspapers, magazines, and books took on an importance they lacked in the old country. Various observers commented that immigrants who had never seen a book became readers in America. While many joined the ranks of what Carlo Cipolla has termed "the intermediate army of the semi-literate," one could find in the Little Italies not a few autodidacts, self-taught intellectuals, among them Bartolomeo Vanzetti.[3]

What was true of the Italians was true of immigrants of other nationalities as well. Contrary to the stereotype of inarticulate, illiterate foreigners, immigrants did read and write. As evidence, they left an enormous library of publications that run the gamut of newspapers, periodicals, almanacs, books, pamphlets, and broadsides. In 1910, over a thousand periodicals in languages other than English had a total circulation of over six million.[4] Such print culture is, in Robert Harney's words, "one of those rare sources through which we can reach some understanding of the mentalités and pyschic maps of immigrants, people, articulate in their own time and culture, rendered silent by historians with inadequate methods for hearing them."[5]

In fact, this incomparable documentation has been too little exploited as a means of "recreating lost ethnocommunities." In 1966, Joshua Fishman observed that little systematic attention had been paid to the ethnic press; Sally Miller reiterated this twenty years later. In this age of multiculturalism, most scholars still seem to be deceived by the "fiction of U.S. monoglottism."[6] True, the mother tongue immigrant press has been consulted by historians in their studies of ethnic groups, but it has been utilized primarily as a source of "factual information." While a legitimate use of the source, this approach rests on the assumption that the print culture is simply a mirror of the ethnic culture. For their part, studies of the immigrant press have remained fixated on the question first addressed by Robert Ezra Park in his classic work, *The Immigrant Press and Its Control:* Did the non-English-language press retard or facilitate the assimilation of the foreign-born?

Recent theoretical approaches to communication studies suggest a more sophisticated perspective on the significance of the immigrant press. Rather than simply serving as transmitters of information, communication media are interpreted as forces actively constructing social reality and identity in the minds of their audiences. Informed by Antonio Gramsci's concept of ideological hegemony, communication is viewed as the means whereby the ruling element manufactures and secures consensus to its view of the world among subaltern groups. Since such hegemonic conceptions are subject to challenges by oppositional views, the media become the site of ideological contestation, of a struggle over meaning.[7]

In this essay, the "critical paradigm" of communications analysis, as Stuart Hall has termed it, is applied to an assessment of the role of the Italian immigrant press in the construction of an Italian-American ethnic identity. Such an analysis conceives of the press as a site of intense ideological struggle for the minds and souls of the immigrants. Among the contestants for hegemony over the immigrant masses were Italian nationalists, Americanizers, Roman Catholic clergy, the *prominenti* (the colonial elite), and the *sovversivi* (meaning radicals of various stripes). By controlling the sources and contents of print culture, each of these contenders aspired to control the consciousness of literate immigrants and, through them, the consciousness of those who lacked direct access to the printed word.[8]

During the immigration phase of Italian-American history (1850–1930), over a thousand periodicals in the Italian language were published in the United States.[9] To be sure, many were short-lived, lasting a few weeks or months, and the majority were weeklies or monthlies. But between 1900 and 1930 some thirty dailies were published in cities with large Italian populations. The circulation of Italian newspapers ranged from a few hundred to many thousands. In 1919, 190 publications had a combined circulation of 800,000. At its zenith, *Il Progresso Italo-Americano* of New York City, the leading daily, attained a circulation of 175,000. Although the Italian press counted a greater number of titles than did the press of comparable immigrant groups, its total circulation tended to be smaller. In 1910, for example, forty Italian publications had a total circulation of 548,000, compared to twenty-three Yiddish publications with a total circulation of 808,000. The fragmentation of the press reflected the factions of politics, ideology, and regionalism among Italian immigrants.[10]

This following analysis focuses on three types of Italian journalism: *exile, prominenti,* and *sovversivi.* Exile journalism was a product of the "heroic immigration" that accompanied the Risorgimento. Beginning in the 1830s, political exiles from the struggle for Italian unification sought refuge in the United States. Individuals of high culture and education, they were well received by Americans and often achieved a relatively high status. These political refugees were accompanied by the pioneers of the mass immigration that was to follow, a modest number of merchants, professionals, peddlers, figurine makers, and street musicians.[11]

The first newspaper of consequence, *L'Eco d'Italia* (The echo of Italy) was established in New York City in 1849 by G. P. Secchi di Casali, himself a Mazzinian exile. Some twenty newspapers of nationalist inspiration appeared in Chicago, San Francisco, and other cities in 1860–80. Their editors, followers of Giuseppe Mazzini and Giuseppe Garibaldi, devoted most of the space to the political and military struggles in Italy and to patriotic exhortations. Divided between republicans and monarchists, they vigorously debated the future of *la Patria*. While they reported commercial news as well as chronicles of colonial life, and thus provided useful information to the Italians scattered about the country, these publications were little concerned with American affairs. In defense of Italian honor, the exiles promoted the earliest Columbus Day observances and responded to anti-Italian slurs in the American press. Predominantly freethinkers, they attacked the Papacy and the Roman Catholic Church in the United States as enemies of Italy and of Italians in America. During this phase, then, an exile mentality dominated Italian journalism, which primarily focused on events abroad affecting Italy.[12]

From the 1880s, the rapid increase in the volume of Italian immigration ushered in the prominenti phase of Italian journalism. Since the majority of the immigrants were now unskilled laborers, they needed middlemen who could provide them with jobs, lodgings, and other services. Thus there emerged the class of prominenti composed of the so-called padrone-bankers and a sprinkling of professionals. Of *piccola borghese* (lower middle-class) background, they enjoyed the advantage of a modicum of education. Literacy was an important source of their power, and in order to extend their influence they established newspapers. Wherever a Little Italy of any size emerged, one or more newspapers were sure to appear. As one commentator observed, periodicals sprang up like mushrooms—and generally lasted as long.

Nearly five hundred publications were established in 1900–1920, most of them weeklies or fortnightlies of four to six pages, over half of which were devoted to advertisements. Many newspapers were one-man operations, the owner being manager, typesetter, printer, and distributor. Few of the owner-editors had pursued journalistic careers in Italy; for many, journalism was a means of escaping from the ranks of common laborers. Largely scissors-and-paste affairs, these gazettes carried news clipped from other materials published in the United States and Italy. With circulations of a few hundred or a few thousand at most, income from sales did not cover costs. Advertisements or patronage by commercial firms or the Italian government were essential. In addition to advertisements for steamship lines, banks, labor agencies, saloons, and stores, such newspapers often carried ads for medical quacks, patent medicines, and real estate promotions (including fraudulent ones). Political support was often sold to the highest bidder, whether Democrat or Republican. After a penurious existence, many newspapers died an early death, to be replaced by publications of a similar character.[13]

Yet some of these prominenti newspapers not only survived but prospered. By the turn of the century, there were some ten dailies; in addition to four in New York City, Boston, Philadelphia, and San Francisco also had daily papers. Together with certain weeklies with circulations in the tens of thousands, such publications became profitable ventures indeed. Although editorial policies varied, these newspapers tended to devote a great deal of attention to political developments in Italy, as well as to news from the immigrants' *paesi* of origin; they also carried reports on community affairs and correspondence from Little Italies in other U.S. cities. Appealing to their readers' appetite for scandal, many featured the *cronaca nera* (black chronicle) of bloody and depraved deeds, both in Italy and America. While denouncing references in the American press to Italian criminality, the Italian papers themselves titillated their readers with lurid accounts of the Mafia and Black Hand. Popular fiction, such as the romance novels by Carolina Invernizio, was often serialized.[14]

The prominenti newspapers could be classified as commercial and personal publications, since their purpose was both to further business interests and to satisfy the vanity of the owners. Carlo Barsotti epitomized the prominente, and his newspaper, *Il Progresso Italo-Americano,* this type of publication. *Il Progresso* was the most long-lived and successful of Italian-American newspapers. Founded in New York City in 1880 as a weekly, it soon became the first Italian daily, continuing publication until 1982. Barsotti, a padrone-banker who had little education, hired others to write for and edit his paper. So long as it promoted his enterprises and lavished praise upon him, he cared little about its contents.

Whether from patriotic or egotistical motives, Barsotti periodically launched campaigns for nationalistic manifestations, including the observance of the Columbian quadricentennial in 1892 and the erection of a monument to Christopher Columbus. *Il Progresso* also raised funds to erect statues to Garibaldi, Giuseppe Verdi, Giovanni da Verrazzano, and Dante, campaigned on behalf of "wrongly" condemned Italians, and championed the claims of Antonio Meucci as the true inventor of the telephone. Although he promoted an Italian hospital, Barsotti, in true prominenti fashion, did not distinguish himself by philanthropic works on behalf of his needy countrymen. His newspaper, like others of its kind, engaged in vicious personal polemics with its rivals that not infrequently resulted in physical attacks or lawsuits.[15]

With the development of mass-circulation publications, opportunities in the Italian-American newspaper business attracted an increasing number of professional journalists from Italy. Agostino De Biasi, for example, after working for a number of newspapers in Italy, was first an employee of *Il Progresso* and then became editor of a new Philadelphia daily, *L'Opinione*. De Biasi espoused a fervent Italian nationalism that evolved into Fascism after World War I. Journalists such as De Biasi brought ideological zeal to their editorial tasks, seeking to uplift the cultural level and instill a passionate patriotism among the immigrants.[16]

The prominenti publications differed from the exile newspapers in their ideological orientation. Although saturated with fulsome nationalistic rhetoric, they recognized that, for an increasing number of Italians, the United States was their permanent home. For such as these, what did it mean to be an Italian in America or an Italian American? Although they did not think of it in those terms, the journalists were willy-nilly involved in the invention of an Italian-American ethnicity.[17] While preaching the gospel of Italian patriotism, they were increasingly concerned with the status of Italians in America. Victor Greene presents a positive view of the prominenti, portraying them as caring leaders who guided their followers to a satisfactory adjustment in the new land.[18] In particular, he depicts them as the artificers of a "dual identity" whereby the Italianness and Americanness of the immigrants would be painlessly reconciled. Speaking of Paolo Russo, a prominente of New Haven, Connecticut, Greene asserts that he "had illuminated the two identities of his people and had shown their compatibility."[19]

I view the role of the prominenti as more problematic. Interpreted from the perspective of Stuart Hall's critical paradigm, their paternalistic "leadership" became the means whereby they controlled the workers, consumers, and voters who were the base of their power; and their success in winning a loyal following testified to the efficacy of their ideological hegemony. Did the prominenti's exhortation of the immigrants to become loyal citizens of the United States while retaining love for Italy resolve the dilemma of dual loyalties? I would argue, instead, that the ambiguity, if not the disingenuousness, of this rhetorical formula smacks of sophistry—a sophistry that was put to the ultimate test in December 1941. The professed affection of the prominenti for the United States is difficult to reconcile with the decidedly anti-American bias of their newspapers. The prominenti press frequently criticized Americans as crude, vulgar, and "puritanical."[20]

Exhortations in the prominenti press to readers of their "sacred duty" to support la Patria, to help Italian victims of natural disasters and wars, and especially to uphold "the good name of the Italians in the United States" have a more sincere ring to them. Celebrations of Italian national holidays such as *la festa dello Statuto* (Constitution Day) on March 4 and *Venti Settembre* (Sept. 20), commemorating the conquest of Rome in 1870, as well as anniversaries of the House of Savoy, annually inspired columns of florid, bombastic prose. If the newspapers vigorously protested abusive treatment of Italians, such as the New Orleans lynchings, they also chastised the *cafoni* (rustics) for behavior that brought shame upon the Italians and entreated them to abjure the stiletto, ragpicking, filth, begging, and the nursing of infants in public. Anxious to win the respect of Americans, the publications espoused standards of bourgeois respectability. Since votes were a source of their power, it is not surprising that the prominenti consistently urged the immigrants to learn English, become citizens, and participate in American politics. Seeking to overcome provincial conflicts (although at times playing on regional animosities), they preached that all Italians should be united as a family; only in that manner could they gain the respect of the other nationalities in America.[21]

Greene is quite correct in portraying the prominenti as seeking to fashion an ideology of accommodation that would bridge the duality of being both immigrants and Americans. For Italians, Columbus served as the epic hero in their origins myth because he embodied the primordial link between Italy and America. Celebrations of Columbus Day, campaigns to make it a legal holiday, the erection of statues of the Great Explorer—all became ritual events in the Italian-American community. The prominenti press was the primary agent in this apotheosis of Columbus, who became the symbol par excellence of an Italian-American identity.[22]

What social reality did the prominenti press present to its readers?

George Pozzetta has argued that, on the whole, these newspapers worked against the best interests of the immigrants. Because newspapers represented the business interests of the prominenti and sold themselves to the highest bidders, political and commercial, they carried misleading items or outright deceptions to the injury of their Italian readers. By and large, the prominenti opposed labor unions and civic reforms and failed to report accurately on labor conditions and strikes. Yet Pozzetta concluded that the press helped create a sense of Italian nationality among the immigrants. John Briggs, on the other hand, concluded that the newspapers he examined took an active interest in civic affairs as well as national politics, provided useful advice and information regarding naturalization and education, and reported on strikes and labor markets. Although I have found evidence of the useful information that Briggs cites, my reading of the press tends to confirm Pozzetta's negative judgment. While *L'Italia* of Chicago (established in 1886), for example, on occasion exposed the nefarious machinations of padrones and politicians, at the same time it carried the ads of labor agents and endorsed candidates who hardly served the interests of the immigrants.[23] A veteran journalist, Giacomo Grillo, observed that although the prominenti were parasitic and preyed upon vulnerable immigrants, the padrone-bankers nonetheless helped the immigrants adjust to this new country.[24] In any event, the prominenti press taught its readers to acquiesce in the status quo, to aspire to bourgeois values, and to love la Patria while also respecting the United States.

Unlike the Slavic immigrants, for whom the Catholic faith was a major source of ethnocultural identity and whose major newspapers were often published under clerical auspices, religious publications were not an important component of the Italian press. Protestant denominations that evangelized the immigrants sponsored publications such as *La Fiaccola*, but these, too, were of limited influence. Largely in response to this challenge, the Catholic church published a number of newspapers, including *Il Corriere della Domenica*, but these papers had modest circulations.[25]

In fact, anticlericalism was a dominant feature of Italian journalism in America. Because the Kingdom of Italy and the Roman Catholic Church remained at odds over the papal territories until the 1920s, Italian nationalists were by definition anticlericals. This sentiment was expressed by much of the prominenti press, particularly as Italian immigrants encountered intense hostility from Irish-American priests. The sovversivi, of course, were sworn enemies of religion of all kinds. In addition to publications in the United States, such as *Libero Pensiero* (Free thought), an anticlerical, satirical magazine, *L'Asino* (of Rome) circulated widely among the immigrants. In 1908, when the papal nuncio in Washington successfully had *L'Asino* banned from entry on the grounds of its alleged pornographic content, an American edition of it was printed in New York City.[26]

Prominenti hegemony encountered an uncompromising opponent in the sovversivi press in America.[27] Although fewer in number and smaller in circulation than the prominenti newspapers, the publications of socialist and anarchist inspiration reached a significant segment of the immigrant population. In a 1920 Department of Justice report, of 222 non-English radical newspapers listed, 27 were Italian—second only to the combined Hebrew and Yiddish total of 35 (and this during the postwar period of repression!). Although 190 Italian radical publications have been identified, many lasted only a few issues, or, for political reasons, the same publication appeared under various mastheads. Circulations were quite limited: *Il Proletario,* one of the most widely circulated and longer-lived, achieved a high point of 7,800 copies in 1916. Even in good times, the condition of the sovversivi publications was precarious. Since they carried no advertisements or only ads that satisfied their test of ideological purity, most journals limped along from issue to issue, covering chronic deficits through contributions and fund-raisers by the faithful.[28]

The sovversivi editors transported to this country the spectrum of radical ideologies from Italy, including several varieties of anarchism, syndicalism, revolutionary socialism, and social democracy. They also brought all the ideological and personal conflicts that plagued the Italian Left. The editors of the radical publications, often political refugees, included outstanding propagandists, such as Luigi Galleani, Arturo Giovannitti, and Carlo Tresca, to name a few. It was said of the radicals that while their bodies were in America their heads remained in Italy. Historians of the sovversivi press have criticized it for its theoretical quality, self-absorption with ideological disputes, and personal polemics. Bruno Cartosio, for example, has remarked upon its focus on struggles in Italy and its disregard for the economic and political realities of America. In a sense, they were American branches of suppressed Italian movements, and they sent their publications clandestinely to Italy. Internationalist in their ideologies, socialist and anarchist journalists regarded their cause as transnational and followed its fortunes everywhere in the world.[29]

Certain publications, such as Luigi Galleani's *La Cronaca Sovversiva* (published for many years in Barre, Vermont), were guilty of abstract and rhetorical disquisitions. However, the socialist and syndicalist papers, in particular *Il Proletario* and *La Parola dei Socialisti,* reported on labor conditions and strikes, especially those involving Italians, often printing reports from comrades on the scene. Although the syndicalists, who were affiliated with the Industrial Workers of the World, dismissed electoral politics as a scam, the socialists, allied with the Socialist Party of America, covered elections and campaigns for its candidates. One of the major purposes of the radical press was to oppose the influence of the prominenti and their publications, that is, to subvert their hegemony. Frequent articles exposed the evil doings of padrone-bankers and ridiculed their pretensions. As antinationalists, the radicals sought to counter patriotic manifestations sponsored by the prominenti, even going so far as to disrupt Columbus Day celebrations. As freethinkers and anticlericals, they mercilessly harassed priests and satirized religious *feste.* The sovversivi press aggressively challenged the hegemony of the prominenti and of the clergy within the Italian colonies.[30]

The radicals believed that education was the key to bringing about the revolution and that essentially this meant liberating the minds of the workers so that they could perceive their class interests. Although lectures were a popular form of propaganda, the sovversivi also had great faith in the printed word. A printing press was an essential weapon in the class war. In addition to newspapers, they printed books, *opuscoli* (booklets), songbooks, almanacs, and broadsides. Among these publications, the theoretical writings of Karl Marx, Mikhail Bakunin, Pyotr Kropotkin, and Errico Malatesta, among others, were published in volumes of several hundred pages or distilled into leaflets of a few pages. Scientific treatises by Charles Darwin and Ernst Haeckel as well as antireligious tracts were prominent in their publication lists. In addition, Henrik Ibsen's plays, Émile Zola's and Jack London's novels, and Pietro Gori's poetry were published and distributed by the radical press. Socialist clubs and anarchist *circoli di studi sociali* (social studies circles) maintained libraries of such literature. In the cigar factories of Tampa, Florida, the *lector* (reader) read from these works as well as from current radical publications. While data are lacking to prove the point, there is reason to believe that immigrants who came under the influence of radical movements acquired a higher degree of literacy than those who did not.[31]

Readers of the sovversivi press encountered a radically different definition of social reality than those who read the prominenti press. Committed to the overthrow of capitalism, the radical publications preached the necessity of class consciousness and class struggle. As internationalists, they rejected all forms of nationalism, including Italian patriotism and American nationalism. The radicals created an oppositional culture with its own anniversaries, heroes and martyrs, rituals and symbols. Rather than Columbus or King Vittorio Emanuele I, they exalted Giordano Bruno, who symbolized free thought, and Gaetano Bresci, the anarchist who shot King Umberto I. Rather than Constitution Day or the Fourth of July, they observed the anniversaries of the Paris Commune and the Haymarket martyrdoms. But *Primo Maggio* (May Day) was the red-letter day in the radical calendar. Celebrated with processions and picnics, it was the occasion to affirm the international solidarity of the working class. The sovversivi press dedicated May Day issues to articles expounding the history and significance of the date and exhorting its readers to observe it in a fitting manner.

Elisabetta Vezzosi, a historian of the Italian-American Left, has criticized the radicals for their violent anticlericalism and abstention from American politics on the grounds that this isolated them from the "complex reality of the Italian American community."[32] However, it is difficult to see how they could have maintained their counterhegemonic posture if they had compromised with the prominenti and the church. The sovversivi and their movements were in fact an integral part of that "complex reality." A more telling criticism is that the destructive internecine warfare among various radical factions dissipated their energies and curtailed their effectiveness. The vituperation with which the radicals attacked each other on personal grounds surpassed even the polemics among the prominenti.

In the words of an archenemy of the radicals, Agostino De Biasi, many Italian immigrants had been bitten and poisoned with antinationalist, anticapitalist propaganda by *"la vipera sovversiva"* (the subversive viper).[33] Writing in the 1920s in the first flush of Fascist victory, De Biasi credited the crushing of the radical movement in the United States to a renewed spirit of *italianità* and devotion to the monarchy among the Italians of America. What really decided the hegemonic struggle between the prominenti and the sovversivi was World War I. Among the working classes in every country at war, the forces of nationalism triumphed over those of internationalism. The question of Italian intervention in the war split the ranks of the radicals in the United States. Some, such as the interventionist Edmondo Rossoni, moved from syndicalism to nationalism to Fascism. The triumph of Bolshevism in Russia brought about yet another split within the diminished ranks of the Italian Left in the United States. Of more direct consequence, the Italian radical press was harshly suppressed during the war by the strict application of the Espionage Act, the Trading with the Enemy Act, and the Sedition Act. Not a few of its editors and writers, such as Galleani, were imprisoned or deported. Meanwhile, the prominenti press, which became a vehicle for the propaganda of the Committee on Public Information, flourished with the patronage of the U.S. government.[34]

Following the war and Mussolini's rise to power, the prominenti press was subsidized and controlled by the Fascist regime. Under such conditions, the hegemonic power of the prominenti over the Italian colonies, while not total, became ever more firmly established. The Italian Left in the United States did not disappear but was reduced to the status of a rear guard of resistance to burgeoning support for Fascism. Ironically, the philo-Fascism of Italian Americans could itself be understood in terms of their growing integration into American society. In many ways, they were making the transition from immigrants to ethnics with a complex and often conflicted Italian-American identity.[35]

Finally, a caveat regarding the study of print culture that can also be regarded as a self-critique of this chapter. While print culture can be read for various ideologies that sought to influence readers, other sources need to be consulted to determine its efficacy. Contemporary observations, oral histories, and behavioral studies (such as on voting or nonvoting) suggest that the influence of the press on the Italian immigrants was limited. Many Italians appear to have remained relatively indifferent to the politicized ethnicities of Fascist nationalism, radicalism, or 100 percent Americanism, holding fast to the traditional, old-country ways of thinking and being. Their minds were not simply a tabula rasa upon which print culture impressed its definition of social reality. Rather, *they* filtered media messages through the sieve of their own experience. Finally, *they* decided what was reality—and its meaning.[36]

NOTES

1. Carlo M. Cipolla, *Literacy and Development in the West* (Baltimore, 1969), 19, 94-97, 127; Ercole Sori, *L'emigrazione italiana dall'unità alla seconda guerra mondiale* (Bologna, 1979), 205-11.

2. Cipolla, *Literacy and Development,* 95, 106; Sori, *L'emigrazione italiana,* 210-11; Alfredo Bosi, *Cinquant'anni di vita italiana in America* (New York, 1921), 118-20.

3. As in the case of Vanzetti, the autodidact was most often a convert to socialism or anarchism. Those movements had as their primary objective the education of the proletariat. Bartolomeo Vanzetti, *The Story of a Proletarian Life* (Boston, 1923); see also Paul Avrich, *Sacco and Vanzetti: The Anarchist Background*

(Princeton, N.J., 1991); Sori, *L'emigrazione italiana*, 205–11; Cipolla, *Literacy and Development*, 11; Robert E. Park, *The Immigrant Press and Its Control* (New York, 1922), 9, 14; Giacomo Grillo, *Cronaca che non e'un epitaffio. I sessantacqinque anni della Gazzetta* (Boston, 1962), 5; Giuseppe Zappulla, "The Italian Press in the United States," 2, and "Tippici aspetti della stampa italiana degli S.U." 1, both in Giuseppe Zappulla Papers, Immigration History Research Center, University of Minnesota (hereinafter cited as IHRC). Both Grillo and Zappulla were old-time journalists who spoke from experience.

4. Joshua Fishman et al., *Language Loyalty in the United States* (The Hague, 1966), 60; Sally Miller, ed., *The Ethnic Press in the United States: A Historical Analysis and Handbook* (New York, 1987), xv–xvii. The latter is a volume of essays devoted to the press of various ethnic groups. Unfortunately, there is no essay on the Italian press.

5. Robert F. Harney, "The Ethnic Press in Ontario," *Polyphony: The Bulletin of the Multicultural History Society of Ontario* 4 (Spring/Summer 1982): 3–14 (quotation from 7). In this provocative article, Harney anticipates in some respects the argument presented in this essay.

6. Fishman, *Language Loyalty*, 61; Miller, *Ethnic Press*, xi. The reference to "the fiction of U.S. monoglottism" is from an announcement by the Longfellow Institute of Harvard University for a seminar entitled "Languages of What Is Now the United States."

7. Stuart Hall, "The Rediscovery of 'Ideology': Return of the Repressed in Media Studies," in *Culture, Society and the Media*, ed. Michael Gurevitch (London and New York, 1982), 56–90; Michael Schudson, "Media Contexts: Historical Approaches to Communication Studies," in *A Handbook of Qualitative Methodologies for Mass Communication Research*, ed. Klaus Bruhn Jensen and Nicholas W. Jankowski (London and New York, 1991), 175–89.

8. For an earlier attempt to analyze the contested nature of Italian-American ethnicity, see my "The Search for an Italian American Identity: Continuity and Change," in *Italian Americans: New Perspectives in Italian Immigration and Ethnicity*, ed. Lydio Tomasi (New York, 1985), 88–112.

9. Pietro Russo, *Catalogo Collettivo della Stampa Periodica Italo Americana (1836–1980)* (Rome, 1983). This definitive union list of Italian-American periodicals cites 2,334 titles. However, all kinds of publications, including those in the English language, are included.

10. Bosi, *Cinquant'anni*, 380–415; Fishman, *Language Loyalty*, 52–60; Park, *Immigrant Press*, 92, 304; Miller, *Ethnic Press*, 52–60; Giuseppe Fumagalli, *La stampa periodica italiana all'estero* (Milan, 1909), 129–34. Fumagalli's report on the Italian periodical press lists 144 publications in the United States with their particular tendencies (liv–lxxiv).

Since this chapter was written, an excellent doctoral dissertation has been completed by Bénédicte Deschamps: "De la Press 'Coloniale' à la Presse Italo-Américaine, Le Parcours de Six Périodiques Italiens aux États-Unis (1910-1935)" (Ph.D. diss., University of Paris VII, 1996).

11. On the "heroic immigration," see Howard R. Marraro, *American Opinion on the Unification of Italy, 1846-1861* (New York, 1932); Joanne Pellegrino, "An Effective School of Patriotism," in *Studies in Italian American Social History,* ed. Francesco Cordasco (Towata, N.J., 1985), 84-104.

12. George E. Pozzetta, "The Italian Immigrant Press of New York City: The Early Years, 1880-1915," *Journal of Ethnic Studies* 1 (Fall 1973): 32-46; Pietro Russo, "La stampa periodica italo-americana," in *Gli Italiani negli Stati Uniti,* by Rudolph J. Vecoli et al. (Florence, 1972), 495-98.

13. Bosi, *Cinquant'anni,* 409-10; Grillo, *Cronaca che non e'un epitaffio,* 3-6, 14; Pozzetta, "Italian Immigrant Press," 35-38; Russo, "La stampa periodica italo-americana," 498-502, 538-45; Russo, "The Italian American Periodical Press, 1836-1980," in *Italian Americans: New Perspectives in Italian Immigration and Ethnicity,* ed. Lydio Tomasi (New York, 1985), 248-53; Stephen Naft, ed., *Gli Italiani di New York* (New York, 1939), 79-85.

14. Fumagalli, *La stampa periodica italiana,* 130; Miller, *Ethnic Press,* 52-60; Pozzetta, "Italian Immigrant Press," 37-38; Russo, "La stampa periodica italo-americana," 505-7.

15. Bosi, *Cinquant'anni,* 382-404; Grillo, *Cronaca che non e'un epitaffio,* 8-14; Fumagalli, *La stampa periodica italiana,* 132; Russo, "La stampa periodica italo-americana," 542; Park, *Immigrant Press,* 343; Agostino De Biasi, *La battalgia dell'Italia negli Stati-Uniti* (New York, 1927), 312. Both Bosi and De Biasi had worked on *Il Progresso Italo-Americano* and observed Barsotti firsthand.

16. Bosi, *Cinquant'anni,* 412-14; Grillo, *Cronaca che non e'un epitaffio,* 6-9; De Biasi, *La battalgia dell'Italia,* 310-13. De Biasi was the founder and editor of the influential literary journal *Il Carroccio,* established in New York City in 1916. It promoted Italian intervention during the war and then Fascism. De Biasi's book (cited above) was adorned with an autographed photograph of Mussolini. For an insightful analysis of De Biasi's relationship to Fascism, see Philip V. Cannistraro, "Toward a History of Italian Fascism in the United States, 1921-1929" (ms. in author's possession).

Other memoirs by intellectuals that depict the trials and foibles of prominenti journalism are Camillo Cianfarra, *Il diario di un emigrante* (New York, 1904); Giuseppe Gaja, *Ricordi d'un giornalista errante* (Turin, c. 1900); and Luigi Carnovale, *Il giornalismo degli emigranti italiani del Nord America* (Chicago, 1909). For astute observations regarding the Italian immigrant press, as well as translated passages from Carnevale's memoir, see Gary R. Mormino, "The Immigrant Editor: Making a Living in Urban America," *Journal of Ethnic Studies* 9 (Spring 1981): 81-85.

17. Kathleen Neils Conzen, David A. Gerber, Ewa Morawska, George E. Pozzetta, and Rudolph J. Vecoli, "The Invention of Ethnicity: A Perspective from the U.S.A.," *Journal of American Ethnic History* 12 (Fall 1992): 3–41; Vecoli, "Search for an Italian American Identity."

18. Victor Greene, *American Immigrant Leaders, 1800–1910* (Baltimore, 1987), 122–37.

19. Ibid., 131.

20. Pozzetta, "Italian Immigrant Press," 247; Charles Jaret, "The Greek, Italian, and Jewish American Ethnic Press: A Comparative Analysis," *Journal of Ethnic Studies* 7 (Summer 1979): 47–70.

21. Bosi, *Cinquant'anni*, 250–53; Grillo, *Cronaca che non e'un epitaffio*, 9, 16–17, 22; Russo, "La stampa periodica italo-americana," 513.

22. Greene, *American Immigrant Leaders*, 135; Bosi, *Cinquant'anni*, 258, 408; John W. Briggs, *An Italian Passage: Immigrants to Three American Cities, 1890–1930* (New Haven, Conn., 1978), 125–26.

23. Pozzetta, "Italian Immigrant Press," 32–41; Briggs, *Italian Passage*, 123–29, 177–89; Jaret, "Greek, Italian, and Jewish American Ethnic Press," 52, 62. The statement regarding *L'Italia* is based on a reading of the newspaper for the years 1886–1915.

24. Grillo, *Cronaca che non e'un epitaffio*, 15.

25. Bossi, *Cinquant'anni*, 410–11; Pozzetta, "Italian Immigrant Press," 40; Russo, "La stampa periodica italo-americana," 528–30.

26. Fumagalli, *La stampa periodica italiana*, 134; Vecoli, "Prelates and Peasants: Italian Immigrants and the Catholic Church," *Journal of Social History* 2 (Spring 1969): 217–68. Copies of the New York edition of *L'Asino* are in the Italian Collection, IHRC.

27. This discussion of the sovversivi press draws on my previously published writings on the topic: "'Free Country': The American Republic Viewed by the Italian Left, 1880–1920," in *In the Shadow of the Statue of Liberty: Immigrants, Workers and Citizens in the American Republic, 1880–1920*, ed. Marianne Debouzy (Saint-Denis, France, 1988), 35–56; "'Primo Maggio' in the United States: An Invented Tradition of the Italian Anarchists," in *May Day Celebration*, ed. Andrea Panaccione (Venice, 1988), 55–83; "Primo Maggio: May Day Observances among Italian Immigrant Workers, 1890–1920," *Labor's Heritage* 7 (Spring 1996): 28–41; "Primo Maggio: Teoria e pratica fra gli immigrati italiani negli Stati Uniti," in *Storia e Immagini del 1 Maggio: Problemi della storiografia italiana ed internazionale*, ed. Gianni C. Donno (Manduria, Italy, 1990), 449–61.

28. Bruno Cartosio, "Italian Workers and Their Press in the United States, 1900–1920," and Elisabetta Vezzosi, "Class, Ethnicity and Acculturation in *Il Proletario:* The World War Years," both in *The Press of Labor Migrants in Europe*

and North America, 1800s to 1930s, eds. Christine Harzig and Dirk Hoerder (Bremen, 1985), 423–42 and 443–55, respectively; and Dirk Hoerder, ed., *The Immigrant Labor Press in North America, 1840s–1970s: An Annotated Bibliography,* vol. 3: *Migrants from Southern and Western Europe* (New York, 1987), 1–10. Hoerder's volume includes an introduction, bibliography, and annotations on almost two hundred publications of the Italian labor press.

29. Cartosio, "Italian Workers," 431; Fumagalli, *La stampa periodica italiana,* 90; Hoerder, *Immigrant Labor Press,* 17–129.

30. Vezzosi, "Class, Ethnicity and Acculturation," 451–53; Vecoli, "The Italian Immigrants in the United States Labor Movement from 1880 to 1929," in *Gli Italiani fuori d'Italia. Gli emigrati Italiani nei movimenti operai dei paesi d'adozione 1880–1940,* ed. B. Bezza (Milan, 1983), 257–306; id., "Anthony Capraro and the Lawrence Strike of 1919," in *Labor Divided: Race and Ethnicity in United States Labor Struggles, 1835–1960,* ed. Robert Asher and Charles Stephenson (Albany, 1990), 267–82; id., "Carlo Tresca," "Alberico Molinari," and "Girolamo Valenti," in *Il Movimento Operaio Italiano Dizionario Biografico,* 5 vols. (Rome, 1975–78); id., "Luigi Galleani," in *Encyclopedia of the American Left,* ed. Mari Jo Buhle, Paul Buhle, and Dan Georgakas (New York, 1990; rpt., Urbana, Ill., 1992), 251–53.

31. On the role of the lector, see Gary Mormino and George E. Pozzetta, *The Immigrant World of Ybor City* (Urbana, Ill., 1987), 102–3. The Italian Collection, IHRC, includes extensive holdings of the sovversivi press as well as other publications of this character. For a description of these materials, see Suzanna Moody and Joel Wurl, comps. and eds., *The Immigration History Research Center: A Guide to Collections* (New York, 1991), 135–200, as well as the Labor Preservation Project, Universität Bremen, *The Newspaper and Serial Holdings of the Immigration History Research Center, University of Minnesota,* pt. 2: *Italian-American Periodicals* (Bremen, 1985).

32. Vezzosi, "Class, Ethnicity and Acculturation," 451–52; see also her *Il socialismo indifferente: Immigrati italiani e Socialist Party negli Stati Uniti del primo Novecento* (Rome, 1991).

33. Di Biasi, *La Battalgia dell'Italia,* 311.

34. Cartosio, "Italian Workers," 434–36; Park, *Immigrant Press,* 434; Miller, *Ethnic Press,* xvii; Vezzosi, "Class, Ethnicity and Acculturation," 443–55; Vecoli, "The War and Italian American Syndicalists," ms., IHRC; William Preston Jr., *Aliens and Dissenters: Federal Suppression of Radicals, 1903–1933* (Cambridge, Mass., 1963; rpt., Urbana, Ill., 1995); John J. Tinghino, *Edmondo Rossoni: From Revolutionary Syndicalism to Fascism* (New York, 1991).

35. Grillo, *Cronaca che non e'un epitaffio,* 23; Adriana Dada, "La Stampa Periodica Italiana negli Stati Uniti," ms., IHRC; John P. Diggins, *Mussolini and Fascism: The View from America* (Princeton, N.J., 1972); Gaetano Salvemini,

Italian Fascist Activities in the United States (Staten Island, N.Y., 1977); Cannistraro, "Toward a History of Fascism."

36. For an elaboration of this epistemological issue, see my "Italian Immigrants and Working-Class Movements in the United States: A Personal Reflection on Class and Ethnicity," *Journal of the Canadian Historical Association* (new
series) 4 (1993): 293–305.

2 Chicago's *StreetWise* at the Crossroads: A Case Study of a Newspaper to Empower the Homeless in the 1990s

NORMA FAY GREEN

We are *StreetWise*.
We walk a different road.
No one knows our journey,
but we walk with faith wherever we go.
We're strong, we're proud.
Keep your head up,
and say it loud . . .
StreetWise . . . IT'S ALL GOOD!
—Vendor chant

In the summer of 1992, when Chicago's homeless population had swollen to an estimated 49,000, a tabloid newspaper debuted to confront the issue that the midwestern metropolis could no longer afford to ignore. Unlike mainstream periodicals that offered occasional dispassionate articles on the crisis as unemployment increased and state aid decreased, *StreetWise* was launched as an alternative monthly devoted to direct reader involvement in empowering the homeless.

This essay is a study of the effectiveness of *StreetWise* in maintaining its initial mission through periods of phenomenal growth, defections, and a rival publication, as well as expanded frequency and distribution, continuing staff turnover, and editorial changes. It examines not only the contents of each issue—including letters to and from the editors, vendor-produced articles, and ongoing commentary from the general media—but it also attempts to chart the dialogue between *StreetWise* and its multifaceted audience. *StreetWise* will be analyzed in the context of "street publications" generally and especially in comparison to New York City's *Street News*, the prototype for several similar newspapers in the United States and Europe.

Like so many periodicals about homelessness, *StreetWise* seemed a natural outgrowth of its founder's social activism. Judd Lofchie, a Chicago lawyer and real estate broker, established the nonprofit People Fighting Hunger in 1987. This was the foundation upon which he launched the monthly newspaper in 1992. Lofchie traced his sense of social responsibility to the mid-1980s when he worked in Washington, D.C., and met an advocate for the homeless, Mitch Snyder of the Community for Creative Non-Violence.[1] Similarly, *Street Heat,* an Atlanta-based magazine, was started in 1990 by the Georgia Citizens Coalition on Hunger.[2] Several such "street publications" were sponsored by grassroots groups;[3] others had religious support.[4] A former missionary in Central America launched *Public Forum,* a newspaper in Los Angeles's skid row in 1990.[5] At least one publication, the *Homeless Report,* is copublished by secular and sacred groups.[6] Both *Street* magazine, dating from the mid-1980s and *Spare Change* newspaper, started in 1992, debuted under the direction of Tim Harris, who was with Boston Jobs with Peace.[7] (He now directs Seattle's *Real Change.*)

Lofchie got the idea to start *StreetWise* from a television commercial for *Street News.*[8] Gordon Roddick was similarly inspired to start the *Big Issue,* a newspaper about homelessness in London, after seeing a copy of *Street News* while on a business trip to New York for the cosmetics company that he and his activist wife, Anita, operate.[9] In turn, his publication is said to have spawned the *Macadam Journal,* after Belgian businessman, Jacques Chamut, saw a copy of the *Big Issue* and longed for a French-language edition.[10] Also, the Dublin-based slick magazine, *Big Issues,* in its masthead admits being "founded on the example of *The Big Issue.* . . . Though separate from its British counterpart, it retains close fraternal links." Lofchie openly acknowledged that both *Street News* and *Big Issue* were paradigms for his Chicago publication.

Thus, *StreetWise* modeled itself after *Street News,* a combination publication and social program created by Ohio musician Hutchinson Persons who began the monthly newspaper in November 1989 when Street Aid, a benefit concert to help the hungry, failed to materialize.[11] *Street News* relied on the homeless of Manhattan to act as independent contractors in selling the newspaper about homelessness to the general public. In the tradition of the Salvation Army's *War Cry* magazine, which was sold on street corners at the turn of the century, the messenger was often the symbolic message, more so than the publication being hawked. Through street sales, the buying public came in deliberate contact with the disenfranchised who moved from the periphery and into the limelight, if only momentarily.

In Chicago, *StreetWise* volunteers set up a folding table on the sidewalk outside their donated office space and recruited vendors from the ranks of homeless men and women. Vendors were given ten free newspapers to sell for one dollar each. They had the option of keeping the proceeds or reinvesting some of the money in more papers to sell. They could buy copies for twenty-five cents each, sell the papers for a dollar, and pocket the other seventy-five cents.[12] Regardless of the varying profit margins at street publications, the vendor program was designed to provide economic self-sufficiency and enhance the self-esteem of its participants. In 1992, a few hundred homeless, formerly homeless, and otherwise economically disadvantaged people started peddling *StreetWise* on downtown byways.

Chicagoans who had felt helpless to change the conditions of the people they encountered daily lying on sidewalks, panhandling, or lining up at overcrowded seasonal shelters and soup kitchens began to show support for *StreetWise*. Some gave the vendors a dollar and lauded their sales savvy but refused the newspaper. Others took the newspaper but later threw it in the nearest trash can.[13] Still others, though, actually read the issue and mulled over the contents, even when it shocked or offended them. "The target audience is anybody who's been asked for a quarter and felt guilty when they didn't give it," declared Kathleen Anne "Casey" Covganka, editor-in-chief at the time of the launch. She admitted that it took a while to override some people's skepticism that vendors were just buying alcohol or drugs with the money. "People thought it was another scam. In American cities, we have lost the sense that we're still a community, a clan and that we have to take care of the weaker. We have to get back to that sense."[14]

StreetWise staffers struggled to find the delicate balance between empowering the homeless and developing a loyal following of paying readers lured by eye-catching graphics and useful information as much as sympathy for the vendor. Resourceful vendors used various techniques to try to get more readers involved. The top-selling *StreetWise* salesman, who made about fifty dollars a day, was a veteran of the Gulf War. Daniel Jackson, dressed in his military fatigues, declared, "I am a soldier. I believe in infiltrating and obtaining my objective."[15] A *Chicago Tribune* reporter who observed Jackson in action noted that his main objective was not just sales. "He wants people to read *StreetWise* to learn from its reports on everything from Cabrini-Green [a public housing project] to the poetry scene in Chicago bars. It bothers him to have people give him a dollar and refuse the paper."[16]

Soon, however, *StreetWise* caught on like a prairie fire and Chicagoans were snatching up all available copies. From an initial print run of 25,000 copies, the fledgling news operation found itself going back to press, selling 60,000 copies in the first five weeks in late August and September 1992 (*StreetWise*, Oct. 1992, 3). The first monthly edition, dated October 1992, sold 75,000 copies with the help of 512 vendors (*StreetWise*, Nov. 1992, 3). By November, it had racked up sales of 230,000 copies (*StreetWise*, Dec. 1993, 3). It peaked at "over 145,000 copies sold by 1,527 vendors" in April 1993 (*StreetWise*, May 1993, 3). It stopped publishing specific monthly circulation information soon afterward, as sales flattened. (By April 1995, circulation was reportedly 120,000 a month.) *StreetWise* struggled to cope with its unbridled growth, paralleling the meteoric rise in circulation of its model, *Street News,* which went from initial sales of 50,000 copies to the 1 million mark just four months later.[17]

Unlike *Street News,* the *Tenderloin Times* of San Francisco, and *Hard Times for Now* of Los Angeles, *StreetWise* did not evolve gradually from a newsletter format.[18] Instead, it arrived in its media market as a full-blown newspaper competing with other paid and free local periodicals available in hundreds of retail outlets and vending machines. *StreetWise* struggled to find its niche in design and content. Volume 1, number 1 of *StreetWise* spelled out an ambitious seven-point editorial mission devoted to diversity:

—Promote empowerment and self-sufficiency of homeless through employment.
—Supply information and support environmental and social issues.
—Advance arts and life sciences.
—Represent cultural diversity in city, country and world.
—Support those seeking to make a difference through volunteerism or positive social change.
—Present information promoting minorities and combating stereotypes.
—Support belief in interconnectedness and interdependence of all living things.

The initial *StreetWise* editors included individuals with general media experience and a commitment to the cause. None were homeless. Covganka, whom Lofchie met through his church,[19] had worked for seventeen years in display advertising at the *Chicago Tribune.* She had worked with people in poverty and welcomed the opportunity to raise consciousness about public policy: "We want to give poor people not only a chance to change their situations but also a chance to help change the backward government that helped put them there."[20] David Whitaker, a former entertainment editor of the *Chicago Suburban Times,* was recruited for an editorial post when he appeared at a volunteer meeting.[21] Neither were on salary until January 1993. Both said that they wanted to help the homeless and to put out a quality publication as well. As Covganka emphasized, "It was important to me to develop a good editorial product that the public would embrace."[22]

While StreetWise had adapted the homeless vendor distribution concept from Street News, it seemed clear that the Chicago publication would have to take a different tack than its New York show-business-oriented cousin when it came to editorial presentation. Circulating in the media capital of the United States, Street News succeeded initially with the motto "Helping America's Hungry" (later changed to "America's Motivational Non-Profit Newspaper" and then "the soul and spirit of the street"). Street News had an editorial mix of job listings, prose and poems by homeless persons, and opinion pieces with celebrity bylines including Paul Newman, B. B. King, Liza Minnelli, Cyndi Lauper, Patti LaBelle, Sting, Gloria Estefan, the Beach Boys, and Melissa Manchester. Critics described it as a "charity gala in print"[23] and "an amalgam of glitz and grit."[24]

Neither Persons, a musician and former designer of hang gliders, nor his codirector Wendy Koltun, a former ballerina and marketing researcher, had any formal journalism training, but they attracted a cadre of eager volunteers who did, "most of whom are in their early 20s from both the [political] left and right."[25] Turnover was high among the volunteer and paid staff as well. After a controversial network television report in May 1990 about Persons's behavior and alleged mismanagement at Street News, eight staff members and two of the five board members quit.[26] Persons himself resigned under pressure after financial records were subpoenaed. That summer, some of the former staffers started a competing publication, Crossroads Magazine, sold by the homeless in Manhattan.[27] The rival enterprise was established as a regular for-profit company allowing vendors to pocket sixty-five cents for every issue they sold for a dollar.

Meanwhile, Street News limped on as sales slumped from a high of 200,000 down to 14,000 per edition.[28] While it garnered favorable publicity initially, public enthusiasm waned after financial investigations began. In 1990, the printer, Sam Chen of Expedi Printing, inherited the vestiges of what had been the media darling of New York. However, the new ownership of Street News came without the nonprofit status that left with Persons. In 1993, the journalist Janet Wickenhaver was brought in as editor and associate publisher to change the newspaper. "I got there with a mission to revamp editorial on the naive theory that good editorial would rescue the business prospects," she explained. "It turned out we needed a whole lot more."[29] Reports of the death of Street News, circulated early in its publishing life, did not seem premature in 1995 when the newspaper admitted great difficulty in maintaining circulation and advertising. Chen published a "Bye Bye" issue in January 1995 but Wickenhaver and four volunteers managed to produce a spring issue, hoping to reinvigorate interest. The editor admitted that *Street News* "can't survive by continuing to appeal to sympathy alone."[30]

Chicago's *StreetWise* struggled with similar peaks and valleys of public acceptance and staff loyalties. Covganka and the rest of the shoestring staff tinkered with copy and layout to attract potential readers and advertisers. The first issue, designed to put a face on homelessness, did so by featuring a front-page photograph of a young, well-groomed white man sitting on a downtown sidewalk with a bag of his possessions, a paper cup for donations, and a handmade sign reading: "I am Homeless. Would you please help me. May God Bless you. Thank you." He stared forlornly into the lens of the camera. Dated simply "Summer edition 1992," the twenty-page issue had a decided arts emphasis and design with large black-and-white photographs offset with bold headlines and wide margins. Verse abounded, supplemented with an interview with a Latino poet and a sidebar on homeless women poets. Mixed in with news on seasonal shelters and a feature on the Great Lakes were articles on an HIV-positive mother, teaching environmentalism to children, reviews of art exhibits, commentary on National Endowment for the Arts grants, and a column called "Speech! Speech!" soliciting reader responses on monthly themes. (The first one was on dating in the nineties.) That latter column never really caught on and was dropped by April 1993 when its monthly topic—favorite pigout food—seemed clearly out of step with the People Fighting Hunger roots of the newspaper.

By June 1993, *StreetWise* had thinned to twenty pages from its regular twenty-four and reprinted an article from its premiere issue on the seasonal shelters. The July 1993 issue had a noticeable feminist bent with cover photograph and seven separate inside features on women, even though the editorial page did not hint at any special theme. By the paper's first anniversary, the original editors, Covganka and Whitaker, had departed, and the newspaper had survived its first editorial crises and a bout of "compassion fatigue" from harassed customers. It seemed that the newspaper, founded in part to provide a vehicle for those who had been voiceless, had suddenly become too noisy.

Chicago's mainstream dailies and weeklies had lavished attention on *StreetWise,* and generally favorable articles were written about it for the first few months before and just after its birth. However, by the beginning of Chicago's bleakest weather, a certain weariness had set in as the newspaper's novelty wore off. The *Chicago Sun-Times* columnist Richard Roeper spoke the heretofore unspeakable: he was tired of *StreetWise*. His biting column reflected the resentment that many citizens may have been afraid to express for fear of being cast as uncharitable curmudgeons. He complained about the noisy vendors spaced too closely together on the major streets and, most damning, he questioned whether the content, which he found too depressing, was actually being read by anyone. He interviewed pedestrians who were not convinced that the paper was a worthy enterprise. Roeper criticized "the relentlessly grim subject matter . . . an odd mix of stories about the homeless, poems by the homeless and attempted humor, all of it's well-intentioned, I'm sure, but not particularly inspiring." He suggested some editorial changes: "I'd rather see classifieds listing the work skills and history of homeless people who want jobs. Statistics proving that not every homeless person is a drug addict or an alcoholic. Stories from the formerly homeless explaining in detail how they got off the street. In short, a paper that isn't so relentlessly . . . homeless."[31]

Reaction to Roeper's column as well as a steady stream of complaints from patrons who were having a hard time coping with increasingly aggressive vendors were grist for the February 1993 editorial meeting that erupted into a power struggle over the direction of the newspaper and its social program.[32] It was clear that *StreetWise* was going to have to change in order to survive. The small staff had been overwhelmed by the phenomenal leaps in circulation. *StreetWise* seemed unwilling to turn away any homeless people who wanted to be vendors, even if it meant saturating the downtown market at a rate of ten to fifteen new sellers a day.[33] There had been hints of trouble controlling vendors as early as the third issue, when Covganka urged readers to greet vendors and buy on the street rather than take the easy way out with a subscription that avoided face-to-face contact (*StreetWise*, Dec. 1992, 3). Ideological conflicts emerged when an angry reader accused Covganka of elitism because the editor complained about the fraudulent use of the *StreetWise* name by unauthorized vendors:

> While your resentment of the unauthorized usage of your name is understandable, the sort of judgmental arrogance that leads to openly hostile references to pan-handlers, scammers, and charlatans is clearly unwarranted. These are people trying to survive in the street, employing tactics essentially no different than those used by anyone else here in our sadly flawed economic system. Your paternalistic dismissal of them betrays the same core ethic espoused by any traditional institution choosing to name its goal, values and practices as legitimate, and any others as inferior or corrupt.[34]

Once citizens heard that the newspaper vendors were able to apply the money they earned selling to pay for room and board and clothing, support increased and more potential vendors clamored for the opportunity. With only a one-day training program, vendors emerged from the *StreetWise* offices in a reconverted theater and nightclub on East 13th Street on the near south side just off Michigan Avenue. Vendors often did not go far, and pedestrians soon found themselves running the gauntlet of a dozen vendors in a single block. Whitaker was appalled by what he witnessed: "We would hear complaints from the public. People were being accosted. There was no time . . . to get to know their names and faces. The paper was getting more important than the people selling it."[35] Also, Whitaker became concerned that *StreetWise* was getting soft on the issues it vowed to cover in its original mission statement. There was resentment that the move toward more upbeat stories was only being done to placate critics. After an unsuccessful takeover attempt, Whitaker and five other original staffers decided to venture out on their own with a more hard-hitting paper and a plan for exclusive sales territories for an initial core group of thirty vendors.[36] Only two issues of *I.D.* were published (April and June 1993) before it folded due to lack of advertising and other financial support.[37]

Whitaker vowed to counter the problems of *StreetWise* with a way to empower the homeless, an objective he felt had been lost in the heady days of initial success. "The project [*I.D.*] is about helping individuals, not selling papers. The paper is just a way to get people in the door," he declared.[38] Part of *I.D.*'s program was designed to offer free health screenings, dental checkups, job training, G.E.D. workshops, and Alcoholic Anonymous meetings as components of a total package to help people break a cycle of poverty and homelessness. The problem with *I.D.*, as well as with *StreetWise*, was finding funds to sustain the effort and restore public goodwill.

Unlike New York's *Street News,* which started with full-page advertisements from mainstream media, real estate developers, and advertising agencies, *StreetWise* published only a few fractional pages of ads in its first months. There were five fractional ads in the preview issue, including one promoting a Chicago walk for the homeless, a trade-in-kind ad for Kinko's Copies (where the tabloid's desktop publishing work was done), two ads for local restaurants, and one for vintage eyewear. These joined two house ads asking for an advertising sales representative and offering charter subscriptions. The first issue of *StreetWise* was financed through a benefit concert, advertising revenue, and contributions from Lofchie. *StreetWise* did not have a full-page ad until its seventh issue. The ad, on an inside page, promoted a Christian Science lecture at a local college. In November 1993, its first full-page back-cover ad appeared for Hopefest, a concert to benefit the Chicago Coalition for the Homeless, sponsored in part by *StreetWise*. Over the months it stooped to the lowly tradition of patronizing advertisers by running editorial features on them close to ads for their establishments. In March 1995, *StreetWise* finally listed an advertising sales representative on its masthead. Shortly thereafter that representative was promoted to manager and two more ad reps were hired. By May, the newspaper was promoting "two ads for the price of one" for potential advertisers.

Plans were underway for a *StreetWise* television campaign,[39] and the first in-house public service ad appeared in the March 1993 issue. The half-page black-and-white horizontal ad showed a man lying on a street under a blanket of newspapers. The headline read: "We created a newspaper to do more about the homeless problem than provide the usual coverage." The tagline read: "*StreetWise*. We're not looking for a handout. Just a hand." The ads were created by Eisaman, Johns, and Law Advertising. In November 1993, a classified advertising section began. On the eve of the second anniversary in August 1994, a new clipboard advertising section of general classifieds, separate from vendor classifieds, began, along with a house ad touting hats, coffee mugs, and T-shirts imprinted with the *StreetWise* logo.

In order to attract advertisers and improve the editorial contents, the newspaper needed to know who was buying it and who was reading it. Initial observations indicated that young white women and college students in general were good customers.[40] The February 1993 issue featured some of the first editorial and sales interaction between vendors and their customers when two sellers (one black, one white) were assigned to interview their mostly white patrons about what Black History Month meant to them. The November 1993 *StreetWise* included a reader survey form. Though the sample size was not revealed, the results indicated that of those who responded 87 percent were college-educated, 25 percent earned more than $50,000, 64 percent were women, 65 percent were single, and readers' average age was 40 (*StreetWise*, Feb. 1994, 10). In a donor newsletter published a year later, more *StreetWise* readership data was published that revealed a slightly different demographic base of support: 69 percent were college-educated, median household income was $40,000 (25 percent reported $75,000), and more than half of those who responded were "regular readers" of *StreetWise*. Also, 71 percent were regular moviegoers, 39 percent were regular theatergoers, and the average *StreetWise* reader bought 14 paperbacks and 10 compact discs each year.[41]

After the negative publicity early in 1993 and the threat of a rival publication, *StreetWise* responded by hiring its first director to coordinate its newspaper and vendor service activities. Christopher Persons came to *StreetWise* from a suburban Chicago office of United Cerebral Palsy where he had been director of development and public relations. Even before he arrived in May, the publication began to feature its vendors more prominently in its pages. One vendor, Joel Alfassa, who had been contributing commentary since the second issue, became a staff writer after his official column debuted in the March 1993 edition. By February 1994, he had built up a loyal following and his column was moved to a prominent position on page three. Later that year, he began writing reviews of budget restaurants, and by November 1, 1994, he was being touted on the cover. Alfassa told the *Chicago Sun-Times:* "I feel I'm writing in their [i.e., the homeless] name, trying to tell people what's going on."[42] One of the first topics he discussed in his column was *StreetWise*'s expansion into the suburbs and his encounters with some less-than-friendly citizens there. While Hutchinson Persons of New York's *Street News* announced plans to distribute that newspaper in major cities across the country and went so far as to open a storefront office in Washington, D.C., *StreetWise* had a less grandiose ambition: to penetrate Chicago's northern and western suburbs with a well-prepared sales force.

In fall 1995, *StreetWise* experimented with a formal northwest suburban vendor partnership with Public Action to Deliver Shelter (PADS). It yielded some mixed reviews on the part of suburban patrons, though a core of five vendors reported selling 600 copies in one week. Beyond the six-county metropolitan area, *StreetWise* tentatively explored expansion to other cities across the country. An article in the *Chicago Tribune*'s business pages on October 2, 1995, stated that *StreetWise* had "its eyes dreamily aimed on expanding its usual non-profit franchise to other urban islands of opportunity like Detroit or Washington, D.C." Two years later, that dream had not yet materialized.

In March 1993 DePaul University sponsored a *StreetWise* "Vendor of the Year" award to motivate the budding entrepreneurs. By August, the formerly homeless Daniel Jackson, who had been appointed community outreach coordinator, announced that the orientation program for vendors had been extended from one day to a full week. The next month, *StreetWise* began a "Vendor of the Month" column profiling one of its hundreds of news hawks. The quotes from vendors were often quite poignant as they reflected on their life before *StreetWise* and the goals they now hoped to achieve. Life stories included a successful accountant forced into homelessness due to medical expenses from a brain tumor, an honors student who turned to drugs, and Vietnam veterans haunted by the war. In the April 1994 edition, one vendor wrote, "I've put down the guns and knives and picked up some *StreetWise*, it's better for us both to point that at you."[43] Another lauded the tabloid: "First of all, it put me back to work. It's a quality paper without sex, prejudice or gangs. The writing is excellent. It's the paper that should be in every home where there are children and in schools."[44]

A new "Heard on the Curb" column was developed to accompany the vendor profiles. It was designed to feature "antidotes [*sic*] you have from the streets. If you witness anything interesting while on your route, jot it down and bring it in. If you have news about yourself, another vendor, your neighborhood or sales territory, bring it in. Also, we are looking for success stories, job and housing announcements, births, deaths, marriages and birthdays" (*StreetWise*, Oct. 1, 1994, 7). In the true community newspaper spirit—and in the spirit of Ragged Dick—there were also stories about good deeds done for customers (rescued children and recovered wallets), good deeds performed by customers (new shoes and a ticket to the opera), news about recovery from surgery, wedding anniversaries, and the birth of kittens. However, not all the news was necessarily fodder for Horatio Alger. The issue of November 16, 1994, featured a story on a suspended vendor and how he was trying to pull his life back together while fighting drug and alcohol addiction.

The vendor Everett Atkinson's commentary debuted in the November 1994 issue, and by February 1995 it had been officially named "The Concrete Word" and was alternating with the vendor meeting summary also penned by Atkinson. The June 1–15, 1995, issue announced that *Street-Wise*'s head cashier and staff accountant was teaching an entrepreneurial course for vendors interested in starting their own businesses. All this seemed to indicate that the tabloid had stabilized to the point where it could expand its vendor services and editorial content.

After Covganka and Whitaker left in 1993, an acting editor, Katy Bruggeman, filled in until Shawn "Cal" McAllister succeeded her in February 1994. McAllister had worked for *StreetWise* as a freelance writer. In October 1993, Bruggeman announced several new features: "In response to reader suggestions, next month we'll be covering some new territory, as yet, sports, astrology and crosswords don't figure into the issue plan— but keep those suggestions coming!" (By the following month, she had to swallow some of her words as a sports column appeared, followed in

December by a horoscope column.) Though most of the content remained nonfiction, *StreetWise* experimented with a condensed novel in its August 1993 edition. This was a precursor to a continuing contemporary fiction serial, "Clark Street Stories," by Kim Clark, debuting on November 16, 1994, and running through mid-1995. More short works of fiction were solicited for use in fall 1995 and a collection of poems from *StreetWise* was printed in a forty-page book entitled *from hard times to hope*. This last was intended as a premium for vendors and bookstores to sell for five dollars during the 1995 holiday season.

A plethora of new columns appeared in fall 1994 after Christopher Persons was fired over conflicts with the board.[45] Just before his ouster he had said, "We want to be a cross between the [Chicago] *Reporter* [an urban affairs magazine] and the *Reader* [a free weekly]. Right now, 75 percent of people buy the paper because it's a nice thing to do, with 25 percent buying it to read. We want to make it 75 percent-25 percent the other way."[46] McAllister and John Ellis IV, whom Persons had hired from *Crain's Chicago Business,* worked as coeditors until Ellis became sole editor in February 1995.[47] In October 1994, new columns appeared on mental health issues and Chicago's theater. In November, "Streetbriefs" debuted as a column of news items on social service agencies serving the homeless community. It was designed to acknowledge the tripartite audience of *StreetWise:* the socially concerned general public, the homeless community itself, and service providers. In January 1995, a Chicago television meteorologist began to contribute a column on the weather, and a column called "Home Free" appeared with advice on successful techniques for pursuing self-sufficiency and an entrepreneurial career.[48] In June 1995, a sports column was revived by a local radio producer.

Following its twenty-page preview issue in 1992, *StreetWise* had twenty-four pages each month through May 1994. In June, it reverted to twenty pages, and since July 1994 it has been sixteen pages per issue. While *Street News* jumped to twice-monthly issues in its first year and London's *Big Issue* waited only eleven issues to go fortnightly, *StreetWise* was conservative in its move to greater frequency. Though it tried to respond to vendor complaints that their sales dropped off after a couple of weeks each month and they needed fresh material to sell, the newspaper did not rush into the two-issue-a-month trend. Instead, it experimented with a second monthly issue in both December 1993 and March 1994, explaining in its December 1993 issue: "We're a frugal bunch though. This 'testing the waters' will be analyzed carefully by our Board of Directors and management staff. If successful—defined by the increase in revenues generated by vendors—we will test the water again in the spring. It is our hope to be semi-monthly by September of 1994."

On the eve of its second anniversary, that hope was realized. The revamped paper made judicious use of color and artwork as well. *StreetWise's* first color appeared as a small inset on the front cover of the January 1993 issue as a teaser to an inside spread on colored lights. In April 1993, it featured another color spread. In February 1994, it began to print its front-page nameplate in color, and by April it was running both the nameplate and "insider" teaser box in color. A year later, *StreetWise* ran its first two-color front page in conjunction with its first-ever special report and a feature, both of which started their text on the cover and continued to several pages inside. Other format refinements included a special four-page pullout section entitled "Street Scene," featuring arts criticism and reviews; it began in June 1994. *StreetWise* also began running script illustrations in the February 1993 edition, and by April 1994 had cartoons on its editorial page. In June 1994, a classified ad appeared that asked for a Spanish-speaking volunteer to coordinate a bilingual portion of the paper (which had not materialized as of 1997).[49]

StreetWise refined and strengthened its editorial stance despite seemingly uncontrolled growth and continued staff turnover that threatened to undermine its mission. Its focus for its second year was to improve content. In November 1993, it shifted from an avowedly "neutral" stance to a position of outright advocacy (*StreetWise*, Nov. 1993, 3). As it celebrated its third anniversary in September 1995, it continued to broaden its base of support. *StreetWise's* masthead started listing the specific affiliations of its board of directors with the February 15, 1995, issue. The board includes members from advocacy groups, government, and corporations, including the Chicago Coalition for the Homeless, the Cook County Board of Commissioners, the Center for Street People, and corporate representatives from Inland Steel, UNE Technology, Spiegel Incorporated, Ringier American, and Deloitte and Touche. An editor's note in the April 1, 1995, issue stated: "*StreetWise* has endured many changes in the nearly three years that it has been serving the Chicago public, vendors and community members. By now, most of Chicago has a basic understanding of how *StreetWise* benefits vendors. . . . What most people don't know is how we contribute to the rest of the Chicago community."

While *StreetWise* was patterned after Manhattan's *Street News*, it managed to adapt the concept to the particularities of Chicago and the Midwest. It did not rely on celebrity bylines but instead took a straightforward, if rough-hewn, substance-over-style approach often fraught with mis-spellings.[50] While some righteous readers decried the "F-word" in poems by the homeless, the use of alcohol as an ingredient in some recipes, and the appearance of an astrology column as unchristian, the paper seemed to lend a sympathetic ear to the previously voiceless as well as the "squeaky wheels."

StreetWise follows in the footsteps of hundreds of other American alternative publications. When the mainstream media ignore, distort, or bury news of an issue such as homelessness, alternative publications spring up to fill the void. For example, commentary in *StreetWise* ridiculed a local television anchorman who attempted to disguise himself as a homeless person in order to do an exposé. Certainly making a profit through street sales or subscriptions has always been secondary to alternative publications in general. While Covganka dreamed about a day when she would "see us eventually luring the homeless as staff, . . . see advertisers and writers flocking to us. The ideal would be to have corporations underwrite publication costs so that the salespeople could keep the entire cover price."[51] All that has not yet happened—but it still could. About 80 percent of its operating expenses are met through paper sales. In 1996, *StreetWise* added a new staff position—director of resource development—to oversee fund-raising, grant writing, and solicitation of in-kind donations.

While New York's *Street News* had considerable mainstream media support, including advertising from the *New York Daily News* and the *Village Voice* and marketing advice and donated promotional merchandise from the *New York Times*, *StreetWise* has gradually built up relationships with the *Chicago Tribune* and *Crain's Chicago Business*. Though not quite as formalized as the *San Francisco Examiner* editor who regularly taught workshops for *Tenderloin Times*'s contributors,[52] staffers from two Chicago mainstream publications routinely volunteer their time at *StreetWise* as editors, writing coaches, and career counselors for fledgling freelancers.

StreetWise hoped to provoke comment and occasionally stir up controversy with its articles. Its first attempt at that dealt with a first-person account of a man's negative experience at Pacific Garden Mission, similar to an editorial strategy used by Boston's irreverent *Street*, which criticized one of its area's biggest shelters.[53] The shelter article in *StreetWise* stirred reader response both pro but mostly con for months. Its longest continuing coverage was of the fatal shooting of one of its vendors and the subsequent trial of the miscreant. So controversy continued into 1997. One reader wrote on January 16, 1995, to complain about the supposed vendor chant: "I am appalled by the recommendation that we ask the vendors to recite that ridiculous little cheer you've designed for them. I hope the staff of this paper is not becoming so full of themselves, due to its success, that they lose sight of why the paper was created."

In its first five years of existence, *StreetWise* wrote about street publications in other parts of the country and the world. In December 1994, it started exchanging stories with *MOB Magazin,* a street paper published in Berlin (now merged with former rival *Haz* into the newly renamed *Motz*).[54] The Chicago newspaper also has written about French street publications[55] and a few in California, Massachusetts, and elsewhere. The April 16–30, 1995, issue reprinted a dispatch from an online version of an Italian street magazine, *Note Sul Disagio, Narcomafie e Nomadismo.* Thanks to Loyola University in Chicago faculty, *StreetWise* connected to the Internet in the spring of 1995 "to trade stories and ideas with other street papers," as well as to offer computer training to vendors who wish to navigate into cyberspace to access job information and to share homeless experiences with the global community (*StreetWise,* May 1–15, 1995, 2). In February 1997, it launched a new column entitled "National Briefs from the Streets: What Other Street Papers Are Saying," featuring excerpts from everywhere, including *Wyoming Winds* in Cheyenne to *Our Voice* in Edmonton and *Homeless Talk* in Johannesburg, South Africa.

In August 1996, *StreetWise,* along with the Washington-based National Coalition for the Homeless and Seattle's *Real Change,* sponsored the first-ever North American Street Newspaper Summit in Chicago, "to allow street newspapers . . . to share experiences." The weekend conference agenda included discussion of technical information on how papers are run, services provided for vendors, empowerment of homeless writers, and political organizing in the homeless community. Ellis moderated a Sunday morning business session attended by more than half of some forty U.S. and Canadian newspapers represented at the conference. They unanimously agreed to form an organization to be known as the North American Street Newspaper Association (NASNA). A temporary steering committee was created. It would be another year before the group name, mission statement, and goals were formally adopted by more than thirty street newspapers represented at the second conference hosted in Seattle by *Real Change* in September 1997.

The vendor columnist Alfassa seems to be most in touch with the growing list of street publications and what he calls "the family of vendors" (*StreetWise,* Aug. 16–31, 1995, 10). *StreetWise* ran an article about the uncertain future of *Street News,* and Alfassa paid tribute to the predecessor publication in his column as well. The March 16–31, 1995, issue mentioned that his column ran in other street newspapers, including the Pittsburgh and Denver editions of *Street Beat Quarterly*. As Alfassa noted: "As the word gets around the country about the potential of these 'street newspapers' to both the homeless and the general public, circulation grows and so does support. . . . I really do believe we have resurrected the American revolution with these street newspapers that are springing up all over the place, recently at the rate of about one a month" (*StreetWise*, Jan. 16–31, 1995, 3).

While the impact of *Street News* on publications in other cities across the world cannot be overstated, publications such as *StreetWise* seem also to have carved a viable niche for themselves, slow and steady as they go. In an ironic twist, London's *Big Issue* planned to colonize its general-interest publication to New York City in 1997 in direct competition with a revitalized *Street News*, which was recognized at the 1997 NASNA conference with an award for pioneering efforts. Publications that rely on volunteer support and public sympathy experience periods of burnout, bickering, and backlash; *StreetWise* has not escaped this cycle. Nevertheless, perhaps it learned from other street publications by rededicating itself to crusading about homelessness as a symptom of bigger social problems.

After months of redesign efforts, the cover of the April 16–30, 1995, issue showed the evolution by featuring reproductions of the last eight front pages of the tabloid and touted "the new, improved *StreetWise*" as a revamped brand of award-winning journalism.[56] The newspaper's centerfold included messages from the staff, volunteers, vendors, and founder Judd Lofchie. The editor Ellis restated the editorial mission: "Our overall goal is to present issues that cut across economic status and culture. We think that everyone is concerned about the spread of AIDS, quality education, affordable housing and other subjects we have tackled with our cover stories. In all our efforts, we are not just pointing to problems, but looking for solutions." The executive director Anthony Oliver noted that the multiple purposes of the publication provide a provocative agenda and journalistic responsibility: "As a newspaper and a social service agency, we are in a unique position to delve deeper into the issues which contribute to the state of homelessness and to educate the public on those issues. . . . The causes of homelessness are complicated and are deeply rooted in problems within society we must consider individually and as a community."[57]

For *StreetWise*, 1996 proved to be a pivotal year. The newspaper staff struggled to produce twice-monthly editions despite a computer crash in January that destroyed its main design system, followed by two burglaries in April that included the loss of $15,000 of computer equipment. Chicago's mainstream press rallied around the underdog publication; the *Chicago Sun-Times* loaned personnel and equipment while other papers donated new equipment and a security system. *StreetWise* kept its local profile high with follow-up coverage and protest marches surrounding the withdrawal of murder charges against an off-duty Chicago police officer accused of fatally shooting a homeless man who happened to be a *Street-Wise* vendor. It continued to publish special reports on topics including domestic violence and regional transportation planning. On the eve of its fourth anniversary in August, it sold its five-millionth copy to a woman in front of the Tribune Tower. The paper changed its front-page motto from "Life on the Streets" to "Empowering People to Self-Sufficiency through Employment." It hosted the North American Street Newspaper Conference in August (described above), and in November its editor John Ellis IV went to London to observe the first general assembly of the International Network of Street Papers, representing sixteen of an estimated sixty such publications in Europe, Australia, and South Africa. Ellis, who had been editor since 1994, resigned at year's end, and the managing editor Jennifer Atkin, hired in 1995, left early in 1997.

In early 1997, *StreetWise* hired Lisa Ely, who had community publication experience, as editor with Brendan Shiller as associate editor. They implemented design changes including computer-generated graphics and an upgrade to four-color, four-page wraps of heavier paper stock for the front and centerfold section, which began with the April 16–30 edition. By June, Ely was gone and Shiller, a Howard University journalism graduate who had been editor of the *All Chicago City News,* became acting editor and eventually editor. Content changes included new columns on housing law and career development as well as vendor-bylined spiritual advice ("The Way of the Mystic"), general advice ("Mr. Wise"), peer advice ("Vendor to Vendor"), and sports views ("Full Court Press"). A new section on nonprofit and community organizations appeared, along with a puzzle page and occasional commentary ("Attuned to the Deaf Rhythm") by deaf writer and *StreetWise* page editor Sally Richards. Its September 16–30 (fifth anniversary) edition featured findings of a planned annual demographic survey sponsored in conjunction with the University of Illinois Research Laboratory to poll people in shelters, transient hotels, and on the streets about the causes of their homelessness and to gather information such as the most recent rent rate paid.

In fall 1997, Shiller shepherded a move to new offices to accommodate the paper's increased frequency, along with an emphasis on exclusive political news stories and special series about gentrification and mass transit cutbacks. The October 1 edition reported that vendors voted 164 to 162 to change from semi-monthly (new editions on the 1st and 16th) to bi-weekly (every other Tuesday) as a prelude to becoming weekly in 1998. This followed the newspaper's move to a rehabbed, three-story, 30,000-square-foot building at 1331 S. Michigan, around the corner from its former facility. The new space housed the newspaper operations as well as StreetWise Work Empowerment Center, which included a Learning Resource Center designed to train vendors with computer-based, self-paced programs in reading and writing, as well as access to Internet-based housing and employment information.

Through its pages and its vendor program, *StreetWise* has tried to foster a caring community to embrace those who have been marginalized. The vendor Elmer Davis, who was profiled in the May 16–31, 1995, issue on the occasion of his "retirement" after two and a half years, likened *StreetWise* to a growing child: "As with all infants, we must learn patience, try to foresee any unexpected turn of events and tolerate certain behaviors. *StreetWise*, like any child, needs time to grow, to find its legs and start making strides of independence. Young as we are, we've had a few hard knocks. But slowly we will become stronger, changing in the areas that need to be corrected. We will grow to where our city can be proud of us."[58]

StreetWise's founder, Lofchie, believes that the paper has been successful in its mission to empower Chicago's homeless. He boasted in general terms, "Hundreds of our vendors have obtained jobs, rooms and apartments, and have reunited with their spouses and children. Many have received alcohol and drug counseling, psychological counseling, haircuts, GEDs and voice mail cards."

In the September 16–30, 1997, issue, *StreetWise*, which touted on its front page "130,000 copies sold monthly," stated that in the last five years it had "developed a solid financial foundation, based mostly on vendor sales of the newspaper." A pie chart showed newspaper sales as $360,132 at the end of 1996. A *StreetWise* press kit distributed at the Seattle conference said the paper "generated over $7 million for the homeless population in Chicago." "What began as a 'street paper' operation, designed to empower the homeless to self-sufficiency has expanded its mission to include those at risk of becoming homeless," Director Oliver wrote (Sept. 16–30, 1997, 2). "In the past five years, *StreetWise* has provided employment opportunities to more than 3,000 homeless men and women." The vendor Isaiah Rogers noted, "*StreetWise* has changed a lot for the better because of new ideas. I think it now does a lot of good, from the things they print to the people they help. But it could go just about anywhere; it depends on the individuals" (6). Editor Shiller said, "Our past—'five years of growth'—has been one of growing pains, triumphs, mistakes, changes and evolution." Fresh from participating in the second annual street newspaper conference, he surmised, "With so much discussion and debate, the right road will eventually become clear. In the mean time, let's all keep an eye on the street."

While *StreetWise* travels the same uncertain roads of all street publications, the feisty tabloid seems ready to enter young adulthood with a renewed sense of purpose about its role in helping Chicago's homeless.

NOTES

1. Edward Walsh, "Chicago's Street-Wise Approach to Helping the City's Homeless," *Washington Post*, Dec. 25, 1992, A3.

2. Lyle V. Harris, "Magazine Devoted to Homeless Thrives," *Atlanta Constitution*, Jan. 13, 1992, C1.

3. Some that cropped up in the 1990s include *Homeless Connection* (Green Bay, Wis., Brown County Task Force for the Homeless); *Homeword* (St. Petersburg, Fla., Advocate for Shelter Action/Policy); *Homeless Times* (Albion, Calif., people of Navarro Beach); *Safety Network* (New York, National Coalition for the Homeless); *Street Beat* (Pittsburgh, Community Human Services); *Street Sheet* (San Francisco, Coalition on the Homeless); *Street Voice* (Baltimore, Center for Applied Nomadology); *Homeless Grapevine* (Cleveland, Northeast Ohio Coalition for the Homeless); *Homeless Reporter* (Los Angeles, Shelter Partnership, Inc.), *Hard Times for Now* (Greater Los Angeles Gray Panthers); *Real Change* (Seattle, Pike Market Senior Center/Downtown Food Bank); and *HOPE*—Helping Ourselves Persevere in Everything (Bloomington [Ind.] Coalition of Low Income and Homeless Citizens).

4. Others with religious roots include the *Dark Night* (published by St. John of the Cross Catholic Worker in Cedar Rapids, Iowa); the *Homeless Express* (distributed by the New Life Evangelistic Center in St. Louis); *Loaves and Fishes* (published by the Elkton, Maryland–based Meeting Ground, "a non-profit religious mission supported through spontaneous gifts of faith and love"); and the historic *Homeless Boy* (published by the Milwaukee Catholic Boys Home in 1907).

5. Bill Boyarsky, "Journalism Comes to Skid Row," *Los Angeles Times*, Mar. 30, 1990, B2.

6. Published jointly by the Minnesota Coalition for the Homeless in Minneapolis and the St. Paul Catholic Charities of the Archdiocese of St. Paul and Minneapolis.

7. Adrian Walker, "*Spare Change* for Sale," *Boston Globe*, Apr. 6, 1992, 21.

8. Janan Hanna, "Homeless Hit the Streets Hawking 'Their' Paper," *Chicago Tribune*, Sept. 12, 1992, 11.

9. Vicky Hutchings, "The Plumber, the Crook, His Wife . . . and the Social Worker," *New Statesman and Society*, Apr. 1991, S29.

10. Alan Riding, "France's Homeless Get Help! Read All about It," *New York Times*, Nov. 10, 1993, A4.

11. Christine McAuley explained: "*Street News* was to be the underground equivalent of Live Aid, the day-long benefit for Ethiopian relief for which Mr. Persons had worked as a coordinator" ("Liza Minnelli Sells Well, Particularly in Subway Trains," *Wall Street Journal,* Feb. 27, 1990, A1).

12. In New York, vendors initially could buy the papers for twenty-five cents and sell them for seventy-five cents, with *Street News* getting twenty cents for paper and costs and five cents to put into an individual savings account for housing. See Kathleen Teltsch, "Tabloid Sold by Homeless Is in Trouble," *New York Times,* May 24, 1990, B6. In Boston in 1990, *Street* magazine charged its vendors just ten cents (for a one-dollar issue), which went to local shelters. See Farai Chideya, "The Kindness of Strangers," *Newsweek,* Aug. 13, 1990, 48. In Oakland and Berkeley, California, homeless vendors of *Street Spirit,* a newspaper started in 1995, were allowed to keep the entire one-dollar cover cost according to Tara Mack, "Spirit of Street Papers Continues to Grow in California," *StreetWise,* Mar. 16–31, 1995, 15.

13. Boston's *Spare Change* editor Marc Goldfinger said his paper, like *StreetWise,* "used to be a charity rag—people would buy it and throw it away. From the responses we get, we can tell people read it now. We're really creating a dialogue between the have and have nots." See Trisha Howard, "Nobody Spared from Boston Street Paper's Critical Eye," *StreetWise,* June 16–30, 1995, 4.

14. Quoted in Walsh, "Chicago's Street-Wise Approach."

15. Quoted in Mary Schmich, "*StreetWise* Seller Is Wise Indeed," *Chicago Tribune,* Dec. 4, 1992, B1.

16. Ibid.

17. Hutchinson Persons, quoted in Paula Span, "For the Homeless, News to Shout About," *Washington Post,* Jan. 1990, D12.

18. Shawn "Cal" McAllister said *Street News*'s Persons had been "keeping investors [in a rock concert benefiting the homeless] informed with a monthly newsletter, which supplemented news of his progress with general information about the homeless crisis in New York ("*Street News* May Fold," *Editor and Publisher,* Feb. 25, 1995, 16). Edward Iwata said, "Since its birth 13 years ago as a newsletter, *Tenderloin Times* has garnered positive reviews in the community" ("Homeless Delivery," *Los Angeles Times,* Feb. 19, 1990, E3). David Cogan said, "Doucette founded *Hard Times* in the spring of 1994. For five years before that, the homeless Santa Monica resident distributed photocopied newsletters and worked to get his plans for a newspaper off the ground" ("The Word from the Street," *LA Weekly,* Jan. 12, 1995, 11).

19. Leah Eskin, "Read All about It," *Chicago Tribune,* May 21, 1993, sec. 5, 1.

20. Jacquelyn Heard, "Hope Hitting the Street," *Chicago Tribune,* Aug. 13, 1992, sec. 1, 26.

21. Eskin, "Read."

22. Mayraw Saar, "Hitting the Streets," *Daily Northwestern,* Sept. 24, 1992, 12.

23. McAuley, "Liza Minnelli."

24. Span, "For the Homeless."

25. "Street News: Down, Not Out," *Economist,* May 29, 1990, 31.

26. McAllister, "*Street News.*"

27. Randy Diamond, "Newspaper Sold by the Homeless Raises Questions," *Christian Science Monitor,* June 19, 1990, 7.

28. McAllister, "*Street News.*"

29. James Barron, "*Street News,* Sold by Poor, Falls on Hard Times Itself," *New York Times,* Dec. 21, 1994, B3.

30. Matthew Leone, "Bye Bye *Street News?*" *Columbia Journalism Review,* June 1995, 22.

31. Richard Roeper, "Word on *StreetWise:* Pipe Down, Will Ya," *Chicago Sun-Times,* Jan. 27, 1993, 11.

32. Eskin, "Read."

33. Greg Burns, "Extra! Extra! Read All about It! *StreetWise* Has Competition!" *Chicago Sun-Times,* May 19, 1993, 55.

34. Lisa Penelton, "Reactions," *StreetWise,* Dec. 1992, 23.

35. Burns, "Extra!"

36. Eskin, "Read."

37. Greg Burns, "*StreetWise* Competitor *I.D.* Closes from Lack of Money," *Chicago Sun-Times,* July 30, 1993, 45.

38. Eskin, "Read."

39. *StreetWise,* Jan. 1994, 24: "Thanks to Go Go Films for donating time and equipment in making the *StreetWise* commercials."

40. Hanna, "Homeless Hit the Streets."

41. *StreetWise Quarterly* 2, no. 4 (1994).

42. Bob Herguth, "Chicago Profile: Joel Alfassa," *Chicago Sun-Times,* June 17, 1994, 8.

43. Timmie Casey, "It's Been Said," *StreetWise,* Apr. 1994, 8.

44. Emilie Smith, "Who Are Homeless People? Please Let Us In," *StreetWise,* Apr. 1994, 23.

45. "*StreetWise* Staffers, Board in Pile-up over Exec's Firing," *Crain's Chicago Business,* Oct. 10, 1994, 8.

46. Leslie Gornstein, "*StreetWise* Seeking a Home in Market," *Crain's Chicago Business,* Aug. 8, 1994, 41.

47. The vertical masthead of September 1, 1994, listed John Ellis IV as assistant editor under managing editor McAllister; the September 16 issue listed McAllister as editor and Ellis beneath him as managing editor; the October 1 issue listed Ellis as managing editor; the October 15 issue listed Ellis and McAllister both as editors and Anthony Oliver's name appeared under the title interim executive director. Ellis and McAllister continued to share the editorship in the December and January issues. Finally, in the issue of February 1, 1995, the masthead was moved from page 3 to page 11 and listed Ellis as sole editor. McAllister was gone.

48. A letter to the editor in the June 1–15 issue criticized the "Home Free" columnist Pierre Clark for being insensitive to homeless people in his business advice.

49. The *Survival News* (West Roxbury, Mass.) includes a Spanish-language section. San Francisco's *Tenderloin Times* may hold the record for multilingual audiences. According to Iwata ("Homeless Delivery"), "Each month, the 24-page paper prints 25,000 issues in English, Vietnamese, Cambodian and Laotian."

50. An ad headlined "Ocashionally We Make Typoz" and asking for volunteers to help edit drew more then seventy responses, according to Laura Larson, volunteer coordinator.

51. Rick Kogan, "Extra! *StreetWise* Set for June," *Chicago Tribune,* Mar. 29, 1992, sec. 13, 2.

52. Sally Jacobs, "Somerville Paper Touts a Prior Claim to Street Beat," *Boston Globe,* July 20, 1990, 15.

53. Iwata, "Homeless Delivery."

54. "German Street Newspapers Merge to Form 'Motz,'" *StreetWise,* Aug. 1–15, 1995, 5. The English translation of the hybrid newspaper's editorial noted: "It is not just the fifth homeless paper of Berlin, but an alliance of the dreamers and the committed. We are neither Mob nor Haz, but the best from the first two 'bum papers' that we want to preserve and continue. Mob ran out of energy, and Haz lacked the will power. But the will power and energy for a new common social project belong to the faithful, loyal and true associates. . . . We are a journal of the poor, but we are rich in ambitious ideas."

55. Cyril Robinson, "On the Streets of the World," *StreetWise,* Mar. 1994, 17.

56. "The National Coalition for the Homeless ranked *StreetWise* the best newspaper in the United States and Canada serving the homeless based on criteria including number of papers sold (125,000 monthly), number of vendors employed (500) and social services provided to vendors." Quoted in news brief in *Crain's Chicago Business,* Apr. 24, 1995, 8.

57. *StreetWise Quarterly* 2, no. 4 (1994).

58. Elmer Davis, "Moving On: Davis Trades Badge for New Opportunities," *Street-Wise,* May 16–31, 1995, 7. In addition to paying tribute to Davis with the profile, the newspaper also devoted a page to his poems, copies of which he was known to give to customers as an unofficial premium.

VIOLET JOHNSON

In 1827, when *Freedom's Journal,* the first African-American newspaper, emerged with its editors' pledge to "plead our own cause,"[1] a tradition of agitation by the black press was set. This commitment to the liberation and advancement of the race resonated in the publications that followed: from Frederick Douglass's *North Star* to W. E. B. Du Bois's and the NAACP's *Crisis* to Marcus Garvey's *Negro World* and Robert Abbott's *Chicago Defender,* to name but a few. In the first half of the twentieth century, Boston, in spite of its relatively small black population, was among the cities notable for this crusading black press. In large part, William Monroe Trotter and his weekly newspaper, the *Guardian,* gave Boston this reputation. Through highly publicized developments such as Trotter's bitter challenge of Booker T. Washington and his philosophy, his leading role in the protest against the showing of the film *Birth of a Nation,* and his assertive denunciation of U.S. hypocrisy in World War I, Trotter's *Guardian* gained national recognition.[2] But also existing alongside the *Guardian* during this period was another black weekly, the *Boston Chronicle,* founded by a group of West Indian immigrants. Although the *Chronicle* never gained the national prominence of the *Guardian,* it symbolized, as much as the *Guardian,* one of the viable institutions of Boston's black community. It was so vibrant that by 1920 even Trotter himself had begun to acknowledge that the *Chronicle* was a formidable competitor cutting into his newspaper's readership.[3]

Piqued by this competition, Trotter accused the *Chronicle* of pursuing "the compromise, expediency, get the dollar, Booker Washington doctrine," with its editors paying no attention to the rights of blacks in the United States or elsewhere.[4] Contrary to Trotter's assessment, a careful examination of the paper reveals a different picture. Its contents speak loudly to the agitational character of its objectives. This element, evident since its founding, became heightened in 1930–50. This was a period when the black population of Boston was grappling with a host of challenges, a situation that the *Chronicle* addressed squarely and within the context of a worldwide black struggle.

As the intellectual center of the abolitionist movement, Boston had a reputation, as "freedom's birthplace," of being an ideal place for black people to live. Nevertheless, the black population remained very small, never exceeding 2 percent of the total population throughout the first half of the twentieth century.[5] Like the Caucasian majority, over three-quarters of Boston's black population by 1920 was comprised of newcomers to that city. In the first few decades of the twentieth century, two black migrations into Boston occurred simultaneously. There was the bigger, more noticeable migration of American blacks from the South and then there was the less visible arrival of black foreigners, mostly from three West Indian islands: Jamaica, Barbados, and Montserrat. Although these black immigrants had begun to come to Boston in the last quarter of the nineteenth century, it was not until the period of World War I that the first major influx occurred. The outcomes of these demographic developments were evident by 1920, as Boston's black population came to be composed of three main groups: the Boston-born, known as "Black Brahmins"; southern migrants, who were dubbed "Homies"; and the West Indian immigrants, who were referred to as "Turks."[6]

Like many other U.S. metropolises, Boston was a city of neighborhoods. In the beginning of the twentieth century, a spatial pattern whereby each major ethnic/immigrant group had established itself in specific areas of the city was unraveling. The North End, which previously had attracted diverse European immigrant groups, became about 90 percent Italian, the other groups having moved out. Other Italian enclaves were formed in East Boston. The Irish also carved their own enclaves in South Boston, Charlestown, and sections of Roxbury and Dorchester. By 1920, Jews, like the Irish, had also moved from the North and West Ends to Roxbury and Dorchester. Blacks, like the Caucasian majority, underwent residential changes as well. For much of the nineteenth century the black population, which was predominantly Boston-born, lived on Beacon Hill in the West End. But at the turn of the century, overwhelmed by the influx of European immigrants in that section of the city, they began to move to the South End. There they were joined by West Indian immigrants, but particularly by migrants from the South who quickly came to constitute the largest segment. Between roughly 1900 and 1950, a new

black neighborhood, with three main subsections, developed: the South
End, where most of the black businesses and entertainment were located, the In Town section, made up of Lower Roxbury and outer South End,
and the Hill, made up of areas in Upper Roxbury and Dorchester. This
third section, previously a staunch Jewish neighborhood, did not become
a black neighborhood until the 1930s, when blacks began to rent and buy
the large Victorian houses that were being vacated as the Jews began
moving into suburbs such as Milton and Randolph, away from the expanding black population.[7]

It was in these black neighborhoods that the black foreigners—West
Indian immigrants—settled. Never exceeding five thousand throughout
the first half of the twentieth century, they constituted no more than 2
percent of the black population.[8] Their small number thus precluded the
development of an easily identifiable ethnic enclave. They not only settled among American-born blacks in the black neighborhoods, the majority of them were confined to the menial, unskilled, low-paying jobs
accessible to blacks—the so-called "traditional Negro jobs" such as manual labor, janitorial work, and domestic service.[9] This residential and occupational pattern largely belied the existence of the foreigners. Prima
facie, a casual observer came out with the impression that an African-
American community was able, because of the structural forces already in
place, to absorb completely the foreign segment, obliterating its identity.
In fact, however, the West Indians, despite their residential and occupational integration into the general black population, were able to evolve
a subculture. This subculture was defined by a church, island associations,
pan–West Indian associations, and cricket sports clubs.[10]

The *Boston Chronicle,* frequently referred to as the West Indian paper,
was one index to the West Indian subculture. It was founded in 1915, just
about the time that West Indian migration to Boston began to peak. A
group of Jamaican immigrants in Boston—Thaddeus Kitchener, Alfred
Haughton, L. Murray, Eleanor Trent Wallace, and Elisha Jackson—together with Uriah N. Murray and Rose Murray of Jamaica, formed the Square
Deal Publishing Company. Headquartered on Tremont Street in the heart
of the business district of the black neighborhood of the South End, the
company launched the *Chronicle,* a paper to be published every Saturday
for the needs of the black community.

As an immigrant paper, the *Boston Chronicle* published news of interest to the West Indian community in Massachusetts and Rhode Island.
The various West Indian associations sent notices announcing meetings
and other scheduled events. St. Cyprian's Episcopal, the West Indian
church in Roxbury, sent church news that normally included activities in

the West Indian immigrant community. Individuals also sent notices announcing births, marriages, deaths, and successful vacations to the homeland. Perhaps most distinctive of the West Indian foreign character was the sports section, comprised almost exclusively of reports on cricket, both in the Northeastern United States League and the West Indies League.

These West Indian traits, as defining as they were, were surpassed by coverage of events, developments, problems—matters pertaining to a much broader black readership. As its editors frequently reiterated, the paper had a mission to enhance the status of blacks not only in the West Indian community but also in Boston, the United States, Africa, the Caribbean, and elsewhere. Its motto conveyed this resolve: "Fearless and Uncompromising—Advocate of Justice, Rights, and Opportunities."

The background of *Chronicle* employees projected its inclusive black orientation. Although the editors and many of the reporters were West Indian immigrants, especially Jamaican, the *Chronicle* used several American-born journalists. Also, the paper consistently utilized the services of members of the New York press, although all the editors in the period under review—Thaddeus Kitchener, Alfred Haughton, and William Harrison—were all Jamaican immigrants settled in Boston. Most of the regular contributors were black journalists or academics connected with some publication or institution in New York. This dependence on New York notwithstanding, the *Chronicle* was a crusading organ in its own right.

Admittedly, the owners, editors, and reporters of the *Chronicle* were middle-class men. Most were professionals, such as Thaddeus Kitchener, a barrister, Uriah Murray, a doctor, and William Harrison, a Harvard graduate. As this study will show, in spite of this socioeconomic background, their publication appealed to a broad section of the black population, which included a significant working-class audience. The reputation that West Indians had earned by then as relentless agitators was one major reason for this appeal. True, the careers of prominent New York West Indians, such as W. A. Domingo, Richard B. Moore, Claude McKay, and of course Marcus Garvey, have mostly been credited with shaping this reputation. But Boston's West Indian society boasted its own firebrands. Significantly, most of them were connected with the *Chronicle*. In fact, some of them were self-proclaimed communists and in that capacity earned the trust of the working class with whom they shared the same neighborhood.

Although many of the *Chronicle* reporters flirted with communism, especially in the 1940s, there was another ideology to which the paper clearly subscribed: Pan-Africanism. Pan-Africanism, many agree, is one of those ideologies that lends itself to several expressions. Very simply defined, it is a notion that stresses the connectedness of people of African descent, no matter where they are settled in the world. This connectedness carries a sense of universality to the experiences of blacks around the world—be it oppression or accomplishment. The exponents of this philosophy in the nineteenth century and the first half of the twentieth century were many. They hailed from Africa and the diaspora: Edward Blyden, W. E. B. Du Bois, Marcus Garvey, Kwame Nkrumah, to name a few. For the present study, Garvey is the most important because he was undoubtedly the strongest force of Pan-Africanism in the careers of the journalists at the *Chronicle*. Some of these journalists were already conversant with the activities of fellow West Indian Garvey's Universal Negro Improvement Association even before they emigrated to Boston. In addition, all of them were connected in varying degrees to the Boston branch of that association. Consequently, they were steeped in the tradition of the universality of the fate of black people that is the core of Pan-Africanism. This orientation is clearly manifested in the character of the *Chronicle*.

Its Pan-African crusade, which was a constant, was most evident in the 1930s and 1940s. Several developments during this period (to be elaborated on below) convinced these journalists of the global domination of blacks and, therefore, the efficacy of a Pan-African solution. The contents of the *Chronicle* in the 1930s and 1940s clearly demonstrate that its main efforts were directed at (1) highlighting the contributions of blacks around the world, with the objective of stimulating black pride, (2) tackling the problems that faced blacks in Boston and the United States, and (3) exposing the insidious nature of European and American imperialism in Africa and the Western Hemisphere.

While focusing on worldwide issues pertaining to blacks, the *Chronicle* directed a great deal of attention at the plight of blacks in Boston and the United States. Contrary to its reputation as a haven for American blacks, Boston was in many ways inhospitable to that segment of its population throughout the first half of the twentieth century.[11] Like Trotter's *Guardian*, the *Chronicle* devoted many efforts to protesting the blatant social, economic, and political injustice directed against blacks of that city.

The 1930s were particularly difficult. With the ravages of the Great Depression permeating every aspect of the American society, blacks found themselves in a bad situation grown considerably worse. Unemployment underscored this desperate situation. As Lance Carden rightly puts it: "The search for jobs preoccupied the entire community."[12] In 1934, almost 34 percent of Boston's black workforce was unemployed.[13] The *Chronicle's* own preoccupation with the situation was amply manifested in its pages, where it continually reminded its readers not only of the high unemployment rate among blacks but also the fact that black workers were consistently confined to menial, low-paying jobs. Throughout the 1930s, the paper reported on the nearly zero representation of blacks in management levels in the big business establishments. On Janurary 23, 1932, the *Chronicle* declared that it would pursue vigorously a policy of exposing those establishments most culpable of excluding blacks, while acknowledging those making strides toward more fair hiring practices. Partly through such agitation by the paper, the First National Stores, a supermarket chain, began an "experiment of preparing Negro managers and salespersons" in 1934. Still, when it faltered, the *Chronicle* reverted to blasting that company (Oct. 13, 1934).

To stimulate action among blacks, the paper started running a front-page advertisement in most of the editions of the 1930s and early 1940s:

NEGROES ARE REALLY WAKING UP!!

THINKING Negroes around Roxbury are now spending their money only in stores owned and operated by Negroes and in other stores where they can find colored help.

Very few Negroes are now spending their hard-earned dollars in places where they haven't a chance to secure jobs for themselves or their children.

This approach was typical of the don't-buy-where-you-can't-work strategy, which defined black protest of the employment situation in the depression era.[14] Investigative reporters studied the situation in a number of stores whose clientele was heavily drawn from the predominantly black neighborhoods of the South End and Roxbury. They concluded that while the mostly white-owned stores relied heavily on black patronage, the only positions they offered blacks were janitor, messenger, or other "low, back room" positions. Admonishing blacks to patronize only those establishments that made serious efforts to give them respectable positions, the paper published its grim findings in a series of editorials and articles in the July and August editions of 1935.

That same year, the paper responded to the appointment of Leon G. Lomax as branch manager of the South End Electric Company and Edward Cooper as the first African-American manager of a First National Stores branch: "Let us get behind Lomax and Cooper and let the white world know with dollars and cents they can get a break when they give us one" (Aug. 3, 1935). Similar observations were made again in the December 19, 1936, issue when the Roxbury branch of the F. W. Woolworth Five and Ten Cents Stores hired "five local colored girls" as part-time clerks.

These "breaks" notwithstanding, for much of the period most of the victories in employment were qualified successes. It was clear by then that a formidable structural pattern of discrimination was firmly in place. Even when the black unemployment rate dropped slightly in 1940 (from 34.0 to 30.3 percent) as a result of the employment of blacks in government projects funded by the Works Progress Administration (WPA), they still compared unfavorably with white groups.[15] White solidarity against blacks in the workplace was one of the major concerns of the *Chronicle*. Readers were encouraged to write to the editor about their experiences in that area. In several articles, the paper exposed the patterns of occupational exclusion launched by whites, especially immigrants—Italians and Irish in particular. For example, in a July 6, 1935, editorial, the paper analyzed how Irish, Italians, and Negroes started off as "underdogs competing for the scraps under the master's table." But through an insidious system of racism the European groups advanced, leaving blacks in the same position of underdogs. In their elevated positions, the editorial went on, white immigrants routinely employed strategies to convey their aversion to a racially integrated workplace.[16]

With such obstacles in the labor market, it is little wonder that self-employment was viewed as one viable instrument of economic progress for blacks. A column in the June 8, 1935, edition expressed this hope: "In a prejudiced white world the Negro is not associated with successful business, consequently every Negro business enterprise drives the wedge a little farther towards breaking down any opposition that confronts the colored man in the commercial field." Convinced of this role of black entrepreneurship, the *Chronicle* promoted self-employment throughout the 1930s and 1940s. One important way that it sought to do this was to ferret out and give some publicity to black businesses in the Greater Boston area. Thus in a series of reports, especially between 1935 and 1948, the paper profiled black entrepreneurs and their establishments' history.

For example, the hairdressing business received great attention. As the paper claimed on November 23, 1935, "The hairdressing industry is an important lifeline among our group and means much to our girls in particular." To underscore its significance, the *Chronicle* ran several pieces about the hairdressing business both in Boston and in the nation in general. It helped its readers understand black women's creative role in this sphere, especially in their formulation of hair care systems. In Boston at the time, two of these were especially popular, the Apex and Poro Systems.

In June 1932, the paper published a detailed interview with the founder of the Apex System and Apex Hair College, Mrs. Sara Spencer Washington. In 1935, a similar piece was done on the founder of the Poro System, Mrs. Annie M. Turnbo-Malone of Chicago. While demonstrating these strides of progress in one industry, the *Chronicle* continued to alert black women to the ever-present threat posed by white competition. On March 30, 1935, it urged the Board of Black Hairdressers to be more assertive about staving off what the paper saw as blatant attempts by whites to co-opt a black economic niche. The brazen assault was explained in an editorial entitled "The Handwriting on the Wall": "Right in our midst two white establishments have been catering to colored patronage, and it is likely that others will follow. Some are sending white girls to have their hair done in colored shops and so learn how it is done, others are hiring colored girls to work in their shops, and will see to it that they teach white girls who will eventually supplant them" (Dec. 7, 1935).

The need for the organized promotion of black business was one of the concerns of the black community in Boston. In fact, when in 1932 Phi Beta Sigma adopted a national resolution to work for "Bigger and Better Business for Negroes," the *Chronicle* devoted some space to explaining the efficacy of that "noble experiment." To ensure continued awareness of the need to develop black entrepreneurship, the second week of April was designated as Bigger, Better Negro Business Week. To commemorate that week the black business community organized seminars, meetings, and other such events to educate blacks about the opportunities available, however scant, to set up and maintain small businesses. For its part, the *Chronicle* ran detailed coverage of these events, delineating useful networks such as "Negro-loving" banks and black credit unions and cooperatives.[17] In 1938 the Bigger, Better Negro Business Week led to the creation of the Greater Boston Negro Trade Association. The *Chronicle* covered the launching of this organization. Urging its readers to support the association, it explained its objectives: "to seek to coordinate and foster the existing colored businesses in the area; promotion of more business for these firms; and the creation of a greater interest in colored business on the part of Boston's public" (June 4, 1938).

The reality of occupational closure and other discriminatory situations within a general context of racism was a constant theme in the *Chronicle*. A major aspect of its crusade on behalf of blacks in Boston and the United States was the exposure of subtle as well as direct violent racist assaults. In 1932, then editor Thaddeus Kitchener affirmed the paper's resolve to expose racist acts against blacks and encouraged readers to send letters to the editor reporting such confrontations. In addition, the *Chronicle* carried out its own investigations. The following is an August 27, 1932, example of a "list of assaults" that frequently appeared in the paper:

1. A group of white men chased, caught, and beat up two Negro men.
2. Negro longshoremen beaten by white strikers and abused by white police. No arrests.
3. Negro women kicked in the stomach on Tremont Street by white gangsters in broad daylight. No arrests.
4. Aged and infirm Negro beaten by white hoodlums.
5. Two Negroes have their skulls split by axe and nightstick when policemen went on a rampage. Negroes were unfairly charged with drunkenness and arrested.

Verbal and physical racial harassment in Boston was most pronounced in the late 1930s and 1940s, a period in which the whole country was experiencing heightened racial and ethnic tensions.[18] In Boston, Jews and blacks were frequently ambushed and seriously beaten by gangs of whites, particularly Irish Catholic youths from South Boston and some districts of Dorchester. While most of the black victims were simple, working-class people, successful, middle-class, prominent blacks were not immune to racial assaults. One good example was the attack on renowned tenor Roland Hayes in 1935, when his home in Brookline Village was vandalized by a group of white youths in what Hayes and many believed was a racially motivated attack (*Chronicle*, May 4, 1935).

Another headline-making attack was on the *Chronicle*'s own editor, William B. Harrison. Harrison had immigrated to Boston with his parents from Jamaica around the period of World War I. He was a Harvard graduate and a respectable leader of the black community who lived in the Humbolt Avenue middle-class area of Roxbury. Moreover, it was even rumored that he sometimes wrote speeches for Mayor James Michael Curley.[19] Yet in April 1947, a group of "black-hating youths" ambushed and beat him severely only a few blocks from his home (*Chronicle*, Apr. 26, 1947).

In addition to these blatant criminal acts of racism, the black community also contended with police brutality. The treatment of blacks by an all-white Boston police force was a thorn in the side of the community throughout the first half of the twentieth century. The *Chronicle*, like its counterpart the *Guardian*, is replete with records and instances of police mistreatment of blacks under the pretext of enforcing law and order.

Convinced that this belligerent atmosphere against blacks was nurtured by tacit encouragement by an unfair justice system, the *Chronicle* frequently investigated the agencies of law and order. Especially during the editorship of Kitchener (he was an attorney, having studied in the law inns of England), the *Chronicle* worked with some local attorneys to assess the fairness of the system in cases involving blacks. One such inquiry led to this conclusion: "A careful survey of all the cases tried before certain judges of the Roxbury District Court shows that there is the cancer of prejudice against Negroes that is wrecking the structure of the great institution of justice" (*Chronicle,* Sept. 17, 1932).

The shortcomings of the federal legal system and its failure to protect blacks on a national level were also frequently tackled by the paper. It covered incidents of racism across the country, from police brutality in New York to lynchings in Indiana to continued enslavement of blacks in Mississippi. But no other incident gave it the opportunity to analyze this dimension as much as the case of the Scottsboro Boys.[20] Like other black publications across the country, the *Chronicle* devoted extensive coverage to the ramifications of that case, which quickly became an international cause célèbre. Besides regular updates of the case's progress, the paper printed the views of its readers as well as feature articles analyzing its many implications. Howard University Dean Kelly Miller, who was also a regular columnist, contributed a series of articles on the issue. He used the Scottsboro case to illustrate the insidious nature of Jim Crow in the South and its northern parallels, the struggle between the NAACP and black communists over control of the boys' defense, and the reactions of African Americans across the country as evidenced by protest demonstrations. In one of his analyses, Miller concluded that "the only way out is getting the Constitution to work for Negroes" (*Chronicle,* Feb. 20, 1932).

Indeed, the search for effective solutions to the problems facing blacks in the United States was a major task the *Chronicle* sought to fulfill. The evidence is ample that the paper did not limit itself simply to identifying the problems. How the Constitution could work for blacks was an important question that was addressed. The writers perceived two major routes to that goal: effective organizing by blacks and active and judicious participation in the political process.

The paper's contribution toward effective organizing lay in its continuous scrutinizing of major black groups such as the National Association for the Advancement of Colored People, the Urban League, and the Universal Negro Improvement Association. Besides performing the obvious function of serving as a vehicle for publicizing events and causes of these organizations, the *Chronicle* undertook critical assessments of their viability. It did not hesitate to point out their shortcomings, as it did when Kelly

Miller, after spending some time studying the effectiveness of black organizations, lamented that "the once radical NAACP was now on the same level as the YMCA" (Mar. 5, 1932).

Reservations over the effectiveness of established organizations were clearly displayed in the 1930s, when the *Chronicle* launched its own campaign to help Boston blacks organize their own civic league. The stimulus was the increasing racial violence in Ward 9, a political district encompassing much of the black neighborhood of Roxbury. Under the leadership of the *Chronicle* editor T. A. Kitchener, the Negro Defense Association was formed to work for "the preservation of peace and safety in the black community" (*Chronicle*, May 14, 1932).

Frequently noting that political apathy was a big impediment to achieving effective solutions, the *Chronicle* attempted to serve as a stimulant of political awareness and action. It is useful to point out at this juncture that all the editors during the period under discussion were active politicians in their own right. Kitchener, Haughton, and Harrison all ran in local elections for seats in Wards 9 and 12, the political districts in which the black neighborhoods were situated. As may be expected, the paper was used as a vehicle for their campaigns. But also, it served as a general sounding board of the political process in Boston and the nation and of how blacks were affected by that process. In typical journalistic fashion, candidates were endorsed and denounced. Political careers were followed with the objective of guiding the black public in choosing political representatives who would seek their interests. For example, it was in this role that the paper ran damaging articles on State Attorney General Joseph E. Warner in 1934, accusing him of discrimination and ingratitude to loyal black voters who had helped him to get elected. It was pointed out that once in office he acknowledged Jews, Irish, and Italians by giving them solid, respectable jobs. On the other hand, he appointed only one black— as a messenger (*Chronicle*, Oct. 20, 1934). In contrast, during the same period, the paper ran articles highlighting Mayor James Michael Curley's good rapport with blacks. In an editorial on October 20, 1934, the paper advised black voters to "disregard allegations of Curley's reputation as dishonest and foremost bankrupter of the city. . . . If the decision is to be based on the honesty of the respective candidates, then we are still of the opinion that our safety is a trifle more secure with Mr. Curley than with the others. For since we think of the whole matter, it is more simple for us to get an audience with James Michael."

It was this practical consideration in voting to which the *Chronicle* appealed throughout the period. The paper consciously spelled out practical demands that black voters must make and consider while they elected their representatives. Reiterating that no demand was too minute, the *Chronicle* guided black voters with lists such as the following one printed on October 20, 1934:

1. That a Negro be appointed as a probation officer in the Roxbury Court at once.
2. That D. A. Foley place a Negro on his staff immediately.
3. That Attorney General Warner drop the bars and add a Negro lawyer to his staff at once.
4. That both a Negro physician and dentist be placed in the Whittier Street Health Unit at once.
5. That Negro men and women be given fairer consideration for general employment in City and State departments.
6. That a Negro lawyer of repute be placed on the Massachusetts bench.

This program and this alone should be the principal basis upon which every Negro voter should base his conclusions. Throw your vote to the major party that acts first and most extensively in these matters.

This pragmatic theme was explicit in the *Chronicle*'s coverage of one of the most significant developments in African-American political history during this period, namely, the defection of black voters from the Republican to the Democratic party. The paper emphasized in its editorials and in a special series by Kelly Miller, under the heading "Why the Negro Should Divide His Votes," that it took the approach that the new affiliation with Franklin D. Roosevelt's party must not preclude consideration of Abraham Lincoln's party. Adhering to this approach, the paper strove to be an informative source for black voters to use in assessing candidates and their programs. In 1932, for example, the paper analyzed interviews with Democrats, including FDR himself, in its attempt, as it put it, "to get into the minds of Democrats." The writers' resolve to play the role of intermediaries was bolstered by the fact that by this time the *Chronicle* had surpassed the *Guardian* in readership and was being referred to as "New England's largest Negro Weekly."[21] On April 23, 1932, Kitchener acknowledged the writers' role: "The plum daddies and mammies—the men and women who go between the masses of voters and political aspirants—are trying to woo us to assess their candidates in favorable light."

Even as the paper encouraged pragmatic evaluation of the two traditional parties, it gave cognizance to the Communist party, which by the 1930s had made some inroads among African Americans.[22] One of the major developments that prompted serious assessment of communism and its relevance for African Americans was the Scottsboro case. The struggle between the NAACP and the Communist party over the boys' defense sparked a debate on the effectiveness of both organizations, not only in pleading the boys' case but in African-American advancement in general. The *Chronicle,* for its part, pursued a policy of providing a forum for the Communist party to publicize its objectives and ideology. To this end, it printed articles on the activities of black communist leaders and even sponsored visits and talks by those communist leaders who were anxious to bring their programs directly to the black public.[23] Commenting on these visits and other activities of black communists, Miller did not hide his concerns about the philosophy and practices of the Communist party. Clearly, though, his disillusion with the traditional political parties and the NAACP forced him to acknowledge the validity of the Communist party as an organ of black protest. On March 5, 1932, he remarked, for example, "Unfortunately, the only radical Black cause is the impossible and irresponsible reds who have a fanatical fringe."

Less ambivalent about their attitude toward the Communist party were some other *Chronicle* contributors who were actually self-declared communists. The most prominent of these was William B. Harrison, editor of the paper in the mid-1940s. Harrison, in fact, ran as a communist for state representative from Ward 12. His editorials underscored his communist leanings. He emphasized a coalition of oppressed peoples—black and white workers, and blacks and Jews. Although in this way Harrison used the paper to further his communist cause, the paper itself cannot be described as the exclusive organ of any of the major political camps. Commitment to readers' rights to decide their own political affiliation was underscored by attempts to give equitable coverage to the various parties and their ideologies. For example, at the height of the 1932 elections, the paper printed what it called a "Political Symposium," designed to present the platforms of all the players. The symposium included articles by Silas F. Taylor, chairman of the Colored Democratic Roosevelt for President League; Mrs. Edna Goodell, alternate delegate at large to the Republican convention; the Reverend James Mitchell, rector of St. Bartholomew Church in Cambridge and member of the Socialist party; and James W. Dawson, candidate for lieutenant governor on the Communist party ticket (Mar. 5, 1932).

Identification of the problems facing U.S. blacks and proposals for solutions pointed to the *Chronicle'*s unwavering commitment to black advancement. But the analyses and interpretations of the sources of those problems were not so unequivocal. The split between the American-born and foreign-born black journalists affiliated with the paper was most evident in their differing views on where the major blame for the black predicament lay. The West Indian journalists, even though they denounced racism, frequently pointed to the role of blacks in creating some of their own problems. Editor Kitchener once pointed out that it was the paper's duty to do just that! On August 20, 1932, he wrote: "The writers of the *Boston Chronicle* will endeavor to praise the accomplishments and denounce without fear the shortcomings of our group." One major query that Kitchener and some of the other writers had was what they saw as the refusal of blacks to exploit their potential to the fullest. In the editorial of December 30, 1933, the *Chronicle* recommended a resolution for the coming year:

> Let us in 1934 utilize what opportunities we have. Let us not merely be satisfied with what we have if something still is withheld from us which is rightfully ours. The Curse of the Boston Negro has been the self satisfaction of its individuals. . . . No distinction is conferred on us Boston Negroes if we live in an atmosphere of culture and do not breathe it.
>
> Here in Boston the *Chronicle* contends, Negroes have the best opportunities to become worthy citizens of a great Commonwealth. Of course the bogey of prejudice is here to hinder us. But we can get here a kind of wealth which thieves cannot filch.

No other writer was more consistent in denouncing such shortcomings as Vere E. Johns, a Jamaican immigrant, actor, and freelance journalist who was based in New York but wrote regularly for the *Chronicle*. In his June 11, 1932, column, "Through My Spectacles," he made clear his conviction that American blacks were to blame for many of their problems, as he put it, in a phrase in his native patois, "Dawg Nyam Dawg" (literally, "dog eat dog"). Although Johns, like most of the Jamaican writers and activists of the period, was familiar with the work of Marcus Garvey and actually embraced Garvey's philosophy of black economic independence, he worried about the ability of American blacks to attain economic self-sufficiency. During the don't-buy-where-you-can't-work campaign, he openly expressed his doubts about whether blacks could really afford to boycott white businesses.[24] Thus, even when the *Chronicle,* as a black paper, endorsed the Phi Beta Sigma's national resolution for Bigger and Better Business for Negroes, Johns continued to express his doubts about blacks' ability to establish successful enterprises. For example, registering his disgust over "perpetual

Negro loitering," he explained how a man took his suit to a Jewish tailor because he was put off by the black tailor "who was jabbering away with a crowd behind his counter" (*Chronicle*, Mar. 5, 1932).

Johns's attitude toward black business failures contrasts with that of the African-American Carter G. Woodson, founder and director of the Association for the Study of Negro Life and History and a fairly regular *Chronicle* columnist. Woodson was aggravated by the unfair assessment of black businesses, a practice that he believed perpetuated the devaluation of black economic efforts. In a June 11, 1932, article entitled "Is the Negro in Business a Failure?" Woodson pointed out: "When a Negro business fails the media is quick to point it out with such headlines as GREATEST NEGRO BUSINESS FAILS; NEGRO BANK ROBBED BY ITS OFFICERS; and THE TWILIGHT OF NEGRO BUSINESS. When the concerns of other races fail, however, you read in the press only a brief mention of it with an expression of regret and it passes from public notice."

Johns's exposure of the shortcomings of blacks sometimes bordered on contempt. For example, he once referred to blacks' attempts at segregation as tomfoolery because "the base of this desire for seclusion is a feeling of inferiority which breeds fear" (*Chronicle*, Jan. 16, 1932). In a similar tone, Johns compared Western Hemisphere blacks, specifically American blacks, with Africans, pointing out that Africans would know what to do in the event of a war. In contrast, he maintained, blacks of Harlem would not know what to do because of "their typical apathy and their shameful failure to keep abreast of developments" (*Chronicle*, Feb. 20, 1932).

Such berating of American blacks frequently elicited reactions from the American-born black writers who used the same *Chronicle* as a conduit for their own counterviews. Kelly Miller, who once described a Negro radical as "an over-educated West Indian without a job," was perhaps the most assertive in responding to the West Indian assault and insult (*Chronicle*, June 1, 1935). The following portion of his May 11, 1935, editorial illustrates his response to Johns:

> When a man gathers his family together and moves to a foreign country; seeks a job, places his children in the schools and establishes a home, in that place should be rooted all his loyalties. No matter what his past affiliations and love for the section from which he departed may have been, he must sever them if he desires to be eligible for the protection and encouragement of the new flag under which he resides. There can be no middle ground in this matter because the initial step implies a desire to become a definite part of the scheme of things.

An even more scathing pronouncement appeared in Miller's article explaining how West Indians "disproportionately swelled the numbers of the ranks of dissatisfied elements in America because they can fight hard here but ran from the British back home" (*Chronicle,* Oct. 13, 1934).

This tension between the two groups of black activists was not unique to Boston. The 1920s and 1930s are notable for the struggle between the two groups for leadership in the quest for black advancement.[25] Much of the conflict was played out by journalists and their publications. A typical example is the counterattack launched by Robert L. Vann, editor of the *Pittsburgh Courier.* Vann took out a full-page advertisement in his own paper in 1934 denouncing West Indians. Later, he continued his attacks in an address before the Harlem Adult Education Convention. His speech read in part: "If you West Indians don't like how we are doing things in this country, you should go back where you came from. We Americans will not tolerate your butting into our affairs. We are good and tired of you. There should be a law deporting the whole lot of you."[26] Responding to this display of anger, George W. Goodman, executive secretary of the Boston branch of the Urban League, registered his disbelief and displeasure over Vann's actions in the *Chronicle* under the heading, "Is Vann Going Mad?" (Mar. 17, 1934).

Another major source of conflict between the two groups of journalists was the debate over the amount of attention given to matters pertaining to blacks elsewhere in the diaspora and in Africa itself. The West Indian founders and writers were activists who, even before emigrating, had been involved in Pan-Africanism and Garveyism, two ideologies that stressed the collective fate of blacks all over the world.[27] This premigration background was reinforced by their affiliation in the United States with organizations such as the Universal Negro Improvement Association (UNIA), whose objectives and deliberations were directly shaped by the strong Pan-Africanist doctrine of its founder, Marcus Garvey, and his followers. Although the UNIA branch in Boston was not nearly as dynamic as the main branch in New York or subbranches in Philadelphia, Chicago, Detroit, and Cleveland, there is evidence that it was an important institution in the life of the West Indian community from which the editors and some of the writers of the *Chronicle* came. Headquartered across from the West Indian St. Cyprian's Episcopal Church, in the heart of the black neighborhood, the Boston branch of UNIA organized several events in the 1920s, 1930s, and 1940s aimed at fostering its objectives. Although nothing like the flamboyant parades that defined UNIA activities in New

York in the 1920s, the efforts of the Boston branch were vibrant and productive. They were mostly lectures, debates, and discussions geared toward fostering awareness of and reaction to the glories, the plight, and the future of African and black disaporic societies.

As evidenced from the emphasis of UNIA and other such Pan-African organizations, one of the fundamental tasks of black people in the quest for liberation and advancement is to recover and display the positive and indispensable contributions of Africa and Africans in world history. The seriousness with which the *Chronicle's* journalists approached this task is clearly reflected in the many columns on the history and people of Africa. The paper solicited contributions from scholars and students of African history and societies. Some of these contributions came from lectures and discussions sponsored by the *Chronicle,* UNIA, and West Indian associations. A few of the speakers were African students or educators: for example, Professor Don Tengo Jabvu from South Africa, who, according to the *Chronicle,* "in impeccable English spoken with a slight accent, discussed conditions in South Africa and pointed to the accomplishments of Africans in that region" (Jan. 16, 1932). Most of the contributors, however, were from the United States—African Americans and West Indian immigrants. One such person was Rayford W. Logan, a prominent African-American historian. In the 1930s, as a graduate student at Harvard, he spoke and wrote frequently on the history of Africa and the black diaspora.

But no other contributor personified this aspect of the character of the *Chronicle* as much as Joel Augustus Rogers. A Jamaican who immigrated to the United States—actually to New York—in the early 1900s, Rogers was a historian, author, and correspondent at large. He dedicated much of his life to researching, writing, and lecturing on African history, especially the significance of Africa's position in world history. His main focus was African personalities and their contributions to important events and developments. Although Rogers was a prolific writer, with over ten books and countless articles to his name, his work did not reach a large audience. Unable to find a conventional publisher for his books, he self-published them and relied on the black press for the publicity needed to disseminate his work. The *Chronicle* was one such vehicle. Rogers's articles and book advertisements were ubiquitous in that publication throughout the 1930s and 1940s: quarter- to half-page advertisements of his *World's Great Men of Color* or some other monograph, excerpts from his published works, feature pieces written specifically for the paper, and notices announcing his visits and talks.[28]

The neglect and malicious distortion of the contributions of blacks to world history is often cited as both the source and outcome of European political, economic, and social domination of the race. With this rationale, the *Chronicle* saw the crusade against European imperialism in Africa and the diasporic societies in the Western Hemisphere as a cornerstone in the black cause. Through feature articles and updates on events and developments in the colonies, the paper challenged the morality and constitutionality of colonialism and revealed the insidiousness and brutality of that system and the resolve of colonized peoples to defy it.

Frequently reminding its readers of the need for concern about the mistreatment of black people on the African continent, the *Chronicle* reported on a vast array of incidents in its efforts to reveal the workings of the colonial system. In 1932, the paper printed a series of articles denouncing the unfair treatment of the natives of the former German colonies in Africa. In this exposé, the paper challenged the constitutionality of the trusteeship of Britain and France, which were still holding them as "mandate colonies." Readers were urged to send petitions to the League of Nations demanding immediate transfer of the former German colonies to the Africans (Mar. 5, 1932). In the same year, the paper exposed accusations of racism made by Africans of Togoland in French West Africa against English missionaries of the Wesleyan Society. Underscoring the gravity of those accusations, one of the articles emphasized that "this is yet another example of world-wide racism and deliberate attempt to check black advancement everywhere" (Apr. 9, 1932). The callousness of colonial administrators was often revealed, as in an article expressing dismay at the unfeeling response of the Portuguese colonial administration to the ravages of locusts and famine in Angola (Mar. 30, 1935).

While the exposure of the victimization of Africans by Europeans was clearly a priority, the paper also found opportunities to show the resilience of Africans in the face of the European assault. For example, it was clearly with some pride that the paper reported on what it called a skirmish in the British colony of Sierra Leone, West Africa. The skirmish erupted because of the natives' protest of the arbitrary installation of a chief who was not in the traditional hereditary line but was in fact hostile to that group. Although the colonial administration eventually put down the resistance, the incident stood as an example of the Africans' willingness to fight for their rights. Pointing this out, the paper noted: "This incident may seem insignificant but it forebodes a grave warning to the European settlement" (July 23, 1932).

Although Liberia was not a colony, it held a special importance in the crusade for freedom, equality, and advancement in Africa. It was always prominent in the Pan-Africanist agenda, starting with the back-to-Africa movement that saw the resettlement of free African Americans (including John Russwurm, founder of the first African-American newspaper) in the early 1800s. In 1851, Edward W. Blyden, known as one of the greatest Pan-Africanists ever, left his homeland of the Danish West Indian island of St. Thomas and moved to Liberia, which he declared his new home and used as his base to develop his doctrine of an African personality.[29] Again, in the early 1920s, Liberia was chosen by Garvey as a Pan-African base, a region in which to resettle diasporic blacks from the United States and West Indies. Garvey saw this as a necessary step toward the liberation of Africa. In 1924, the plan disintegrated as the Liberian government, distrustful of Garvey's motives and influenced by behind-the-scenes maneuvers by Garvey's opponents, such as Du Bois, changed its mind and withdrew permission for UNIA to establish the proposed settlement.[30] As heavy a blow as this failure was, it did not eliminate the focus on Liberia, even in the 1930s and 1940s, when Garveyism was clearly on the wane.[31]

The *Chronicle*'s editors and writers, most of whose careers (as pointed out earlier) had been influenced by the Garveyite tradition, demonstrated this continued focus. By this time, they were not proposing a settlement in Liberia; instead they were concerned about the shaky sovereignty of that republic. As a September 24, 1932, editorial pointed out, Liberia's independence was nominal. The ruling oligarchy, made up of Americo-Liberians, descendants of those free blacks who had emigrated in the back-to-Africa movement, was accused of being a puppet of European powers and Euramerican business interests. By 1932, Liberia's economy was in so much trouble that the League of Nations voted to "supervise its finances." To the *Chronicle,* this was like declaring a protectorate over a supposedly independent African nation and thus a good example of the Euramerican threat to Liberia's sovereignty. Closely following the protests launched by the native Liberians, the *Chronicle* joined in the crusade. Its articles dissected the problem, revealing that Liberia's economy was in trouble in the first place because of the meddling of white foreigners, especially America's Firestone Rubber Company (Sept. 24, 1932). Joining forces with associations such as UNIA, Jamaica Associates, and the Women's International League for Peace and Freedom, the paper organized lectures and discussions throughout 1932 to address the issue of Liberia's sovereignty. As may be expected, announcements of these events as well as resolutions and other decisions made at meetings appeared regularly in several editions.

The incident that provided the greatest opportunity for the journalistic crusade against European domination of Africa was the Italian invasion of Ethiopia in 1935. When Mussolini's Fascist forces overran Ethiopia, forcing Emperor Haile Selassie into exile, as John Hope Franklin and Arthur Moss Jr. observe, "almost overnight even the most provincial among black Americans became international-minded."[32] The overriding factor responsible for this remarkable increased awareness was the publicity and fight launched by the black press. General histories of African Americans and of Pan-Africanism, discussing the role of the black press, often mentioned publications such as the *Amsterdam News,* the *Pittsburgh Courier,* and the *Chicago Defender* but usually ignored the *Chronicle.* Despite this lack of national prominence, however, there is overwhelming evidence that the *Chronicle* served the same purpose as the better-known publications. It sought to rally blacks to the Ethiopian cause.

The invasion was symbolic. As the only sub-Saharan African region to escape colonization (Liberia's independence was often seen as dubious because of the American factor), Ethiopia stood as a beacon for blacks everywhere. This caught the attention of Pan-Africanists, who saw Ethiopia as testimony of Africa's past glories and projector of its ultimate future. Given this significant position, it is not surprising that the *Chronicle* had been covering events related to Ethiopia even before Mussolini invaded. Like most black publications of the period, the *Chronicle's* most extensive coverage of Ethiopia started with the lavish 1930 coronation of Haile Selassie as Negus Nagast (king of kings). This emphasis on Ethiopia's prestige and splendor, in an Africa then overrun by European monarchies and governments, led to further interest in emigration to Africa. In the early 1930s, a small group of black New Yorkers, mostly Jamaicans and Barbadian immigrants who were also Garveyites, set up an African-American immigrant community in the Ethiopian capital of Addis Ababa. The experiences of this group of returnees constituted one main focus of the *Chronicle* before 1935. Most of the articles on the subject pointed to the reciprocal relationship that existed between the diasporic blacks and their hosts. For example, in a December 31, 1932, account riddled with sarcasm, the paper reported on the experiences of an African-American returnee:

A school teacher from Chicago, widely travelled, decided to emigrate to Abyssinia to help the people there. This is an altruistic action. The natives and customs of Africa, especially, have been of interest to us. It may be atavistic or the urge of consanguinity, but we have always wanted to know more of the communal life of the Africans. Are they in constant fear of the sweating behemoth and other wild beasts or do they regard them with the same equanimity as we do the hit and run driver thundering along in his snorting juggernaut?

Are they as much in terror of their lives from the crabbed disposition of a chief who does not brook the violation of a ceremonial kowtow as we are from inadvertently sitting in a section of a car in Southern cities reserved for whites?

Would a tribe aid a helpless and badly wounded member of a friendly tribe by taking her into their hands and allow the ministrations of the medicine chief, or would . . . ? But why ask other questions? After all, there must be some good points which the untutored savage could teach the civilized Christians.

After the invasion, reporting on Ethiopia took a more serious turn. Like the other black publications across the country, the *Chronicle* broke the somber news of the European assault on the beacon of the black race. Providing updates as the conflict escalated, the paper published articles educating readers on the events that led to the invasion and on the meaning of the assault for Ethiopia, Africa, and the diaspora. One of the main points that it tried to hammer home was the fact that the event represented a conspiracy by a white-dominated world against blacks. The failure of other European powers, the United States, and the League of Nations to castigate Italy was seen as testimony of their tacit complicity.

Several black organizations, such as the Boston branch of the NAACP, the Urban League, and West Indian associations, in conjunction with the *Chronicle,* organized events that addressed the crisis. The Boston UNIA branch was especially active in this endeavor. For example, Garvey Day, May 31, 1936, was devoted to the Italo-European crisis. Details of events, especially statements, resolutions, and petitions were printed regularly in the *Chronicle.*

Also printed were feature pieces by experts on African affairs. Again, J. A. Rogers was most prominently represented in this endeavor. Although the *Pittsburgh Courier* sponsored Rogers financially to go to Ethiopia to cover the crisis, as an international correspondent at large, his findings were disseminated in many black newspapers, including the *Chronicle.* And Boston was one of Rogers's stops in his post-trip lecture tour. He also published his findings in a booklet entitled *The Real Facts of Ethiopia.*[33] As with his other publications, the *Chronicle* not only advertised the work but also printed excerpts from it. These excerpts mostly painted an uplifting, though somewhat unrealistic, picture of Ethiopian superiority on the battlefield.[34]

Although the Italo-Ethiopian crisis unified blacks around the world, there were still signs of division over the issue of how representative of blacks were Haile Selassie and the ruling elite. This situation was amply portrayed in the *Chronicle* not only in its editorials and feature articles but also in the letters that it encouraged its readers to write on the issue. Although the returnee community in Addis Ababa had accused Ethiopians of denying their blackness,[35] it is also clear that the white world at times exploited the problem to reduce the potency of Pan-Africanism. This strategy was more commonly employed by European colonial administrators in Africa and the West Indies. For example, pointing out that the ruling class in Ethiopia, being of mixed ancestry, deliberately suppressed the blacks of that country, the white editor of the *West Indian Review*, a monthly published in Kingston, Jamaica, observed: "It surely has the flavor of ironic comedy for British subjects, safe and secure under the British flag, enjoying freedom and equality that makes them the envy of subject races to be attempting to make a common cause with a country like Abyssinia" (*West Indian Review*, Nov. 1935).

While the *Chronicle* did not ignore the problematic nature of Ethiopians' perception of their racial identity, it certainly did not view the West Indians in the colonies or those in the United States as the envy of others. Instead, like other organs of black activism in that period, it saw the invasion as an assault on blacks regardless of where they were or how they perceived their identity.

By 1941, when Mussolini finally withdrew his forces, coverage of the crisis had dwindled, as evidenced by the decrease in the number of letters to the editor and articles devoted to that issue. The diminished interest notwithstanding, the paper continued to remind its readers of the necessity of the crusade with the following phrase to open the section on international news: "FREE ETHIOPIA, FREE AFRICA, ADVANCE THE RACE."

The European domination of Africa was only part of the imperialist saga. Also of great importance to the *Chronicle* and the West Indian community was the colonial situation in the West Indies. In the period under review (1930–50), two main developments captured the journalists' attention: the strikes and riots that engulfed the whole British West Indies in the 1930s and the agitation for federation and self-government in the 1940s. Throughout the 1930s, the paper reported extensively on the disturbances as they spread in the Caribbean region.[36] The *Chronicle* boasted of getting speedily updated information from its contacts in the West

Indies, among whom was T. A. Kitchener, former editor of the *Chronicle,* who was now editor of *Plain Talk,* a publication in Kingston, Jamaica.

As active members of the various West Indian associations in Boston, the editor at the time, Alfred Haughton, and many of the columnists were instrumental in organizing events designed to address what they termed "the trouble in the tropics." In these events, resolutions and petitions were drawn up to be sent to the respective colonial administrators in the islands and to the British consul in New York. Details of these were of course printed in the *Chronicle.* As Haughton frequently maintained, the paper was obligated to explain the trajectory of events not only for the benefit of the West Indian immigrants but also for the information of the majority of its readers who were American-born blacks. In many reports, the paper took pains to illustrate the similarities in the plight of blacks in the United States and those of the West Indies. The following excerpt from a July 24, 1937, editorial illustrates that endeavor: "Too long have those regions [the West Indies] been crushed under the heel of oppression and exploitation. True, the ruling classes (and we are sorry to say they are black and white) do not lynch the masses nor do they openly Jim-Crow and insult them, but they keep them in such abject poverty that segregation is achieved by a mere flick of the coin."

The unrest of the 1930s was among the key factors that convinced the British government to embark on constitutional reform. But this road to reform was just as bumpy. Although the process involved roundtable talks and negotiations between the British government and the West Indian activists, violent confrontations continued, and some of the activists, such as W. A. Domingo, were jailed for their radicalism.[37] In response to this torturous route to self-government, and thanks to the efforts of Richard B. Moore and Domingo, a Pan-Caribbean movement was launched in the United States.[38] The *Chronicle* became an effective vehicle in Boston for the propagation of the agitational agenda of the West Indies National Council and the American West Indian Association on Caribbean Affairs, the two organizations that, though based in New York, sought to unite West Indians living in the United States around the struggle for West Indian constitutional reform.

A significant component of the Pan-Caribbean agenda was the education of West Indian immigrants and their African-American sympathizers on the situation in the islands. The *Chronicle* performed this function by carefully explaining what constitutional reform entailed. The following exemplifies the tone of many of the editorials dealing with the issue: "It is important that we know exactly what is going on. Britain must move towards constitutional reform in order to broaden the suffrage, give more responsibilities to the natives, and overhaul the agricultural system to alleviate the problem of the single crop economy. To see this happen, you must register protests at the British embassy in Washington and with the colonial office at Whitehall, London" (Feb. 27, 1943).

In the now-typical pattern of cooperation between the paper and West Indian associations, speakers were brought in to educate the West Indian community and the black community in general on the reform process. The following personalities were among the most prominent: Dr. Eric Williams, who later became the first prime minister of independent Trinidad, came in 1943, when he was still an associate professor of social science at Howard University. He talked about the economic implications of constitutional reform (*Chronicle,* June 5, 1943). Richard B. Moore, vice president of the West Indies National Council, visited in 1942 to talk about the repressive measures adopted by Britain to lessen the pace of change. He focused especially on the case of W. A. Domingo, who was in jail in Jamaica at the time (Mar. 14, 1942). Norman Manley, leader of the People's National Party of Jamaica, was invited in 1945 under the combined auspices of the *Chronicle* and Jamaica Associates to give a firsthand account of current political affairs in Jamaica (Mar. 17, 1945).

In hosting speakers and providing a forum for petitions, resolutions, statements, and opinions, the *Chronicle* served as an organ of protest in the West Indian colonial struggle with Britain. Largely because of the size of the West Indian immigrant community in New York and the national prominence of its leaders,[39] the West Indian–owned newspaper in that city, the *Amsterdam News,* is often acknowledged as a critical part of the protest. But a careful examination of Boston's *Chronicle* reveals that it too articulated the cause of the homeland.

When it came to imperialism in the Western Hemisphere, although the primary focus was on European powers (specifically Britain), the United States did not escape the critical attention of the *Chronicle.* In its collaboration with Moore and the West Indies National Council, the paper pledged to monitor U.S. conduct in the West Indian bases it acquired from Britain in the Bases-for-Destroyers agreement in 1940. In December of that year, the *Chronicle* published a letter to Franklin D. Roosevelt, signed by W. A. Domingo on behalf of the members of the West Indies National Council, demanding assurance from the U.S. government that the insidious practice of racism would not be extended into the islands on which the bases were situated: "We want to safeguard our fundamental right in the lands of our birth" (Dec. 26, 1940).

In 1942, even with Domingo in jail, the *Chronicle* was still committed to evaluating U.S. activities in the West Indian bases. In March of that year, Jamaica Associates called a mass meeting on "The Caribbean Peoples and the Defense of America," to which it invited the Barbados Union, Montserrat Progressive League, Bermudan Associates, and NAACP. Richard Moore, one of the key speakers, addressed the vitality of the bases in the islands and their relevance to the defense of the Panama Canal and the Western Hemisphere. Commenting on the event, the *Chronicle* editor Alfred Haughton, also a prominent member of the Jamaica Associates, emphasized that the bases were yet more proof of the vitality of black people in world affairs. He therefore admonished his readers to "embrace this knowledge with confidence and always take interest in the happenings there so that the U.S. will be reminded of who needs who when they tend to forget it" (*Chronicle,* Mar. 21, 1942).

Some of the most scathing criticism of U.S. imperialism in the Western Hemisphere was vented in the paper's coverage of the American occupation of Haiti. Indeed, some of the meetings organized by the West Indian associations and the *Chronicle* to address Liberia's sovereignty cited Haiti, a black republic that was nominally independent, as a parallel situation in the Western Hemisphere (Apr. 2, 1932).

As U.S. withdrawal became imminent, the paper covered the situation, urging its readers to rally to the cause of their Haitian brothers and sisters by putting pressure on the U.S. government to follow through with its plans to withdraw. In a series of articles under the title, "Respite in Sight for Haiti," the *Chronicle* recalled the U.S. occupation of Haiti as a period defined by brutality and exploitation. Reviewing the whole picture, it concluded that the brutality far outweighed whatever benefits the United States may believe came out of occupation (Sept. 10, 1932).

Thus, Haiti, Jamaica, Sierra Leone, Ethiopia, Liberia, Scottsboro, and Boston—any place with a significant black presence—drew the attention of the *Boston Chronicle.* Unfortunately, its frequent description as the local West Indian paper belied this diffuse focus. Furthermore, the national recognition attained by the *Guardian* before 1920 continued, unfairly, to undercut the viability of the *Chronicle* as an organ of black protest. By 1934, when the *Guardian's* founder, William Monroe Trotter, died in what may have been suicide, his paper's reputation had slipped.[40] The other black newspaper of the city, the *Chronicle,* on the other hand, had gained ascendency as New England's largest black weekly, even though it still was not nationally recognized.

The intraracial diversity of the employees of the *Chronicle* was what added richness and focus to its efforts. There was, of course, the West Indian core, the editors and writers who worked closely with the local West Indian associations. But there was also the group of well-known African-American literary figures who were closely affiliated with the paper. As the contents of the paper clearly reveal, each group, though in agreement about several issues, also freely diverged in their opinions. In the 1930s and 1940s, such events as the Great Depression, the Italian invasion of Ethiopia, and the rise of nationalist movements in Africa and the Caribbean provided them with the opportunity to express these opinions and to contribute toward black advancement everywhere.

Pan-Africanism as an ideology has manifested itself in several different forms. One of the earliest of these was the back-to-Africa movement that sought to link diasporic blacks physically to the homeland. Political manifestation came in the form of the Pan-African congresses held in Europe in the first half of the twentieth century, the Organization of African Unity, and even Malcolm X's Organization of Afro-American Unity, which had hoped to work with the newly independent African states in the United Nations to force the United States to address the plight of American blacks. Pan-Africanism has even manifested itself in religious forms such as Ethiopianism and in literary and art forms such as Negritude and Rastafarianism. All of these forms were expressed mainly through an important forum of Pan-Africanism: journalism. Print journalism has always featured prominently in the Pan-African endeavor of bringing dispersed African people together. Although the *Chronicle* of Boston never attained the stature of Garvey's *Negro World*, it nonetheless performed similar functions. As one Bostonian who was a teenager in the 1940s remembered it: "The *Chronicle* was more than a newspaper at my house. It was a source of geography, history and political science which educated us on blacks all over the world."[41]

NOTES

1. This pledge was made by the founders and editors of *Freedom's Journal*, Samuel E. Cornish and John B. Russwurm, in the first edition (Mar. 16, 1827). Cited in Lerone Bennett Jr., *Before the Mayflower: A History of Black America* (New York: Penguin, 1984), 174.

2. The classic work on Trotter and the *Guardian*, which details the significance of these and other developments, is Stephen R. Fox, *The Guardian of Boston: William Monroe Trotter* (New York: Atheneum, 1970).

3. Ibid., 267.

4. William Monroe Trotter to George A. Towns, Jan. 23, 1914, quoted in Ruth Worthy, "A Negro in Our History: William Monroe Trotter, 1827–1934" (Master's thesis, Columbia University, 1952), 36.

5. Andrew Buni and Alan Rogers, *Boston: City on the Hill* (Boston: Windsor Publications, 1984), 118.

6. Anthony Lukas, *Common Ground: A Turbulent Decade in the Lives of Three American Families* (New York: Alfred A. Knopf, 1985), 58–59.

7. For more on the evolution of Boston's ethnic neighborhoods in 1900–1950, see Thomas H. O'Connor, *Bibles, Brahmins and Bosses: A Short History of Boston* (Boston: Boston Public Library, 1984), 119–52; and Andrew Buni and Alan Rogers, *Boston: City on the Hill* (Boston: Windsor Publications, 1984), 88–95.

8. These data were computed from statistics in the U.S. census published in 1922, 1932, and 1943, and from community data supplied by West Indian associations.

9. Stephan Thernstrom, whose statistically loaded work is still the most empirically conducted investigation of Boston's ethnic groups, paints this picture. He demonstrates the economic predicament of the overwhelming majority of the black population in much of the first half of the twentieth century. For details, see his *The Other Bostonians: Poverty and Progress in the American Metropolis, 1880–1970* (Cambridge, Mass.: Harvard University Press, 1973), 176–219.

10. The West Indian church, St. Cyprian's Episcopal Church, was built by mostly Jamaican and Barbadian immigrants in 1924. Situated on Tremont Street in Lower Roxbury, it was actually the first black church in that neighborhood. There were three major island/national associations before 1950: Jamaica Associates, Barbados Union, Inc., and the Montserrat Progressive Association. There were also Pan-West Indian associations, of which two major ones were the West India Aid Society and the Boston branch of Marcus Garvey's Universal Negro Improvement Association. Cricket clubs, most symbolic of West Indian leisure, were also very crucial to the community. In fact, cricket clubs, such as the Windsors, West India A, West India B, Standards, and Wanderers, were formed before the national associations. For more on the associational life of the West Indian community in Boston in 1900–1950, see Violet Johnson, "The Migration Experience: Social and Economic Adjustment of British West Indian Immigrants in Boston, 1915–1950" (Ph.D. diss., Boston College, 1992), esp. chap. 3.

11. Buni and Rogers, *Boston,* 118.

12. Lance Carden, *Witness: An Oral History of Black Boston, 1920–1960* (Boston: Boston College Press, 1989), 19.

13. Charles H. Trout, *Boston: The Great Depression and the New Deal* (New York: Oxford University Press, 1977), 193.

14. For useful analysis on the rationale, strategies, strengths, and weaknesses of the don't-buy-where-you-can't-work campaign of the depression era, see August Meir, Elliot Rudwick, and Francis L. Broderick, *Black Protest Thought in the Twentieth Century* (Indianapolis: Bobbs-Merrill, 1983), 122–31.

15. Trout, *Boston,* 193.

16. A good example of this was a case the *Chronicle* investigated in 1933 in which a Canadian construction company refused to hire two black men because, as the supervisor blatantly explained, his workers, who were all white and mostly Irish, would not work with them (*Chronicle,* June 10, 1933).

17. The Atlantic National Bank on Huntington Avenue in the South End was touted as being good to blacks. Two of the black credit unions were the Boston Progressive Credit Union and the Excelsior Credit Union.

18. The racist ideologies of Nazism and Fascism were becoming increasingly apparent in the United States in that period. Emblematic of this development was the Detroit "radio priest," Father Charles E. Coughlin, and his "Social Catholicism." Coughlin used his weekly broadcasts, which reached an audience estimated at 30–45 million listeners, to disseminate his anti-Semitic and anticommunist sentiments. Most cities in the United States, including Boston, reflected these racist currents in the marked increase of attacks on Jews and blacks.

19. Victor Bynoe, interview by Violet M. Johnson, South End, Mass., Aug. 6, 1989; Carden, *Witness*, 53.

20. In April 1931, the trial of nine black youths began in Scottsboro, Alabama. They were accused of raping two white women in a freight train. The charges, which were controversial since the onset, elicited rage among blacks around the country and the world.

21. Robert C. Hayden, *African-Americans in Boston: More than 350 Years* (Boston: Boston Public Library, 1991), 116.

22. For a detailed case study of African Americans and communism, see Mark Naisson, *Communism in Harlem during the Great Depression* (Urbana: University of Illinois Press, 1983).

23. One of the black communist leaders who came to Boston on several occasions, under the auspices of the *Chronicle* and some West Indian associations, was Richard B. Moore, a Barbadian immigrant in Harlem and one of the best-known black communists in the 1930s.

24. In the March 19, 1932, issue of the *Chronicle*, for example, Johns emphatically asserted that the *Harlem Home Journal and Business Informer's* appeal to blacks to shun white businesses was reckless. He envisioned severe reprisals and repercussions because blacks could not do without white businesses.

25. A useful study of this aspect of black protest in the United States is Keith S. Henry, "The Black Political Tradition in New York: A Conjunction of Political Cultures," *Journal of Black Studies* 7 (June 1977): 455–84.

26. Cited in the *Chronicle*, Mar. 17, 1934. For more on Vann and the *Pittsburgh Courier*, see Andrew Buni, *Robert L. Vann of the Pittsburgh Courier: Politics and Black Journalists* (Pittsburgh: University of Pittsburgh Press, 1974).

27. A concise yet informative study of Garveyism and Pan-Africanism is Horace Campbell, "Garveyism, Pan-Africanism, and African Liberation in the Twentieth Century," in *Garvey: His Work and Impact*, ed. Rupert Lewis and Patrick Bryan (Trenton, N.J.: Africa World Press, 1991), 167–88.

28. For more on Rogers, see John Henrik Clarke, "J. A. Rogers: In Search of the African Personality World History," *Black History Is No Mystery* 1, no. 2 (Feb. 1990): 16–19.

29. For more on the life of Blyden, see H. R. Lynch, *Edward Wilmot Blyden* (London: Oxford University Press, 1967).

30. Imanuel Geiss, *The Pan-African Movement: A History of Pan-Africanism in America, Europe and Africa* (New York: Africana Publishing, 1974), 268–71; Campbell, "Garveyism, Pan-Africanism, and African Liberation," 174.

31. For a brief analysis of the significance of Liberia in Pan-Africanism, see R. D. Ralston and Albuquerque Mourao, "Africa and the New World," in *General History of Africa*, vol. 7, ed. Adu Boaher (Berkeley: University of California Press, 1985), 747–49.

32. John Hope Franklin and Alfred A. Moss Jr., *From Slavery to Freedom: A History of African Americans* (New York: McGraw-Hill, 1994), 433. For a detailed examination of the African-American response to the Italian invasion of Ethiopia, see William R. Scott, *The Sons of Sheba's Race: African Americans and the Italo-Ethiopian War, 1935–1941* (Bloomington: Indiana University Press, 1993).

33. J. A. Rogers, *The Real Facts of Ethiopia* (New York: J. A. Rogers Publications, 1936).

34. Rogers has been criticized for producing colorful, exaggerated reports to please a hopeful black public. See Scott, *Sons of Sheba's Race*, 198–99.

35. The friction between the two groups—Ethiopians and the African-American immigrants—is addressed in ibid., 189–91.

36. Disturbances occurred in Trinidad, British Guyana, Barbados, St. Vincent, and St. Lucia in 1935 and in Trinidad, Barbados, and Jamaica in 1937 and 1938.

37. W. A. Domingo was a prominent Jamaican immigrant in New York who had gone back home to participate in the political process.

38. For more details on the career of Moore and his role in advocating change in the Caribbean and elsewhere, see W. Burghardt Turner and Joyce Moore Turner, eds., *Richard B. Moore, Caribbean Militant in Harlem* (Bloomington: Indiana University Press, 1988).

39. Examples of this West Indian leadership in the 1930s and 1940s include Richard Moore, W. A. Domingo, Cyril Briggs, C. L. R. James, the Rev. Ethelred Brown, Claudia Jones, and Ferdinand C. Smith.

40. Fox, *Guardian of Boston*, 266–72.

41. Colin B., interview by Violet Johnson, Roxbury, Mass., Feb. 2, 1990.

4 San Francisco's *Chung Sai Yat Po* and the Transformation of Chinese Consciousness, 1900–1920

YUMEI SUN

In the early twentieth century, America's Chinese immigrants were socially, economically, linguistically, and psychologically isolated from the greater American society. As a result of their insularity, the Chinese in America were stigmatized as a people self-confined to their own world. Many people assume that the Chinese in America carried on their own lives, detached from U.S. social and political life, indifferent to American values, and impervious to assimilation. Gunther Barth has articulated the popular view of the early Chinese immigrants, which has often been used to describe the entire Chinese immigrant population. Unlike other immigrant groups, Barth wrote, the Chinese came to the United States with a different goal in mind: "The newcomers came with a vision; they would make money to return to China with their savings for a life of ease, surrounded and honored by the families which their toil had sustained."[1] This assumption was widely held in the nineteenth century and well into the twentieth. Thus, as late as 1976, Stanford Lyman could declare that "the Chinese as a stranger in America was in the society but not of it."[2]

In point of fact, much of this isolation was more the result of racial discrimination and discriminatory legislation at the city, state, and federal levels than of anything inherently Chinese. What follows is an examination of how one influential institution—a Chinese-language newspaper entitled *Chung Sai Yat Po*—negotiated the chasm between the Chinese community and mainstream American society and how, in the early 1900s, it helped the Chinese to break through their social and cultural isolation and, in effect, to become Americans.[3]

Chung Sai Yat Po (China West daily, hereinafter abbreviated *CSYP*) provides an insider's view into what indeed seemed, to most outsiders, a closed community. Published in San Francisco's Chinatown from 1900 to 1951,[4] the newspaper was one of the longest running and most popular

Chinese dailies in the United States. *CSYP* was published and managed under the editorship of Ng Poon Chew, who had been raised in China to become a Buddhist monk. He converted to Christianity shortly after immigrating as a youth, subsequently became a Presbyterian minister, and remained a devout Christian throughout his life.[5] He was one of the first Chinese in America to cut off his queue—both as an act of defiance of the Qing Dynasty and as an act of assimilation into American culture. Ng spoke fluent English and lectured extensively throughout the United States.[6] He was respected and well known both within and outside the Chinese community; for example, he became a thirty-second-degree Mason, active in the Lakeshore Masonic Lodge of Oakland.

Ng was committed to assimilation. He saw his paper as a beacon of journalistic integrity in an age of yellow journalism and racism. Ng described *CSYP* this way: "It is peculiar, but nevertheless true, that in San Francisco the yellow man gets out the white paper and the white man gets out the yellow paper. We run a conservative paper in every way. It is cleanly edited and our whole aim is to educate and elevate the Chinese people; to make them better citizens and better people."[7]

Ng was "the driving force behind the paper's success," but his staff at *CSYP* also had considerable exposure to American culture, for many of them were graduates of American schools.[8] In addition, *CSYP* enlisted as its literary advisor John Fryer, a professor of Chinese literature at the University of California.[9] This step perhaps aimed at both indicating the approval of an American educational institution and incorporating the input of a non-Chinese.

CSYP's situation was not unique, in that American society had a profound impact on the development of the Chinese-language press itself— for the political freedom and the availability of technology and information contributed to the rise of the foreign-language press in general.[10] America's first Chinese-language newspaper, *Kim Shan Jit San Luk* (Golden hill news), was established shortly after the arrival of the first wave of Chinese immigrants in California.[11] Though *Kim Shan Jit San Luk* was short-lived,[12] a string of other bilingual and Chinese-language newspapers followed, apparently in response to the community's need for news and information. As Robert Park defines it, news is a kind of "urgent information that men use in making adjustments to a new environment, in changing old habits, and in forming new opinions."[13] Like other immigrant groups, the Chinese took advantage of an environment conducive to newspaper publishing. Indeed, as the historian Him Mark Lai points out, it is not surprising that "the first Chinese daily was founded in the

United States, for this was the first country in the West where the Chinese settled in great numbers and where they had excellent opportunities to observe and learn from the Western press."[14]

Before continuing, let us look at a few facts that may help to illustrate *CSYP*'s impact on the community (see table 4.1). From 1900 to 1920, *CSYP* enjoyed an average circulation of about 4,000 in a community of about 10,000.[15] The *Chinese World,* another popular Chinese-language daily, claimed a circulation of 3,000. Though the circulation figures for the two other papers in San Francisco, the *Chinese Free Press* and the *Radiator* (a weekly), are not available, the combined readership for *CSYP* and the *Chinese World* alone accounted for over half the Chinese population in San Francisco.[16]

In addition, the circulation figures for *CSYP* and the *Chinese World* reflect only sales as reported by the newspaper publishers. Actual reader-

Table 4.1. Chinese Population and the Distribution Figures of Chinese-Language Newspapers, 1900–1920

	Chinese Population		Chinese-Language Newspapers		Total of Available Circulation Figures
	San Francisco	California	San Francisco	With Circulation Figures Available	
1900	13,954	45,753	3	1	600
1901			4	1	600
1902[a]			4	2	3,100
1903			3	1	2,500
1904			3	1	3,500
1905[b]			4	2	4,850
1906			4	2	5,900
1907			3	2	11,756
1908			3	2	13,756
1909			4	2	6,500
1910	10,852	36,248	4	2	6,500
1911			5	3	8,050
1912			5	4	12,550
1913			5	4	12,631
1914			5	5	16,250
1915			4	4	14,800
1916			4	4	18,150
1917			4	4	22,627
1918			4	4	23,000
1919			4	4	24,100
1920	7,744	28,812	4	4	25,500

a. This is the first year that *CSYP*'s subscription figures were available. *CSYP* enjoyed a steady readership and stayed on top in subscription volume throughout most of its history.

b. This is the first year that the figures for *Chinese World,* another popular Chinese-language newspaper, became available.

ship was surely much larger, due to pass-along effects in the communal dwellings of the bachelor society. Even assuming that some Chinese had multiple subscriptions and that the circulation figures may have been inflated by the publishers, the total percentage of Chinese who read at least one Chinese newspaper was still impressively high.[17] A contemporary journalist bore witness to *CSYP*'s popularity. He wrote in 1922 that "[one could] scarcely enter a Chinese home in California without seeing a copy of [*CSYP*'s] famous sheet. . . . Among the upper classes even the ladies read [*CSYP*] as they sip their tea and nibble their moon cakes."[18] Advertisements for books and textbooks in *CSYP* suggest that there were learning activities closely linked to assimilation. Throughout its first two decades, *CSYP* periodically displayed advertisements for "all varieties of books." A typical ad (such as one from November 1906) listed the availability of English readers, English-Chinese dictionaries, and English-language textbooks.

Thus, if *CSYP* is any indicator, print culture was not only an integral part of the lives of the Chinese in America, it also played a leading role in shaping the thinking of the Chinese community. This fact is made more significant because, for many of the Chinese, *CSYP* was one of the few sources of news to which they had access. The linguistic barrier obviously contributed to the high demand for Chinese-language newspapers. Social and sometimes literal isolation—as when Chinatown was under quarantine at the height of the plague scare in 1900—further enhanced the visibility and impact of these newspapers.

Even for Chinese immigrants who could read English, *CSYP* was still indispensable because it provided them with information that could not be found in English-language newspapers. *CSYP*'s news of China, for example, was tailored specifically to the interest of Chinese immigrants, most of whom came from Guangdong Province. Much of the news of China was sent by *CSYP*'s own correspondents stationed in China and transmitted via cable.[19] *CSYP* reported daily, and in great detail, wars, natural disasters, important political developments, and educational and economic progress in China and in the immigrants' hometowns. Likewise, *CSYP*'s U.S. news section addressed the diverse interests of the Chinese community in America. National news, for example, paid special attention to federal, state, and city laws and regulations that had a direct bearing on Chinese immigrants. Regulations restricting the importation of Chinese food staples, real or rumored changes in immigration laws, incidents of Chinese lawbreakers, and various legislative proposals relevant to Chinese immigration were usually translated and printed verbatim. Specific cases of harassment of Chinese in the United States received considerable attention, as did disputes, petty offenses, and violent crimes in Chinatown. America's international relations, particularly its policy toward China, its purchase of Chinese goods, and other such national headline news were thoroughly covered.

Despite the heavy emphasis on matters directly related to Chinese immigrants, the connection between the Chinese-language press and its American counterpart was noteworthy. It is not surprising that *CSYP* and other Chinese-language newspapers reported more news of particular interest to the Chinese in America; what is less known is that most of the Chinese-language newspapers actually relied on wire services—notably the Associated Press and United Press—as their primary sources for national and international news.[20] Thus, though the selection of news printed reflected the editors' concerns, ultimately the news itself derived from the same sources that American mainstream newspapers were using.

In addition to being a news source, *CSYP* also sought to encourage the assimilation of the Chinese community through its front-page editorials.[21] Year after year, for example, *CSYP* editorialized on the significance of national holidays, such as the Fourth of July, Lincoln's and Washington's birthdays, and Christmas. The editorials, mixing holiday celebration with criticism of Chinese society, revealed *CSYP*'s deeply felt admiration for the American way of life. A typical editorial described the joy of July 4: "Americans stand tall on this earth, proud and spirited; every one of them carries the air of being above everyone else. Even women and humble children entertain no thought of living under anybody" (July 5, 1911). Each editorial exploring American values also pointed out lessons for the Chinese in America. The July 5 editorial was no exception: "The Chinese in America have been in this country for decades. We have witnessed firsthand how Americans celebrate their Independence Day for dozens of times. Do we feel nothing after the smoke from the fireworks drifts away? Do we not feel moved? Do we not wish that our country has a day like this?"

On February 15, 1911, a *CSYP* editorial described Lincoln's life—his humble origins, his desire to help the poor, his advocacy of equal rights for all people, and his leadership in the Civil War—and then went on to explain his relevance to the Chinese: "Our fellow countrymen who live in this country must encourage each other with humanitarianism, so that we can enjoy the blessings of humanitarianism. That way, we can truly benefit from the great humanitarian Lincoln's legacy."

In the age of John Dewey, *CSYP* viewed education as the solution to many of the problems the Chinese faced in America. "Everything begins with education," declared an October 3, 1911, editorial. "Talented people are created through education," said another (Apr. 16, 1907). In a January 12, 1911, editorial entitled "On Getting Our Children into Public Schools as the First Step to Removing the Exclusion Laws," *CSYP* reemphasized the need for education in the context of anti-Chinese discrimination: "We Chinese are mistreated by the white people because we are more ignorant than the whites; we are ignorant because we Chinese have never had any basic education. If we are to get rid of the Exclusion laws, we must nurture the intelligence of the Chinese children. To nurture the Chinese children's intelligence, we have to give them a regular education. Therefore, the first thing to do to get rid of the Exclusion laws is to get our children into public schools."

Many of *CSYP*'s editorials directly addressed political issues of the day that were widely debated among the Chinese. Each time, *CSYP* encouraged its readers to explore further the debate in the context of American history. For example, on the eve of the 1911 Revolution, some Chinese expressed doubt about the Revolution's viability, pessimistically saying that there was no George Washington among China's revolutionaries. *CSYP* took the opportunity to bring the American Revolution into clearer focus: "For one Washington to succeed in the Revolution, there must have been many Washingtons that helped," said an August 7, 1911, editorial, emphasizing that a democratic republic could only be built through the participation of many people. In this context, *CSYP* refuted those who hailed George Washington but hesitated to support the revolutionaries in China. If these Chinese had lived through the American Revolution, *CSYP* asked rhetorically, "Would they really have thought of Washington as a revolutionary? Or would they have called him a subversive bandit?"

The fundamental principles of the U.S. Constitution and justice system framed many of the editorial discussions in *CSYP*. In the early years, when denouncing the mistreatment of the Chinese in America, the paper often criticized the United States for failing to abide by the Burlingame Treaty (1868) between the United States and China. A decade later, *CSYP*'s criticism gradually shifted to constitutional issues; it held the United States up to its own moral standards, which led to bitter complaints about American hypocrisy and injustice in the treatment of Chinese immigrants. *CSYP* denounced the tendency among some Americans "to subjugate and ultimately deprive the humanity of its birth-right to freedom" (Feb. 15, 1911). The anti-Chinese Labor Party, for example, "treat[ed] other races as their enemy" (Apr. 28, 1911). "The United States is a free country. So doesn't it put a dirty spot on the American freedom when a party repeatedly invades and violates other people's freedom?" (Apr. 28, 1911).

Similarly, the irony of suffering from discrimination in the land of Lincoln did not escape *CSYP*. Its celebration of Lincoln's Birthday in 1915 led to the poignant statement, "What people are celebrating [here] we overseas [immigrant] Chinese cannot enjoy" (Feb. 12, 1915).

CSYP's appeal to the Constitution became apparent in the aftermath of the 1906 earthquake and fire in San Francisco. Shortly after the destruction of Chinatown, discussions of relocating the Chinese appeared in English-language newspapers. Many in the city's government supported this approach. In an attempt to gain voice, some Chinese suggested that they should appeal for the intervention of the Chinese counsel in San Francisco. *CSYP*, on the other hand, asked the Chinese to place their faith in American constitutional protections. In one of its first editorials after the earthquake, *CSYP* addressed the proposed Chinatown relocation:

> The Chinese here have discussed measures to have the consul negotiate with the San Francisco city government. . . . But they do not know that this matter does not lie in the hand of the consul. Officials from [the Chinese] government have no rights to haggle with the San Francisco city government on matters regarding Chinatown. . . . The city government or the administration have no power to force the Chinese to live in a place they designate. According to the U.S. Constitution, Americans and foreigners in the United States are both protected by its provisions to choose freely where they want to live. Therefore, the city government cannot tell the Chinese where they should relocate; we Chinese can simply ignore them as well. (May 1, 1906)

As a start, *CSYP* suggested that the Chinese should contact the insurance agencies in order to recover some money and encouraged those with financial resources to help those who had none. Both of these measures would help finance the rebuilding of Chinatown. *CSYP* also suggested that people should contact their former landlords prior to the rebuilding to ensure their space: "It is not necessary to rent the entire section of Chinatown. We only need to rent a few houses in a row and leave the rest vacant. The Westerners do not wish to live near us, so that the owners of those vacant houses [nearby] will certainly let us rent them" (May 1, 1906). *CSYP* thus refocused the crisis from one that accentuated the marginality of the Chinese to one that empowered them through an understanding of American constitutional freedoms and guarantees. In hindsight, *CSYP*'s viewpoint prevailed. What contemporary journalists (and, later, some scholars) described as a random act when the Chinese happened to drift back into Chinatown did not in fact happen by accident. The Chinese took an assertive, if not aggressive, stance and re-claimed their homes, confident that their action was protected by the Constitution.

Even in matters without a clear-cut victory, *CSYP*'s efforts to educate its readers with regard to their constitutional rights were significant. The exclusion of Asians from land ownership, for example, was discussed at great length. In the first decade of the twentieth century, when the issue was brought up again by the California state legislature, a *CSYP* editorial once again explained that such exclusions violated the Constitution:

> Property ownership is what lawyers call land ownership. All foreigners residing in the United States, regardless of whether they are citizens, as long as they are obligated to pay taxes, have the right to own property; that is, they can enjoy land ownership. . . . Readers: please do not think that I am simply giving a high talk—the United States is a republic where the people have the right to make regulations and the right to repudiate them. (Mar. 29, 1911)

In the same editorial, *CSYP* called an emergency meeting to devise a contingency plan: "The best idea is to hire a legal advisor from among those who are honest and fair and who are not prejudiced against other races; he should evoke the constitutional rights for the people. We should select a representative to go with this legal advisor to meet with the state representatives. Those state representatives who believe in human rights will have a reason to help us." Even though it was not clear how long they could keep the anti-Asian forces at bay, *CSYP* recognized the ultimate benefits of spreading the word about the Constitution. In an April 1, 1911, editorial review, *CSYP* praised the accomplishments of the state legislature:

> Of all the legislative measures passed, none is anti-Asian; before the closing of the Congress, the labor unions clamored around; one day they wanted to take away the voting rights of the American-born Chinese; another day they wanted to forbid Asians from owning land altogether; yet another day they wanted to ban selling medicinal drugs without license. From our perspective, the issues over the voting rights of the American-born and the sales of medicinal drugs without license failed to win because of our great effort. This reflected the progress in our political thinking and the progress in our thinking on issues of rights.

During the 1911 Revolution in China, when interest in the home country was high, *CSYP* repeatedly discussed issues related to the formation of a new Chinese government, using the U.S. Constitution as a model. Many Chinese felt new hope that as citizens of a republic, their lot in the United States, one of the world's oldest republics, would change. There was a euphoric sense that China and America had finally found an important common link: "Cheers! Cheers! Our country has suddenly become a democratic republic after thousands of years of dictatorship. Cheers! Cheers! The New World created a complete republic over a hundred years ago; the Old World finally has created a complete republic in the beginning of the twentieth century" (Oct. 31, 1911).

The establishment of the Chinese republic, above all, gave many Chinese in America a new angle on things. There was an increased awareness of the affinity between the two countries as republics. In their view, the United States had the closest ties to China and was a natural ally. As *CSYP*'s editor Ng said, their expectations were high: "[The Chinese people] have an eye on America. . . . We want this country to bid us Godspeed. It is only right: we are entitled to expect that. America is in duty bound to give moral support and sympathy to us in our fight for a government patterned on the principles of the American fathers of 1776."[22] Amid great anticipation of the possible changes in China, *CSYP* began to reflect upon the Chinese community. *CSYP* realized, perhaps for the first time, that the political apathy prevailing in the Chinese community contributed to their lack of understanding of how the U.S. government worked. That, in turn, played a role in the marginal status of the Chinese in America:

> Our people have been coming to the United States for over one hundred years. We have done much business; we have had many achievements, and we should, logically, enjoy equal rights. However, instead of having the same rights, we have been cruelly and meanly treated by Americans. The United States can betray humanity as such, because our people have no political awareness, no concept of how a government works, and we have contributed to our situation by giving up many of our rights. Otherwise, why am I afraid we will never have any hope of electing a president? Why would we have no part in the state legislature? Not to mention having those anti-Asian people envious of our basic rights such as land ownership and wanting to take it from us forever. What a shame! (Apr. 6, 1911)

This concern with political participation reflected an evolution in *CSYP*'s political thinking, particularly with regard to second-generation Chinese. In early 1906, amid discussions of education for Chinese children, *CSYP* urged that youngsters maintain their ties to China. *CSYP*'s reasoning was that, with both American and Chinese educations, these children would grow up to serve China, should the need occur. Less than a decade later, however, the paper had begun to look toward the second-generation Chinese, who were entitled to U.S. citizenship through birth, with the hope that their political participation in the United States would effect change.

Editorials began to target Chinese Americans, calling on them to participate actively in the political process as a way of gaining respect for all Chinese in America: "Our only hope is with the men and women who were born in the United States and reside here who must be given citizenship. Those American-born Chinese who are above the legal age can participate in elections, which is a comforting thought" (Feb. 28, 1911). In this, the newspaper was not alone. The Chinese American Citizens Alliance was engaged in similar activities, and *CSYP* commended them for their role in educating the Chinese during recent elections. The purpose of political participation was clear: "[The American-born Chinese] can regain various rights for us; in addition, those whites in power will not dare to neglect us any more; instead, they will respect these native-borns" (Feb. 28, 1911).

CSYP's editorials reflected the deepening of Chinese immigrants' understanding of the complex problems of race and power that were at the basis of the Exclusion Laws and discrimination. Though "Westerner" was still used to refer to non–Asian Americans, the word "race" appeared more and more frequently in the editorials—in discussions of the alien Manchu rulers versus the ethnic Chinese, for example, and, more significantly, in discussions of the anti-Asian sentiment in the United States. On several occasions, *CSYP* condemned the prevailing racial discrimination against immigrants as well as people of color and predicted that social control based on race would be more difficult in the future (Mar. 19, 1918).

In the decade bracketing World War I, the content of *CSYP*'s news and editorials began to reflect more loyalty toward the United States among the Chinese in America, as well as the relevance of American social and political affairs in their lives. After the U.S. entry into the war, *CSYP* published an editorial entitled "Urging Our Overseas Chinese to Buy Liberty Bonds." Quoting President Woodrow Wilson, it argued, "These bonds are matters of our nation's lifeline, and matters of the freedom of humanity, and therefore are of great importance." Furthermore, Chinese in America should purchase Liberty Bonds: "We overseas Chinese are protected by the American flag. Enemies of the United States are our enemies. We overseas Chinese benefit from every victory the United States has over her enemy" (Oct. 17, 1917).

CSYP promptly printed official announcements for enlistment registration procedures for eligible citizens as well as discussions on whether noncitizens were required to enlist. Despite its enthusiasm, *CSYP* was not unaware of the problems posed by compulsory military service—among Americans as well as Chinese. It reported the various incidents of draft resistance by Americans and the consequences of eligible men avoiding registration. In this context, its editorial of September 11, 1918, was all the more significant, for it explained how the registration was to be conducted and then called on the Chinese in the United States to join the armed forces: "We overseas Chinese who reside in the United States are protected by the American flag (stars and stripes) and must abide by the order to register for enlisting and must not evade in any way. Those born in the United States must take the lead." *CSYP* indicated that more than two hundred Chinese had already enlisted in America's armed forces and that their effectiveness at the front was "no less than white soldiers." Their sacrifices, their glory would "bring honor to the people of our race." Noting that though non-U.S. citizens did not have to enlist, *CSYP* urged all Chinese in America to "do all we can if the U.S. government requests our help, in order to end the war soon" (Sept. 11, 1918). *CSYP* frequently reported news of the Chinese in America supporting military service, as in one case (admittedly somewhat extreme) of a Chinese man in his late fifties who tried in vain to join the army because of his "patriotic feelings" (Dec. 1, 1917).

Chung Sai Yat Po had an undeniable role in the transformation of Chinese immigrant society in the United States. Through its reporting and editorial policies, the paper affirmed what it considered to be positive actions by the Chinese in America. It took strong stands on controversial matters and stood firmly by what it touted as American principles. As one of the few sources of information in Chinese, *CSYP* provided news about China, San Francisco, and the United States to those not yet able to cross the linguistic barrier. It informed them of laws and regulations, both state and national, that affected their lives; it sought to teach them about the U.S. Constitution and patriotic holidays; it published news of the triumphs of the new Republic of China as well as injustices inflicted upon their fellow countrymen in North America. In its own way, *CSYP* provided leadership to the community in times of need and distress. It also served as one of the community forums where Chinese organizations and individuals presented their public grievances, negotiated resolutions, attempted reconciliation, and announced their affiliation or severance from various associations. It was a bulletin board where Chinese professionals, practically excluded from doing business outside Chinatown, advertised their trade; and it was a forum where Chinese writers voiced their opinions and exercised their literary skills.

Through it all, *Chung Sai Yat Po* actively participated in and chronicled events. It engaged the Chinese community in a reflexive process of self-examination that led, inevitably, to greater assimilation. It took pride in its role as a community leader as well as a source of news; it was a fundamental agent of change in the transformation of the Chinese community in San Francisco. Like the newspapers published by and for America's other immigrant groups, *Chung Sai Yat Po* facilitated and took a leading role in the eventual assimilation of the Chinese in America. Most importantly, together with other Chinese-language newspapers, *CSYP* provides a valuable but all too rare glimpse into the thinking of the early twentieth-century Chinese immigrants in America.

NOTES

1. Gunther Barth, *Bitter Strength: A History of the Chinese in the United States* (Cambridge, Mass.: Harvard University Press, 1964), 1.

2. Stanford M. Lyman, "The Chinese Diaspora in America, 1850–1943," *The Life, Influence and Role of the Chinese in the United States, 1776–1960: Proceedings, Papers of the National Conference Held at the University of San Francisco, July 10–12, 1975* (San Francisco: Chinese Historical Society of America, 1975), 131.

3. My approach in this essay is evidential and descriptive. Recent works in the area of the formation of cultural identities could inform this study, but because of the scope of this study they have not been included. Both Werner Sollors, *Beyond Ethnicity: Consent and Descent in American Culture* (New York: Oxford University Press, 1986), and Mary C. Waters, *Ethnic Options: Choosing Identities in America* (Berkeley: University of California Press, 1990), give excellent overviews.

4. Shih-shan Henry Tsai places *CSYP*'s demise as Jan. 1, 1951. See his *Chinese Experience in America* (Bloomington: Indiana University Press, 1986), 130. This is the only date I have located.

5. Corinne K. Hoexter, *From Canton to California: The Epic of Chinese Immigration* (New York: Four Winds Press, 1976), 274.

6. In his lifetime, Ng made eighty-six transcontinental speaking tours (ibid., 258).

7. *New York Eagle*, Oct. 9, 1909. Ng's reference, of course, is to yellow (i.e., sensational) journalism.

8. Charles F. Holder, "The Chinese Press in America," *Scientific American*, Oct. 11, 1902, 241. This article bears considerable resemblance to Ednah Robinson's "Chinese Journalism in California," *Out West*, Jan. 1902, 33–42.

9. Holder, "Chinese Press," 241.

10. Robert Park, *The Immigrant Press and Its Control* (New York: Harper and Bros., 1922; rpt., Montclair, N.J.: Patterson Smith, 1971), 9.

11. *Kim Shan Jit San Luk* was a bilingual weekly that began publication on April 22, 1854, and continued for about three months. See Karl Lo, "*Kim Shan Jit San Luk:* The First Chinese Paper Published in America," *Chinese Historical Society of America Bulletin* 6 (Oct. 1971).

12. According to Lo, *Golden Hills News* was published by Howard and Lersner and printed by F. Kuhl in San Francisco. Lo, "*Kim Shan Jit San Luk.*" Its English transliteration varied, but *Gold Hills News* and *Golden Mountain News* are most commonly used.

13. Park, *Immigrant Press*, 9.

14. Him Mark Lai, "The Chinese-American Press," in *The Ethnic Press in the United States: A Historical Analysis and Handbook,* ed. Sally M. Miller (New York: Greenwood Press, 1987), 27–43.

15. The Chinese population in 1900 was 13,954; in 1910, it was 18,850; and in 1920, it was 7,744. *Ayer's and Son's Directory* for 1910 registered 3,500; the figure in the 1911 directory was even higher: 4,000.

16. The figure accounted for one-sixth of the Chinese population in California and about one-ninth of the Chinese in the United States.

17. By 1910, New York City had already had some Chinese newspapers, such as *Chinese Reform News,* a semiweekly. By 1913, Chinese dailies appeared in New York City. The subscription figures for the San Francisco Chinese newspapers did not show any significant decline as a result.

18. Jessie Juliet Knox, "A Chinese Horace Greeley," *Oakland Tribune Magazine,* Dec. 3, 1922; rpt. in *Chinese Historical Society of America Bulletin,* Apr. 1971, [1–4].

19. M. B. Levick, "A Maker of New China," *Sunset,* May 1912, 599–610.

20. Tung Chen Chiu, "Chinese-Language Daily Newspapers in the United States" (Master's thesis, Indiana University, 1949), 23.

21. In fact, except for the advertisement, they were the only items on the first page. News was printed on the second and third pages.

22. Levick, "Maker of New China," 601.

PART 2

Discovering the Reader: Texts of Class, Race, and Gender

5 "The World We Shall Win for Labor": Early Twentieth-Century Hobo Self-Publication

LYNNE M. ADRIAN

James Buchanan Eads is an example of a self-made, self-educated American in the tradition of Benjamin Franklin. Born in Indiana on May 20, 1820, Eads was forced to leave school at age thirteen to help support his poor merchant family. After working for three years as a purser on a Mississippi river boat, he patented a diving bell and founded a steamboat salvage company, earning a fortune before his fortieth birthday. Then, in 1862, Eads emerged from five years of semiretirement to become a major producer of armor-plated gunboats for the Union Navy. In 1865 Congress approved a plan for a bridge across the Mississippi, with a 500-foot center span and fifty feet of clearance. Twenty-seven leading civil engineers deemed the project impossible, but Eads secured the contract and successfully completed the bridge in 1874. In the process, he achieved international acclaim as a bridge engineer, expanded his already considerable fortune, and made a lasting contribution to the American landscape: the Eads Bridge at St. Louis, still admired for its ruggedness and beauty.

James Buchanan Eads's bridge amassed a family fortune. His grandson and namesake, James Eads How, spent a fortune trying to construct another kind of bridge. How's newspaper bridge, the *"Hobo" News,* connected America's migratory workers to one another and to the larger labor movement; today it lies virtually forgotten, in a remote corner of the St. Louis Public Library. Though trained as a doctor, How spent his lifetime giving away money rather than earning it. Attracted to Christian socialism, he tried unsuccessfully to start a monastic order. Then, convinced that his inherited wealth was undeserved, he turned his efforts to helping hoboes. How founded the International Brotherhood Welfare Association (IBWA) in 1906, sponsored its publication of the *"Hobo" News* from its debut in 1915, and funded the Migratory Workers Union (MWU) throughout its organizational existence. Most of his power within the hobo subculture came from his control of the purse strings of so many hobo organizations. He died penniless in 1930, having poured his entire fortune into a movement for hobo organization and self-expression while living as a hobo himself.[1]

Though How's *"Hobo" News* is yellowed and largely crumbling, it can still connect modern readers to the millions of young men who wandered America as hoboes during the last decade of the nineteenth and the first two decades of the twentieth century. While the majority of settled Americans praised mobility in the abstract and valued hoboes' unskilled labor, they also often regarded the representatives of mobility as threats to their values and menaces to their lives. Hoboes, often incorrectly referred to as "tramps" or "bums," were a migratory labor force that moved freely and frequently among agricultural, rural construction, and urban manual labor jobs. About 90 percent of hoboes were young males, usually unmarried and lacking home ties; they were overwhelmingly of English-speaking, working-class origins. Though the number of hoboes and the individuals who were part of the subculture changed continually, their presence was a constant fact of American life. Essentially, they formed an unskilled, almost invisible adjunct to the nation's workforce.

The problems involved in reconstructing the hobo subculture are amply illustrated by tracing the history of the *"Hobo" News* and *Hobo World,* which provide most of the available information. (These seem to have been alternate titles carried by the same monthly publication that ran from 1915 until at least 1930.) Only nineteen copies of the newspaper survive in the New York Public Library (NYPL), most in extremely deteriorated condition.[2] Many of the microfilm holdings were photographed from ephemeral sheets that could not be reassembled into complete issues, and many issues could be dated solely on the basis of internal evidence. As early as 1922, the NYPL requested back numbers from the International Brotherhood Welfare Association so that the library could compile a complete run. The organization responded half-heartedly, merely requesting that members send in their extra copies. It is probable that the IBWA did not itself have a complete archive. Since the NYPL collection ends in 1923, it may be that the library became discouraged and discontinued its collecting efforts.[3] Later, two additional copies turned up in the Military Intelligence Records in the National Archives. Until quite recently, these scattered but tantalizing fragments represented all that was known about the hobo newspaper.

In July 1989, I contacted a St. Louis researcher and requested copies of some otherwise unobtainable biographical data on James Eads How. Unexpectedly, I received not only the requested biographical material but also clippings from unknown issues of the *"Hobo" News*. Subsequent calls revealed a cache of sixty-three issues, fifty-four of them previously uncollected, beginning with volume 1, number 1, April 1915, five years earlier than any previously known issues. Unaware of their value, the St. Louis Public library had left the newspapers stored on open stacks, and the manuscript librarians I contacted were unaware of their existence. The first half of the issues were copied and returned to circulation; the next day all were missing. Fortunately, the issues were recovered in the Popular Science Reading Room, where, librarians theorize, they had been taken by a homeless person looking for something to read. The sixty-three issues are now stored in the Special Collections of the St. Louis Public Library, which plans to catalog them and make them available to researchers.

Many aspects of hobo life can be recreated by a careful study of the *"Hobo" News*. For present purposes, analysis of the *"Hobo" News* will be confined to the role of storytelling and oral traditions within the hobo subculture, the existence of organizations for hoboes separate from their participation in the more well-known Industrial Workers of the World (IWW), and the importance of money as a source of power for James Eads How within the subculture itself.

The publication history of the *"Hobo" News* is curious and uneven. Roger Bruns, a popular historian of the hoboes, writes, "In May 1913 the IBWA issued *The Hoboes Jungle Scout*, a sheet which later became the *'Hobo' News*."[4] The only information available on this precursor is contained in a July 1920 article in the *"Hobo" News* entitled "The Editor on a Rambling Tour": "It was this great flood of 1913 that first put Dayton on the map of the hoboes as the first page of the first issue of *The Hoboes Jungle Scout*, the short-lived predecessor of the *Hobo News* (May 1, 1913), was devoted to the rotten conditions of the stomache [*sic*] robbing camps of the reconstruction work as reported to the present editor, by John J. Murray and James Scott on a postal card." In May 1915, the *"Hobo" News* notes:

> James Eads How, moving spirit and "angel" of the Brotherhood Welfare Association, yesterday kept the first of the promises he made to his migratory brethren when recently he came into a fortune under his mother's will. He said he would publish a newspaper for the benefit of his organization of the unemployed and Volume 1, Number 1 of the *"Hobo" News* was the fulfillment. . . . The [editorial] writer admits that he doesn't like the word "hobo," but philosophically concludes: "We have got it and we are going to make it respectable."

A letter "To Our Readers, Contributors and Subscribers" (Aug. 1917) stresses the communal effort represented by the paper: "We greet you all with this number, No. 5. This means that we have struggled along for two years and have started the third, with the prospects bright before us. It was hardly believable two years ago when the first number was issued, that a paper of this class could be made to go. But it does go and go well. The last number was oversold, but this seems to be a regular thing with us now and we are getting used to it."

In the July 1920 issue, however, the masthead states that the paper was in its "Eighth Year, Number 7, Established June 1913." Apparently, publication of the paper became more frequent and regular over time. By the second issue (May 1916), the paper had expanded to sixteen pages. All issues after June 1913 were sequentially numbered on a monthly basis (e.g., June 1921 is vol. 9, no. 6). Though the precise origin and development of the *"Hobo" News* can no longer be traced, such internal evidence seems to indicate strongly that early publication was more problematic and less regular. By 1920, the paper had apparently established itself as an ongoing concern, though probably not on a firm financial footing.

Two of the first questions to arise regarding publication of the *"Hobo" News* are who was writing for the paper and to what degree it represented hoboes rather than served as a vanity press for How and his associates. In order to determine the breadth of contributors, I randomly selected and entered into a database program fifty-four issues of the paper, representing approximately 70 percent of the extant issues. How and twenty-nine other individuals appear at some time during the paper's run in a variety of offices: president, vice president, treasurer, secretary, trustee, and organizer. How appears as president only once and is on the list of officials only part of the time. Clearly, his influence stemmed more from the force of his personal example and finances than from any organizational role or title.

It is also evident that the choice of what to publish in the paper sometimes created conflict. Though it contained nothing signed by Nicholas Klein, page 15 of the September 1915 issue notes: "The article in this number by Comrade Nicholas Klein of Cincinnati, is printed without the consent of Dr. How. He has not seen it, but it is felt by the management that such an article is necessary in view of the fact that the paper is booming. We feel that you thousands of people who are helping along our work by paying your nickels for this paper are entitled to know the truth as to this Hobo problem and why a paper 'OF THE HOBOES, BY THE HOBOES AND FOR THE HOBOES' is being circulated."

The application of the term "Comrade" to Klein may indicate tension concerning Klein's Marxist political position. The efficacy and limits of How's influence are highlighted in the passage. Apparently he entrusted the paper's publication to an editorial group that felt free to override their patron when it would help achieve the paper's agreed-upon goals.

Of the thirty men and women listed in leadership roles at various times, eighteen apparently never wrote for the *"Hobo" News*. Eight more appear fewer than five times. Three men, John X. Kelly, Nicholas Klein, and William Schweitzer appear between ten and fifteen times. Most of their articles appear in 1915-17, the years in which the paper was establishing itself and, presumably, before many hoboes were sending in written contributions. Schweitzer, however, made a number of additional contributions in 1918-19, discussing the U.S. role in World War I and the Russian Revolution. The two IBWA leaders who made significant written contributions to the paper were Bill Quirke and How, who contributed short reports of their activities and letters to the members. In total, the thirty IBWA leaders represent only 140 signed entries in the *"Hobo" News*. This diversity of authorship and representation of the readers is particularly remarkable because the fifty-four issues entered in the database included 226 pages with signed articles, 142 pages containing signed organizational news, 92 pages with poems, and 110 pages with short stories. Organizational news and articles were included only if they were individually signed. This conformed to the editorial policy stated in August 1916: "All signed articles are duly credited to the writers thereof and are printed, not because they are endorsed by the management, but because it is considered that they are of interest to those in the great movement. *All unsigned articles are by the Editor and the paper is responsible therefore.* They are written around the principles of Brotherhood as laid down by the International Brotherhood Welfare Association" (emphasis added). Approximately half of each issue was thus composed by the editorial committee; in most issues no editor is identified.

The number of authors represented is significant for two reasons. First, it indicates that the *"Hobo" News* functioned primarily as a published version of a more oral format—meaning the campfire tale-telling and political discussion of the "hobo jungle." Second, the number of authors gives some clue to the paper's readership. Enough people were purchasing and reading the paper to produce a sizable pool of authors. Most of those who published are unknown in any other literary or political context. Whether or not they were paid is unknown.

The 226 signed articles cover a wide range of topics and represent a large number of authors. Several were submitted under noms de plume, such as "Hoosier Drifter," "Organizer," or "Caveat." This accords with an IWW tradition of anonymous publication, and it is likely that some writers contributed to both the IWW press and *"Hobo" News*. After the deaths of several IWW members in Everett, Washington, an obituary appeared, noting that one of the slain men contributed to the *"Hobo" News* under a pseudonym (Jan. 1917).

A number of articles in the *"Hobo" News* are by well-known figures in anarchist and socialist circles of the period, including, for example, Nina Van Zandt Spies, widow of one of the Haymarket anarchists, Volterine de Cleyre, and Eugene Debs. Some of this material—Debs's contributions in particular—probably was made available to a wide range of socialist, IWW, and independent leftist papers.

The poems published in the *"Hobo" News* fall into two general categories, approximately equal in frequency. About half are reprints of well-known authors' work, perhaps because they were in the public domain. Notable examples include Rudyard Kipling, "The Sons of Martha" (July 1915), Alfred Tennyson, "The New Year" (Jan. 1918), and the frequent reprinting of Robert Service, "The Man Who Won't Fit In." Some of the pieces have obviously been taken from other published sources. Charlotte Perkins Gilman's song "To Labor," Edwin Markham, "Man with the Hoe," and Maxim Gorky's essay "Russia" are prime examples of such borrowing. Henry Herbert Knibbs's poem "Rags" was listed as a copyrighted poem reprinted by permission of *Popular Magazine*. In this case, the *"Hobo" News* observed formal publishing conventions, implying that the authors knew their material was being reprinted and that they probably approved.

A second category of poems included those published by what can best be characterized as amateur writers. Some of these poets, such as Volterine de Cleyre, appeared fairly frequently in the leftist press, but most were unknown. Others published only one or two occasional poems, either writing in general terms about the heroic struggle of labor and the hard lot of the workers or more specifically about the hobo subculture. Within leftist circles, the most famous of these poems was undoubtedly W. E. Jones, "The Bum on the Rods and the Bum on the Plush" (June 1916), which was also frequently reprinted in IWW publications. Some, such as Wilby Heard, "The Blanket Stiff" (Apr. 1917), were designed to be completely anonymous. Many of the most technically sophisticated poems were written by Bill Quirke, who used the *"Hobo" News* as a venue to develop his writing talents and to experiment with different forms.

The editors intended to have the readers contribute a large percentage of the paper's contents. Such an attitude corresponded with the importance of oral traditions and storytelling in the hobo subculture. Indeed, the paper occasionally printed traditional hobo folksongs, such as "The Hobo's Last Lament" (June 1917) and "The Rock-Candy Mountains." It also published "A Hobo and His Friends," by Norman Scott (Oct. 1917). Though set in a city restaurant, this song followed the standard format of the "monicker" songs, constructing a tale from the men's road names.[5]

Publication of work by the men on the road also was dictated by a practical consideration: hoboes were the best source of concrete information about constantly changing job conditions in far-flung places—something necessary to people seeking work. For example, in July 1915 the second page of the paper featured a boxed special notice: "This is our POVERTY EDITION to be sold up till August 10th. The August number will be issued on that day and tell you all about the harvest Stiffs. All the boys out in the fields are requested to send their story in to the Editor."

The same edition contained an unsigned article entitled "Straight Stuff from a Hobo with Brains in His Head." It detailed the author's experiences traveling from St. Louis to Kansas City, complete with notations about which towns' railroad policemen to avoid. As the paper's circulation grew, a larger share of the text was written by hoboes themselves:

> We ought to call this our special "Hobo" number. It is written almost entirely by the "men on the road" or the men who have been on the road. We say nothing of erudition and "high-brow" language. Perhaps these are lacking.
>
> But the "Hobo News" cares little for these things. We propose to show you in plain unvarnished language the great truths of things as they are, by the men who are on the bottom of this social system. (Nov. 1916)

Unfortunately, the readers did not always seem to come through for the editors, for a later editorial noted:

> There is a dearth of material for the "Hobo News." What is the matter with the hoboes? Are there no more employment sharks down whose throat you can jump, more flop-houses against which you can raise your voices, no more feasts and famines which move you to rush into verse? Draw a cartoon, write a story, a poem that has an unforgettable ring and rhythm, a slashing indictment of the social system, funny story, something short and snappy, full of fun and color, and send it to us. We'll make you famous. Write and tell us what you are doing. We are always interested. We love all hoboes and if they want a friend they will always find one here.[6]

The editors wanted the paper to do a great many things, as witnessed by the announcement of a poetry contest offering a five-dollar prize "to the writer of the best short poem of hobo interest" (loose page, c. 1920). They wanted "songs to voice the thoughts you feel," preferably songs of twenty-four or forty-eight lines, and they prohibited those that exceeded a hundred lines (ibid.). Although the published poems have been lost, the contest can be dated from a later announcement that "the prize of five dollars for the best Hobo Poem has been won by Edward Connor, 119 North Thirteenth Street, St. Louis, whose two poems will be found on another page" ([Oct. or Nov.] 1920).

The "Special Notices" was also effective in generating other material. "We thank very cordially all those who responded so readily to our appeal for contributions," it stated. "Our difficulty in this number has been to make room for all that has been sent us. One of our best contributors, a most eloquent Irishman, has, I think, been trying to save us the expense of papering the walls of our office" (ibid.).

Only one call for story contributions has been discovered: "We want to hear from all of you. Straight, clean cut, original stories of Hobo life and death. But in a small paper like this," the editor warned, "it is not advisable to try to run serial stories. So please remember the cost of paper and keep as nearly as possible within a thousand words. Shorter than that if possible" (Nov. 1916). In general, the published stories are each two or three pages in length.

All the stories share two notable characteristics: (1) the protagonist is always from the working class, such as the noble "gandy dancer" (a railroad track worker) who delights in reading Thoreau and Whitman; and (2) the stories are overwhelmingly sentimental. The plots often involve romance. For example, true love saves both a gandy dancer and the streetwalker with whom he falls in love; a miner buys his dream cottage, only to find that his younger fiancée has eloped with another and it is her mother he truly loves. The other main plot involves cosmic retribution against those who have exploited the hobo. In one of the most notable examples, the son of an employment agency owner dies as a result of being sent to a phony job by his father's own employee. All of the stories are designed to provide a highly romanticized, sentimental portrayal of working-class life. One of the few unsentimental stories, and truly amusing, is T. O'Donnell's "Autobiography of the Crum Family," written from the perspective of the lice that made the hobo's life so miserable (Mar. 1918).

Such contests and notices may have had more long-range success in generating contributions than the editors ever imagined. In *Knights of the*

Road, Roger Bruns remarks, "The *News* gave many hobo writers their first opportunity to publish."[7] This assertion appears to be true. Over eighty writers were represented, excluding pieces less than one column in length, signed letters, and anonymous and untitled material.

One author who seems to have used *"Hobo" News* to develop and publish a major opus was William Quirke (perhaps the prolific Irishman referred to above), who also published as Bill or Will J. Quirke. He produced a mixture of autobiographical vignettes, short stories, and a few poems. His short stories are among the better ones in the hobo genre, and his personal tales were written with verve and a keen eye for detail. Though Quirke was consistently listed as a member of the executive committee, his work commanded publication on its own merit. Quirke's writing is all the more remarkable in light of his life. He was never particularly active organizationally because he insisted on traveling constantly and working at only the heaviest jobs as the one true way of maintaining his working-class allegiance. It is impossible to say whether or not he could have made the transition to wider publication (as Harry Kemp did earlier), because in December 1921 Quirke was hit by a car and killed. In "Loving Memory" the paper noted of him: "He got nothing for his share but hardships and poverty, but thousands are richer that he lived. He loved to do the hardest, dirtiest, worst paid work in the world—he claimed there was a fascination in it—that he, too, might suffer with his fellow slaves and be able to describe it truthfully and convincingly. True to the end to Life's hardships. Earth knows no better friend than that" (Dec. 1921).

Not only the authors but the paper in general was geared toward working-class men. From its inception, the *"Hobo" News* cost five cents an issue, or fifty cents for a yearly subscription. In 1919, the price was raised to ten cents per issue, or one dollar for a yearly subscription, to cover the increased cost of paper (Oct. 1919). Sales appear to have been strong for a paper of this type from its beginning. In July 1915, the editors noted, "This paper is only a baby. We circulated 6,700 copies of the June number." In fact, this figure may be low; by February 1917, the Chicago local claimed to have sold 3,000 papers a month. Despite these circulation claims, however, the paper often ran in the red (Oct. 1915) and repeatedly emphasized obtaining subscriptions for a more consistent flow of funds, indicating its dependence on street sales.

Every issue encouraged readers to get out and sell the paper, both as a way to help the cause and to earn individual income: "Comrades of the East, we are getting out the best paper in the movement and you should sell thousands. . . . And remember, Boys, the Hobo News is the only paper published for the purpose of breaking up the Bread lines, and if you do your work as you should, we will break them up, just as sure as the sun shines" (June 1915). While the official price of an issue was still five cents, a 1917 editorial noted that a "single copy often sells for a quarter at some of the big camps so eager are the Boes to get it" (Dec. 1917), allowing substantial individual profit to sellers, even when the cost for a bundle of a hundred papers rose to $1.50 (Jan. 1917). Such income-earning potential was built into the political enterprise, and in "'Quit Moochin,' by the Business Agent" (Dec. 1916), the paper emphasized its significance: "The public will more generously respond to your invitation for help when you offer them something of real merit like the 'News,' than for a straight handout. For this very purpose the News was ushered into the Journalistic field. It offers you all the profits if you are willing to prove your willingness to help yourself by offering it for sale."

The paper thus reached hoboes with its ideological message and served as a means of assistance. In some cases, this economic appeal became part of how the IBWA sponsored its city meeting places, often called "Hobo Colleges." In the October 1915 issue, Bill Quirke proposed that hoboes could finance the Philadelphia branch because "after that [three days' free lodging] he must become a member of our order and agree to contribute 10 cents a month to the cause when he gets a job. We will be able to pay the rent by all working together this winter gathering up old clothes, waste paper and selling the monthly magazine called the Hobo News."

Selling the *"Hobo" News* for income could pose a risk, however, particularly after the paper took on its more militantly leftist tone in the 1920s. In "Beware of the Bulls!" E. Kaprall wrote:

> I'm on the road from N.Y. Well, as I hit Cumberland I got pinched trying to get a hot shot out. The R.R. Bull took me to the station and talked pretty nice until he looked over the "Hobo" News, and read "Black and Tan, American Style" [an article extremely critical of railroad security officers].
>
> Then the fun began. He played a tattoo on my head with his club, pinched me and burned up in my presence 80 copies of the "Hobo" News. (June 1922)

The paper also contained an interesting contradiction regarding audience. While written by and for hoboes, to function financially and redefine "hobo" more positively, the *"Hobo" News* also had to reach a large number of nonmigratory readers. In several cases, the editor directly addressed this settled audience: "Now, there are, in this country, over two millions, as a vast army of men who live the life of the casual, migratory and most of the time, unemployed men, whom you call the HOBOES. They are doing the work of the World, and you have never been given a chance to understand them until you bought this paper" (Oct. 1915). In "Of the Hoboes, by the Hoboes, for the Hoboes" (Oct. 1917), the address to the nonhobo reader was even more explicit in regard to social status:

> You bought this paper for a nickel. You got your money's worth and you did a good thing. Yo [sic] helped some poor man to make a few pennies for his lunch and you helped to give yourself an education.
>
> We care not whether you be an aristocrat or a plebeian, a priest or millionaire, a professional man or worker—it is necessary for your welfare and all your fellow-citizens, that you should be in touch with the evils of the hobo life.

The problematic nature of the *"Hobo" News's* relationship to its wider audience was indicated in the protracted struggle with postal authorities over second-class mailing privileges. The paper was entered for second-class postage November 28, 1916, and received second-class certification in February 1917, as noted in that issue. The editors seemed very anxious to specify that the paper was respectable enough to warrant mailing privileges: "The Socialist and Radical papers are having a great deal of trouble and loss on account of the postoffice, whose officials make arbitrary and unconstitutional rulings. . . . The Hobo News has no complaint to make for itself. It was our mistake in overlooking one of the rulings of the postoffice laws that the trouble has occurred which mixed up our last two numbers" (May 1919).

The cause of the mix-up was never clarified. Even such tenuous respectability was short-lived, however. In May 1919 the paper again carried a plea to "Make This Paper Pay." That the financial difficulties were not due to mismanagement is immediately clear:

> We have withdrawn from the second-class mail, not because we wanted to, but because we jolly-well had to. But, that difficulty has been overcome by mailing the subscription numbers by the third-class mail and the bundle orders by express.
>
> This paper has lost circulation through not being properly pushed; when the war broke out the police became very officious and in many cities threatened, and in some cases, arrested our hustlers. This hurt badly. But the paper does not propose to go back on any of the principles of the International Brotherhood Welfare Association, of which the chief is that the workers shall never take up fire-arms or the tools of production against

their fellowmen. But that does not mean that we are traitors or German spies or any such arrant nonsense. The paper is gotten out solely for the benefit of the hobo class and is read widely by them.

Apparently, the reference to not taking up arms or tools of production against fellow workers was too much for the postal authorities, who interpreted the pledge as precluding IBWA members' participation in the war effort because it was being fought against German workers. The federal government considered internationalism subversive and sufficient to warrant revocation of a paper's mailing privileges and often used such charges against socialist or allegedly pro-German newspapers.

Local police were also suspicious of any form of internationalism. The April 1919 issue of the *"Hobo" News* describes simultaneous raids by the Kansas City police to break up separate meetings of the IWW and of the IBWA where James Eads How was speaking on "Internationalism."[8] While *"Hobo" News* was quite sympathetic to the plight of the IWW, the final paragraph took great pains to dissociate the two organizations: "The I.B.W.A. men, who have nothing whatever to do with the I.W.W., come in for their share of the persecution, just the same, although they teach nothing but Brotherhood and Justice. The principles of the International Brotherhood Welfare Association will live forever."

The original intention of the IBWA pledge is unclear. R. W. Irwin, in "The Advance Guide and the International Brotherhood Welfare Association: An Answer," put a decidedly conservative and noninternationalist interpretation on it in July 1919:

This obligation has caused us much trouble during the war; as the jingoes and so-called patriots have insisted that it meant we were teaching men to shirk their military duty during the war. Of course, this is arrant nonsense and too far-fetched for sensible men to credit. This obligation means that the migratory workers will never hurt a union man in any way, either by taking his job from him or joining the thug detectives to shoot strikers down. It means that even if a man is poor and down and out he will scorn to advance himself by being a traitor to his class.

After the U.S. Post Office suspended the publication's second-class mailing privileges in 1919, distribution proceeded via express shipment, though the paper unsuccessfully tried to use the postal system again in 1921. Bundles of papers were shipped to each local headquarters, and individuals would "push" the paper on the street, just like Horatio Alger's ambitious newsboys. Thus, the listing of IBWA locals also indicated where hoboes could get copies of the paper to sell.

The relationship between the paper and the International Brotherhood Welfare Association was both changeable and problematic—as reflected in the masthead of the paper. The importance of retaining the official IBWA seal in the 1922 convention fight indicates that masthead changes probably reflected ideological and personnel changes in the organization. In August 1917, and again in April, May, and July 1919, the paper was "Published for the International Brotherhood Welfare Association" and listed its business address in St. Louis. In July 1920, however, the masthead proclaimed that the *"Hobo" News* was "Published by the Press Committee of the International Brotherhood Welfare Association in interest of Casual and Migratory Workers and the Solving of the Problem of Unemployment," and the paper's address was listed as Cincinnati, Ohio. These differences may reflect changes in personnel and attitudes. The July issue featured an article on the IBWA picnic as its cover story, complete with a photograph containing many women and children; it seems more concerned with "homeguards" (nonmigratory workers) than hoboes.

By November 1920, the paper had undergone numerous changes. It contained no masthead on the cover and the title was printed as *Hobo News,* rather than *"Hobo" News.* The back cover contained the paper's manifesto: "Published Monthly in the Interests of the Casual and Migratory Workers—The Hobo Class—the Modern Journeyman. To enlighten the Public in General and Organized Labor in Particular on the conditions that this Class is up against and the slumbering powers it embraces." The more radical tone of the statement is unmistakable.

The November 1920 issue is anomalous in two additional ways. It is the only extant hobo paper to carry multiple advertisements. The ads included in the few surviving pages are for the *Vote,* an English women's suffrage journal, the *New York Call,* and William Z. Foster's book, *The Great Steel Strike.* The leftist character of the ads was matched by the articles' rhetoric. The other striking fact is that only this issue and the July 1920 issue listed an editor. Despite the vast gap between an issue featuring a picnic in the woods and one featuring a well-known communist, A. Schiermeyer edited them both. No other issues had a designated editor, and Schiermeyer's name did not reappear until after the IBWA split in 1922 when he wrote one article for each issue of *Hobo World.*[9]

By December 1920, the paper had changed again. The masthead again read "Published *for* the International Brotherhood Welfare Association" (emphasis added), and the publishing address was back in St. Louis. Even this change was not permanent, however. Beginning in June 1921 the masthead read "*Official* Organ of the International Brotherhood Welfare

Association" (emphasis added), apparently remaining that way through February 1922. The first information clearly indicating the paper's address again is in July 1921. According to the addresses listed, the business offices were in Cincinnati, but editorial comments and contributions needed to be sent to St. Louis, thus splitting the paper's functions.

In May 1922 this relatively stable publishing situation again dissolved. The masthead still read "Official Organ of the International Brotherhood Welfare Association," but the editorial page said the paper was "Published monthly *for* the International Brotherhood Welfare Association" (emphasis added) and carried a statement that "this number of the 'Hobo' News is issued by the orders of the Holding Committee, 119 N. Thirteenth Street, St. Louis, Mo." Thus, the office had again shifted completely to St. Louis from Cincinnati, and the use of "Holding Committee" may indicate economic difficulties or renewed internal ideological conflict.

The *"Hobo" News* continued to be "Published for the International Brotherhood Welfare Association" until the final split occurred within the IBWA itself, late in 1922. The last, extant regularly numbered issue of *"Hobo" News* is volume 11, no. 2, February 1923. Only one later copy exists, datable by internal evidence to either February or March 1929. The paper included no volume or issue numbers or masthead, but the cover carried the official IBWA seal that had appeared on all earlier issues. This undated issue listed no business or editorial offices but printed a conference call, whose signatories included Jacob Coxey and How, and gave a Cincinnati address. Whether the paper was regularly published from 1922 onward, or continued at all after 1929, is unknown. Given the financial dependence of both the paper and the IBWA on How, it is unlikely that the paper survived long after his death in 1930. In his autobiography, Benjamin Benson speaks of selling the *Hobo News* during the 1930s and 1940s.[10] He refers to it as a paper published in New York and describes its contents primarily as jokes and snappy stories. Probably it was another publication entirely that reincarnated only the name *Hobo News*. So far as is known, no copies of it exist.

The *"Hobo" News* can be read not only as a window on life within the hobo subculture but also as a means of shedding light on the complex relationship between migratory workers, their organizations, and general working-class organizations. To date, the organization of hoboes has always been viewed as an adjunct of the Industrial Workers of the World (IWW). Even during the early IWW conventions, the leadership saw potential in "Overalls Brigades" of migrant workers from the western United States who rode the rails to Chicago and sang "Hallelujah, I'm a Bum."[11]

Historians have reinforced this view.[12] In fact, focus on the IWW has prevented scholars from acknowledging the parallel development of an organizational movement among the motley army of hoboes. As a result, they have severely underestimated the autonomy and distinctiveness of the hobo subculture.

During 1893–1932,[13] at least four distinct hobo organizations arose: the Tourists Union, Local No. 63 (always listed in this manner), the International Brotherhood Welfare Association (IBWA), and the Migratory Workers Union (MWU). All of these organizations were quite distinct from the IWW in their philosophy and intent; they purported to represent only the migratory worker, while the IWW, however great its migrant membership, avowedly represented all members of the working class. The hobo subculture assumed a very different position in an organization that viewed hoboing as a distinct, valid way of life rather than just an extension of working-class oppression. To those who saw positive attributes in the hobo's mobility, classification with society's "submerged tenth" was not particularly desirable, though organizers were often quite susceptible to the argument that hoboes were at the vanguard of the workers' revolution. However closely related, the IWW, with its diverse and primarily nonhobo leadership, was not an inherent part of the hobo subculture.

The Tourists Union and IBWA originated in the first decade of the twentieth century. These dates seem more than coincidental, since the founding convention of the Industrial Workers of the World opened in Chicago on June 27, 1905, and reflects a widespread tendency toward unskilled workers' activism that extended beyond the hobo subculture. This trend emerged against a background of conflict within the labor movement itself, frequently typified by the Western Federation of Miners' struggle against both Samuel Gompers's political conservatism and the strictly craft orientation of the American Federation of Labor (AFL) and the "aristocracy of labor" it represented. To men who changed occupations almost as often as they changed locations, such craft preoccupations of the homeguard could seem only retrograde and divisive.

From its founding, the IBWA, and particularly James Eads How, saw the organization as separate from the IWW. Indeed, as early as 1911 the IWW also saw itself as competing with the IBWA for the allegiance of hoboes. Bruns writes:

> Although James Eads How's organization of hoboes, the International Brotherhood Welfare Association, was not essentially a labor union but a fraternal society, and although How had encouraged hoboes to support the

labor movement, IWW leaders saw fit to attack him as a "faddist" with half-baked schemes likely to injure the hobo cause rather than help it. That IWW leaders felt obliged to attack How was a measure of his influence among the hobo community, an influence which Wob leaders saw damaging their own recruiting efforts.[14]

The IBWA itself was determined to maintain its identity as a separate organization. The August 1917 issue of the *"Hobo" News* included two articles defending the organization's integrity. A lengthy editorial stated, in part:

> We wish to observe for the benefit of our readers, some of whom seem to get things mixed, that this paper is published for the International Brotherhood Welfare Association, affectionately called by its members the I.B.W.A. It has nothing to do with the Industrial Workers of the World, called the I.W.W., or by the Capitalist Press, the I won't works. There is nothing in common between the two organizations. We do not believe in their so-called sabotage. We do not burn down fences nor fill fruit trees with copper nails for spite. These things are foreign to the I.B.W.A. man who has taken an obligation to be kind and courteous to all his fellow men. Therefore, we print in this number a short article on the aims and objectives of the International Brotherhood Welfare Association so that there can be no mistake about it. At the same time we believe that a lot of injustice is done and lies fostered by the Capitalist Press about the I.W.W. movement.

The first IBWA conference, held in Baltimore in 1915, involved a protracted struggle between How and IWW sympathizers. As the *"Hobo" News* reported it in "Side-lights on the Conference" (May 1915):

> The two sessions yesterday were taken up chiefly with the war of words and ideas between the pacific Socialists of the James Eades [*sic*] How stripe, and the little band of firebrands from Philadelphia who wanted to make the association an adjunct to the Industrial Workers of the World, advocates of "direct action" in wresting the industries from the capitalist class. This little group made a lot of noise and spoke frequently with fire and fervor of their alleged wrongs, but they seemed to have very little effect on How, whose smiles and forgiveness were ever on tap, like his coffee and sandwiches for the unemployed. . . . For the present, he [How] said, the work of the Welfare Association ought to consist of practical aid to the unemployed, the fight against vagrancy laws and the bringing together of the workingmen into solidarity as principles and methods by human kindness and brotherly love.

After the decimation of the IWW by the Espionage Act of 1917, the IBWA gained public visibility and seems to have taken up the torch that had been struck from the IWW's hands by government agencies. The increased importance of leftist ideology within the IBWA, as shown in its newspaper, coincides with the demise of the IWW. There is both a clear shift in tone and a change in the format and appearance of the *"Hobo" News* in 1918–19. In 1919 the paper first used a cover that included a masthead and a political cartoon. Even more significantly, the articles in the magazine began to be accompanied by graphics—simple, rather generic pen-and-ink renderings. The most frequently used of these drawings is the bust of a ragged man captioned "A Blanket Stiff."[15] This drawing is significant because previously it was a standard graphic in an IWW publication, *Industrial Worker*. Once adopted, this drawing and others were used throughout the run of the *"Hobo" News*.

While the evidence of increasing IWW influence in the IBWA is suggestive, it is not definitive. The *Industrial Worker* and the *Masses* were the first leftist magazines to use graphics as effective propaganda devices, and their model was followed by many subsequent groups. For example, as late as 1977, the Revolutionary Communist Party (RCP), a Maoist group, was reproducing a lightly edited version of the IWW graphic, "The Hand that Will Rule the World—One Big Union" in its publications, posters, and memorabilia.[16]

Many of the poems and song lyrics printed in the *Industrial Worker* were gleaned from a variety of radical sources. "We Have Fed You All for a Thousand Years," for example, is an IWW adaptation of a Polish workers' song; an updated version of this song was used as recently as 1976.[17] The Military Intelligence Division Files of the War Department contain a one-page handout entitled "Songs of the Hobo Colleges—Care of International Brotherhood Welfare Association." The collection date on this flier is 1924. Of the six songs printed in the flier, four ("Hold the Fort," "The Hope of the Ages," "The Internationale," and "Solidarity Forever") appear in the ninth edition of the *I.W.W. Songbook*, first published in 1916.[18] In the September 1917 issue of *"Hobo" News* are published four songs from the Hobo Colleges, none of which are IWW songs—perhaps indicating that the IBWA continued to write songs independently of the IWW.

Again, the overlap in songs is interesting but not definitive. "Hold the Fort" and "The Internationale" were European imports. By the 1920s, "Solidarity Forever" had also become a worker's "standard" through its use in countless strikes. Leftist movements seemed to find a continual need to sing and lacked enough composers to engage in sectarian musical struggles. However, the IBWA was not ready to yield the musical field entirely to the IWW. One of Bill Quirke's most notable contributions to the *"Hobo" News* was "A Brotherhood Anthem," sung to the tune of "Annie Rooney" (loose sheet, n.d.).

> Under this flag we've taken our stand;
> Onward we march, a conquering band;
> Gladly we'll follow a slogan so grand,
> The world we must win for Labor.
> Turning our backs on all that is wrong,
> Trusting each other in union we're strong,
> Upward we climb, a conquering throng.
> The world we must win for Labor.
>
> CHORUS:
> Labor, labor shall be king.
> The I.B.W.A. to it we'll cling,
> Clasp hands in Brotherhood, never to part,
> United for Justice, we'll win every heart.
>
> In every conflict let this be our shield,
> Brotherhood Welfare to naught will we yield,
> Gladly [illegible] for it in the field,
> The [world we] must win for Labor.
> Strong [illegible]t, each working with will,
> The f[ertile s]oil for those only who till,
> March [o]n, lead where it will,
> T[he world we m] ust win for Labor.

The organizational conflict between the IBWA and IWW stemmed from the fact that they had very different goals. The IWW always intended itself as a union of all workers: the "One Big Union" with many branches. As Father Thomas J. Hagerty's famous wheel of organization proposed, the IWW sought to act as a union that fulfilled all the worker's practical needs.[19] It sought to do this without acknowledging management's right to exist and control the workplace, which more conservative AFL unions granted. As explained by R. W. Irwin in the July 1919 issue of *"Hobo" News,* the IBWA saw its purpose as entirely educational:

> The International Brotherhood Welfare Association is not a Labor Union. It is a clearing house for labor. It plows the field and plants the seeds so that Organized Labor can reap the benefit. It works toward one end and one end only and that is, the complete emancipation of the Migratory

Unskilled and often Unemployed workers. It helps the Unions in every way possible. At all meetings the great principles of organization and co-operation are expanded upon and taught with conviction.

In the beginning union labor was so busy with its own affairs that it left the migratory workers to shift for themselves as best they might. But a broader view is prevalent now. Thotful [sic] union men see that they are never safe and their organizations are always in danger while there are hundreds of thousands of migratory workers ready to take their places. Labor could have its demands complied with at once if there were no scabs, and we try to eliminate this evil. There is only one way, and that is by education.

The International Brotherhood Welfare Association goes farther than that; if it only preacht [sic] these ideals it would sow some good seed. But it is practical, too, and we ask all union men to note this. Every member is forced to take this solemn obligation: "I will never be guilty of taking up fire-arms or the tools of production against my fellow workers."

The method of the IBWA was further underscored by How's article entitled "A New Truth" in the same issue:

Time and tide does not wait—big events cast their shadows before us today. We need confidence and it is for us workers to clasp hands and educate ourselves, our sons and daughters—educate the "COMING PEOPLE."

To this end we need a Hobo College in every town—a PEOPLES' HOUSE—a LABOR TEMPLE. We must have our printed word—our "Appeal," our "Call," our daily press in every town. How else can the masses of the people learn?

The hour has struck—the psychological moment is here. It calls for economic education. It calls for the organization and for intelligent action.

Interestingly, How considered the *"Hobo" News* as the hobo equivalent of the *Appeal to Reason* or the *Call.* Both of these papers were socialist and published in opposition to mainstream American ideology. It is never clear whether How saw the *"Hobo" News* as distinct from other leftist papers in primarily its ideology or its audience. Numerous internal references to the *"Hobo" News* as a paper specifically for hoboes, rather than for workers generally, suggest that How was probably referring to audience. It is entirely in keeping with his Christian socialist beliefs that he sought change through education and that most of his effort and finances went in this direction.

If the hobo subculture distinguished its organizations from the IWW, the distinction was largely lost on the rest of American society. Those who opposed all radical activities regarded the IBWA, MWU, and IWW as closely related. During World War I and the subsequent Red Scare, the Military Intelligence Division of the War Department monitored all three groups. In an April 7, 1921, letter about IBWA activities in Cincinnati, Mathew C. Smith noted: "A recent report concerning the International Brotherhood Welfare Association is to the effect that radicals of all organizations apparently have a common meeting place at its headquarters at 320 W. Second Street, Dayton, Ohio. Mail sent to this address indicated that it is a stopping place for radicals of other organizations. Copies of postal cards indicate that men who are in the field selling the 'Hobo News' are also spreading I.W.W. propaganda."[20] Earlier memos from Sergeant Lynn D. Copeland, Corps of Intelligence Police, noted: "Immediately upon arrival in Baltimore he went to the 3rd floor of a building at 502 East Fayette St.—the Baltimore Headquarters of the I.B.W.A. and the M.I.U. [probably the Migratory Workers Union]." Copeland also remarked that John X. Kelly was both an organizer for the MWU and an official of the IBWA and that his headquarters in Cincinnati was the same for both activities.[21]

In a previous report, dated July 21, 1919, Copeland made an even stronger case for the practical and ideological connections among the IBWA, MWU, and the IWW:

The writer has met and talked with many men who are connected with the "I.B.W.A." and the "M.W.U." and they openly assert that they are in favor of a Soviet form of government for all nations and they also uphold the Bolshevik governments of Russia and Hungary. It is not a concealed fact that the radical Socialists are in favor of this movement and that they offer their assistance and support to this organization. Even the National Secretary of the Socialists in his 4th of July speech in St. Louis . . . commended the "work being done" by the I.B.W.A. and declared himself in favor of all such organizations. It is also apparent that radical Socialists and former I.W.W.'s are affiliated with this organization and they will tell you, if they think you are a prospective member or a radical, that they have the "best plan on earth to put over I.W.W. organization and further the cause" under the guise of a "Welfare Association" and an "Unskilled Labor Organization." . . . They boast that they have 300,000 members and that they "can be depended upon in a crisis" and that each one of these members "will have a clearly defined duty to perform." . . . This organization supposed to have been founded by "a harmless hobo" whose motives were to help and assist unfortunates is now being manipulated by unscrupulous agitators and being used for propaganda purposes to stir up unrest and dissatisfaction and foster the principles of the Soviet form of government.[22]

Within the IBWA, the debate over the purpose of the *"Hobo" News* continued into 1921 despite, or perhaps because of, the wide range of contributions it received. The paper's increasingly leftist tone sharpened the discussion. In July 1921, the paper published a letter to the editor from Harvey A. Gordon that stated, in part:

> I surmised from the name that it [the paper] was written by and in the interest of the hobo workers.
>
> With the excepting of one or two articles there was nothing in it to justify its name. Homeguard spittoon philosophy, scientific socialism and its technical term does not appeal to the average working stiff and there are hundreds of papers that specialize in that stuff.
>
> The average bo is a surface thinker. . . .
>
> We need a hobo magazine that will express the life and labor and fight our battles. When the "Hobo News" makes that its function and gives us a magazine written of the hoboes, by the hoboes and for the hoboes, it will be supported, read and distributed in every camp, jungle and slave market in the United States.

This criticism apparently stung the paper's editorial staff. In the same issue, a sharp reply appeared before the original letter:

> A Bo writes us to publish his complaint "in the hope that we may get some of the dead ones to use their thinking boxes." Say, bo, that's just where we are trying to get, see? Do you think we can get people to use their think boxes if we get out a paper full of Weary Willie dope? . . .
>
> The average hobo is inarticulate, a brute with brute strength of labor; he has suffered so much and so long that he is accustomed to his wrongs and will stand for almost anything. . . .
>
> And that explains why The Hobo News receives so many articles on Socialism, Marxism, Anarchism and many another ism. There are bright minds in this struggling mass and they try to explain to their fellow boes how and why things are. It may create some confusion for the time being, but every protest counts and every thought lives somewhere. The hobo element through their bright minds in its own ranks is making itself heard and will continue to do so until this wicked and wasteful system of producing and distribution of the world's goods is changed for the better.
>
> We invite stories from the road; but we welcome the philosophy of the down and out who has the foresight to see better things and how to get them.

As a putative workers' organization, the IBWA existed in constant tension with both the political left and the labor movement. From the beginning, the IBWA also used the *"Hobo" News* to express the belief that "the migratory and casual workers MUST be recognized as a part of the whole or the whole fabric of unionism will fall to the ground. Get together, and get together quick" (Sept. 1915). The relationship between the IBWA and the rest of organized labor was probably more problematic than How cared to admit. That Eric Anderson also carried a membership card for the Jewelry Workers Union when he was arrested in 1917, that the Colorado Springs IBWA local operated out of the Union Printers Home, and that several IBWA conventions were held in labor temples—all this indicates that the relationship could be positive and that some individuals probably moved from the IBWA to a more traditional labor union when the situation demanded. But in other cases, closeness to local union members could be problematic for the IBWA:

> In behalf of the I.B.W.A. of Toledo I desire to report that there seems to be quite a sprinkling of members although they are not keeping in contact with the national organization and can therefore not be considered as a group of that body as they have no charter. I observed further from conversation with some of those who laid claim to such membership that they have been working altogether from the wrong end. That is to say that they have been trying to organize within, or drawing their membership from, other organizations instead of acting as feeders to such other organizations. Hence to do successful work in Toledo it is necessary that a new field of operation be selected—separate and away from the Labor Temple. (*"Hobo" News*, July 1920)

Even those committed to working for the hobo could fall prey to the lure of the comparative ease of organizing the homeguard. Conflicts with organized labor probably would have been more frequent and of greater magnitude had the IBWA been a larger or more effective organization. Indeed, writers in the *"Hobo" News* were not above occasionally blaming organized labor for the failure to pull migratory workers the rest of the way into the union fold after the Hobo Colleges had educated them about the brotherhood of working men. As one example, Henry A. White writes, in "What of the 'Hobo'" (July 1921):

> But not every migratory worker is a potential strike breaker. The International Brotherhood Welfare Association recognized the fact that "in every man is the good," the hobo as well as the millionaire, and fifteen years ago organized the very class of workers which the unions despised. . . . Although this organization has no connection with organized labor, yet its work is along union lines and it has laid the foundation for the effectual unioniza-

tion of the migratory workers, and now it is up to organized labor to complete the work.

White seems to blame unionized labor for not having built on the organizing efforts of the IBWA. In effect, he was encouraging unions to practice dual unionism by recruiting members of the IBWA. This possibility seems as unlikely as readers of the *"Hobo" News* agreeing to the good in every millionaire. The fact that the IBWA regarded itself as an educational organization and specifically eschewed active organizing of migrant labor left an opening for the founding of the Migratory Workers Union in 1918: "It is time that the migratory workers, the skinners, the muckers, ice harvesters, berry grabbers, oyester [*sic*] glommers, apple knockers, spud diggers, hop pickers, etc., through an organization demand better conditions."[23] The MWU claimed to be a national "general labor organization" and demanded:

1. A shorter work day.
2. Free transportation to and from the job.
3. The abolition of all privately owned employment agencies.
4. The commissary food and supply companies to be eliminated on all construction work.[24]

As early as 1915 all of these were also goals of the IBWA. The Migratory Workers Union stuck, quite literally, to "pork chop unionism." It was not concerned with general education or raising class consciousness, as was the IBWA. Nels Anderson asserted that the MWU was organized within the IBWA in 1918, largely to reassert the importance of the migratory worker and give a group of more radical, dissident members of the IBWA a membership and financial base outside of How's direct control.[25] As Anderson put it: "Between the M.W.U. and the I.B.W.A. there is considerable antipathy, yet the M.W.U. cannot stand alone and will not cooperate with the parent organization."[26] The conflict between the two was clearly related to economic problems and power struggles within the hobo movement itself.

The early rhetoric of the *"Hobo" News* reflected How's ideology of Christian socialist uplift. His early attitude is probably best shown in a letter to the editor entitled "Capital, Labor, Golden Rule, Conscience" written by Francis B. Livesey in the *"Hobo" News* of May 1919:

The new religion now called for and based on conscience makes easily possible the acceptance of the Golden Rule, but the churches have not and will not bring it. N. O. Nelson, once a millionaire manufacturer of East St. Louis, is now a pauper as a result of applying the Golden Rule to his employees; and the last I heard from him he was living on the charity of Upton Sinclair. Now, Sinclair says Mr. Nelson and James Eads How are the only two conscientious millionaires he has ever known.

How's identification with, and aid to, migratory workers—the lowest workers of all on America's economic ladder—seemed to derive more from the social gospel of Walter Rauschenbusch and Washington Gladden than from the class-conscious theories of the anarchists, Marxists, or IWW. When traveling overseas and attending labor and unemployed conferences, How seemed primarily interested in orchestrating the passage of resolutions requesting clemency for political prisoners such as Debs and Mooney or trying to negotiate a settlement to World War I.[27] Even as How was about to enter Soviet Russia for the first time, the closing lines of one of his letters to the paper, published in October 1921, recall the New Testament more than Marx: "May the light of Comradeship and Brotherhood be like a Light through the Universe!"

How's quiet Christian attitude seems to have caused trouble as the IBWA organization grew. This conflict between Christian socialism and more militant Marxist socialism was particularly pronounced after 1920, when many in the organization had been influenced by Marx, Lenin, and the Russian Revolution. By May 1922 even How noted, in "Solidarity and the May-Day Conference," that these tensions were ready to explode:

> There appears to be an effort at this time on the part of some Local Groups to go it alone—an effort that is fine in certain ways.
> What new group and what husky kid don't grow restless and want to be his own boss and "go it alone," particularly if the goings [sic] good?
> Perhaps it is up to us as the I.B.W.A. elders to endeavor to open up our minds so as to appreciate the new spirit of abandon and let them "bring up dad."
> Nevertheless it is good to keep the family together or, now and then, to get the members all together for a sort of reunion. . . .
> So this is the reason why some of us are boosting for a "get-together" for a May-Day Conference the last of the month and the first of May in Cincinnati. . . .
> A larger measure of solidarity ought to come from such a conference even if it develops a tendency to hew to the line and to separate out some of us elderly or possibly less militant elements.
> As for me, if that is progress and leads on to a larger solidarity, I must not fight against it.

How's tone is extremely ambiguous. The proposed conference (which may or may not have taken place) might be regarded as How's attempt to try to rescue a deteriorating situation. It can also be read as a plea for cooperation, or even as acquiescence in a new order.

The next event at which large numbers of hoboes gathered was the Buffalo Conference, July 4, 1922. Henry A. White's reports on this conference in the *"Hobo" News* were light and good humored, and he stressed unity throughout:

> There is no place where extremes are so sure to meet as at a hobo conference, and the one held in Buffalo was no exception to the rule. Old, white-haired men and callow youths meet on a common ground, that of making the life and lot of the hobo—the man who does the absolutely necessary, the disagreeable and dirty, the hard and laborious work of the world—better. The most radical communist and the most conservative churchman vied with each other in this task harmoniously and enthusiastically. (Aug. 1922)

It is ironic that White managed to express so clearly the lines of tension while trying to maintain (or create) a feeling of unity. These tensions finally boiled over at the opening session of the IBWA convention of October 28–November 1, 1922, held in Columbus, Ohio: "The split in the ranks of the 'Hoboes' came with the opening of the convention Saturday morning [when Vice-President Joe Ormond of Toledo . . . refused to accept the credentials of the delegates who rally around the How standard.] . . . After heated debate, during which coats were removed, force was used and a general melee ensued, three of the How delegates were able to take their seats—the remainder representing Baltimore, Washington, Chicago, Denver, Oklahoma City, Muncie, Ind., and other cities were denied the right of franchise and participation in the convention."[28]

The status of the *"Hobo" News* was also a large matter of contention during the morning session. The Ormond faction declared that the paper was no longer the official organ of the IBWA; the How delegates demanded to know "by what authority and under whose direction the official stamp of approval was withdrawn." When the convention resumed that afternoon, the anti-How faction discredited and displaced some of the past officials for failing to function properly. The How faction then refused to accept the treasurer's report without a hearing. When such a hearing was denied, "a general exodus took place." As Cleveland Red reported in the November 1922 issue: "Miss Inez Newton, of Oklahoma City, who is a member of the Holding Committee of the International Brotherhood Welfare Association, explained that all of the pyrotechnics were the result of a warring faction's desire to rid themselves of Dr. James Eads How, who, she declared, was the originator of the association and its greatest financial supporter."

Who ultimately "won" the conflict is not clear. In November 1923, there appeared suddenly a "Convention Special" of *Hobo World, "Official Bulletin Published Monthly of, for, and by the Migratory Workers."* The publication's address was listed as Cincinnati, and the new editors clearly stated their editorial policy: "The press Committee is not responsible for and may not agree with the ideas conveyed in some of the articles appearing in these columns. Such articles simply convey the idea of the author, and are presented to you through these columns for consideration and reflection. THE HOBO WORLD is open to all who have anything of interest to [share with] the Migratory Workers in particular and the working class in general." Ties to the old paper were still strong enough, however, that it included the New York Public Library's call for back issues of the *"Hobo" News.*

Only one other issue of *Hobo World,* the Holiday Special of December 1923–January 1924, has survived, and the lack of further issues may be due to more than collection problems. The editorial page of this issue carried the following notice: "WE CAN NOT GUARANTEE REGULARITY OR PUNCTUALITY OF PUBLICATION, as our finances sometimes get strained, but WE DO GUARANTEE TWELVE (12) CONSECUTIVE NUMBERS TO THOSE WHO WISH TO SECURE THE HOBO WORLD THROUGH THE MAILS." There is no way of knowing if twelve more numbers of the paper were ever printed; none apparently survived.

It is interesting and suggestive that distinctively set off on page eight of the final extant issue of *Hobo World* is the old Knights of Labor slogan: "An Injury to One Is the Concern of All." Perhaps the slogan indicates a retreat to an earlier, populist interpretation and away from a more radical, syndicalist position as expressed in the IWW transformation of the slogan into "An Injury to One Is an Injury to All." Evidence here is unclear, however. The slogan's change may simply represent a blending of traditions or rhetoric.

The fact that, in 1923, issues of both *"Hobo" News* and *Hobo World* were printed seems to indicate that the groups did not completely reconcile. Since the 1929 *"Hobo" News* carried How's call for a convention, the anti-How faction is probably represented by the *Hobo World.* Once such deep ideological divisions were aired, they could never be completely pasted over. Certainly, such a split greatly hampered the efforts of a movement that was already marginal.

The conflict between the IBWA and the MWU was clearly related to economic problems and power struggles within the hobo movement itself. In a crucial sense, then, the very significance of the hobo movement was its weakness. In seeking independently to represent migratory unskilled workers as a group with specific interests as members of the working class, and with separate interests as a functioning subculture, movements such as the IBWA rendered themselves even more marginal than the IWW. Their marginality made them exceptionally vulnerable to organizational splits based on personality and finances as well as on ideology. It also made their publications far more ephemeral than IWW publications. Given this lack of effectiveness in organizing rootless hoboes and the difficulty in preserving their publications, it is not surprising that historians have overlooked them for so long. However, the importance of the *"Hobo" News* in creating and maintaining a self-conscious subculture is worthy of further study. James Eads How's bridge among hoboes may have been ephemeral but, as a field for research, it provides a sturdy route into the past for contemporary scholars.

NOTES

1. "James E. How Dies, Friend of Hoboes," *New York Times,* July 23, 1930.

2. *National Union Catalogue, Pre-1956 Imprints* (New York: Roman and Littlefield, 1963–   ).

3. The issues of the *"Hobo" News* now available are Apr.–Oct. 1915; Apr.–Aug. and Oct.–Dec. 1916; Jan.–June and Aug.–Dec. 1917; Jan.–Apr., July, Sept., and Nov. 1918; Jan., Apr.–May, July, and Oct.–Dec. 1919; Jan., Mar.–Apr., July, and Nov.–Dec. 1920; Jan.–Dec. 1921; Jan.–Dec. 1922; Jan.–Mar. and Nov. 1923; a Dec. 1923–Jan. 1924 issue; and an undated, post-1928 issue. Copies of *Hobo World* exist only for Nov. 1923 and a New Year's issue for Dec. 1923–Jan. 1924. A single copy of *Hobo News/Review* was located in the Billy Adams Papers, Archives of Industrial Society, University of Pittsburgh. In the case of the NYPL collecting the *"Hobo" News,* it is possible that police raids on the IWW, and the loss of source material they entailed, stimulated librarians to collect more radical and ephemeral materials. Thus, what is being measured is not activity but library collection and preservation.

4. Roger A. Bruns, *Knights of the Road: A Hobo History* (New York: Methuen, 1980), 112.

5. For an analysis of moniker songs, see Richard Phelps, "Songs of the American Hobo," *Journal of Popular Culture* 17 (Fall 1983): 15–16.

6. "Special Notices," *"Hobo" News,* loose page, probably from 1920, New York Public Library.

7. Bruns, *Knights of the Road,* 112.

8. Mathew C. Smith, Apr. 7, 1921, Military Intelligence Division Files, Record Group 165, War Department Files, National Archives, Washington, D.C. (hereinafter cited as MIR).

9. "A Bowery Meeting," *"Hobo" News,* July 1921, 4, 11, also mentions in passing that distributing the coffee was "Miss Laura Clark, slender, spectacled, formerly Editor of *Hobo News."*

10. Benjamin Benson, *500,000 Miles without a Dollar* (New York: n.p., 1942).

11. Paul S. Brissenden, *The I.W.W.: A Study of American Syndicalism* (New York: Russell and Russell, 1919), 221–24.

12. Robert L. Tyler, *Rebels of the Woods: The IWW in the Pacific Northwest* (Eugene: University of Oregon Press, 1967), 24–25.

13. The Hoboes of America, Inc., appears to have been founded in the 1930s. By 1932, other political groups were largely supplanted by unemployment councils that assumed a more geographically stable constituency. While comparisons of these unemployment councils to hobo organizations is a fruitful field for future inquiry, it is beyond the scope of this study.

14. Bruns, *Knights of the Road,* 151.

15. "The Blanket Stiff," *Industrial Worker,* Apr. 23, 1910, n.p., in *Rebel Voices: An IWW Anthology,* ed. Joyce L. Kornbluh (Chicago: Charles H. Kerr Publishing, 1988), 70.

16. "The Hand that Will Rule the World—One Big Union," *Solidarity,* June 30, 1917, in Kornbluh, *Rebel Voices,* 25; and logo for the RCP Labor Day Conference, Chicago, 1977.

17. Prairie Fire, "We Have Fed You All for a Thousand Years," *Break the Chains* [phonograph record] (San Francisco: One Spark Music, 1976).

18. "Songs of the Hobo Colleges—Care of International Brotherhood Welfare Association," Record Group 165, MIR.

19. Kornbluh, *Rebel Voices,* 10.

20. Smith, Apr. 7, 1921, MIR.

21. Copeland to Major Henry G. Pratt, Military Intelligence Division, Dec. 9–10, 1919, MIR.

22. Copeland to Pratt, July 21, 1919, MIR.

23. "Leaflet No. 3 Issued by the Migratory Workers Union," *"Hobo" News,* May 1919, 11.

24. Nels Anderson, *The Hobo: The Sociology of the Homeless Man* (Chicago: University of Chicago Press, 1923), 240–41.

25. Ibid.

26. Ibid., 247.

27. Laura Clarke, "What the Out-of-Works Are Doing in England," *"Hobo" News,* Oct. 1921, 12–13.

28. Cleveland Red, "Hobo Session Is Upset—Factions in a Row—Break over Delegates," *"Hobo" News,* Nov. 1922, 9.

6 "The Morning Cometh": African-American Periodicals, Education, and the Black Middle Class, 1900–1930

MICHAEL FULTZ

It is not known whether J. Max Barber, editor and guiding spirit of the *Voice of the Negro,* ever read "Shall the Wheels of Race Agitation be Stopped?" an article written by John Mitchell Jr. and published in the *Colored American Magazine* in September 1902. By repeatedly answering his own rhetorical question, Mitchell, the well-known and well-regarded editor of the *Richmond Planet,* a black weekly newspaper, sought to emphasize African Americans' responsibility to maintain an abiding vigilance against the perils of racism and discrimination as well as against efforts to silence their protests. "The watchman must wait upon the wall until the night of oppression shall have passed," Mitchell declared. "I have never lost faith in my people. They have been hampered by poverty and blinded by ignorance, but—the day is now breaking. . . . The morning cometh."[1]

This last phrase, "the morning cometh," was the title of J. Max Barber's editorial in the inaugural issue of the *Voice of the Negro* in January 1904. In a brief, self-congratulatory essay, Barber wrote, "To the casual observer there is nothing new in the launching of a Negro magazine; but to the philosopher of history, to him who is a reader of the signs of the times it means much. It means that culture is taking a deep hold upon our people. It is an indication that our people are becoming an educated, a reading people, and that is a thing of which to be proud." He added: "We hail with delight the opportunity to help run a magazine which shall stand as the vanguard of a higher culture and a new literature. . . . We want to make it a force of race elevation. We want it to be more than a mere magazine. We expect to make of it current and sociological history so accurately given and so vividly portrayed that it will become a kind of documentation for the coming generations. . . . The morning cometh."[2]

The intent of this study is to take advantage of Barber's foresight: to survey and explicate the major educational issues and themes not only in the *Voice of the Negro* but also in eight other black monthly periodicals published between 1900 and 1930. Together, these nine monthly magazines provide the primary data for this examination of African-American intellectual history. They present a chorus of voices that, in discussing and interpreting the issues of the day, make up a rich—yet unfortunately seldom acknowledged—heritage of penetrating analysis and thoughtful discourse. But it is important to be clear about the nature of these "voices." As will be seen, the arguments and opinions projected by these periodicals were articulated largely by a small but increasingly influential group of middle-class and professional African Americans who were coming into their own around the turn of the century.

Through migration, urbanization, and subsequent occupational differentiation, the years 1890–1920 saw the development of new African-American enclaves and new social and economic leadership groups in black communities throughout the nation. In particular, as the result of the creation of mass urban markets and the availability of new job opportunities, the economic base supporting the black class structure shifted. A new black middle class and professional group arose, supplanting the "Old Settlers," especially in northern urban communities. This new middle class and professional group was distinct from the older African-American upper class in several ways, notably in terms of their racial philosophies and their relationship with the existing black community. Among other traits, they were decidedly race conscious, and they forcefully advocated self-help, character-building, social uplift, and race patronage and solidarity. Another notable attribute of this new black middle class was that they were institution builders, committed both ideologically and practically to creating an infrastructure that would sustain African Americans in their oppressive urban enclaves as well as advance their social, economic, and political interests. As the urban historian Allan Spear has observed, "The physical ghetto was the product of white racism, but the institutional ghetto was the creation of Black civic leaders."[3]

The journals reviewed here form a subset of the black press in the United States, and, like black newspapers, they were established to demonstrate the race's capabilities and to disseminate the African-American point of view. They fostered the creation of what has been called a "universe of discourse" for the black middle class,[4] allowing this group (and implicitly, though indirectly, the race as a whole), to debate the burning issues of the day, to protest injustice in its myriad forms, to illuminate the path to progress and uplift, to define and promote shared meanings, to celebrate their achievements, to encourage artistic and literary expressions, and to articulate to both black and white America the terms of compatible coexistence. My intention is not to criticize the black middle class, nor to disparage their attempts and achievements in institution building, of which the black press itself was one positive outcome. Rather, by acknowledging the class-based "voice" articulated by African-American periodicals, I am simply adopting one analytic lens through which to better understand and explicate the essential educational themes and issues during this period.

Before elaborating upon the issues and themes addressed, a brief overview of the nine periodicals is in order. All were edited by blacks, published monthly, and intended for a general reading audience.[5]

THE PERIODICALS

The *Colored American Magazine* (May 1900–Nov. 1909) was initially established in the spring of 1900 as a journal that would "intensify the bonds of racial brotherhood" through a blend of African-American fiction and political commentary.[6] Especially noteworthy among the individuals associated with the journal in its early years was Pauline E. Hopkins, who progressed from a frequent and prominent author to general editor, making her one of the few African-American women editors of the period.[7] In 1904, however, the *Colored American Magazine* was secretly acquired by Booker T. Washington and subsequently moved to New York. National Negro Business League organizer Fred R. Moore, a close Washington ally, was installed as publisher and general manager, and the emphasis of the periodical changed to feature "the doings of the race along material lines."[8] Under Moore's stewardship, the journal reportedly reached a circulation of 15,000–17,000.[9]

The *Voice of the Negro* (Jan. 1904–Oct. 1907), applauded by W. E. B. Du Bois as "the greatest magazine which the colored people had had," featured a broad range of articles on the political, social, and economic concerns of African Americans, in addition to occasional poetry, humor, and artwork.[10] The Atlanta-based journal had ongoing difficulties in its relations with Booker T. Washington; as Louis Harlan has documented, "Washington first tried to force the *Voice* to sing his song and then tried to silence it."[11] Although the *Voice*'s editor J. Max Barber was initially independent in his political beliefs, repeated clashes during the journal's first year with board member Emmett Scott, Washington's personal secretary, moved Barber into a more "radical" posture. He joined with W. E. B. Du Bois as a founding member of the Niagara Movement, and the *Voice* itself became the unofficial political organ for that group. Rumors of his involvement in the Atlanta riot of 1906 forced Barber to leave Atlanta for Chicago, where he unsuccessfully attempted to reestablish the periodical.[12] Its maximum circulation was said to be 15,000 for the May 1906 issue.[13]

Alexander's Magazine (May 1905–Mar./Apr. 1909) is another example of Booker T. Washington's efforts to control the contours of African-American political thought in the early twentieth century through surreptitious control over the black press. In this case, in 1904 Washington recruited Charles Anderson, a graduate and former employee of Tuskegee Institute, asking him to return to Boston to oppose the threat of William Monroe Trotter's vitriolic *Boston Guardian*.[14] *Alexander's Magazine* was an undistinguished periodical featuring articles on a broad range of topics. The journal flirted briefly with the Niagara Movement and, likewise, briefly promoted the black emigrationist cause but mostly toed the Tuskegee line.[15] In 1907, circulation was estimated at 5,000.[16]

The Horizon: A Journal of the Color Line (Jan. 1907–July 1910) was W. E. B. Du Bois's second attempt at journalism during 1900–1910.[17] It was a unique publication. Published in Washington, D.C., with Lafayette Hershaw and F. H. M. Murray as coeditors, the journal carried virtually no full-length articles but rather reviews of the white and black press, together with considerable gossip and commentary on the political leanings of various prominent members of the African-American middle class. Its slogan was "Seeking the Seldom Sought." Circulation data are unavailable.

The Crisis: A Journal of the Darker Races (Nov. 1910–present) was guided by Du Bois from its inception until his somewhat bitter departure from the NAACP (National Association for the Advancement of Colored People) in July 1934. The journal exuded the aggressive, authoritative, and acerbic style of its uncompromising editor. As Du Bois wrote in his opening editorial, "The object of this publication is to set forth those facts and arguments which show the danger of race prejudice, particularly as manifested today toward colored people."[18] Circulation grew by leaps and bounds, paralleling the growth of its editor's stature within African-American leadership and intellectual circles: from an initial run of 1,000 in November 1910, its readership grew to 15,000 by July 1911, to 30,000 in April 1913, to 54,000 by December 1917, and to an average of 94,400 in 1919, with the May issue of that year reaching 100,000 (about 80 percent of its readership was black in 1916).[19] After 1919, however, circulation dropped precipitously, averaging only 62,000 in 1920 and slightly under 50,000 in 1921; by 1924, it had dropped to 35,000 and by 1930 to 30,000.[20] It is the only periodical reviewed herein that is still published.

The *Half-Century Magazine* (Aug. 1916–Jan./Feb. 1925) represents a gauge of the growth, consolidation, and depth of the African-American middle class. Published by Anthony Overton, a wealthy Chicago cosmetics manufacturer, and edited by Katherine Williams-Irwin, the *Half-Century Magazine* was intended for the new middle-class black woman. It was a decidedly race-conscious magazine, yet its limited political commentary paled in importance in relation to regular features on domestic science, beauty hints, fashion trends, etiquette, and ever-present short stories on love and romance. It was, as it occasionally called itself, a "Colored Magazine for the Home and Homemaker." A June 1919 advertisement for the journal claimed a monthly circulation of 47,000. No other circulation data are available.

During its eleven-year existence, the *Messenger* (Nov. 1917–May/June 1928) evolved through three distinct phases. From its inception in late 1917 through approximately 1921–22, it was the voice of black radicalism: "The Only Radical Negro Magazine in America," as it called itself. From 1921–22 to around 1925, a moderated tone made it indistinguishable from other African-American periodicals, a transformation captured by the change in subtitle to "The World's Greatest Negro Monthly." And from 1925 until its demise, it became, for all intents and purposes, the publicity organ of the Brotherhood of Sleeping Car Porters.[21] The New York–based journal is best remembered in its radical heyday when, jointly edited by A. Philip Randolph and Chandler Owen, it provided the spiritual leadership for the "Messenger crowd" of young black intellectuals and socialists. In those times of heady postwar fervor, the *Messenger* ardently advocated trade unionism, repeatedly attacked "Old Crowd" black leaders such as Du Bois, and touted the militancy of "New Negroes."[22] In 1919, the U.S. Department of Justice labeled it "the most dangerous of all the Negro publications."[23] Circulation reached its peak in 1919, when 21,000–26,000 copies were sold monthly. In the 1920s, however, its monthly circulation apparently never exceeded 5,000.[24]

The *Competitor* (Jan. 1920–June 1921) was published and edited by Robert Vann, best known for his editorship of the *Pittsburgh Courier* newspaper. It was the shortest lived of the journals reviewed, lasting only eighteen months. It carried a wide array of articles on black life, stressing social, cultural, and business concerns over political commentary. It also featured more news on African-American sports than any other black periodical. The journal's assimilationist theme was striking in the degree to which it was emphasized.[25]

Opportunity: A Journal of Negro Life (Jan. 1923–Winter 1949) was the organ of the National Urban League (NUL) and took its name from that organization's motto, "Not Alms, But Opportunity." From its inception through mid-1928, the journal was edited by Charles S. Johnson, the NUL's director of research and investigations. After Johnson left the Urban League to head Fisk University's department of social sciences, Elmer Carter became editor.[26] *Opportunity* sought to articulate an interpretation of black social problems based upon the findings of social science research. "[The magazine] will aim to present, objectively, the facts of Negro life," Johnson stated. "It hopes, thru an analysis of these social questions, to provide a basis of understanding; encourage inter-racial co-operation in the working out of these problems, especially those surrounding the emergence of the Negro into a new industrial field and the consequent reorganization of habit and skill."[27] Like the Urban League itself, *Opportunity* tended to emphasize social and economic concerns over political issues. Its tone, as the historian Nancy Weiss remarks, was generally not one of protest but rather of "conscious optimism."[28] Johnson also did much to promote the Harlem Renaissance then in vogue; Langston Hughes once commented, "Mr. Johnson, I believe, did more to encourage and develop Negro writing during the 1920s than anyone else in America."[29] Johnson opened the pages of *Opportunity* to a broad spectrum of black artists and writers. The journal presented an outstanding selection of poetry, and its cover illustrations were quite avant-garde. But circulation was never high. From an initial run of 6,000, *Opportunity* reached its peak average monthly circulation of approximately 11,000 in 1927–28.[30]

THE MIDDLE-CLASS FRAMEWORK: HIGHER EDUCATION

Gunnar Myrdal's insightful discussion of the black press in *An American Dilemma* explicitly addressed the issue of whose "voice" is heard in these periodicals. Myrdal commented: "The Negro press is primarily controlled by the active members of the upper and middle classes of the Negro community. . . . These classes make up a great part of its subscribers. The people who publish and write the Negro newspapers belong to the upper class. It is the doings and sayings of the people in the upper and middle classes that are recorded in the Negro press. They, therefore, set the tone."[31]

Similarly, E. Franklin Frazier acknowledged the class-based nature of the black press, making it a central element in his stinging critique of the African-American middle class in the twentieth century. "Although the Negro press, including magazines as well as newspapers, claims to be published in the interest of the 'race'," Frazier charged, "it represents primarily the interests of the black bourgeoisie and promulgates the bourgeois values of the make-believe world of the black bourgeoisie."[32] Like Myrdal, Frazier noted that the black press relished items that depicted noteworthy accomplishments and related the activities of African-American "society," but he condemned its tendency to highlight "petty achievements . . . as if they were of great importance." Overall, he described both emphases as aspects of a semipathological "wish-fulfillment."[33] Frazier overlooked Myrdal's discerning observation that "Negroes stress 'society' because whites deny them social prestige. They have to create prestige and distinctions of prestige among themselves, *and there is an element of caste protest in demonstrating that they have done it*" (emphasis added).[34]

These considerations provide an important framework for an interpretation of the treatment of educational issues in the black monthly periodical press in 1900–1930. Without question, these journals were the means through which the black middle class and black professionals defined their vision and disseminated their views. Their pictures appeared on its pages; their achievements, petty or not, were duly noted. They wrote the articles and likely provided a substantial proportion of the reading audience. This was perhaps even more true for black periodicals than for black newspapers. As Charles S. Johnson observed in 1928 in "The Rise of the Negro Magazine," "If there is a clear distinction between a newspaper and a magazine, it is in the more deliberate and cultural quality of the latter." He added, "A mellowed literacy is required for the appreciation and support of the Negro magazine."[35]

The essentially middle-class orientation of the periodical literature in 1900–1930 can perhaps most clearly be observed by contrasting the journals' discussions of African-American common schools with their treatment of higher education. Given the deplorable conditions and discriminatory funding that characterized black common schools in the South during this period, one might imagine that strong, vigorous, unrelenting protest would have been the order of the day. Yet this was decidedly not the case. None of the periodicals surveyed publicized the plight of black common schools with any degree of consistency. The *Messenger,* for example, published only one full-length article in its eleven-year history on the underdevelopment of African-American schools in the South. The article discussed the situation in only one state, provided no comparative racial data, and presented an overly optimistic assessment.[36]

The *Crisis,* on the other hand, considered fairly regularly the plight of common school education for southern African-American children, although, like the other black journals, it rarely did so in full-length articles and discussions. Only in the mid-to-late 1920s, when the journal published a five-part series of investigatory articles that amounted to a shocking exposé of educational conditions for African Americans in Georgia, Mississippi, North Carolina, South Carolina, and Oklahoma, did the *Crisis* present what might be considered an in-depth, comprehensive account.[37] On the other hand, an examination of the *Crisis* during the 1920s reveals that, on the whole, the treatment accorded to black common schools paled in comparison to the NAACP's strenuous (though ultimately unsuccessful) efforts to win congressional passage of a federal anti-lynching law. In no individual magazine reviewed, nor even in combination, did discussions of black common schools over this thirty-year period approach the level of a full-fledged protest campaign.

By contrast, college attendance among African Americans was consistently publicized and celebrated. In 1900–1910, for example, lengthy profiles of the black colleges and universities formed the centerpiece of the coverage of African-American educational concerns for the *Colored American Magazine, Voice of the Negro,* and *Alexander's Magazine.* Given the political differences among these journals, this similarity in their educational emphasis speaks to an overarching orientation not subsumed in the famous debate between Booker T. Washington and W. E. B. Du Bois. From 1910 to 1920, the prominent treatment of black higher education is most noticeable in Du Bois's spirited promotion of it. The importance of higher education, of course, had long been a central theme for Du Bois, and although he did not attempt to sustain his famous "Talented Tenth" argument in the *Crisis,* he celebrated enthusiastically black higher education. Indeed, his strident criticisms of Booker T. Washington and the disturbing trends of organized philanthropy were only the flip side to his efforts to safeguard and encourage the full development of black intellectual talent. Throughout 1910–20, in fact, he unleashed a string of stinging invectives, less in the direction of Washington than toward the General Education Board (GEB), regarding its advocacy of industrial education as a substitute for adequate education and its obstinate refusal to support adequately African-American colleges and universities. As he angrily remarked on one occasion: "The great dominating philanthropic agency, the General Education Board, long ago surrendered to the white South by practically saying that the educational needs of the white South must be attended to before any attention should be paid to the education of Negroes; that the Negro must be trained according to the will of the white South and not as the Negro desires to be trained. It is this board that is spending more money today in helping Negroes learn how to can vegetables than in helping them to go through college."[38] Despite outcries such as this, Du Bois soon returned to his principal theme: "If the Negro is to survive in this world as a man of thought and power, a co-worker with the leading races in civilization, a free, independent citizen of a modern democracy, then the foundations for this must be laid in the Negro University."[39]

Although the editor of the *Crisis* did not present feature-length profiles of individual institutions, beginning in 1912 he designated the July edition of the *Crisis* as the annual "Education Number" devoted to data and commentary on trends in African-American collegiate enrollment.[40] Readers might have sensed Du Bois's personal pride when he commented on the photographs of college graduates that appeared in these July issues: "Here are a group of healthy, bright-eyed, clear-brained young folk of Negro descent, who are going to make the cheating, lynching and oppression of Black folk more difficult in the future than in the past."[41]

During 1920–30, in addition to the bouquets Du Bois continued to bestow upon higher education for blacks, the importance of college-going was reinforced by the black press in several indirect but conspicuous ways. First, the strikes and protests by African-American college students at such prestigious institutions as Fisk University, Howard University, Hampton Institute, and Lincoln University were all extensively publicized, especially in the *Crisis,* but also, though to a lesser extent, in *Opportunity* and the *Messenger.* Although the specific issues included acquiescence to segregation, draconian campus policies, and the need to hire black administrators and professors, the major interpretive theme in these protests has been the newfound self-determination on the part of African-American middle-class parents and students of the 1920s.[42]

It was no accident that Howard and Fisk Universities, in particular, experienced major campus protests in the mid-1920s. Both schools were well known for attracting students from black middle-class backgrounds, adolescents and young adults more attuned to the spirit of freedom on college campuses nationwide and more likely to express their dissatisfaction with notions of piety that they deemed increasingly irrelevant to the maintenance of their social status. They were also more likely to know of the protest tradition articulated by Du Bois and others and to have soaked up the anger and frustration of the postwar tumult.[43] Unlike the situation at industrial Hampton, where parents and alumni turned against the students, the support of activist, concerned, middle-class alumni and parent groups at Howard and Fisk was instrumental in the successful campaign to change allegedly repressive administrations.

Other aspects of the journals' treatment of black higher education in the 1920s also reflect the heightened sense of security and influence among the black middle class. Articles discussing black colleges and universities, for example, no longer contained elaborate justifications for college-going or defensive counterarguments against the alleged academic inferiority of African Americans. Moreover, the common formula of the 1900–1910 profiles—a "thrilling history" of the institution, statements of "unswerving fidelity" to the aims and goals of a particularly illustrious abolitionist founder or early president, pious assertions of the "noble work" and "positive influences" of its graduates—gave way to discussions that explored black higher education from new angles. Such fresh approaches included articles on the need for research-based black studies programs, the value and meaning of a doctoral degree, new techniques to orient freshman to the college scene, and the social and service activities of black fraternities and sororities.[44] To be sure, these new interests also reflected the fact that African-American college attendance was itself on far firmer footing during the 1920s than ever before. As Du Bois crowed, "Who would have dreamed at the beginning of the 20th Century, when all the 'best friends' of the Negroes were sneering at Negro colleges because they had few students, that in 1927 we would find in Negro colleges alone ten thousand students of full college grade! . . . The revolution of Negro education is astonishing."[45] In sum, higher education was a continuing source of pride among the black middle class and professional group, as their periodical literature abundantly attests.

The reasons for the discrepancy in the treatment of higher education as compared to common schooling relate to concerns about race, class, and status. First, since particularly during 1900–1910 the black middle class perceived that they, and their race as a whole, were "on trial" and needed to "measure up," higher education figured prominently in providing "evidence" to whites that blacks had the ability, discipline, and brains to achieve academic distinction. This is an important consideration, and it reveals a significant theme in pre–World War I African-American literature. Throughout the first decade of the twentieth century, there was considerable discussion of the need for African Americans to "place ourselves in the proper light before the world" and that through such displays of capabilities whites would change their stereotypes of black inferiority.[46] "There is a battle to be fought," stated Cyrus Field Adams of the Afro-American Council, "not with swords and guns on bloody fields, but in the arena of public opinion."[47] This theme flowed smoothly into the self-help motif characterizing much of African-American social thought during 1900–1910. But it also took a special twist: "The Negro must stand alone and prove his case."[48] In a time of ugly and rancorous negrophobia, with

African Americans openly condemned as "brutes" and "beasts," with the very provision of schooling for African Americans vigorously contested, the heavy didactic overlay in the periodical literature is unsurprising. It is as if African Americans in the prewar period—especially, in this case, the newly emergent black middle class—needed to affirm repeatedly the educational and moral roots of their accomplishments. The reiteration of those accomplishments, such as college attendance, was itself the reverse echo of the extent to which these attributes were denied by southern whites and by many northerners as well.

Given the temper of the times, education was one of the few means available to African Americans with which to prove their detractors wrong. To be sure, declining illiteracy rates were frequently noted. Given the advances since the benchmark days of slavery (so the argument went), "who can then say we are a race of ignoramuses?"[49] But this form of "evidence" did not lead into discussions of the possibilities and cruel limitations of black common schools. The argument was not made, for example, that literacy rates would have improved even faster if the poor conditions of African-American elementary schools had been improved. Instead, college-going was *the* powerful symbol evoked, highlighting in particular the worthy accomplishments, and the ability to "measure up," of the black middle class.

Second, since education was an important basis of status and stratification within the African-American community, college-going both reflected and justified the middle-class position as a black elite. In a review of sixteen empirical studies of prestige criteria among African Americans—ranging from Du Bois's *Philadelphia Negro* in 1897 to an investigation of the New Orleans black community in 1960—the sociologist Norval Glenn found that education was emphasized more than any other standard. Glenn hypothesized that African-American differentiation in educational levels may be the most significant explanation for its consistency as a highly valued prestige criterion. E. Franklin Frazier, August Meier, and others have noted that the black middle class and professional group came into prominence at the turn of the century in part through a process by which the older upper class was supplanted as a result of the changing economic base in black communities in 1890–1920. Glenn's findings support their views. He noted, "Income, occupation, and education emerged as the dominant criteria only where and when the Negroes became fairly well-differentiated in these attainments. Perhaps, in most places, the educational differentiation proceeded most rapidly."[50]

Other studies agree on the importance of college attendance as a status symbol among the black middle class. In his article on social stratification in black society, for example, Edward Shils pointed out that for the "already arrived" black upper class, higher education provided an "index of superior personal qualities." For those aspiring to enhance their place, on the other hand, it acted as a "certificate of admittance."[51] Langston Hughes's delightful satire of Negro society in Washington, D.C. (1927), is a source of anecdotal data on this point. Hughes wrote: "In no other city were there so many splendid homes, so many cars, so many A.B. degrees, or so many people with 'family background.' . . . She is a graduate of this . . . or he is a graduate of that . . . frequently followed [an] introduction. So I met many men and women who had been to colleges,—and seemed not to have recovered from it."[52]

DECLINE IN PRESCRIPTIVE AND DIDACTIC DISCUSSIONS

The consistency with which black higher education was featured in black periodicals was only one of the ways the black middle class shaped the journals' treatment of educational issues and concerns. By the 1920s, for example, when the middle class was more secure in its leadership position in the black community, the highly prescriptive discussions of education so characteristic of 1900–1910 had virtually disappeared. This is not to say that all of the earlier social and cultural themes were absent in 1920–30. Occasional discussions of the need to "measure up" were still evident, as were notions of "service to the race" and, especially, the overarching emphasis on "character" development that had marked the earlier period.[53] No doubt these prescriptive, didactic discussions declined in part because the very provision of education for African Americans was no longer as fiercely contested as it had been at the turn of the century; commentators no longer had to plead the case for the purposes and benefits of schooling for a "despised race."

Nonetheless, the search for identity of the black middle class and black professionals was more clearly defined in the 1920s than it had been in the 1900s. "Signposts" in the form of clearly delineated social and moral "duties" were no longer needed; as exemplified by the black college protests, the pieties of yesteryear had lost their burning immediacy and had become outmoded.

In fact, the decline in prescriptive discussions of education is related to the convergence of three trends: the increased security of the black middle class, the lessening of southern white hostility to the rudimentary education of African Americans (albeit by degrees), and the emergence of a highly educated cohort of young black social scientists who undertook analyses of black social issues and conditions in an academic, scholarly manner strikingly different from their predecessors. In this regard, *Opportunity* was in the vanguard, though its intellectual debt to W. E. B. Du Bois must be recognized. Under Charles Johnson's leadership, the journal of the Urban League provided a much-needed outlet for a new voice among the African-American middle class and professional group—a cohort of young black social scientists, trained largely in graduate facilities in northern universities. Not coincidentally, this cohort, more or less consciously recognizing its unique role as the intellectual segment of the black middle class, first achieved distinction by defending African Americans against the invidious racial implications drawn by the intelligence-testing movement.[54] Du Bois's drive to push forward the development of a "Talented Tenth," his call "to study the facts, any and all facts, concerning the American Negro and his plight . . . primarily with the utilitarian object of reform and uplift; but nevertheless . . . to do the work with scientific accuracy," saw its initial fruition with the emergence of this group of African-American intellectuals.[55] As Richard Bardolph noted in *The Negro Vanguard:* "The maturing of Negro American civilization . . . fostered by well-defined Negro communities in Northern cities and by advances in education and occupational differentiation . . . produced 'functional leaders.' . . . In the new era the Negro artist, scientist, or scholar was to be less and less an untaught prodigy pushed forward by latter-day abolitionists beseeching the world to measure him against his handicap. In growing measure he was a trained specialist."[56]

E. Franklin Frazier has elaborated on this point, specifying its ties to the black middle class:

> The development of the present Negro leadership . . . represents to some extent the social transformation of the Negro in general, but in the main it presents a picture of the social differentiation of the growing civilized minority. This social differentiation is due in large measure to urbanization, which is requiring a new type of leader. The most significant aspect of this development is the emergence of an intellectual leadership which is not dependent for status upon the colored group but stands upon the intrinsic worth of its achievements. The new leadership who are participating in all the activities of American life have destroyed the prospects of any social policy that looks toward confining the whole colored group within a lower caste.[57]

CONCLUSION

Several questions arise when considering the overall treatment of education by the black journals during the thirty years reviewed. What role was played by education in the nexus of political, economic, and social issues that confronted black America between 1900 and 1930? Where did education stand among the priorities of the fledgling civil rights movement? What impact did the black journals have?

Regarding the latter question, as Frederick Detweiler noted regarding black newspapers, "Instead of merely reflecting 'life,' the newspapers, in setting themes for discussion and suggesting the foci of attention, help powerfully to create that life."[58] Likewise, Myrdal observed: "*The press defines the Negro group to the Negroes themselves.* The individual Negro is invited to share in the sufferings, grievances, and pretensions of the millions far outside the narrow local community. This creates a feeling of strength and solidarity. The press, more than any other institution, has created the Negro group as a social and a psychological reality to the individual Negro" (emphasis added).[59]

Although the ultimate impact of this discourse cannot be measured, education clearly played a central role in the social, moral, and status considerations of the black middle class and professional group of the period. Over the course of thirty years, black monthly periodicals publicized and promoted schooling at all levels and in all forms. Despite variations in their treatment of educational issues—occasionally accusatory, often celebratory, sometimes unduly optimistic—education was implicitly and explicitly promoted as a positive, valued endeavor in the struggle for racial uplift. Segregated schools in the South may have been a conceded issue, and some topics may have been downplayed from time to time, but the drive for schooling itself continued.

How deeply were African Americans in general imbued with similar values? The answer is complex. Undoubtedly, the vast majority of black people saw education as a path toward a better life and saw a certain degree of literacy as a goal in and of itself. Yet, just as contemporary educational policy research has pointed out that some segments of the African-American community deprecate standard educational achievement as "acting white," so too did Shils point out, "The Negro lower class does not share the beliefs of the Negro upper and middle class regarding the indispensability of education and good breeding and in many instances comes to derogate them as a reaction formation."[60] Moreover, the journals' treatment of the intraracial battles over school segregation in the 1920s (with only the prointegration opinion, generally the black middle class position, publicly presented) indicates that the African-American community was significantly divided in its opinions on certain educational concerns.[61] Issues such as these limit the extent to which the findings of this study can be generalized without qualification.

What can be asserted without reservation is that between 1900 and 1930 the black middle class created a "universe of discourse" through its monthly periodical literature, and within this African-American arena of intellectual discussion and debate, educational concerns and higher education in particular figured prominently. Celebration blended easily with agitation in the black journals, since both were joined in a vision of racial advancement. As Myrdal has suggested in his observation about the coverage on African-American society, the celebration of college achievement in the black press contained elements of accomplishment and self-assertion that were their own forms of tacit protest.

By 1930, black America as a sociological and psychological entity continued to develop as a "Nation within a Nation." Emphases within each of the journals reviewed here reflect this phenomenon. Blacks had their own baseball league (*Competitor*), their own romantic fantasies (*Half-Century*), their own radical movement (*Messenger*), their own social scientists (*Opportunity*), and their own outspoken, iconoclastic editors (*Crisis*). Within this African-American world continually growing in complexity, black periodicals served as mediums of internal communication, defining the issues and framing the social and political debates for informed opinion and literary appreciation. Though black commentators were still defending the race against malicious allegations, and their treatment of some subjects was somewhat muted, in general, discussion of educational issues was more sophisticated than it had been in the past. A broader range of concerns was addressed; self-determination joined self-help as a central theme; and the commentary was less rhetorical. The cohort of black social scientists that achieved prominence during the 1920s symbolized the enhanced maturity of black middle-class professionals and their ability to articulate educational issues in the language of the modern university.

Education was not the sole item on the African-American agenda, and it was often overshadowed by other more pressing topics—jobs, lynching, social services, housing—in the panoply of issues that made up the generalized demand for "justice." Though it may not have ranked consistently as the number one concern, education was nonetheless a ubiquitous theme. The articulation of educational concerns in and by the black monthly press in the 1900–1930 period powerfully illuminated a distinct meaning of progress and helped to define a vision of social uplift.

NOTES

An earlier version of this essay appeared in the *Journal of Negro History* 80.3 (1995). Used by permission.

1. John Mitchell Jr., "Shall the Wheels of Race Agitation Be Stopped?," *Colored American Magazine* (hereinafter cited as *CAM*) 5 (Sept. 1902): 391.

2. J. Max Barber, "The Morning Cometh," *Voice of the Negro* 1 (Jan. 1904): 38.

3. Allan Spear, "The Origins of the Urban Ghetto, 1870–1915," in *Key Issues in the Afro-American Experience*, vol. 2, ed. Nathan I. Huggins, Martin Kilson, and Daniel M. Fox (New York: Harcourt Brace Jovanovich, 1971), 154. See also August Meier, "Negro Class Structure and Ideology in the Age of Booker T. Washington," *Phylon* 23 (Fall 1962): 258–66; E. Franklin Frazier, *The Negro in the United States*, rev. ed. (New York: Macmillan, 1956), 547–63; Allan H. Spear, *Black Chicago: The Making of a Negro Ghetto, 1890–1920* (Chicago: University of Chicago Press, 1967); St. Clair Drake and Horace R. Cayton, *Black Metropolis* (New York: Harcourt, Brace, and World, 1962).

4. David Gordon Nielson, *Black Ethos: Northern Urban Negro Life and Thought, 1890–1930* (Westport, Conn.: Greenwood Press, 1977), 50.

5. With three exceptions (*Half-Century Magazine, Competitor,* and, to a lesser extent, *Horizon*), the remaining six journals are generally considered the major monthly periodicals of the period. See W. E. B. Du Bois, "The Colored Magazine in America," *Crisis* 5 (Nov. 1912): 33–35; Charles S. Johnson, "The Rise of the Negro Magazine," *Journal of Negro History* 13 (Jan. 1928): 7–21; Abby Arthur Johnson and Ronald Maberry Johnson, *Propaganda and Aesthetics: The Literary Politics of Afro-American Magazines in the Twentieth Century* (Amherst: University of Massachusetts Press, 1979); Penelope L. Bullock, "The Negro Periodical Press in the United States" (Ph.D. diss., University of Michigan, 1971). For the purposes of this essay, note that the *Southern Workman,* a monthly journal published by the white administration of Hampton Institute, is not considered a black periodical. Detweiler explicitly excludes the *Southern Workman* as a "Negro publication," while neither Johnson nor Du Bois mentions it in their overviews of black periodical literature. See Frederick G. Detweiler, *The Negro Press in the United States* (Chicago: University of Chicago Press, 1922), 40.

6. "Editorial and Publishers' Announcements," *CAM* 1 (May 1900): 60; William Stanley Braithwaite, "Negro America's First Magazine," *Negro Digest* 6 (Dec. 1947): 21–26.

7. See Ann Allen Schockley, "Pauline Elizabeth Hopkins: A Biographical Excursion into Obscurity," *Phylon* 33 (Spring 1972): 22–26; and Abby Arthur Johnson and Ronald Maberry Johnson, "Away from Accommodation: Radical Editors and Protest Journalism, 1900–1910," *Journal of Negro History* 62 (Oct. 1977): 325–38.

8. See August Meier, "Booker T. Washington and the Negro Press: With Special Reference to the *Colored American Magazine,*" *Journal of Negro History* 38 (Jan. 1953): 67–90; and Emma L. Thornbrough, "More Light on Booker T. Washington and the New York Age," *Journal of Negro History* 43 (Jan. 1958): 34–49. On Moore's denial of Washington's ownership, see "Publishers' Announcements," *CAM* 7 (Sept. 1904): 606.

9. "Publishers' Announcements," *CAM* 7 (Sept. 1904): 606.

10. Du Bois, "Colored Magazine." Even Washington held the *Voice* in high esteem, believing that in "breadth, dignity and form" it was a better journal than *CAM*. See Louis Harlan and Raymond Smock, eds., *The Booker T. Washington Papers:* vol. 8, *1904-6* (Urbana: University of Illinois Press, 1979), 571.

11. Louis R. Harlan, "Booker T. Washington and the *Voice of the Negro, 1904-1907," Journal of Southern History* 45 (Feb. 1979): 46.

12. J. Max Barber, "Why Mr. Barber Left Atlanta," *Voice of the Negro* 3 (Nov. 1906): 470-73; Harlan, "Booker T. Washington," 45-62.

13. Barber to Du Bois, Mar. 2, 1912, in *The Correspondence of W. E. B. Du Bois,* ed. Herbert Aptheker (Amherst: University of Massachusetts Press, 1973), 176-77.

14. Louis R. Harlan, *Booker T. Washington: The Wizard of Tuskegee, 1901-1915* (New York: Oxford University Press, 1983), 58-61.

15. Bullock, "Negro Periodical Press," 161-65; see also Edwin Redkey, *Black Exodus: Black Nationalism and Back-to-Africa Movements, 1890-1910* (New Haven, Conn.: Yale University Press, 1969).

16. Bullock, "Negro Periodical Press," 162.

17. See Paul G. Partington, "The Moon Illustrated Weekly—The Precursor to the *Crisis," Journal of Negro History* 48 (July 1963): 206-16, for a discussion of what was actually the precursor to the *Horizon.*

18. Du Bois, "The Crisis," *Crisis* 1 (Nov. 1910): 10.

19. *Crisis* 1 (Feb. 1911): 3; 5 (Apr. 1913): 301; 15 (Feb. 1918): 163; and 19 (Feb. 1910): 198. See also Charles Flint Kellogg, ed., *NAACP: A History of the National Association for the Advancement of Colored People,* vol. 1 (Baltimore: Johns Hopkins University Press, 1967), 149-53.

20. *Crisis* 19 (Jan. 1920): 198; 23 (Mar. 1922): 214; Du Bois, "Editing 'The Crisis,'" in *Black Titan: W. E. B. Du Bois,* ed. John Henrik Clarke, Esther Jackson, Ernest Kaiser, and J. H. O'Dell (Boston: Beacon Press, 1970), 268-73. See also Du Bois's explanation for declining circulation in Eliott M. Rudwick, "W. E. B. Du Bois in the Role of Crisis Editor," *Journal of Negro History* 43 (July 1958): 234.

21. Theodore Kornweibel Jr., *No Crystal Stair: Black Life and the Messenger, 1917-1928* (Westport, Conn.: Greenwood Press, 1975), 42-61; Theodore G. Vincent, ed., *Voices of a Black Nation: Political Journalism in the Harlem Renaissance* (San Francisco: Ramparts Press, 1973), 18-38.

22. Chandler Owen, "The Failure of Negro Leaders," *Messenger* 2 (Jan. 1918): 22-23; "The Crisis of the *Crisis*" and "Who's Who," *Messenger* 2 (July 1919): 10, 12, 27; and "Du Bois Fails as a Theorist," *Messenger* 2 (Dec. 1919): 7-8.

23. Department of Justice, *Investigative Activities of the Department of Justice,* 66th Cong., 1st Sess., Senate Documents, 12, doc. no. 153 (Washington, D.C.: Government Printing Office, 1919), 172.

24. According to a letter sent to Detweiler, the *Messenger* had a peak circulation of 26,000 in mid- to late 1919; his correspondent added, "Its readers are about ⅓ white and ⅔ colored" (Detweiler, *Negro Press,* 171).

25. "Why This Magazine—Our Policy," *Competitor* 1 (Jan. 1920): 2.

26. *Opportunity* 6 (July 1928): 219.

27. "Why We Are," *Opportunity* 1 (Feb. 1923): 3.

28. Nancy J. Weiss, *The National Urban League, 1910-1940* (New York: Oxford University Press, 1974), 224.

29. Langston Hughes, *The Big Sea* (New York: Hill and Wang, 1940), 218.

30. Weiss, *National Urban League*, 221.

31. Gunnar Myrdal, *An American Dilemma* (New York: Pantheon Books, 1944), 910.

32. E. Franklin Frazier, *Black Bourgeoisie: The Rise of a New Middle Class* (New York: Free Press, 1957), 179.

33. Ibid., 180.

34. Myrdal, *American Dilemma*, 919.

35. Johnson, "Rise of the Negro Magazine," 8, 21.

36. James E. Shepard, "These Colored United States: 'North Carolina—Its Educational Progress,'" *Messenger* 8 (Mar. 1926): 81, 90–91.

37. "The Negro Common School, Georgia," *Crisis* 32 (Sept. 1926): 248–64; "The Negro Common School, Mississippi," *Crisis* 33 (Dec. 1926): 90–102; "The Negro Common School in North Carolina," *Crisis* 32 (May 1927): 79–81, 96–97; (July 1927): 117–18, 133–35; "South Carolina Negro Common Schools," *Crisis* 32 (Dec. 1927): 330–32; and Horace Mann Bond, "The Negro Common School in Oklahoma," *Crisis* 35 (April 1928): 133–36, 138; (July 1928): 228, 243–46.

38. Du Bois, "Negro Education," *Crisis* 15 (Feb. 1918): 177.

39. "Self-Help," *Crisis* 16 (July 1918): 114.

40. In the second issue (Dec. 1910), advertisements appeared for Howard, Atlanta, and Fisk Universities. These college ads evolved into what was called the "Educational Directory." Eventually moved to a position of prominence at the front of the journal, right after the table of contents, by the end of the decade the directory contained ads for twenty-four institutions, including sixteen colleges and universities, four industrial schools, two nurses' training schools, and two stenographers' schools.

41. "The Year in Colored Colleges," *Crisis* 4 (July 1912): 134.

42. Raymond Wolters, *The New Negro on Campus* (Princeton, N.J.: Princeton University Press, 1975); E. Franklin Frazier, "The American Negro's New Leaders," *Current History* 28 (Apr. 1928): 56–59.

43. As Wolters has commented, "The spirit of W. E. B. Du Bois hovered over the black college rebellions of the 1920s" (*New Negro on Campus*, 18).

44. Horace Mann Bond, "Human Nature and Its Study in Negro Colleges," *Opportunity* 6 (Feb. 1928): 38–39, 58; Harry W. Greene, "The Ph.D. and the Negro," *Opportunity* 6 (Sept. 1928): 267–69; Ambrose Caliver, "The Freshman," *Opportunity* 5 (Sept. 1927): 261–63; "The Program of the Young College-Bred Negro," *Opportunity* 2 (June 1924): 172–74; "Fratres and Sorors," *Crisis* 29 (Feb. 1925): 151; "What Good Are College Fraternities?" *Messenger* 9 (June 1927): 179–81.

45. Du Bois, "Higher Education," *Crisis* 34 (Sept. 1927): 239. As the *Crisis's* annual reports on black graduates indicated and as subsequent data confirmed, black college attendance rose spectacularly in the 1920s. Du Bois's 1900 study, "The College-Bred Negro," reported a total of approximately 2,500 black college graduates from 1826 to 1899; in the five-year period 1921–25, 3,338 African Americans received academic degrees (bachelor's, master's, or doctoral degrees), while for the decade as a whole the figure was 10,707. See Du Bois, *The College-Bred Negro* (Atlanta University Publications, no. 5; rpt., New York: Arno Press, 1969). In fact, as Charles S. Johnson notes in his authoritative work *The Negro College Graduate* (College Park,

Md.: McGrath, 1938), 8, 20: "There were more graduates during the eleven-year period from 1926 through 1936 than there were during the one-hundred-year period from 1826 to 1925."

46. "Loyal Legion of Labor, U.S.A.," *CAM* 5 (Aug. 1902): 305. See also George Gilbert Walker, "Our Ideals," *CAM* 14 (Apr. 1908): 183–85; and S. Laing Williams, "The New Negro," *Alexander's Magazine* 7 (Nov. 1908): 18–19.

47. Cyrus Field Adams, "The Afro-American Council," *CAM* 6 (Mar. 1903): 332. As others similarly noted, "Public sentiment in this country is higher than the law" (Adams, "What Things the Race Should Emphasize," *CAM* 12 [June 1907]: 407).

48. William Pickens, "Southern Negro in Northern University," *Voice of the Negro* 2 (Apr. 1905): 234.

49. "Negroes Crowding the Schools," *CAM* 11 (Nov. 1906): 286.

50. Norval D. Glenn, "Negro Prestige Criteria: A Case Study in the Bases of Prestige," *American Journal of Sociology* 68 (May 1963): 655. See also Frazier, *Negro in the United States;* and Meier, "Negro Class Structure," 258–66.

51. Edward A. Shils, "The Bases of Social Stratification in Negro Society" (paper prepared for the Carnegie-Myrdal Study, 1940), 37 (available on microfilm, Schomberg Research Library, New York).

52. Langston Hughes, "Our Wonderful Society: Washington," *Opportunity* 5 (Aug. 1927): 226.

53. Service to the race and the importance of "character" were the central social and cultural themes through this entire thirty-year period. Delegates at the National Negro Baptist Convention in 1903 resolved, "The education that does not draw out our love for service . . . is a Christless, useless gift, that is a curse, rather than a blessing to the possessor." See Woolford Damon, "Twenty-third Annual Session of the National Negro Baptist Convention," *CAM* 6 (Nov. 1903): 788. Character was the ubiquitous ideal, both a "moral force" and "the end and aim of all education." See R. M. Hall, "The Future of the Afro-American," *CAM* 3 (July 1910): 204; and Edith Millan, "Discipline in Modern Education," *CAM* 13 (Dec. 1907): 425.

54. *Opportunity,* in fact, launched a veritable crusade against the dangers of the mental-testing movement from the journal's inception in January 1923. Eight of its first twelve issues contained articles that sharply attacked the myths and allegations of black intellectual inferiority that so frequently highlighted white researchers' conclusions. Among those who wrote on the issue of intelligence testing and race classifications in *Opportunity* were: Horace Mann Bond, University of Chicago, M.A. (1926) and Ph.D. (1936), who became the first black president of Lincoln University in 1945; E. Franklin Frazier, Clark University, M.A. (1920), University of Chicago, Ph.D. (1931), who later headed Howard University's sociology department; Howard H. Long, the Harvard Graduate School of Education's first black Ed.D. in 1933 and later assistant superintendent for research in the Washington, D.C., public schools; Ira de A. Reid, the Urban League's industrial secretary, University of Pittsburgh, M.A. (1925), Columbia University, Ph.D. (1939); Alain Locke, Harvard University, Ph.D. (1918), and in 1925 editor of the classic volume *The New Negro;* and, of course, Charles S. Johnson, editor of *Opportunity* from 1925 to 1928, University of Chicago, Ph.D. (1918).

55. Du Bois, *The Autobiography of W. E. B. Du Bois* (New York: International Publishers, 1968), 206. Ironically, Du Bois initially scoffed at the very idea of intelli-

gence tests, commenting, "Is it conceivable that a great university should employ a man whose 'science' consists of such rot?" ("Race Intelligence," *Crisis* 20 [July 1920]: 119).

56. Richard Bardolph, *The Negro Vanguard* (New York: Vintage Books, 1959), 133.

57. E. Franklin Frazier, "American Negro's New Leaders," 59.

58. Detweiler, *Negro Press,* 268.

59. Myrdal, *American Dilemma,* 911.

60. Shils, "Bases of Social Stratification," 26; John U. Ogbu, "Variability in Minority School Performance: A Problem in Search of an Explanation," *Anthropology and Education Quarterly* 18 (Dec. 1987): 312–34.

61. Although historians have noted that African Americans were often divided over the issue of mixed or segregated schooling, an interesting aspect of the treatment of this issue is the unanimous support lent by the black periodicals to the integrationist position.

ELIZABETH MCHENRY

Let us begin with three scenes from African-American literary history:[1] In June 1832, the abolitionist and editor William Lloyd Garrison reported in the "Ladies Department" of the *Liberator* his visit to "a society of colored ladies, called the FEMALE LITERARY ASSOCIATION," in Philadelphia. "The members assemble every Tuesday evening," he told his readers, "for the purpose of mutual improvement in moral and literary pursuits. Nearly all of them write, almost weekly, original pieces, which are put anonymously into a box, and afterward criticized by a committee. If the traducers of the colored race could be acquainted with the moral worth, just refinement, and large intelligence of this association, their mouths would hereafter be dumb." Garrison's impression of the literary society resulted not only from the "intellectual promise" he perceived in the group's conversation; he was equally impressed by the very fact of their coalition. "Having been permitted to bring with him several of [their] pieces [of writing]," Garrison "commence[d] their publication [in the *Liberator*], not only for their merit, but in order to induce the colored ladies of other places to go and do likewise."

The second scene reports another literary gathering, this one fictionally cast in the pages of Frances E. W. Harper's novel *Iola Leroy; or, Shadow Uplifted* (1892).[2] The chapter "Friends in Council" depicts the meeting of a community of blacks distinguished by their northern, private-school educations and professional lives as educators, ministers, and doctors. Harper's description of Iola's evening suggests the liveliness of the meeting, held in "Mr. Stillman's pleasant, spacious parlors," which Harper described as "overflowing with a select company of earnest men and women." The evening's "program" included the reading of papers written by the group's membership, on topics ranging from "Negro Emigration" and "Patriotism" to Iola's paper on the "Education of Negro Mothers." Lively discussion of the issues raised followed each reading, and the recitation of poetry and other genres was interspersed with the essays. One regular member of the group who regrettably could not attend the meeting contributed a poem that another member read. Members leaving Mr. Stillman's house at the end of the evening remarked how "interested and deeply pleased" they were with the proceedings. For her part, Iola left the session deeply inspired to "do something of lasting service for the race."

Our third scene provides yet another glimpse of literary community: a report of the meeting of Georgia Douglas Johnson's literary society, the Saturday Nighters, in Washington, D.C., June 4, 1927. Gwendolyn Bennett set the scene in her literary column, "Ebony Flute": "E. C. Williams with his genial good humor; Lewis Alexander with jovial tales of this thing and that as well as a new poem or two which he read; Marieta Bonner with her quiet dignity; Willis Richardson with talk of 'plays and things' . . . and here and there a new poet or playwright . . . and the whole group held together by the dynamic personality of Mrs. Johnson." Bennett's account goes on to note that Charles S. Johnson was the guest of honor, "some poems by Langston Hughes were read," Angelina Grimke was "particularly pleasing," and the whole company was "a charming medley."

While the recent "recovery" and reprinting of various texts from African-American literary history has increased our access to such literary creations, these opening scenes serve as reminders that we remain less cognizant of the variety of processes of intellectual production and exchange that have existed within African-American communities—processes through which texts were both created and read. Regardless of the fact that these formal and informal literary societies were ubiquitous in urban, African-American communities throughout the nineteenth and twentieth centuries and of the fact that these societies served as intellectual centers for individuals who *were,* to quote Iola Leroy, inspired to do things "of lasting service to the race," they have long suffered from scholarly neglect.[3]

This neglect is due only in part to the scarcity of documents that might definitively chronicle the activities of African-American literary societies throughout the nineteenth and early twentieth centuries. Equally relevant is the influence of a series of misleading and misrepresentational assumptions about African Americans and their literary habits. Historically, much has been written about the *absence* of literacy skills among African Americans. While their verbal performance arts, from folktales and proverbs to testifying and rapping, have received wide recognition, the singular identification of African-American culture as "oral in nature" has obscured facts surrounding other language uses—especially those related to reading and writing.[4]

Despite evidence to the contrary, the notion that African Americans are a "nonliterary" people is as much a part of the legacy of slavery in the United States as it was a part of the institution itself. The argument that "blacks and other people of color could not [read or] write" initially supported the theory that the natural condition of blacks was enslavement.[5] It also authorized their exclusion from the terms of the new nation's Declaration of Independence and Constitution. The hypocrisy of this reasoning is revealed in the fact that, to guard against the "inconveniences" of a literate black population, many states passed legislation making it a crime to teach blacks to read and write.[6] Given these impediments to even the most basic education, it is no wonder that much current work on the history of literacy, especially for "minority" populations, has emphasized the instrumental purposes of reading and writing—to enhance schooling and obtain a job. The writings of particular individual figures from nineteenth-century African-American history, including Frederick Douglass, have been mined for their linkage of literacy with freedom and economic opportunities.[7] These perspectives have contributed to a sense that there are few significant *differences* in African-American literary history regarding the uses of reading and writing and the development of their literary tradition.[8]

But what of those African Americans who, as early as 1830, chose to write and read in groups in the hope that these activities might help to enlighten others? What of those individuals who used their literary reading to promote discussion and inspire their own writing? We are hardly aware that such a group existed—in part because, in the words of Bayard Rustin, a "sentimental notion of black solidarity" has perpetuated the fiction that, especially before emancipation, black culture consisted of an illiterate mass undistinguished by differences of experience, privilege, or class. Only persistent scholarship has exposed the "significant and illuminating distinctions in background, prestige, attitudes, behavior, power, and culture" that have always composed African-American communities.[9] Primarily in the northern states before the Civil War, merchants, shipbuilders, ministers, and printers in urban areas formed an elite group of educated and active African Americans who sought to be recognized as citizens. During and after Reconstruction, their numbers were swelled by members of the legal and medical professions, politicians, and landowners who highly valued education, literature, and music.

For this substantial group within American society, reading literature and taking part in reading and writing groups provided from the early decades of the nineteenth century a central orientation to being literate, aiding self-improvement, and moving social justice ahead with additional "voice." From the 1830s on, African Americans formed literary societies that encouraged reading and writing by their members, developing a nationwide literary community with authors, editors, and publishers who shared an interest in their literature. Proponents of building this community urged the merits of individual and group expression for informing, exploring, and validating their unique identity as "Colored Americans" while asserting their right to full U.S. citizenship.

Recent efforts to restore accuracy and cross-class representation to the history of African Americans in the United States has allowed us to know something of the many "free" black communities that existed prior to the Civil War.[10] Formed in large part by the wave of abolitionist sentiment that provoked thousands of manumissions and schedules to abolish slavery after the Revolutionary War, urban communities offered free blacks conditions for potential employment and the promise of fellowship with others of African descent. Although not enslaved, these blacks hardly enjoyed the freedom and equality that the Constitution of the United States "ensured" all of its citizens. Yet this constitutional ideal, and the very concept of "citizenry" with its accompanying rights and responsibilities, captured the imagination of and was embraced by both whites intent on creating a democratic republic and blacks, whose aspirations focused on inclusion in the ideals of citizenship at the heart of the new nation.[11]

This study argues that African-American literary societies and the literary habits promoted by these institutions had social and political dimensions through which the desire for civic participation was both expressed and actively pursued. Drawing on the status of reading and writing in antebellum America and the development of African-American literary societies in that context, it augments our understanding of the connections among reading, writing, and responsibility as identified by middle- and upper-class African Americans throughout the nineteenth century. I argue that nineteenth-century African-American literary societies served as particularly important entry points to a literary and intellectual world otherwise inaccessible to their membership: they provided "a means of access to social and political events from which [African Americans] were . . . largely excluded."[12]

This function became particularly clear in black women's discourse about their collective literary activities in post-Reconstruction America, a period marked by the Supreme Court's nullification of the restrictive features of the Civil Rights Act of 1875 and the withdrawal of the last federal troops from the South in 1877, effectively ending the use of force on behalf of southern blacks. Largely if not entirely disenfranchised from the workings of the dominant culture, members of African-American literary societies continued to utilize collective reading as a means of keeping their social, political, and economic desires alive. During the last decade of the century, black women were especially successful in deriving from their literary activities forms of political agency associated with citizenship. Through an exploration of the publication of a representative black women's literary society, the Woman's Era of Boston, I suggest how literary interaction provided space—both physical and psychological—for a public and political discourse on the issues that most concerned African Americans and their status in America.

◫

From the beginning of the nineteenth century, free blacks could not *but* be aware of the centrality of the nation's founding documents to the question of African-American citizenship and oppression. Although their perceived illiteracy helped authorize their exclusion from the terms of the new nation, this alienation from society probably made African Americans understand writing and print more clearly as technologies of power. David Walker revealed this consciousness in his radical assessment of the condition of people of African descent, *Appeal to the Colored Citizens of the World.*[13] Published privately by Walker in 1829, the appeal delivered a furious indictment of American slavery and racism. It urged Americans of African descent to overcome the psychological weight of servility and prepare to fight their oppressors. This revolutionary message was not solely responsible for the incendiary nature of Walker's pamphlet: he also instructed blacks to read and study Thomas Jefferson's *Notes on Virginia,* especially spotlighting the famous passage: "I advance it therefore as a suspicion only, that blacks, whether originally a distinct race, or made distinct by time and circumstances, are inferior to whites in the endowments of both body and mind."[14]

Walker satirizes this passage in the appeal when, after reviewing the history of whites both as pagans and Christians, he advances his own "suspicion of them, whether they *are as good by nature* as we are or not." But Walker's master stroke against Jefferson and the hypocrisy of America comes at the very end of his pamphlet where he quotes Jefferson's Declaration of Independence and then cries out: "See your Declaration, Americans!!! Do you understand your own language?"[15]

Walker's attack on the unfulfilled rhetoric of the Declaration of Independence suggests his keen understanding of the role of print culture in the early United States. Protesting the structures of monarchy and religion with pamphlets and broadsides—and finally, with a formal declaration—the colonies had established themselves as a place where freedom and independence were first and foremost rhetorical acts. In such an environment, reading, writing, and public discourse were considered essential to the advancement of both proto-nation and individual.[16] Later, printed documents such as the Declaration of Independence and the Constitution were essential to maintaining the status of slaves and free people of color in the United States, for although the framers had focused the Declaration on the words "all men are created equal," they failed to include people of African descent in this distinction. Likewise, when the phrase "We, the People" was adopted to identify the collective body in the U.S. Constitution, the framers made no mention of who "We, the People" excluded.[17] Walker's *Appeal* reflects an understanding that these written documents had to be challenged and reconfigured if slaves and free blacks were to be considered Americans. In the words of the literary critic Houston Baker, the *Appeal* illustrates Walker's awareness that "he had to master the very forms of enslavement in order to write the African body in empowering forms."[18]

While most blacks were eventually legislated into illiteracy, the acquisition and use of letters came to be considered a fundamental responsibility of all white male citizens across social classes and roles, and the essence of "civic responsibility" was active participation in the public sphere through reading and publication.[19] Early Americans considered literary skills and the ideals of citizenship so inseparable that the writers of "literary" texts were not considered creators of original thought but disseminators of crucial information; because texts were designed to assert and sustain political discourse, authors were viewed as "minor participant[s] in the process of literary manufacture."[20] Focus was instead directed toward the variety of genres that might prove instrumental to their objectives: more often than fiction and poetry, these were the treatise, the direct essay, the letter, address, declaration, or appeal—all of which came to be defined as "literary." The task of these literary undertakings, then, was to establish and present an authoritative, legitimate voice capable of capturing an audience. The "publication" of this voice took several forms. With the meaning of the word "publish" not yet fixed in its modern meaning of "making public exclusively by means of print," the difference between written and oral presentation was indistinct.[21]

In an effort to cooperate in promoting their own interests and supporting their financial and material needs, free blacks in northern cities organized themselves into mutual aid societies in the last decades of the eigh-
teenth century.[22] But to effectively develop an American identity, African
Americans needed to enter an arena largely untouched by these insular
communities. Despite their strengths, mutual aid societies lacked opportunities for the kind of activities that might allow others to see them as
citizens. But "speaking"—in oral or written form—was a public act, an
assertion of cultural and political authority. As early as 1809, select mutual benefit societies began to call for the revision and expansion of their
functions to include more deliberate reading, writing, and public presentation of their condition. In an address to the New York African Society
for Mutual Relief, William Hamilton commended an essay cowritten by
two "colored" men of the community, citing not only its important subject, the abolition of the slave trade, but also its form as an example of the
kind of writing in demand. He urged others to write equally carefully constructed and powerful essays: "If we continue to produce specimens like
these," he said, "we shall soon put our enemies to the blush; abashed and
confounded they shall quit the field, and no longer urge their superiority of souls." Hamilton expressed concern that "we have not produced any
to excel in arts and sciences" and challenged his audience with the following rhetorical question: "What station above the common employment
of craftsmen and laborers would we fill, did we possess both learning and
abilities?" Although the subject of mutual aid remains the focal point of
Hamilton's address, the benefits of "being united in social bodies" for
improvement—not just survival—are at the heart of his words.[23]

Despite difficult access to literary texts, free blacks increasingly expressed their awareness of living in "the golden age of Literature" and
subscribed to the theory that interaction with "the Literature of the
day . . . brings in regular succession the condensed learning of past ages;
and all the erudition of the present."[24] In the midst of a dominant society for whom knowledge of the arts, sciences, and literature was distinctive, blacks increasingly believed that they needed to read widely and
produce documents that were sophisticated not so much in their presentation, as was the style of the day, but in their content. "The age in which
we live is fastidious in its taste," acknowledged William Whipper in an
address to an early literary society in Philadelphia in 1828. "The orator
[and writer] must display the pomp of words, the magnificence of the
tropes and figures, or he will be considered unfit for the duties of his profession." But, he continued, "such high-wrought artificial [presenta-

tions] are like beautiful paint upon windows, they rather obscure than admit the light of the sun. Truth should always be exhibited in such a dress as may be best suited to the state of the audience, accompanied with every principle of science and reason."[25]

Concern for intellectual stimulation and American identity, then, prompted those African Americans with economic security and sufficient leisure time to establish coalitions around reading and writing. Their societies were constructed as formal and informal and large and small discussion groups. Libraries and reading rooms were also considered literary societies—places people both found/stored books and read them collectively. Some instructed beginning readers while others supported those more advanced. Literary societies planned reading lists and schedules; they provided regular opportunities to "publish" original creations and audiences to encourage, discuss, and criticize the ideas and presentation. Typically, literary society members paid one dollar as an initiation fee and a monthly membership fee of twenty-five cents.[26] The bylaws of one early Philadelphia society, the Colored Reading Society, emphasize that the focus of a literary society was to be *literary* and not more generally social or beneficent: "All monies received by this Society," read items 4 and 5, "is [*sic*] to be expended in useful books, such as the Society may from time to time appropriate. . . . All books initiated into this society shall be placed in the care of the Librarian belonging to said institution, and it shall be his duty to deliver to said members alternatively, such books as they shall demand, with strict regard that no member shall keep said book out of the library longer than a week, without paying the fine prescribed in the constitution." The members of the society agreed to "meet once a week to return and receive books, to read, and express whatever sentiments they may have conceived if they think proper, and transact the necessary business relative to this institution."[27]

The guiding principle of Philadelphia's Colored Reading Society, which exemplified the many reading groups in northern cities such as New York, Boston, and Pittsburgh, was that "the station of a scholar, highly versed in classic lore, . . . is indeed higher than any other occupied by man." Members of the Reading Society adopted a "course of study" that would allow them "to fix the attention, to strengthen the memory, and to form habits of analyzing, comparing, abstracting, and correct reasoning." They were particularly interested in how these goals might be achieved through the reading of classical texts, which they defined as essential on a number of levels. From these texts, a "fund of ideas [is] acquired on a variety of subjects; the taste is greatly improved by conversing with the best models, the imagination is enriched by the fine scenery with which the classics abound; and an acquaintance is formed with human nature, together with the history, customs and manners of antiquity." By working collectively toward these goals, members could help one another "discipline the mind."[28]

The Philadelphia society subscribed to at least two important journals of the time: the first African-American newspaper, *Freedom's Journal*, and the *Genius of Universal Emancipation*.[29] Through their reading and discussion, members could "[analyze] and [compare their] ideas on different subjects," both contemporary and historical.[30] Members of the society also addressed the larger black community, informing them of their activities and generally supporting the pursuit of education.

For African Americans in the early nineteenth century, these societies offered a protected, collective environment in which to develop a literary background as well as the oral and written skills needed to represent themselves with confidence. Nowhere is this more clear than in the description of the Female Literary Association, the organization highly praised by William Lloyd Garrison in the pages of the *Liberator*. In an address to its members on the occasion of the first anniversary of their coalition, words written "by a member" and later published in the October 13, 1832, issue of the *Liberator* draw a parallel between the role of the literary society for its members and the "vault" Demosthenes built to provide him with the needed privacy to overcome the defects of his speech. "On his first attempt to speak in public, he was hissed," the member wrote; but Demosthenes, in private, perseveres and ultimately develops his speaking skills. By referring to this particular story in her anniversary address, the writer argues that the "brilliant success" resulting from Demosthenes's "seclusion" is also available through the protective "vault" created by the women's literary society itself. She equates the words Demosthenes masters during his time spent in the vault with powerful weapons: as the "first orator of the age," his "eloquence was more dreaded . . . than all the fleets and armies of Athens."

For African-American women, literary societies were especially important popular resources. In 1831, the number of female mutual aid societies outnumbered male mutual aid societies, twenty-seven to sixteen.[31] This figure is not surprising, given that two-thirds of Philadelphia's black population in the 1820s was female. Evidence suggests that from 1830 to 1850 women's literary societies may have outnumbered men's, not on the basis of size or prominence but on the sheer number of their societies. The differences between men's and women's literary societies were in keeping with a gendered notion of civic participation. Whereas men's literary societies typically had a large membership and sponsored public lectures and debates, women's societies were more likely to assemble in small groups in members' homes. In contrast to the formal documents that represent many of the men's literary societies, one-line announcements in journals of the day are often all that remains to mark the existence of early African-American women's literary societies. One such entry in the August 24, 1827, issue of *Freedom's Journal* reads, "A Society of Young Ladies has been formed at Lynn, Mass., to meet once a week, to read in turn to the society, works adapted to virtuous and literary improvement."[32]

⌐

Artifacts from the turn of the century serve as vivid reminders of the myriad ways blacks were characterized as lazy, ugly, lascivious, violent, and, most fundamentally, intellectually inferior. The rapid resurgence of racial tension and bigotry in both the North and South during the post-Reconstruction era effectively undermined the social, political, and economic progress blacks had anticipated during Reconstruction. Northern communities that had mobilized against the injustices of slavery and the treatment of blacks in the South before the Civil War seemed suddenly paralyzed by their preoccupation with adjustment to the abrupt social and economic changes accompanying industrialization. Although blacks in the northern cities did not suffer the same injustices as their southern counterparts, everywhere African Americans fought a common battle against the *concept* of "the Negro." The results of this perspective were debasing both psychologically and materially. Upper- and middle-class blacks redoubled their efforts to prove themselves capable, creative, and productive Americans. Association with literature remained one way of doing so.

For black women, engagement with the written word had always represented a means of acquiring knowledge. Before formal educational opportunities became available, a woman's reading and the intimate discussions it prompted with other women were synonymous with her education. Through a wide variety of activities, literary societies educated middle- and upper-class black women beyond what was considered their "proper sphere," preparing them instead to participate in the "gentleman's course" of study at schools such as Oberlin College in the 1860s.[33] As "school[s] for the encouragement and promotion of polite literature,"[34] literary societies served as the institutional bases from which black women could claim an education and thereby distinguish themselves. Black women considered the benefits of reading and writing to be transindividual, even expansive:

through their literary efforts and influence, "colored" people would become "highly distinguished and intelligent people."[35]

Despite claims by historians of the book that, by the late nineteenth century, reading had shifted from a public to a private practice, it remained a social and collective as well as an individual endeavor for African Americans. Although black men maintained their interest in literary communities, it was middle- and upper-class black women who more often expressed their understanding that reading could be used to realize an active role in promoting change.[36] Although one purpose of their literary activities was to "diversify the ceaseless [sic] monotony o[v]erhanging [them]," their reading was not an idle practice.[37] Rather, collective literary activities incited them to realize active roles in combating public perceptions and media claims that they were promiscuous, slothful, and less capable than all other Americans: reading was a means of clarifying and stimulating their political desires, not pacifying them. Shared reading, writing, and discussion allowed black Americans to reimagine themselves and their possible agency in the struggle for equality. It led them to public and political discourse on issues that most concerned African Americans and their status in the United States.

In the 1890s, the discourse circulated by black women concerning their reading and literary activities took on a new dimension. Increasingly, these women communicated to one another the importance of becoming readers and taking their literary activities seriously. In this way, reading was encouraged: "Great care should be taken in cultivating the habit of reading, for without reading it is impossible to ever be [a] 'full man'."[38]

In these instructions the link established between a woman's reading and her achievement of "full manhood" is an oddly phrased yet particularly relevant concept for understanding the importance of literary coalitions for black women at the turn of the century. In her study of the cluster of the domestic novels published by black women writers in the 1890s, Claudia Tate identifies a historical moment in the hostile interracial climate of the end of the nineteenth century when the equation between "home and state, between ideal domesticity and moral civil polity," was shattered. Tate suggests that the disassociation of idealized womanhood from political ambition and politicized discourse prompted a shift from the Victorian understanding of womanhood as "half of the mutually complementary public/male and private/female spheres of social, moral, and political influence."[39] This shift theoretically eliminated black women's political agency, depoliticizing their activities and erasing their ability to express political desire.

Rather than being silenced, middle- and upper-class black women "embraced the rhetoric of manhood as an emancipatory discourse to be mediated by both men and women."[40] If a woman's reading might enable her to become a "full man," it also authorized her to reimagine herself in a variety of unfamiliar ways. This "transformation" offered more opportunities for political power, not fewer; for, while the public activity and political agency of black men were severely limited at this time, both were certainly far greater for a black man than for a black woman. Occupying a theoretically marginal position "out of the thick of the fight," women used their literary activities and writing to "slip in and glide along quietly" in a political arena traditionally occupied by (white) men. With the attention of black men's societies focused elsewhere, black women had space to "think over [their] thoughts, and carry out [their] purposes" through professionally "published" and nonpublished essays, short stories, novels, and poetry and, increasingly, through publicly delivered lectures and speeches.[41]

Nowhere is the paradoxical power of this position more apparent than in the activities of the Woman's Era, a representative black women's literary society organized in Boston in 1892. In 1894, the society's membership began to publish a journal called The Woman's Era. Because each issue of The Woman's Era reported the activities of black women's literary societies throughout the country as well as those in Boston, the journal offers an especially detailed perspective on the relationship black women cultivated during this time between literary interaction and cultural authority.[42] Virtually every issue of The Woman's Era contains at least one article reminding women of the power of literature and the importance of "cultivating the habit of reading." "No kinder or wiser friend can one have than a good book," counsels Sarah Tanner in her article, "Reading," "for a book which is worthy for us to take as a companion is the embodiment of the noblest thoughts of which that life was capable."[43] Reports printed in the journal indicate that the reading interests of literary societies included not only the classics of English literature but other fields and genres as well, such as "Afro-American Literature." Announcing a "splendid programme" for its ninth season, New York's Brooklyn Literary Union lists the broad spectrum of suggested books. It included English, French, and American literature, biography, children's literature, and Afro-American literature. Larger societies assigned committees to prepare and then lead meetings on the various literary periods or genres.[44]

While the notion that, by reading "the masters" of English literature, African-American women would "learn to appreciate the good and beautiful" remained one reason for literary study, the importance of literature in the development of critical thinking skills and the ability to articulate one's views became increasingly important during this time.[45] Black women put into words what had been a significant aspect of their literary societies from their beginnings: "The chief benefit derived from the study [of literature] was . . . being able to form and hold one's own opinion."[46] "In order that the women may become educated in thought," reads one society's correspondence with *The Woman's Era,* "an original paper is prepared and read by some member each week. A discussion follows."[47] What would in earlier times have been known as a "meeting" of a literary society became increasingly referred to in *The Woman's Era* as a "class"; like the literary society meetings, "classes" were organized and conducted by the members themselves.[48] Missing a class was met with disapproval; the May 1895 issue of the journal reports that, at the Woman's Era's own literary meeting, two "thoughtful" papers were "prepared and eloquently presented": both addressed the topic "Our Opportunities." "Owing to small attendance," the announcement reprimands, "it is proposed to have the papers read again, that a larger number may be heard in the discussion of this important subject."

Although literary programs were meant to challenge women, they were not intended to foster competition. Rather, the women of the Woman's League of Denver, Colorado, expressed their belief that "nothing so stimulates and creates enthusiasm as . . . contact and friction with other minds. To learn to work harmoniously is education of a higher order."[49] That the activities and the benefits of literary societies were firmly rooted in relationships and associated with an atmosphere of sympathetic female peers should not be underestimated. Black women relied on the *combination* of intellectual challenge and emotional sustenance for their developing sensibilities. In the company of other black women, members found support for their thoughts and ambition: like-minded peers met their enthusiasm with enthusiasm. It is the success of this aspect of the Woman's Era literary society that was particularly celebrated on the occasion of the society's second anniversary: "The especial aim of this club," reads a notice in *The Woman's Era,* "is to promote and foster a spirit of unity and helpfulness in every needed direction among its members, to discover and uncover hidden capacities." Through literary activities, the society aimed "to foster . . . ambition" and to bring "to the light talent among our women which had only to be discovered to reflect credit on any people."[50]

That the Woman's Era literary society felt the need, within just two years of its organization, to publish a journal is testimony to the extent that reading and conversation, reading and writing, reading and *ambition* were not discrete activities but existed on a continuum. Reading offered "subjects for thought and hence for conversation."[51] History suggests that these "conversations" were "heard"—not only by other black women in the protected environments of their literary societies but also by a wider audience through publications such as *The Woman's Era*. After only a handful of issues, the journal was described by one reader—"a gentleman of large experience and fairly cultivated mind"—as "the finest thing in the way of a paper or journal the race has ever put forth."[52]

One of the most valuable aspects of the publication was its ability to indicate the sheer number of black women's literary coalitions throughout the nation. The May 1895 issue reports that in Denver alone, black women's literary societies included "the Fortnightly and Monday Literary clubs, both having been formed about 1881."[53] In addition to these, in Denver there were "dozens of study and reading clubs all over the city," including the Clio Club, Round Table Club, and Friday Morning Club. The same issue carries Ohio news of Toledo's Dickens Club and Springfield's Lovers of Wisdom, as well as the Augusta, Georgia, Phillis Wheatley Club. For those wanting to study literature but not engaged in a local society of their own, *The Woman's Era* periodically reprinted reading lists and study questions from the society's own meetings, extending its local literary exchange to the journal's subscribers nationwide.[54]

Despite the important sense of coalition conveyed by the proliferation of black women's literary societies at the turn of the century, the difficulties associated with literary study for women were not easily dismissed. Writers for *The Woman's Era* crafted clever rhetorical ways to ease the anxieties of black women and encourage them to persist in their literary studies. Mary Church Terrell's monthly column in the journal often turned what she called "conversations" into fables. A story about a "young woman of [her] acquaintance," for instance, articulated this concern: "I want to hear something which will remove the feeling that my inability to express myself well is due to ignorance and stupidity." It is not surprising that Terrell attributes the "moral" of the story to "a little woman, reputed to be something of a book worm." Says the "book worm" to the distressed woman: "Whoever is a master of language hath his mind full of ideas, [and] will be apt in speaking to hesitate upon the choice of both." Another such "fable" dramatized a conversation between two women over their household duties in order to encourage black women to "arrange [their] work so as to leave a certain amount of time each day for study."[55]

Although *The Woman's Era* contains occasional advertisements for such "female concerns" as "diet," "healthful dressing," and "chest expansion,"[56] the journal also reflects that the central interest of the societies it represented was not a black woman's personal appearance but her determination to change her role in what one writer identified as "the American scheme of life."[57] "Colored women come last in the American scheme," wrote Dora J. Cole, editor of the "Pennsylvania" column of *The Woman's Era*. It was the duty of middle- and upper-class African-American women to change this by abandoning "the pedestal of statue-like inactivity in the domestic shrine, [not] daring to think and move and speak."[58] Literary study was seen as an alternative to—or, indeed, the opposite of—cultivating "ladylike" inactivity. One literary woman, Mrs. N. F. Mossell, expressed the understood connection between literary study and *action* in this way: "Any achievement of man embodied in literary expression becomes in large degree fixed and settled, and is a point of departure for new achievements."[59]

Indeed, the activity encouraged through collective reading and writing in African-American literary societies transformed a generation of black women writers into "activists," giving them the textual responsibility of defending the race and speaking out for sexual justice. As educated readers, writers, and lecturers, literary society members became conscious of their roles as agents responsible for the creation, preservation, and transmission of "the records, books and various publications" that would represent the race for future generations.[60]

⅃

There is no doubt that the creation of a "lasting history" of the African-American race presented itself to middle- and upper-class black women at the turn of the century as "the highest privilege": indeed, there was "no greater responsibility." The very real proliferation of literary productions by African-American women at the turn of the century should not overshadow the fact that, as much as anything else, this period established black women as public figures and placed them in positions of great public appreciation and demand. If "Race Literature" was to be effective, many writers had to double as paid speakers who toured the country and presented their ideas at well-attended public lectures. Their resulting notoriety and the distinct sense of political purpose behind their work proved to be a double-edged sword for many literary women of the time. In many respects, urgent political need for their writing contributed to a sense that there was no "literary atmosphere" during the very time when the greatest percentage of elite African-American women were involved in literary societies.

Faced with the need to write literature and participate in forums that might encourage conversations around issues of gender and the reimagination of African Americans' role in society, black women readers and writers were often frustrated by the nature of their literary interaction. "It has been a bitter disappointment to me," wrote Mary Church Terrell in her autobiography *A Colored Woman in a White World*, "that I did not succeed as a short story writer."[61] Terrell, a popular essayist and orator who aspired to write imaginative literature, found it difficult to focus on her own fiction and "refuse to be called upon by everybody who asks me to assist in the thousand and one things which we try to do to promote the welfare of the race."[62] Her regret was the result not only of a sense of missed artistic, but also political, success: "I have thought for many years that the Race Problem could be solved more swiftly and more surely through the instrumentality of the short story or novel than in any other way."[63]

Terrell's personal correspondence and memoirs leave an especially detailed record of one writer's frustration with the public and political demands placed upon the literary creations of all African Americans, female and male, by the social and political climate at the turn of the century: the very diversity of these responsibilities made their literary lives all the more difficult. Terrell was only one of many would-be African-American imaginative writers, for instance, who gave voice to individual laments over the lack of any strong role for African-American imaginative literature in the public arena at the time. By speaking frankly about her literary disappointments, Terrell put into perspective the limitations that resulted from laying claim to a collective, black public voice:

> If I had lived in a literary atmosphere, or if my time had not been so completely occupied with public work of many varieties, I might have gratified my desire to "tell the world" a few things I wanted it to know. I do not regret the time and energy consumed serving others. I cannot help wondering, however, whether I might not have succeeded as a short-story writer, or a novelist, or an essayist, if the conditions under which I lived had been more conducive to the kind of literary work I so longed to do.[64]

In spite of Terrell's repeated efforts to publish her short stories and other fictional works, she met constant rejection from publishers who repeatedly advised her to address "the Race Problem" through her lectures and occasional essays. Overwhelmed by or uninterested in the potential political power of Terrell's fiction—writing that she recognized as a vehicle for reporting, critiquing, and reflecting on the sociohistorical circumstances of black people in America—publishers criticized and refused to print her creative works. Terrell's personal archives are filled with rejection letters that echo the words of one publisher: "Perhaps you are too intent on reforming this world than on creating an imaginary world of your own, after the artist's fashion."[65]

Inherent in this typical dismissive editorial response to Terrell's fiction is the debate on the powers of written expression and the relative effectiveness of different genres for the promotion of causes linked to the black race. Terrell's conviction that short stories and novels could act to promote conversations around and, eventually, introduce solutions to the "race problem" was due in part to her impression that these genres would reach those unlikely to attend lectures or read political treatises or pamphlets. She believed a "conspiracy of silence"[66] existed on the part of the American press, which resisted presenting literary materials that would set forth the "conditions under which Colored people actually live today—their inability to secure employment, the assault and battery constantly committed upon their hearts, their sensibilities and their feelings."[67] Terrell wished to recreate fictionally not only those major characters whose lives of impoverishment and exploitation challenged them to survive as individuals but also portraits that would accurately represent the range of backgrounds and social and occupational contexts of African Americans.

The history of African-American women's interaction with literature and involvement in literary societies in the nineteenth century suggests that no African-American reader or writer, however privileged individually, could totally escape the collective historical experience of oppression. This history exposes two contradictory claims on the African-American "literary woman": (1) the fundamental human need to affirm specificities of one's personal experience, however "typical" or "atypical," through reading and writing, and (2) the equally compelling imperative to use literature to express solidarity with those whose lives and sufferings take similar forms from similar causes. For the African-American woman writer of the late nineteenth and early twentieth century, these claims are such that the gift of reading and writing, especially in coalition, became a tool for both individual therapy and gratification as well as the means to make a political statement.

The development of their literary societies and literary lives indicates that, although literary societies introduced black women to public voice and greater political power, it did not always give the luxury of freely representing their own individual voices. Frequently, they were forced to supply a unified and seemingly uniform narrative that might establish collective experience. Mary Church Terrell's autobiography reveals the bitterness resulting from the ambiguous status of the *individual* stories of African Americans: "Nobody wants to know a colored woman's opinion about her own status or that of her group. When she dares to express it, no matter how mild or tactful it may be, it is called 'propaganda,' or is labeled 'controversial.' Those two words have come to have a very ominous sound to me. I cannot escape them; they confront me everywhere I go."[68]

Had they been published, such personal narratives and fictional accounts of the lives of African Americans would have left a more complete portrayal of the various ways in which literature, among other things, figured into the ambitions, goals, and aims of readers and writers from different classes and social backgrounds. Terrell's sense of herself as "trapped" by the particular demands placed upon her by the political and literary worlds that she traversed reflects the literary tensions of the period in which she lived. Despite her frustration, however, Terrell never abandoned her interest in reading, writing, and the power of literature. She found refuge and support for her reading and writing through active membership in Washington's Book Lovers' Club.[69]

The role of imaginative literature envisioned by Terrell and others became possible for the writers of the Harlem Renaissance in large part because of institutions such as literary societies and through instruments like the literary journals begun by their nineteenth-century counterparts. Without the self-conscious reflection of nineteenth-century African-American women writers on what their reading and writing could do for their own psychosocial struggles as elite African Americans and as disappointed citizens for whom the promises of Reconstruction did not hold, the literature of the Harlem Renaissance could not have successfully negotiated a balance among expressing the variety of African-American experience, removing prejudice, and educating "outsiders." For the writers of the Harlem Renaissance, literary work continued to be a way to ground themselves and establish their roots and identities, as both blacks and Americans. Like those of their predecessors, their literary activities were committed to moving the black community forward in the struggle for civil rights by using the powers of fiction, drama, essays, and poetry to engage attention, to arouse empathy, and to move readers—black and white—to thoughtful reflection and meaningful action.

NOTES

1. I have borrowed this model from Richard Brodhead's introduction entitled "On the Idea of a Culture of Letters" to his *Cultures of Letters: Scenes of Reading and Writing in Nineteenth-Century America* (Chicago: University of Chicago Press, 1993).

2. Harper's novel is reprinted in *Three Classic African-American Novels*, ed. Henry Louis Gates Jr. (New York: Vintage, 1990), 227–463, quotations from 431–44.

3. A notable exception to this is Dorothy Porter's article, "The Organized, Educational Activities of Negro Literary Societies, 1828–1846" (*Journal of Negro Education* 5 [Oct. 1936]: 555–76), in which she identified almost fifty "Negro Literary Societies" that existed in northern cities in 1828–46. According to Porter, her research on these societies was incomplete; although she gives an overview of the activities of early literary societies, she herself has said that she never had time to fully explore their framework or context in African-American and American literary history. Organized as it is by city, state, and dates of formation, however, the list proves that African Americans created an active intellectual life through literary study long before the Civil War.

Despite Porter's article, scholars of African-American literary history seem unaware of the societies' existence. Even Hazel Carby's groundbreaking critical study of African-American women in the late nineteenth and early twentieth century, *Reconstructing Womanhood: The Emergence of the Afro-American Woman Novelist* (New York: Oxford University Press, 1987), overlooks early African-American women's literary societies. Although Carby's study has been extremely instructive to my own, she incorrectly identifies the turn of the century as "the years of the first flowering of black women's autonomous organizations" (7).

4. In "The Literary and the Literate: African Americans as Writers and Readers, 1830–1940" (*Written Communication* 11 [Oct. 1994]: 419–44), Shirley Brice Heath and I argue for a balance to this image by laying out historical evidence on the literate values and habits of African Americans since the 1800s.

5. Henry Louis Gates Jr., "Writing 'Race' and the Difference It Makes," in *"Race," Writing, and Difference*, ed. Henry Louis Gates Jr. (Chicago: University of Chicago Press, 1985), 1–20.

6. "Inconvenience" is not my word but was used in a 1740 South Carolina statute prohibiting the teaching of reading and writing to slaves. The first part of the statute reads as follows: "Whereas the having of slaves taught to write, or suffering them to be employed in writing, may be attending with great inconveniences" (quoted in ibid., 9).

7. See, for example, Houston Baker Jr., *Blues, Ideology, and African American Literature: A Vernacular Theory* (Chicago: University of Chicago Press, 1984).

8. Critical scholars and feminist theorists have recently opposed this singular perspective as the "imposition" of literacy in the struggle for freedom and civil rights, as well as for its failure to distinguish between the conditions and results of literacy for males and females. Valerie Smith, in *Self-Discovery and Authority in Afro-American Narrative* (Cambridge, Mass.: Harvard University Press, 1987), is one of few to suggest that there exist a *variety* of ways literacy and the idea of literacy has been used within the tradition of African-American letters. Katherine Bassard, in "Gender and Genre: Black Women's Autobiography and the Ideology of Literacy" (*African American Review* 26 [Spring 1992]: 119–29), examines the texts of several black women autobiographers to see how they perceived "both the potential and limits of the ideology of literacy" (120). "It was much easier," she suggests, "for a male slave narrator like Frederick Douglass to 'cash in' on the investment of literacy than it was for Harriet Jacobs or Harriet E. Wilson" (119). She finds that "[their] views about themselves as writers and the purposes of their written texts reflect a broad range of positions vis-à-vis literacy, and even language itself. These women are keenly

aware," she continues, "of the limits of the literacy-as-freedom ideology, due to their multiple marginalized positions in the social order, and they express everything from mild tension to outright suspicion of the power of the Written Word to provide freedom, economic security, and a restructuring of social formations of power" (120).

9. Bayard Rustin, quoted in Willard B. Gatewood, *Aristocrats of Color: The Black Elite, 1880–1920* (Bloomington: Indiana University Press, 1990), ix.

10. See, for example, James Oliver Horton and Lois E. Horton, *Black Bostonians: Family Life and Community Struggle in the Antebellum North* (New York: Holmes and Meier, 1979); James Oliver Horton, *Free People of Color: Inside the African American Community* (Washington, D.C.: Smithsonian Institution Press, 1993); Julie Winch, *Philadelphia's Black Elite: Activism, Accommodation, and the Struggle for Autonomy, 1787–1848* (Philadelphia: Temple University Press, 1988); and Gary B. Nash, *Forging Freedom: The Formation of Philadelphia's Black Community, 1720–1840* (Cambridge, Mass.: Harvard University Press, 1988).

11. Not all blacks were interested in remaining in the United States. Waves of emigrationist sentiment also swept through black communities in antebellum America, as did various movements to return blacks to Africa. The American Colonization Society, organized in 1816, was at the forefront of this project.

12. Here I am quoting Cathy Davidson, *Revolution and the Word: The Rise of the Novel in America* (New York: Oxford University Press, 1986), 10, whose specific argument refers to the role of the novel in the nineteenth century. She suggests that the novel became a form of education, especially for women and others excluded from institutions of higher learning; I argue that literary societies functioned similarly for African Americans in the nineteenth century.

13. See David Walker, "Walker's Appeal to the Colored Citizens of the World," 1829; rpt. in Herbert Aptheker, *One Continual Cry: David Walker's "Appeal to the Colored Citizens of the World"* (New York: Hill and Wang, 1965).

14. Thomas Jefferson, *Notes on Virginia*, 211n., quoted in Walker, "Appeal," 26.

15. Walker, "Appeal," 17, 75.

16. Recent literary and historical studies of American culture, such as Jay Fliegelman, *Declaring Independence: Jefferson, Natural Language, and the Culture of Performance* (Stanford, Calif.: Stanford University Press, 1993); Thomas Gustafson, *Representative Words: Politics, Literature, and the American Language* (New York: Cambridge University Press, 1992); and Michael Warner, *The Letters of the Republic: Publication and the Public Sphere in Eighteenth-Century America* (Cambridge, Mass.: Harvard University Press, 1990), trace America's political development in terms of its use of language as representative of the union and its people. They identify numerous projects in revolutionary and early national history that reflect the dimensions of early U.S. literary culture.

17. For an exploration of how the framers of the Declaration of Independence and Constitution used rhetoric to leave the place of African Americans ambiguous, see Robert Ferguson, "'We Hold These Truths': Strategies of Control in the Literature of the Founders," in *Reconstructing American Literary History*, ed. Sacvan Bercovitch (Cambridge, Mass.: Harvard University Press, 1986), 1–28.

18. Houston Baker Jr., "There Is No More Beautiful Way: Theory and the Poetics of Afro-American Women's Writing," in *Afro-American Literary Study in the 1990s*,

ed. Houston Baker and Patricia Redmond (Chicago: University of Chicago Press, 1989), 135–63 (esp. 140).

19. In an essay on nineteenth-century concepts of writing and education, Shirley Brice Heath notes that concepts of literacy were closely linked with ideals of "citizenry." See her "Toward an Ethnohistory of Writing in American Education," in *Writing: The Nature, Development, and Teaching of Written Communication,* ed. Marcia Farr Whiteman (Hillsdale, N.J.: Lawrence Erlbaum Associates, 1981), 25–45.

20. Davidson, *Revolution and the Word,* 30.

21. See the *Oxford English Dictionary*'s history of the word "publish," as well as Raymond Williams's discussion of "literature" in *Keywords: A Vocabulary of Culture and Society* (New York: Oxford University Press, 1976).

22. The first mutual aid society was formed in Newport, Rhode Island, in 1770. A similar organization formed in 1787 in Philadelphia (the city with the largest population of free blacks) and another in Boston in 1796. These "free African societies," as they were called, as well as the hundreds of smaller mutual aid societies that developed in the early nineteenth century, worked on much the same principle: members paid a sum to join and a monthly fee that was held "for the mutual benefit of each other." The society was then able to "hand forth to the needy" a certain amount each week or at a time of crisis, "provided this necessity [was] not brought on them by their own imprudence." See William Douglass, *Annals of the First African Church, in the United States of America, Now Styled the African Episcopal Church of St. Thomas, Philadelphia . . .* (Philadelphia: King and Baird, 1862), 16.

23. William Hamilton, "An Address to the New York African Society, for Mutual Relief, Delivered in the Universalist Church, January 2, 1809," rpt. in *Early Negro Writing,* ed. Dorothy Porter (Boston: Beacon Press, 1971), 36–37.

24. William Whipper, "An Address Delivered in Wesley Church on the Evening of 12 June, before the Colored Reading Society of Philadelphia, for Mental Improvement, 1828," rpt. in *Early Negro Writing,* ed. Porter, 105–19, quotation from 107.

25. Ibid.

26. My records indicate that the payment of one dollar at initiation and twenty-five cents as a monthly fee was standard for societies established around the same date in the northern cities. But without some indication of the average income of free blacks, these figures carry little meaning. Studies of the economic conditions for African Americans in the antebellum United States reveal little about the actual wages earned by free blacks in their various occupations. My research in this area is ongoing. Property-holding statistics suggest that very few free blacks were financially secure; for the most part, blacks were restricted to the fields of domestic service and common labor. In northern cities, the African-American job-seeker faced competition from European immigrants; although technically "free," blacks were subject to hostility and bitter discrimination.

27. Whipper, "Address," 107–8.

28. Ibid., 109–11.

29. "Original Communications," *Freedom's Journal,* June 20, 1828, 98.

30. Whipper, "Address," 110.

31. "To the Public," *Hazard's Register,* Mar. 12, 1831, 163–64.

32. The largest women's literary societies in the 1830s and 1840s seem to have consisted of about thirty members. In *Sketches of the Higher Classes of Colored Soci-*

ety in Philadelphia (Philadelphia: Merrihew and Thompson, 1841), Joseph Wilson outlines the organization and activities of the Minerva Literary Society, an association formed by thirty African-American "ladies" in October 1834. In Boston, the Afric-American Female Intelligence Society, founded in 1832, maintained a comparable membership during this period. Similar New York societies included the Ladies Literary Society (1834) and the Female Literary Society (1836).

33. In her first column in *The Woman's Era* (Nov. 1894), Mary Church Terrell reported the death of Mary J. Patterson, "the first colored woman [to] receive her A.B. in the United States." Patterson had received her degree from Oberlin College in 1862. Terrell noted the importance of this accomplishment not only for African Americans but for women generally: "When Oberlin College opened its doors to women, she was courageous, indeed, who dared to brave public opinion by taking what was commonly called the gentlemen's course, on the principle that it belonged exclusively to the lords of creation, and that no women need apply" (5). Anna Julia Cooper also commented on the controversial admission of "ladies" to the "gentleman's course" of education in her essay "The Higher Education of Women" (in her *Voice from the South by a Black Woman of the South* [1892; rpt., New York: Oxford University Press, 1988]), suggesting the importance of the preparation offered by literary societies in her comments on the anxieties that surrounded the introduction of women to higher education: "It was thought to be an experiment—a rather dangerous experiment—and was adopted with fear and trembling by the good fathers, who looked as if they had been caught secretly mixing explosive compounds and were guiltily expecting every moment to see the foundations under them shaken and rent and their fair superstructure shattered into fragments" (49).

34. Wilson, *Sketches of the Higher Classes*, 108.

35. Maria Stewart, "An Address, Delivered before the Afric-American Female Intelligence Society of Boston," in *Productions of Mrs. Maria Stewart, Presented to the First African Baptist Church and Society* (Boston: Friends of Freedom and Virtue, 1835), 60.

36. From one woman's perspective, the turn of the century found black men "hampered by their contentions with their white brothers." See Mrs. N. F. Mossell, *The Work of Afro-American Woman* (1894; rpt., New York: Oxford University Press, 1988), 100. This seems to be one reason reading, writing, and other literary exercises served less and less frequently as the "glue" holding men's "literary" societies together.

37. "The Woman's Mutual Improvement Club," *Woman's Era*, Feb. 1895, 15.

38. Sarah E. Tanner, "Reading," *Woman's Era*, June 1895, 13–14.

39. Claudia Tate, *Domestic Allegories of Political Desire: The Black Heroine's Text at the Turn of the Century* (New York: Oxford University Press, 1992), 131.

40. Ibid., 132. Tate's study focuses particularly on the African-American woman novelist's ability to maintain agency by recasting political desire through fictions of domestic life.

41. Mossell, *Work of Afro-American Woman*, 100.

42. Although the journal was eventually adopted as the unofficial and then official publication of the African-American women's club movement generally, *The Woman's Era*'s beginnings as the publication of a literary society, its focus on liter-

ature, and its frequent reports on the activities of literary societies point to a continued understanding of the importance of literature and dedication to literary study during this time.

43. Sarah E. Tanner, "Reading," 13–14.

44. Reporting on the organization and upcoming season of the Brooklyn Literary Union, Victoria Earle commented on their plan to subdivide the literature they studied into fields. "Such an innovation has many advantages," she wrote. "It will not only concentrate the efforts of progressive minds, but bring them into more immediate touch with the people, and thereby develop much that is latent among us, besides giving impetus to intellectual activity. Victoria Earle, "New York," *Woman's Era*, Feb. 1895, 2.

45. Tanner, "Reading," 14.

46. "The Woman's Era Literature Department," *Woman's Era*, June 1896, 2.

47. Elizabeth Piper Ensley, "Colorado," *Woman's Era*, May 1895, 9.

48. "One distinct feature of these evenings," wrote Sara Iredell Fleetwood of her involvement in the Washington, D.C., Mignonette Club, "is the well understood fact that no refreshments will be furnished, a decision that does much to insure the permanency of these entertainments" (quoted in Dorothy Sterling, ed., *We Are Your Sisters: Black Women in the Nineteenth Century* [New York: Norton, 1984], 431–32). The impulse to treat their meetings as "classes" and to keep them from becoming socially oriented is especially characteristic of black women's literary societies during this time. While records indicate that between 1870 and 1910, men's literary societies became primarily social clubs, women chose in their literary societies to maintain and increase their focus on literature, facing directly through it the political and social justice issues of the time.

49. Ensley, "Colorado," 9.

50. "England's Attitude," *Woman's Era*, Feb. 1895, 12.

51. "University Extension Work and Its Mission," *Woman's Era*, May 1895, 20.

52. "New York," *Woman's Era*, Dec. 1894, 2.

53. Ensley, "Colorado," 9.

54. See, for example, "The Woman's Era Literature Department," *Woman's Era*, June 1896, 2–3.

55. Mary Church Terrell, "Washington," *Woman's Era*, Feb. 1895, 4, and Terrell, "Washington," Dec. 1894, 7.

56. Elizabeth Piper Ensley, "A Rare Opportunity," *Woman's Era*, May 1895, 9.

57. Dora Cole, "Pennsylvania," *Woman's Era*, Dec. 1894, 14.

58. Cooper, *Voice from the South*, 121–22.

59. Mrs. N. F. Mossell, "Life and Literature," *A.M.E. Church Review* 14 (Jan. 1898): 318–26.

60. Perhaps the definitive contemporary statement of this is Victoria Earle Matthews's 1895 article "The Value of Race Literature: An Address Delivered at the First Congress of Colored Women of the United States, at Boston, Massachusetts, July 30, 1895" (rpt., *Massachusetts Review* 27 [Summer 1986]: 169–85). Matthews outlined the role played by black female readers and writers in promoting a new purpose to literature and literary study and production during this time. She coined the term "Race Literature" to suggest that literature by and about African Americans would be a significant reporting medium "for the unnaturally suppressed inner

lives which our people have been compelled to lead." In answering the question "What part shall . . . women play in the Race Literature of the future?" Matthews singled out *The Woman's Era* as instrumental in signifying women's responsibility for the advancement of both race and gender issues in their literary efforts: literature must provide the motivation for both interaction and action (173).

Matthews echoes Mossell's publication of a year earlier, *The Work of Afro-American Woman* (1894), as well as those of Anna Julia Cooper, whose chapter "One Phase of American Literature," in *A Voice from the South* (1892), recognized the importance of "Race Literature" by concluding "that an authentic portrait . . . representing the black man as a free American citizen . . . has not yet been painted" (222–23).

61. Mary Church Terrell, *A Colored Woman in a White World* (1940; rpt., Salem, N.H.: Ayer, 1986), 234.

62. Terrell to Mr. Reid, Dec. 19, 1921, Mary Church Terrell Papers, Library of Congress, Washington, D.C.

63. Terrell, *Colored Woman*, 234.

64. Ibid., 237.

65. J. E. Spingarn to Terrell, May 24, 1922, Terrell Papers. Spingarn wrote to Terrell in his official capacity as the editor of Harcourt, Brace, and Company, Publishers.

66. Terrell to "the Editor of Harper's Magazine," Mar. 29, 1922, Terrell Papers.

67. Terrell to F. Arthur Metcalf, President, Home Correspondence School, May 25, 1916, Terrell Papers.

68. Terrell, *Colored Woman*, 234.

69. Organized in 1894, the club met twice each month to "pursue courses of reading and study for higher culture." Various pieces of information on the Book Lovers, including several "programs of study" and the club's creed, are available in the file of Ida Gibbs Hunt, who was a member. These are in the William H. Hunt Papers, Moorland-Spingarn Research Center, Howard University, Washington, D.C.

8   Better than Billiards: Reading and the Public Library in Osage, Iowa, 1890–95

CHRISTINE PAWLEY

On December 15, 1892, a woman calling herself "Gertrude B." addressed a letter to the readers of the "Woman's Kingdom" column in the *Mitchell County Press,* a weekly newspaper published in Osage, Iowa. "Sisters," she wrote, "the thought has often presented itself to my mind that our public library should be open oftener than one half-day a week, to afford an opportunity for the reading citizens, boys and girls. Not only ought more books of a better quality to appear on the shelves but a small part of the fund on hand might be used to light and warm the library two or three nights a week for a reading room. So long as two billiard rooms are running in full blast the duty of providing something of the kind for those who have higher aspirations ought to be self-evident."

Gertrude was articulating a belief commonly held by middle-class Americans at the end of the nineteenth century: that reading constituted a "safe," morally uplifting activity that ought to be encouraged, particularly among the young. Libraries stood in marked contrast to those dangerous places, billiard rooms, and even worse, saloons, where the young and not-so-young might be diverted from the pursuit of "higher aspirations." Whether or not the users of the public library actually followed the precepts of the advocates of moral improvement is another matter, and one that until now has been largely a topic for conjecture.

We know very little about the place of reading in the lives of "ordinary" Americans living in small towns at the turn of the century. To date, the history of reading in America has tended for the most part to be the history of the middle class in northeastern cities before 1876. Because researchers have had to rely on diaries, letters, and autobiographies (less readily available for the less wealthy and for those in the South, Midwest, and West), they have either inferred the reading practices of the great mass of the population from publishers' sales figures or else ignored them entirely.

Despite the fact that for over a century the American free public library has provided reading materials and facilities to men, women, and children of many races and classes in towns large and small across the country, historians have ignored the records of the public library. My aim here is to demonstrate these records' potential by illustrating their use in my own larger study of reading in one small rural midwestern community: Osage, Iowa.[1] By focusing particularly on gender, age, class, and religious affiliation, we can see how the accessions and circulation records of the public library, combined with library board minutes and census data, can shed light on two principal questions: Who used the public library? And what did they read?[2]

THE COMMUNITY

Osage is a small northern Iowa town that even today numbers only about 3,700 people. In the 1890s, its population was about 2,000. (The desirability of increasing the population was frequently discussed among the community's business leaders.) The story of Osage's beginnings conveys a picture of intense activity by a group of highly energetic people. The first white settlers arrived in the area in 1853, and the town was platted three years later. According to one historian of Mitchell County, "Osage was inhabited by land seekers, surveyors and speculators. In the spring of 1857, there were an estimated 1,500 people in Osage in addition to the regular residents. That spring, over one million dollars changed hands in Osage due to these extra people and the sale of several townships of land."[3] Grist, flour, sorghum, and saw mills, carpentry, wagon and shoemaking shops, smithies, a foundry, and hotels opened for business. The Cedar Valley Seminary (a Baptist school that combined a high school and a junior college) opened in 1863. In 1869 the Illinois Central Railway Company chugged into Osage from the south, and (after much local dispute) Osage became the county seat in 1870. Thus firmly rooted in commerce and government, Osage began to flourish. In 1871, leading citizens formed the Osage Library Association, a subscription library selling shares for five dollars each. In 1876 the city council accepted all the books from the library association as a startup collection for the newly formed Sage Public Library (named after Orrin Sage, an eastern philanthropist who donated land to the town for the benefit of the public library).

The public library was just one of several developing local institutions through which the inhabitants of Osage expressed their intention to stop their westward movement and build a permanent community. By 1891, with the coming of electric lights and a second railroad, the Winona and Southwestern, the Osage Board of Trade expressed the hope that "a new era has dawned upon us, and ere the year 1891 is past, many new industries will be brought to our beautiful city, and her population greatly increased."[4]

The directory accompanying the board of trade's report included an impressive list of professional services and businesses. In addition to two banks and four hotels, it lists a dozen attorneys, four physicians, two dentists, two veterinary surgeons, and six publishing and printing firms. Businesses included dry goods and groceries, lumber merchants and livestock dealers, carpenters, coal dealers, blacksmiths, milliners, tailors, druggists, masons, barbers, livery stables, harness makers, photographers, and a "News and Book" store.

To what extent do the people of Osage in the late nineteenth century constitute the "ordinary" folk about whose reading we know so little? While it is true that almost all of the primary sources provide information about the reading of the wealthier members of the community and very little about what poorer people read, there is another sense in which all the people of Osage were nonelite. Even the most affluent citizens of Osage could not be described as more than "middle class." Compared with the wealthy social elites of the East Coast, the town's inhabitants were irredeemably rustic. The sons and daughters of successful merchants and professional men did not attend Ivy League schools. Local colleges, such as Cornell and Grinnell, were the height of educational ambition for most, while a scant handful of highfliers went to the University of Chicago. They bought their clothes in local shops, visited friends in neighboring towns, and spent their summer vacations camping nearby. A journey farther afield than Minnesota or Wisconsin was extremely unusual, while trips abroad were almost unheard of. In their lifestyle, the people of late nineteenth-century Osage were representative of a large but historically neglected group: inhabitants of small towns.

Did the public library succeed in attracting clientele away from the highly successful billiards rooms? Without a study of the users of billiards facilities, this question is unanswerable, but apparently Gertrude B.'s suggestion that library services at least be extended went unheeded, for three months later, another correspondent wrote to complain that the Sage Public Library still lacked basic amenities. In the March 16, 1893, issue of the *Mitchell County Press,* one library patron queried,

> Who are the members of the library committee? For two weeks or more the library has been so cold that it is an unpleasant task to go after a book, to

say nothing of trying to read. On inquiry, found that the librarian has no kindling, nothing but heavy wood and it is such big pieces that it required help to get them in the stove, and no poker, using the broom handle. Can not the room be opened more than one afternoon a week, and cannot the front stairs be kept free from lime? Those passing might think it summer by the cob-webs hanging filled with flies from the hall windows, but alas winter reigneth at least in the reading room.

Who were the people who braved the cold and the spiders to borrow books from the public library in Osage during the early 1890s? Were they bent on the self-improvement recommended by Gertrude B.? Were they seeking relief from the rigors and confinements of life in a small community in rural Iowa? What sort of lives were they seeking to enrich through reading? And what did they read? Did they check out mainly fiction or nonfiction, and if the latter, what were the topics of most interest? What sort of fiction were people reading? Did men and women prefer different sorts of fiction? Was children's reading clearly differentiated from that of adults?

While an extensive answer to these questions is beyond the scope of this chapter, some preliminary results illustrate a process whereby more complete answers can be provided through an analysis of library records combined with the manuscript schedules of the population census.

WHO WERE THEY?

The ideal census records for this study would have been the federal census of 1890. However, since the manuscript records for Mitchell County are among those which have been lost, the next best records available are the Iowa state censuses of 1885 and 1895.[5] The 1885 data include name, address, age in 1885, sex, color (i.e., race), marital status, occupation, place of birth, parentage (native- or foreign-born), eligibility to vote and for military service, and details of literacy—whether those over the age of ten could read but not write, or whether they could do neither. There is also a category called "Deaf and dumb, blind, insane or idiotic" (happy to say, mostly blank in the case of Osage). The number of Osage inhabitants recorded in 1885 is 1,848. The 1895 data include all of the above, with the important addition of "Religious Belief." In 1895 the census count stood at 2,448, an increase of 600, or roughly a third, during the decade 1885–95.

In constructing a profile of the inhabitants of Osage during 1890–95, I used both sets of census data separately, referred to as "1885 population" and "1895 population." I have also combined the census data sets to form a "pool" of inhabitants who occupied Osage during 1885–95, supplementing this with information from a city directory (1899) and two business publications (1890 and 1891), as well as church and school documents. I have included in the pool 169 library patrons who appear in library circulation records, but who are not included in either of the two censuses (see below). The combined pool from all sources contains a total of 3,779 persons.

The library circulation records for 1890–95 yield a group of 607 library users, all but 169 of whom appear in one or other of the two sets of census data (mentioned above). Generally, the only information I have about this group of 169 library patrons is whether they are male or female (inferred from first names or from the titles Mr., Mrs., or Miss)—and in the case of 19 patrons, not even that. Sometimes, however, information from other sources tells us a little more about members of this group; for example, from a locally written history of the Osage Baptist Church we can discover that Reverend C. J. Pope was its pastor in 1889–93.

Counting library patrons is one way of measuring patron use of the library. In this method, each patron counts equally, whether he or she was a onetime user of the library in the five-year period or a frequent visitor who checked out many books over several years. An alternative method of measuring use is to count the number of charges made and then make comparisons among users; for example, between males and females. For purposes of comparison with the group of general library users, I also decided to construct a subgroup labeled "Frequent Users." I assigned patrons to this group if they met one of two criteria: either they had checked out an average of thirty-five or more books a year for two or more years, or they had used the library for four out of the five years under consideration. This group contained 105 members.

Gender

Slightly over half the total pool (51.33 percent) was female. (In 1885, 49.51 percent had been female, but in 1895 the balance had shifted to 50.48 percent female.) This contrasts with the group of library patrons, of whom 384 (63.26 percent) were female. Women also accounted for about 68.35 percent of the charges, so not only were they more likely than men to use the library in the first place, but they were also likely to charge out more books than men readers. Among the frequent users, however, the discrepancy was not so great: 61.90 percent of this group were women.

Age

The population of Osage grew by over 30 percent between 1885 and 1895. In both 1885 and 1895, Osage was a town of young people. In 1885, 44 percent of the population was aged 20 years of age or younger, while 64 percent were 30 or younger. It was much the same story in 1895: over 40 percent were 20 or younger and nearly 60 percent were 30 or younger. At the other end of the age spectrum, 6.79 percent in 1885 and 9.43 percent in 1895 were over age 60. That left less than 33 percent of the population aged 31–60 in both 1885 and 1895.

The library patrons were also mostly under age 30. Of the 443 library users (72.98 percent) for whom we have information on age, 33.18 percent were aged 10–20, and a further 23.47 percent were 20–30. Thus, well over half the library users were under age 30. Figure 8.1 compares the distribution of age among the library users and the frequent users with that of the general population as measured by the 1895 census. A total of 1,939 people were potential library users in 1895 (meaning that they were aged 10 or over). About 20 percent of the potential library users was under age 20, but over 33 percent of the library users and over 36 percent of the frequent users fall into this age category.

Another way to show the disproportionate use of the library by the young is to compare the proportions of each age group that are library

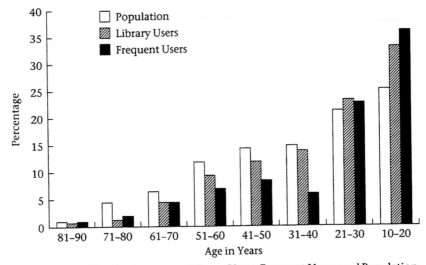

Figure 8.1. Age Distribution among Library Users, Frequent Users, and Population, 1895

users. Of all those aged 10–21 in 1895, 30 percent were library users, compared with lower percentages for all the other age groups. Excluding the elderly (those over age 71), who were much less likely to use the library, the proportions from the other age groups varied from about 17–25 percent.

While these quantitative data show that younger members of the community were more likely to use the library, it is important to note that elderly people were also users and, in some cases, heavy users. Three were in their eighties by 1890, and one of these, Artemus S. Hubbard, was a frequent user. Born in Vermont in 1808, by 1885 Hubbard was a widower living with a son, A. J. Hubbard, a carpenter and builder of windmills. Both father and son were considerable readers. Artemus used the library for each of the five years under consideration and, on average, checked out more than twenty-seven books a year. Five other patrons were in their seventies during this period, including two frequent users, Lorenzo D. Rice (born in Ohio in 1818) and Mary Warburton (born in England in 1817), both widowed. These older citizens made the effort to climb the lime-bespattered library stairs week after week, often braving the cold and ice of an Iowa winter, to select and charge out a new book or to renew an old one. Clearly, the library played an important part in their lives, something that might be overlooked by concentrating only on the averages.

Origins

Neither state census lists parents' country of origin and thus cannot be used to analyze the original nationality of second-generation immigrants. The use of surnames as a guide to ethnic origin is fraught with problems, especially for married women. Therefore, I have confined analysis of the regional origins of the people, whether native- or foreign-born, to first-generation immigrants.

Although race, in the broad sense of white or nonwhite, can be assessed directly from the census entries, it is not very relevant here, since the population of Iowa, then as now, was almost entirely white.[6] Two families were listed as "colored" in the 1885 census. One of them, the Burrs, had originated in Kentucky but were no longer living in Osage ten years later. The other family, the Martins, were included in both censuses. John Martin was born in Georgia in 1850, very possibly into slavery. His wife Julia, who was eleven years younger, had been born in Norway, and they had several children. John Martin was listed in 1885 as a farmer, but in 1895 his occupation had changed to laborer, which suggests either that the two categories were somewhat interchangeable, or that the family had fallen on hard times during the intervening decade. No members of the Burr or

Martin families appear in library records. All other Osage inhabitants were listed as white, despite the fact that the newspapers in the early 1890s occasionally mention Chinese owners of restaurants and laundries.

Not surprisingly, in 1885 and again in 1895, less than half the population had been born in Iowa, though the proportion had increased slightly by 1895 (45 percent as against 41 percent in 1885). Of the 1,109 Osage residents in 1895 who had been born in Iowa, only 303 (27 percent) were born before 1875 and even fewer (92, or 8 percent) were born before 1865. Some 72 percent of those aged thirty or under had been born in Iowa, while older members of the community had mostly come from elsewhere.

Among the native-born, the state of New York was the place of origin for the largest single group (371), with Wisconsin a relatively close second (331). No other state came near to these two. Illinois was next, with only 160, while 108 came from Vermont, 99 from Minnesota, 98 from Pennsylvania, and 97 from Ohio. Very few came from the South, although 13 were born in Kentucky, including such diverse inhabitants as the African-American Burrs, Nancy Nichols, wife of a prominent physician, and Louise Abernethy, wife of the Cedar Valley Seminary principal. The 1895 census includes a scattering of children born in Nebraska, Kansas, and the Dakotas, youngsters whose families had possibly continued the westward drift in the late 1880s, searching for cheaper and better farming opportunities, only to be driven back by the harshness of frontier conditions and the economic depression of the early 1890s. One child had the distinction of having been born in Los Angeles, another in Oregon.

Foreign immigration was of major political concern in the United States of the 1890s. While Osage contained a number of foreign-born inhabitants, none was from the group of southern and eastern European immigrants that aroused such nativist passions in the eastern United States. Indeed, the Osage Board of Trade sought to reassure potential investors: "There are settlements of Germans, Norwegians, Bohemians and Irish. These are enterprising, law-abiding people, the settlements having their church buildings in their respective neighborhoods."[7]

In fact, there were also large contingents of people from Great Britain and Canada living in Osage, but clearly they did not qualify for mention, possibly because their Anglophone Protestantism made them less visible (and perhaps less threatening) than immigrants from central or eastern Europe. About 13 percent of the total pool were foreign-born, about 40 percent of these being English-speaking (including 31 Irish). Scandinavians—some Danish, but mostly Norwegian and Swedish—formed the largest single group of non-English speaking immigrants: 203, or about 43 percent.

Another large group (75, or about 16 percent) came from Germany. There was a handful from Austria-Hungary, France, Italy, and Switzerland. One woman with an Anglophone name had been born in South America.

Did the foreign-born make use of the library facilities? On the whole, the answer is a definite "no." Since there were no foreign-language books or periodicals in the library collection at this time, language may explain why only one person of German origin and only six from Scandinavia (3 percent) used the library at all. On the other hand, only five from English-speaking Canada (7 percent), eight from Britain (9 percent), and none at all from Ireland were library users.

The lone patron of German origin, Mrs. Mary E. Starr, used the library a great deal, however. Born in 1833, Starr was a widow by 1895, living with her son James, a student. In 1890–95, she used the library constantly, charging out an astonishing annual average of forty-one books (including renewals) during each of the five years. One of the English-born readers was Mary Warburton, the elderly resident mentioned above. Another was Phebe Greenhalgh, a middle-aged woman married to a businessman; she checked out an average of thirty-five books per year over a three-year period. The two borrowers of Norwegian origin were Mr. and Mrs. Hovelson, probably John, a grain dealer, and his wife Jane. They had six children in 1895, one of whom was also a library user, while another worked as a teacher. Like other families in Osage, the Hovelsons were in the process of establishing a middle-class lifestyle; use of the library may have seemed to them an integral part of this effort.

Class

Class poses even more problems than ethnicity. It, too, is a category that cannot be drawn directly from the census, so I have had to infer class principally from three other criteria: (1) occupation, (2) whether or not a servant is living in the household, and (3) photographs of leading citizens included in a publication by the Osage Board of Trade that I used to assess the social standing of wealthier members of the community.

There are a number of problems with the use of occupation as a criterion, in part because the census data are hard both to read and to interpret. Difficulty in reading arises from the fact that, unfortunately, the manuscripts for 1895 were so tightly bound that much of the "Occupation" category was all but lost when the records were microfilmed. For most entries, only the last few letters are legible. In many places, enough of the entry is visible for a confident guess to be made—as when, for example, the entry reads " borer," or " eacher." Happily, the 1885 census presents no problems in this respect, and I have been able to supplement data from the two sets of censuses with information from city and business directories and from the two weekly newspapers, the *Osage News* and the *Mitchell County Press.*

There are further problems with interpretation. Women (especially if they are married) are rarely listed as having an occupation other than "Keeping House." This is used whether the woman employed servants or not, though clearly the activity is very different. The status of women is therefore almost always tied to that of their husbands or fathers. Neither do married women appear in the 1899 city directory. Even women such as Laura Eaton or Clarinda Hitchcock, who occupied major positions as leaders of local women's groups such as the Woman's Christian Temperance Union or, after 1895, sat on the library board, were unlisted in the directory. Of course, there were no photographs of women in the business publications of the Osage Board of Trade, although small businesses owned by women were listed in the 1891 publication.

Other problems stem from the difficulty of classifying occupations a hundred years after the fact. For example, the term "carpenter" may seem to denote a working-class occupation, until another source reveals that this particular carpenter was actually a building contractor with several employees. How does one classify occupations that no longer exist and for which we have little frame of reference, such as "teamster," "harness maker," "brick maker," and "section foreman"?[8] Another problem arises from the fact that although a household may employ several servants, if they do not "live in" they do not appear in the census as linked to a particular household.

This difficulty is partly a reflection of the fluid situation in late nineteenth-century Osage. What *is* possible, without ambiguity, is to define the poles of the class continuum. At one end is the middle class: successful lawyers, physicians, store owners, real estate agents, and bankers. At the other is the working class: laborers, teamsters, and domestic servants. In between are those whose class position is more ambiguous—the skilled craftworkers, many of whose occupations would become obsolete in the next two decades, as the automobile replaced the horse as a means of personal transport and as mass-produced and mass-distributed goods replaced locally produced goods.

I have constructed a loose typology of class, using five general categories. At one end of the spectrum is the middle class, labeled as groups 1 and 2. Group 1 consists of men and their families, plus one woman physician, who follow the traditional professions of law, medicine, and the church, those with live-in servants, and owners of large businesses. In group 2 are white-collar workers such as clerks, insurance agents, teachers, and owners of smaller businesses. In group 3 are the families of skilled manual workers such as blacksmiths, harness makers, masons, dressmakers, and milliners. Group 4 consists of the families of unskilled workers: laborers, teamsters, foundry workers, coopers, and domestic servants. Farmers pose an almost insuperable problem, since the occupation can cover such a variety of economic circumstances. Faced with this dilemma, I have placed farmers and their families in a totally separate category, group 5. While this means that farm families cannot be included in assessments of the class structure of Osage, it does have the advantage of identifying a group of those who perhaps lived a more rural lifestyle.

Figure 8.2 compares the distribution of the five groups in the population as a whole with that of the library user group. The proportion of inhabitants in group 1 is about 16 percent for the whole pool, whereas for the library group it is about 28 percent. Group 2 is also relatively overrepresented in the library user population—37 percent as opposed to 31 percent in the general population. Among the other three groups, library users are underrepresented, most strongly in the case of Group 4. About 15 percent of the general population consists of laborers, teamsters, or domestic servants and their families. Among the library user group, the proportion is 5 percent.

Religion

Along with gender and age, religious affiliation was recorded on 1895 census schedules and can be supplemented, in the case of a few individuals,

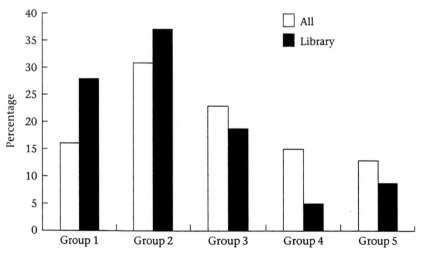

Figure 8.2. Social Groupings: Population and Library Users, 1895

by data from church documents and newspapers. While the 1895 state census lists the religious affiliation of most adults, that of children is generally unlisted, though the practice is far from uniform; on the whole, the column is left blank in the case of children under the age of about fifteen. One might be tempted to assume that the children follow the religion of their parents, and in most cases this is probably correct. However, there are enough examples of married couples listing different religions, and indeed of several members of the same family listing different religions, to suggest that this temptation should be resisted. The family of Hover Holvelson (a different Hovelson family than above) is a case in point. Hover, born in Norway, is listed as Lutheran. His wife Sarah, born in Wisconsin, is listed as Baptist. Three of their five children, however, all born in Iowa, chose to be Congregationalists (the remaining two children were very young in 1895). Similarly, in the Fessenten family, Eli is a Universalist and his wife, Harriet, a Congregationalist; one daughter, Lolo, is a Methodist while the other, Hattie, is a Baptist. The effect of this exclusion of children from the data on religious affiliation is to confine the information, on the whole, to the adult population. This restriction affects the comparison between the general population and the library users, since so many of the library users were young people aged ten to twenty.

While members of the same family might differ as to denomination, there are few differences within families, and indeed within the population as a whole, as to broader allegiance. Apart from one Jewish family, one Spiritualist individual family, and those who responded "None" to the religion question, the population of Osage was entirely Christian. Within the Christian group, the biggest division was between Protestants and Roman Catholics. Five cases existed where one spouse was Protestant, the other Catholic.

There is quite a variety of denominations listed, including Christadelphian, Adventist, Restitutionist, Episcopalian, Quaker, and Unitarian. Most people, however, belonged to one of the major denominations that had built a church and supported a clergyman: Baptist, Congregationalist, Methodist, Roman Catholic, and Universalist. There was also a sizable community of Lutherans, who in 1895 were in the process of buying land to build a church. Figure 8.3 shows the distribution of the major denominations among the general population, compared with the distribution among library users.

As the figure shows, among the general population, Methodists, Congregationalists, and Baptists were most numerous, although nearly 10 percent of the population were Catholics and Lutherans and over 6 per-

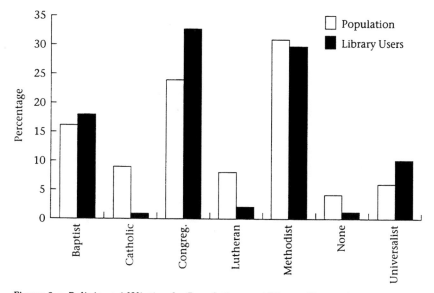

Figure 8.3. Religious Affiliation by Population and Library Users, 1895

cent were Universalists. Congregationalists are not only the largest single denomination among the library users but are disproportionately represented by comparison with the whole population: 33 percent, as opposed to only 24 percent of Osage inhabitants in general. On the other hand, Catholics and Lutherans were considerably underrepresented in the library user group. Of ninety-five Catholics living in Osage in 1895, only two were library users, and one of these, Ella M. Johnson, was married to a Lutheran. Language difficulties can probably be ruled out at as a reason: only eleven Catholics (15 percent of the total) were born in non-English-speaking countries. Twenty were born in Ireland, four in Canada or England, and all the rest (52 percent) were native-born Americans—thirty-two of them (44 percent) from Iowa. Neither can class entirely account for the lack of library use by Catholics. As figure 8.4 indicates, the proportion of Catholics in the middle-class groups 1 and 2 was fairly close to that of Catholics in the population as a whole. There was not an overwhelming preponderance of Catholics in working-class occupations, although they are certainly overrepresented in group 4.

Catholics undoubtedly felt themselves excluded from the Osage establishment, of which Sage Public Library, with its origins in the Protestant-defined and -dominated past, was clearly a part. Up to this point in the town's history, no Catholics had sat on the city council or (therefore) served

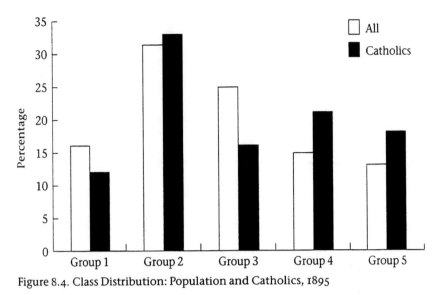

Figure 8.4. Class Distribution: Population and Catholics, 1895

on the council's library committee. Nor were any of librarians Catholic. Catholics may not have been formally shut out of the Sage Public Library, but at this juncture they only participated at the margins of the dominant culture that produced the library—either in its control or its use.

Another possible explanation for the lack of library use by Catholics may lie in the authoritarian position of the Roman Catholic Church with respect to reading. What Catholics might or might not read was carefully controlled by the church hierarchy. Whereas for Protestants the Sage Library represented a place of moral safety (especially when compared to billiard halls), among Catholics, the Protestant-controlled public library may have been viewed as a place of moral danger.[9]

The explanation for relative lack of use of the library by Lutherans is probably more straightforward. Seven Lutherans were library users, of whom four were born in Iowa. However, of the 138 Lutherans living in Osage in 1895, 109 (79 percent) were born in non-English-speaking countries. Thus, language was probably more of a barrier for Lutherans as a group than it was for Catholics. There were also fewer middle-class Lutherans living in Osage at this time.

Lutherans were much more likely to work as skilled craftworkers or unskilled laborers than the rest of the population (fig. 8.5). Of the 28 people (all women) listed as domestic servants in the 1895 census, 15 (54 percent) were Lutherans. The underlying factor here is undoubtedly immigrant status. More than any other religious group, Lutherans were associated with a particular ethnic origin: they were overwhelmingly Scandinavian and to a lesser extent German. As recent immigrants, largely from rural backgrounds, they were at the bottom of the social and occupational heap. A few individuals, such as John H. Johnson (American Express agent in 1891, treasurer of the Osage School Board throughout the later 1890s, and president of the Farmers' National Bank by 1899), succeeded in breaking into the elite group of Anglophone males, most of whom were of New England or New York origins and had affiliations with other mainstream Protestant churches. Another prominent Scandinavian, Otto Rundborg, a dry goods dealer, had joined an established mainstream church (Methodist). The majority of Scandinavian immigrants in the 1890s, however, were just beginning to feel their way around the power structure of Osage society. Buying a plot of land and building an institution all their own—a Lutheran church—was just a beginning.

CLASS AND THE LIBRARY

For the most part, Osage was a community of the middle class, including professionals, merchants and other white-collar workers, and skilled artisans whose collective task was to service the needs of the producers living in the surrounding countryside. However, since "class" is a relational concept, not a series of static categories, evidence of class emerges not simply from a study of the census data but also, and perhaps more effective-

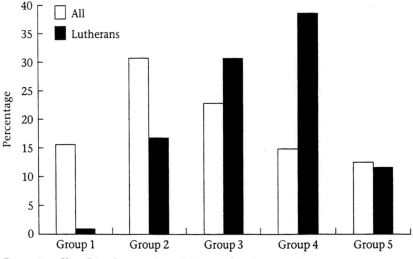

Figure 8.5. Class Distribution: Population and Lutherans, 1895

ly, from a picture of people's activities. That is, I am less interested in classifying Osage residents according to a rigid structural scheme than in uncovering how the dynamics of class formation and reproduction played out in people's daily lives, by investigating who was, and was not, included in the institution-building activities of the dominant group. One of these institutions was the public library.

In 1890–95, the library was still controlled by a subcommittee of the Osage City Council, which was, of course, a group of men elected by men. In 1894, a new state law permitted the establishment of library boards separate from, although still elected by, city councils. In 1895, a nine-member Osage Board of Library Trustees was elected by the city council; it included four women and five men. In the early 1890s, the unreformed library committee still consisted of three members of the eight-member city council, who proposed measures concerning the library for a vote by the council as a whole.

Generally speaking, the members of the library committee and the city council were not library users. Of nineteen men who served on the council between 1890 and 1895, only five checked out library books. The most frequent user was Charles H. Bacon, who used the library over a two-year period (1893–95), checking out a total of fifty-seven books. John Haight, a tinsmith born in England, used the library once. John Davis, a blacksmith, also of English birth, checked out thirty-nine books in the library year 1890–91. W. H. H. Gable, a physician who checked out ten books in 1890, served repeatedly on the city council, though not on the library committee. But Gable was clearly a friend to the library. In 1891, the library committee reported that "there is a special and urgent need of improving and replenishing the City Library by the rebinding or replacing of a large number of books which have become unfit by constant use for further reading, and by the purchase of new volumes for the use of the people of Osage, especially the young people who desire to avail themselves of the privileges of a good library." The committee voted four to three to authorize three hundred dollars for the purpose. Gable then proposed increasing the sum to a thousand dollars. His motion lost on a vote of three to four, the library committee voting with the nays.[10]

While the men who controlled the public library tended not to be library patrons, the same is not true of their wives and children. Colonel Alonzo Abernethy's teenaged children, Clara and Herbert, were frequent users, as were John C. Davis's son, Louie, and daughter, Dottie. Eleven out of the nineteen councilmen had wives or children who used the library to some extent.

The city council employed a librarian at a monthly salary of four dollars. The librarian's job was to open the library one-half day a week (on Saturdays) and to take charge of the circulation and accessions records. The election of the librarian was highly politicized and, on occasion, the subject of repeated balloting. The librarian was always female, usually young (in her twenties), single, and a member of the middle class (groups 1 or 2). She had no other formal employment, and as four dollars a month was not enough for self-support, even in the 1890s, she had to rely on someone else—usually her father—for her living expenses. Her position was also formally powerless; it was not she but the city council who decided what books to purchase. Thus, although the city council members themselves were often not patrons of the public library, they controlled not only the sums to be spent but also what books should be made available for the residents of Osage to read.

I have found little evidence of the book selection process. Selection guides for libraries were not common in this period; the first American Library Association guide was not published until 1893.[11] An earlier guide by Frederic Beecher Perkins, first published in 1876, came out in several subsequent editions, including one in 1886, and classified titles according to literary merit.[12] There is no mention of these or other guides having been purchased for use in Osage, but the 1876 subscription library collection did include Charles H. Moore's *What to Read and How to Read*. Moore aimed his 152-page volume at "the inexperienced reader to direct and shape his studies amid the immense mass of literature now before the public."[13] The Osage library committee may have also relied upon reviews in journals or more informal methods such as simply asking wives, offspring, or friends for advice. An 1896 book committee report to the library board suggests that the committee may have used mail order catalogs as a selection guide: "Your subcomittee would respectfully report that they have made lists of books and obtained prices from: American Baptist Society, Montgomery Ward, A. C. McClurg & Co."[14] By whatever means the books were selected, the collection in the early 1890s consisted of about sixteen hundred volumes, mostly fiction, biography, history, poetry, religious works, and self-help.

LIBRARY RECORDS

Toward the end of the nineteenth century, with the spread of bureaucratic practices, it became standard practice for American public librarians to record in an accessions book the bibliographic data on every title acquired by the library. At the same time, circulation records were also being standardized through the use of registers on which was recorded such information as patron's name, book identification number, and borrowing date. In the 1890s the Sage Library started to buy record books for recording both circulation and accessions from Library Bureau, a Boston company that supplied library furniture and materials.

The circulation book was purchased first. In the 1880s, circulation had been recorded in a series of notebooks, such as might have been used by schoolchildren. The librarian recorded the patron's name, number of the book borrowed, and date on which the book was charged out. Beginning in 1890, she entered the same information in the new ledger but in a much more organized fashion. Now she allocated a double-page spread to each letter of the alphabet, so that, for instance, all the patrons whose names began with "A" were entered on the same page. Across the top of the page were printed the weeks of the year (numbered 1 to 52); a rubric informs us that the "library year" began on April 1. Book numbers were entered in the columns under each week. An entire year's borrowing record for an individual patron appeared therefore on a single page.

The first entries in the new circulation record were made in the first week of April 1890. The librarian continued to make entries in this book until March 1896, that is, the end of the library year 1895–96, when a new circulation system was adopted. Minutes of library board meetings show that in February 1896 the board agreed to order 1,000 charging cards, borrower cards, and Acme pockets from the Library Bureau. Once the library adopted the new system in April 1896, library records immediately (and unfortunately) became more ephemeral. The librarian entered books' names on a card that stayed in a pocket pasted in the book while it was on the shelf. When the book was charged out, the borrower's name was entered on the card and the card would be kept at the circulation desk until the book was returned. The cards would therefore record a list of names of borrowers of that particular book. After a card was filled, it was discarded and a new one inserted in the pocket. There is no indication that the librarian retained these cards. In all probability, they were thrown away at once. There is just a small window of time, therefore, during which the circulation records are available for analysis.

The first purpose-made accessions book that survives (and there is no record of an earlier book having been bought) dates from 1893. The accessions ledger was also bought from the Library Bureau and it too contains a two-page spread for each entry. Each page is organized with the accessions number printed on the extreme left. Columns to the right provide space for author's name(s), book title, assigned book number, class number, publisher, and so on. The librarian's first task when a new book arrived was to enter it into the existing collection. She did this in approximately alphabetical order by title, so that the first two thousand or so records show the collection as it existed in 1893. After these books were entered, the librarian entered new books in accession order.

The key to creating book-borrowing profiles for individual patrons is the "book number." It is not clear on what basis the librarians of the 1880s and early 1890s assigned these numbers, but it is likely that these too represent an early accession order. In any case, the book number is the basis of the borrowing system, since it is the book number entered against the patron's name in the circulation register. Two problems emerged with respect to the book numbers. The first might be described as the "Case of the Missing Book Numbers." As systematic circulation records were begun in 1890 and accessions records in 1893, there is a gap of three years before the two sets of records begin to overlap, which means that some of the book numbers entered in patrons' circulation records have no counterpart in the accession records. A second problem arises from the fact that sometimes the librarian assigned the same book number to two books, or even to three or four—probably a clerical error since there seems to be no relationship between titles with the same book number. This affects as many as 135 of a total of 1,608 borrowable titles, or about 8 percent of the collection in 1893.

These two difficulties reduce the proportion of analyzable charges to about 68 percent of the total. This is serious, but not devastating, in view of the fact that there are approximately 19,000 charges in the database, of which about 13,000 can be related to their specific titles. After all, even 68 percent of the borrowing profile seems a reasonable "response rate." It should be borne in mind, however, that the profiles only allow us to draw conclusions about what we know patrons charged out, not about what was apparently missing. The absence of a best-selling title from the 1893 accessions register does not mean that it had not previously been part of the Sage collection; it may have been withdrawn before 1893. Also, titles that did appear in the accessions register, but that shared a book number with one or more other titles, have had to be discounted in the analysis.

Since the 1893 accessions records are organized in alphabetical order by title, not by book number, the two sources of records (accessions and circulation) can only feasibly be connected by using a computerized relational database. I have created two electronic files based on library data. The first contains information about the books, such as author, title, book number, class number if known, and odd pieces of information such as pseudonyms, whether the book is a duplicate, queries about the title, and so on, in a memo field. The second contains information about circulation: patron name, book number, and charge date. The common field is the book number. I have used the census data to compile a third file containing information about individuals. This allows me to combine all three files (using the "name" field as the common field relating the third file to the circulation file), so that I can look for borrowing patterns based on such variables as gender, age, religion, and so on.

A file of 13,000 charges contains a huge amount of data, and so far I have only begun to scratch the surface. However, some preliminary findings have emerged that relate reading preferences to gender, age, class, and religious affiliation.

WHAT DID PEOPLE READ?

The single unadorned answer to this question is fiction. The library users of Osage almost without exception concentrated their reading on novels. This is not to say that they did not also read history, biography, and inspirational writing, but fiction was the main choice for most of the men and women of all ages and classes, most of the time.[15]

Table 8.1 shows the most popular titles, measured by number of charges, in 1890–95. Of the sixteen titles listed, all but three (Froude, *History of England;* Talmadge, *Series of Sermons;* and J. S. C. Abbott, *History of Napoleon Bonaparte*) are novels. Several were best sellers or near best sellers, though not many are familiar titles today.[16] *Ben Hur* was a best seller in 1880, but *Airy, Fairy Lilian* was a "better seller" in 1879. *Faith Gartney's Girlhood* had been a best seller as early as 1863, but it was still being read avidly in Osage twenty years later. Several of the other titles were by authors who had attained best or better seller status for other books, such as E. P. Roe (*Barriers Burned Away* [1872] and *Driven Back to Eden* [1885]) and Susan Warner (*The Wide, Wide World* [1850] and *Queechy* [1852]).

According to Michael Denning, Bertha M. Clay was a pseudonym, first for titles pirated from England and supposedly by an author called Charlotte M. Brame, but then carried on by the publishing house Street and Smith, long after Brame herself had died in 1884. The men who wrote under Clay's name were house novelists who succeeded in imitating what was supposed to be a "feminine style."[17]

These were the only two Clay titles in the Sage Public Library collection, but they were clearly very popular, although they were far from the

Table 8.1. Popular Titles, 1890–95

Title (Author)	Number of Charges
An Original Belle (E. P. Roe)	92
Airy, Fairy Lilian (Duchess)	90
For Another's Sin (Bertha M. Clay)	90
History of England (James Froude)	90
A Brave Lady (Miss Mulock)	87
Ben Hur (Lew Wallace)	79
Series of Sermons, vol. 1 (Thomas Talmadge)	79
A Broken Wedding Ring (Bertha M. Clay)	74
Daniel Deronda (George Eliot)	65
His Own Master (J. T. Trowbridge)	64
Sights and Insights (A. D. T. Whitney)	64
History of Napoleon Bonaparte (J. S. C. Abbott)	63
The Virginians (W. Thackeray)	61
Diana (Susan Warner)	60
Faith Gartney's Girlhood (A. D. T. Whitney)	60
The Letter of Credit (Susan Warner)	60

sort of book that was recommended by Frederic Beecher Perkins and the *Catalog of "A.L.A" Library.* Denning points out that stories by Clay and the Duchess were often ridiculed by "advocates of reform stressing the sensational and immoral character of working-class reading," and he cites the critical judgment of observers such as Walter Wyckoff who came across an Irish logger "on a rainy day, 'reading a worn copy of one of the Duchess's novels, which is the only book I have so far seen in camp.'"[18]

The middle class may have criticized the working classes for reading dime novels by the Duchess and Clay, but workers were by no means the only "guilty" parties. In Osage, about 65 percent of Clay's readers were middle class (from groups 1 and 2), and another 23 percent came from the skilled craftworker class (group 3). Only 2 percent of the readers came from the working-class group 4, while 10 percent came from farm families. The 82 readers of the Duchess show a roughly similar class distribution: 32 (61 percent) were from the middle class (23 percent from group 1, 38 percent from group 2); another 12 (23 percent) were from group 3; 6 (11 percent) from group 4; and 3 (6 percent) from group 5.[19] These numbers are too small for general conclusions to be drawn, but they do suggest a substantial middle-class readership for the cheap fiction denigrated by the proponents of "self-improvement."

The readers of both authors were predominantly female—85 percent in the case of the Duchess, 73 percent for Clay—but not entirely so. Clay's male readers included the octogenarian Artemus S. Hubbard, John D.

Wing (an insurance agent in his late fifties), John C. Davis (a blacksmith in his forties who was a sometime member of the city council), and Frank Bronson (also in his forties and clerk of the court). Nor were the readers entirely from the younger age groups: 23 percent of Clay's readers were over forty by 1890 and about half of those were over fifty.

At the other end of the cultural spectrum, ninety library patrons checked out one or more volumes from the twelve-volume set of James A. Froude's *History of England*. (The first charge was not until February 1894, which suggests that it had only just been acquired.) During 1894 there were sixty-six charges of volumes from this set and a further thirty-four charges in the first three months of 1895, which is as far as the database records go. The readers were mostly women (66 percent) and mostly from the middle class (72 percent from groups 1 and 2). Thirteen readers (16 percent) were from group 3, four (5 percent) from group 4, and five (6 percent) from the farming group. Two-thirds of the readers were older teenagers (born in or after 1875), the youngest being thirteen-year-old Max Katz, who charged out two volumes in March 1894 and another three in March 1895, renewing one of them once. Were the young people using the books for their school work? Very possibly they were, except that ten (29 percent) of thirty-five charges by young people occurred during the summer months of July and August 1894, when school was closed. Among the older readers were the Norwegian-born Mrs. Hovelson, the Catholic Anne Sheehan, the fifty-five-year-old farmer Byron Benedict, and the women's leader Clarinda Hitchcock as well as her daughter Augusta.

Another way of looking at what people chose to read is to look at the popularity of authors as opposed to single titles (table 8.2). Some authors had written a number of books, but no single title stood near the top of the popular title list. Who were the readers of books by the pseudonymous Miss Mulock (Mrs. Dinah Craik), the British author of such best sellers as *John Halifax, Gentleman* (1856) and *The Ogilvies* (1849)? Pansy (the pseudonym of Isabella Alden) wrote stories with a Christian message for young people. Were they read only, or even mainly, by the young?

Readers of Miss Mulock, whose books are generally classed as domestic fiction (and therefore targeted at women readers), came from all age groups. Some 37 percent were over age 40, but another 41 percent were teenagers. Moreover, 37 percent of the teenagers (15 percent of the total) were boys. Miss Mulock was much less popular with young men in their twenties, however. Of the 100 readers (28 percent of the total) aged 21–30 in 1895, only 15 percent were male. There were nineteen titles by Miss Mulock in the Sage Library, one of which has to be discarded since it was

Table 8.2. Popular Authors, 1890–95

Author	Number of Charges
Miss Mulock	538[a]
Pansy	525[a]
E. P. Roe	416[a]
W. Wilkie Collins	399
A. D. T. Whitney	379
Susan Warner	323
E. Kellogg	297[a]
Harriet B. Stowe	292[a]
Oliver Optic	282
Sophie May	223[a]

a. These numbers probably understate the actual number of charges; some titles by these authors have been affected by the "multiple book number problem" and therefore were omitted from the calculations.

affected by the multiple book number problem. It was common for patrons to read as many as four of these books. Ella M. Johnson (Catholic, twenties, married to a clothing merchant but with, as yet, no children) read the largest number: eight. Several other young women read six or seven. A couple of men—Frank O. Bronson (the clerk of court mentioned above) and William F. Hunt (twenties, son of a stonemason and listed, unusually, as a "student")—each read five.

There were thirty-three titles by Pansy in the collection, although five of these were affected by book number problem. Of the remaining twenty-eight, two women each read thirteen: Ruby Hoag (Methodist, later thirties, married but childless) and Kittie Kathan (Congregationalist, early twenties, unmarried, daughter of a successful horse trainer, and the library user group reader who checked out the most books). Charles H. Bacon (Baptist, early fifties, city council member) read eleven titles, and Ella G. Benedict (Baptist, early forties, matron of the Cedar Valley Seminary, unmarried) read ten. Pansy had a wide readership, despite her stated aim of bringing a Christian message to the young. While 31 percent of the readers were in the under 20 age bracket, 29 percent were over 40 and 5 percent were over 60. Women were the great majority—over 81 percent. Most readers were also middle-class (25 percent from group 1; 48 percent from group 2). However, a great many people with relatively diverse characteristics read one or more titles, including Max Katz (Jewish, teenaged, son of a cold-storage proprietor), Dr. W. H. H. Gable (Methodist, physician, late forties), Alvin B. Bisbee (a Methodist farmer, sixties, read seven Pansy titles), Lelia O. Goldsworthy (Baptist, thirties, Osage's only woman physician), and Erika Anderson (Lutheran, late thirties, Swedish-born wife of a laborer).

This diversity vanishes when one concentrates only on the stereotypical (and largely conjectural) picture of Pansy's readers as young, middle-class females. Although accurate, as far as it goes, such a picture lacks the details that bring to life the reading practices of the Osage inhabitants.

CONCLUSION

These tentative explorations of the library collections and the demographics of Osage, Iowa, are still too fragmentary to permit any general conclusions about Americans' reading habits at the turn of the century. These findings are, so to speak, test borings. But, if nothing else, they suggest that we should carefully reexamine, and perhaps revise, our conjectures about what sort of books were selected for reading by women, by the young, and by working people at any given time and place. The analysis of the library records and census data reveals that specific groups of people used the library most: women, members of British-origin Protestant churches, the young, and the middle class in general. The Sage Public Library was a place where, on a Saturday afternoon and evening at any time of the year, young women in particular could expect to encounter their relatives, friends, and acquaintances. However, the library user population was not entirely homogeneous. Some male, elderly, and less wealthy people also made extensive use of the library. The records suggest that the library played an important part in their lives, which could be overlooked by concentrating only on the average categories of library users. Those who did not fit the majority profile were the elderly Artemus S. Hubbard, Lorenzo Rice, and Mary Warburton, middle-aged men such as Clerk of the Court Frank Bronson, the working-class Benjamin W. Johnson, the Catholic Anne Sheehan, and immigrants such as German-born Mary E. Starr. The place of reading in the lives of these "anomalous" patrons challenges the view of the library as the site of middle-class Protestant domination. While this domination undoubtedly existed, it was far from complete, and it is through these interstices that we can glimpse the operation of individual choice and action.

The analysis of patrons' choices shows that although the cultural authorities' rhetoric supported an educative, high-culture role for the public library, the Sage Library users generally ignored this advice. Osage readers were thoroughly exposed to an ideology of self-improvement through reading, but they possibly did not recognize the discrepancy between their own choices and the recommendations of "experts." Perhaps they assumed that books by the Duchess and Bertha M. Clay were acceptable not only in Osage but also in urban cultural centers throughout the nation. After all, the heroes and heroines of the most frequently charged romances were usually wealthy, titled Anglophones, thus confirming their readers' understanding of what it meant to be part of the dominant culture. Moreover, although the public library was a potential source of diverse reading matter, within the reader group, differences between men and women and between people of different ages and from different class backgrounds tended to fade. Most of the Sage Public Library users were fairly eclectic in their reading, suggesting that they tended not to draw the same distinctions between different types of books that we do today. A patron might read a relatively "high" culture novel such as *Daniel Deronda* and the following week check out a "low" culture book such as *Airy, Fairy Lilian*. Male readers chose much the same books as female readers. Books for children, such as those by Pansy and Oliver Optic, were also read by adults. Books that the moral improvement advocates would certainly have considered "detrimental" (to use Perkins's expression), such as those by Clay, were popular with those who also read books with a Christian message, such as Thomas Talmadge's sermons and Pansy's books.[20]

The main point of this essay is not, however, to draw specific and detailed conclusions about readership and reading in a small midwestern city a century ago. Instead, the examples should be taken as illustrations of what can be done with a relational database created from library records and census schedules. In addition to providing details on patrons and their reading choices, the database is also a source of information about the collection, itself an expression of what those in control of library spending believed should be made available for the reading public. The questions multiply endlessly. How much of the collection circulated? Which books never left the shelves? What was the balance between fiction and nonfiction? What sort of nonfiction was collected?

Researchers may also seek answers to questions about book publishing and distribution in the United States. Which publishers were represented in the collection? How long did it take a best-selling book to arrive in the collection? What regional patterns emerge from an analysis of their place of publication?

The records of the Osage library, like the records of the various layers of class, status, and government that encompassed the town and its people—to say nothing of the analogous records of other such communities—hold tremendous potential for extracting detailed empirical answers to many of the questions currently being posed by historians of the book. Indeed, such records hold so much potential that it is hard to understand why this source of primary data has been neglected for so long.

NOTES

1. Christine Pawley, "Reading on the Middle Border: The Culture of Print in Osage, Iowa, 1870 to 1900" (Ph.D. diss., University of Wisconsin, Madison, 1996).

2. This is the first study attempted for a public library; while many claims have been made about the differences in, say, men's and women's reading practices, until now there has been little evidence to support or reject these assumptions, at least for small-town Americans at the end of the nineteenth century. My dissertation (ibid.), of which this essay is a part, also utilizes several other primary sources, including newspapers, a city directory, business directories, and church records. I have used some information from these sources to supplement findings described in this essay.

3. Leona Montag, *Mitchell County History* (Dallas: Curtis Media, 1989), 45.

4. Osage Board of Trade, *Resources and Advantages: Mitchell County, Iowa* (Osage, Iowa, 1891).

5. Many of the manuscript schedules of the 1890 federal population census were destroyed by a fire in 1896. See Carroll D. Wright, *The History and Growth of the United States Census* (Washington, D.C.: Government Printing Office, 1900).

6. Similarly, the literacy categories of the census are largely redundant: the Osage population appears to have been overwhelmingly literate.

7. Osage Board of Trade, *Resources and Advantages: Mitchell County, Iowa* (Osage, Iowa, 1891).

8. Two publications by the U.S. Census Bureau are of help here. In Part 2 of the printed population schedule of the 1890 census is a section (xciv–xcix) that shows how uses of certain occupational categories by previous census were standardized for use in the 1890 census. The second document is a book by the statistician Alba B. Edwards, *A Socio-Economic Grouping of the Gainful Workers of the United States* (Washington, D.C.: U.S. Department of Commerce, 1938). Although the time period is considerably later, and many of the occupational categories are inappropriate in the context of the 1890s, the classification scheme was constructed in order to make a comparison between the results of the 1930 census with the censuses of 1910 and 1920. This brings the time frame a little closer to my period of interest.

9. For Protestants, print and reading were an integral part not only of their cosmology but also of the process of establishing their churches in Osage. For Roman Catholics, on the other hand, the relationship of their church to print was more uneasy. In the Protestant tradition, literacy was a guarantor of religious purity and loyalty, and the written word was a powerful symbol of Protestant theological superiority. However, even in late nineteenth-century America, individual Catholics' reading was carefully controlled, not so much by the indirect moral exhortations of the establishment as by more direct efforts of the church hierarchy, through the production of approved literature that was often sealed by archdiocesan imprimatur. See Natalie Zemon Davis, "Printing and the People," in *Rethinking Popular*

Culture: Contemporary Perspectives in Cultural Studies, ed. Chandra Mukerji and Michael Schudson (Berkeley: University of California Press, 1991), 65–96, for the Roman Catholic Church's response to the challenge of print at the time of the Reformation. See also the discussion in David Vincent, *Literacy and Popular Culture: England, 1750–1914* (Cambridge: Cambridge University Press, 1989), 5–6.

10. Osage City Council, minutes, Oct. 15, 1891, Archives, City Hall, Osage, Iowa.

11. *Catalog of "A.L.A." Library: 5,000 Volumes for a Popular Library* (Washington, D.C.: U.S. Bureau of Education, 1893).

12. Frederic Beecher Perkins, *The Best Reading: Hints on the Selection of Books; on the Formation of Libraries, Public and Private; on the Courses of Reading, Etc.* (New York: Putnam, 1886).

13. Charles H. Moore, *What to Read and How to Read, Being Classified Lists of Choice Reading, with Appropriate Hints and Remarks* (New York: D. Appleton, 1871), 9.

14. The committee decided to place an order with McClurg and Company of Chicago and were still ordering from this supplier the following year. Sage Library Board, minutes, Nov. 2, 1896, and Nov. 15, 1897, Archives, Sage Public Library, Osage, Iowa.

15. I am making the assumption that people read what they checked out. My larger study contains arguments that I believe validate this assumption but for which there is not space here. However, it is a common assumption of those who study publishers' sales figures and other sources of information on reading practices that purchasing a book is at least a fair indicator of reading it.

16. For a definition of the criteria for best seller or "better seller," see Frank Luther Mott, *Golden Multitudes: The Story of Best Sellers in the United States* (New York: Macmillan, 1947), 303, 315.

17. Michael Denning, *Mechanic Accents: Dime Novels and Working-Class Culture in America* (London and New York: Verso, 1987), 23–24. See also Mary Noel, *Villains Galore: The Heyday of the Popular Story Weekly* (New York: Macmillan, 1954), 186–90. The two titles in the Sage Public Library were from Bertha M. Clay's earlier period. Originally published in England, they are catalogued by the British Library under the pseudonym Charlotte M. Brame.

18. Walter A. Wyckoff, *The Workers: An Experiment in Reality: The East* (New York: Charles Scribner's Sons, 1898), quoted in Denning, *Mechanic Accents,* 33.

19. Charges must be distinguished from readers here. *Airy, Fairy Lilian* was charged out ninety times, but this figure includes renewals, thus reducing the number of individual readers. However, patterns of family use show that close relatives often visited the library together. Although only two library cards were issued to each household, undoubtedly books brought home were shared among family members before being returned the following week.

20. In his selection guide, Perkins included a group of books that he considered "less desirable, but which may, in most cases, be added without detriment, to an extended collection of fiction" (*Best Reading,* 105). Books by Clay and the Duchess were not included in this selection.

PART 3

Constructed Events:
Reexamination through Different Lenses

9   Unknown and Unsung: Contested Meanings of the *Titanic* Disaster

STEVEN BIEL

The *Titanic* disaster, the subject of hundreds of books, is the stuff of what academic historians sometimes refer to, condescendingly, as "popular history," in which complex processes are ignored in favor of antiquarian stories or are reduced to single dramatic moments. Academic historians are uncomfortable with unselfconscious narrative, with arguments that seem insignificant, or with arguments that seem too bold. A statement such as Walter Lord's—"The *Titanic* more than any other single event marks the end of the old days, and the beginning of a new, uneasy era"—makes us squirm. The disaster actually changed very little except shipping regulations. It did not, as Wyn Craig Wade has written, produce a "loss of innocence" and replace American certainty with doubt. Nor was it "the birth cry of a growing animosity" between Great Britain and Germany. Despite Charles Pellegrino's suggestion, the *Titanic* wireless operator's snub of his counterpart on the *Frankfurt* had nothing to do with the coming of World War I.[1] Any search for the social effects of the disaster is bound to yield facile generalizations and tenuous connections.

But the importance of an event does not reside solely in its effects; we need not treat the *Titanic* disaster as the "end of an epoch" to recognize that it did, in fact, have cultural significance. It was, as Lord and others have noted—but as professional historians have not—an event of deep and wide resonance in Progressive Era America. Besides shock and grief, the disaster produced a contest over meaning that connected the sinking of an ocean liner on calm seas in April 1912 with some of the most important and troubling problems, tensions, and conflicts of the day. If it was not a transformative event, it was nonetheless a highly dramatic moment—a kind of "social drama" in which conflicts were played out and American culture, in effect, thought out loud about itself.[2] Whatever "timeless" messages the disaster may convey about heroism or cowardice, about complacency or technological hubris, it tells us a great deal about the workings of American culture in the Progressive Era.

At the center of the contest over the disaster's meanings was a conventional narrative that emerged in the commercial press, genteel magazines, poems, popular songs, pictures, eulogies by public officials, sermons by mainstream religious leaders, and efforts to build memorials to those lost on the *Titanic*. I use the term "conventional" to describe an interpretive framework that affirmed existing power relations—that made sense of the disaster according to dominant conceptions of gender, class, ethnicity, and race. I also call it conventional because it was pervasive, defying clear-cut divisions between conservatives and reformers, between high and low cultures, between staid and sensational reporting, between sections and regions of the country. It was a collective work of interpretation (though the interpreters often claimed to tell only the truth), constructed and re-inforced in the days, weeks, and months after the wreck by people who consciously or unconsciously needed to understand and represent a shocking event in familiar and comfortable terms.[3]

Briefly summarized, this conventional narrative was centered around a myth of the heroism of the first-cabin male passengers—a myth based on reports that women and children had survived in much greater numbers than men. According to this myth, wealthy and successful men willingly gave up their lives so that their weaker charges might live. Repeated celebrations of their chivalry and Christian sacrifice reinforced conservative views of gender and class relations in which both women and workers were best served by accepting the authority and protection of paternalistic elites. The myth emphasized natural and immutable gender differences while it denied class differences. Meanwhile, any incidents of panic were attributed to "crazed" or "frenzied" immigrants and stokers. The first-cabin men and the ship's British officers were credited with preserving order when chaos threatened. Chivalry was often described as an exclusively "Anglo-Saxon" virtue. Probably the most succinct version of this narrative is a wire service report that appeared in papers across the country on April 17—two days before any reliable information, except for lists of survivors, had reached shore. The report declared,

> The picture that invariably presents itself, in view of what is known . . . is of men like John Jacob Astor, master of scores of millions; Benjamin Guggenheim of the famous family of bankers; Isidor Straus, a merchant prince; William T. Stead, veteran journalist; Major Archibald W. Butt, soldier; Washington Roebling, noted engineer—of any or all of these men

stepping aside, bravely, gallantly remaining to die that the place he otherwise might have filled could perhaps be taken by some sabot-shod, shawl-enshrouded, illiterate and penniless peasant woman of Europe.[4]

If the conventional narrative met the expectations of most Americans, it did not meet the expectations of all. Marginalized people and oppositional groups responded differently, drew their own implications from the *Titanic* story, and constructed alternative narratives of their own. I want to explore three sets of counterresponses to the disaster—the reactions of feminists, African Americans, and labor radicals.

It is not hard to imagine how the *Titanic's* gender lessons readily lent themselves to a more specific political stance, namely, opposition to women's suffrage. The *St. Louis Post-Dispatch* made the point in verse:

"Votes for women!"
Was the cry,
Reaching upward
To the sky.
Crashing glass,
And flashing eye—
"Votes for women!
Was the cry.

"Boats for women!"
Was the cry,
When the brave
Were come to die.
When the end
Was drawing nigh—
"Boats for women!"
Was the cry.[5]

Suffragists drew their own implications from the disaster by accepting the chivalric myth and then redirecting it to their own purposes. Suffragism intersected with a much larger set of reform movements in which women were the leading activists, and it was in the context of reform that women described displays of male chivalry as the exception rather than the rule. Moving beyond the call for specific reforms concerning ship speed, number of lifeboats, and wireless transmissions, suffragists read the disaster as a lesson in the need to extend protective legislation to cover all aspects of American life.

To these women reformers, memorializing the *Titanic* meant more than paying lasting tribute to the "noble altruism" of the first-cabin heroes. A poem in an Anti-Saloon League journal, for example, used the disaster as an argument for temperance:

> Women and Children First, 'tis the law of the sea,
> But why not make it the rule wherever a man may be?
> Let it become the law where roisterers quench their thirst,
> Emblazon it over the bar—"Women and Children First."[6]

Reformers with larger agendas played off the same phrase. Rheta Childe Dorr chose "Women and Children First" as the title of an article that described her experiences working in a "dismal" sweatshop in Brooklyn with its "foul odors" and "locked doors" that prevented mothers from going home to take care of their children. She bluntly concluded: "The law of the sea: women and children first. The law of the land—that's different." Dorr converted the claim that the men on the *Titanic* had sacrificed themselves for motherhood and childhood from celebration into criticism: "It is known on land as well as at sea that the race is carried on by children and that women are needed to care for the children," yet only in a rare circumstance, she added, had men acted on this knowledge.[7]

Alice Stone Blackwell, editor of the National American Woman Suffrage Association's *Woman's Journal,* generously noted that "chivalrous things were done even by men who had not been chivalrous in their past lives, as well as by those who had always been so," and she was touched "to see how many people were able to die bravely though they had not been able to live bravely." Blackwell went beyond the conventional homage to call for a "new chivalry" that would transform protection into a general principle and apply it universally. The only way to achieve such a goal, she contended, was through women's votes.[8] Inez Milholland argued that the best way to "inculcate" the heroism and chivalry of the *Titanic* men "in a more widespread fashion" was to give women the freedom to exercise and extend these admirable qualities.[9]

The chivalry displayed on the *Titanic,* which proved to some that women did not need the vote and that American society was basically sound, demonstrated precisely the opposite to feminists and reformers such as Milholland, Blackwell, and Dorr. Comparing a captain of a ship to a captain of industry, Blackwell observed,

> The "law of the sea" is quite different from the custom on land. The captain is expected to be the last man to leave his ship; all other lives must be saved before his. The captain of industry makes sure first of a comfortable

living for himself, even if the workers in his employ die of tuberculosis through insufficient food and unsanitary conditions. The chivalry shown to a few hundred women on the Titanic does not alter the fact that in New York City 150,000 people—largely women and children—have to sleep in dark rooms with no windows; that in a single large city 5,000 white slaves die every year; that the lives and health of thousands of women and children are sacrificed continually through their exploitation in mills, workshops and factories. These things are facts.[10]

An editorial in the *Progressive Woman* went further in contrasting chivalry at sea with exploitation on land by exposing the hypocrisy of the *Titanic* heroes themselves. "Most of those men, no doubt, stubbornly opposed the idea of the rights of women in participation in governmental affairs. Exploited them in industry, voted for the white slave pen, sent the daughter to the street, the son to the army, the husband to tramp the streets for a job."[11] The men may have redeemed themselves in the end, but their lives up to the moment of redemption had been anything but chivalrous. It was women who were best equipped to universalize the self-sacrificing behavior that surfaced only rarely in men.

Male chivalry, for example, had done nothing to prevent the disaster, only to mitigate its effects. Such "wholesale, life-taking disasters must almost be expected," wrote Agnes Ryan, as long as "the laws and the enforcement of the laws are entirely in men's hands." Drawing an analogy between the *Titanic* and the ship of state, Ryan described the disaster as "typical" of the needless waste of life under the rule of men. "The need of women in all departments of human life to conserve life itself is pitiful. More than anything else in the world the Votes for Women movement seeks to bring humaneness, the valuation of human life, into the commerce and transportation and business of the world and establish things on a new basis, a basis in which the unit of measurement is life, nothing but life!"[12]

Beginning by paying tribute to the *Titanic*'s heroes, suffragists and reformers turned the chivalric myth against itself. Male chivalry was exceptional and inadequate. To make care and protection the rule required an active role for women in public life. Deference to men may have saved some lives on the *Titanic*, but only empowered women could initiate the real work of lifesaving. In this version of the disaster, the emphasis on gender differences served radical ends. Women's supposed special qualities justified participation rather than paternalism.

Dorr and Blackwell invoked chivalry only to note its limitations. Other feminists praised the *Titanic* heroes and then suggested alternative models of conduct. "Chivalry, no doubt, has its attractive, romantic side," admitted the *Progressive Woman*, "but just plain common sense would serve social progress so much better!" Charlotte Perkins Gilman and Anna Howard Shaw demanded a single standard of "loyalty, courage and devotion." Shaw declared that the men on the *Titanic* "acted from the loftiest motives, and no word of praise is too great for their sacrifice," but went on to explain that "woman does not want a standard which sets her apart." Lida Stokes Adams dispensed with the homage to chivalry and said that "women should have insisted that the boats be filled with an equal number of men and women, or that the men should have had an equal chance of saving themselves, even though in brute strength they are stronger." Such a demonstration "would have been a wonderful thing for the suffrage movement." For Inez Milholland and Grace Guyton Kempter, women displayed equal heroism on the *Titanic,* and attention to this fact would advance the suffrage cause.[13]

Suffragists' and feminists' most common response to the disaster was to accept the conventional narrative's version of events while redirecting it to an alternative set of conclusions. A few, however, rejected the narrative outright by debunking the chivalric myth. Letting women and children into the lifeboats was the least the men could have done. "After all," an anonymous woman wrote in the *Baltimore Sun*, "the women on the boat were not responsible for the disaster," and it would have been "gross injustice to decree that the women, who have no voice in making and enforcing law on land or sea, should be left aboard a sinking ship, victims of man's cupidity." Another anonymous letter-writer wondered "how much of this heroism was due to the belief in the unsinkable qualities of the ship, or what part pistols played into converting cowards into brave men." Perhaps the most subversive opinion of all was that of a Maryland suffragist who questioned the entire premise of extracting lessons from the tragedy. It was, she wrote, "a desecration to inject the question of woman suffrage into the Titanic disaster."[14] This was asking the impossible—sorrow and grief alone, without political and social implications. Suffragists, feminists, and women reformers knew that political battles extended into the cultural realm. They knew, too, that to acquiesce in the conventional narrative of the disaster would be to concede a defeat at the height of their struggle.

⌐

What does silence mean in the face of what an editorial called the "Greatest of All News Stories?"[15] Indeed, in most of the black press, the *Titanic* was not news at all. To be sure, black journalists knew about the disaster; occasional editorials discussed it without elaborate explanation. It is possible that given the massive coverage in the commercial press, black newspapers decided that carrying the story would be redundant. It is equally possible that for many African Americans, there was no immediacy to the disaster, nothing momentous or instantly meaningful about it. The black press continued to focus on matters that directly touched its constituency: the presidential campaign, state and local elections, Booker T. Washington, lynchings, church and lodge news, the International Negro Conference, the NAACP convention. What deeply engaged white Americans did not affect black Americans in the same way; what seemed universal to some—"Titanic Disaster Hits Home of the Entire Nation" read a typical headline—was actually a matter of perspective.[16]

Silence, on the other hand, was not the only African-American response to the disaster. Where the *Titanic* resonated with blacks, it did so primarily in religious terms, and the predominant theme was not Christian sacrifice or redemption—as it was in the conventional narrative—but rather God's majesty. The empty pride of power and wealth, the illusion of security, and the deflation of pretensions were messages that black audiences could readily accept. If the disaster was not quite divine retribution, it nonetheless functioned as a warning about what the Rev. L. Z. Johnson, citing Jeremiah 9:23, called the false "glory of self-sufficing wisdom and might and riches." The *Richmond Planet* compared the *Titanic* to Belshazzar's Feast: "Joy was unconfined and God was apparently forgotten" and the "hand-writing" was "on the wall." The ladies in their evening dresses and the men in "their full dress suits," the "diamonds everywhere glittering and the pearls told their own stories." God had taught the rich and powerful a lesson in humility: "He is not interested in the increase of millionaires, so much as He is in the increase of righteousness and the well being of the poor of the earth, equally the objects of His love as are the 'rich.'"[17] Couched in general terms of man's pride and God's majesty, African-American sermons and editorials indirectly but perceptibly addressed issues of race, class, and power.

Nowhere is this intersection of religious, racial, and class critiques more evident than in the many African-American folk songs about the *Titanic* disaster. The black press—middle-class, literate, self-consciously literary, and dominated by Booker T. Washington's "Tuskegee machine"—tended toward conservatism. Folk songs, by contrast, were largely working-class, oral, and collective forms of expression. In a few such songs, the possibility of redemption remains open. "De Titanic," which originated in Georgia and was sung by black troops bound for Europe in World War I, ends with a standard image: "De people was thinkin' o' Jesus o' Nazaree, / While de band played 'Nearer My God to Thee!'" But most of these songs cast doubt on redemption. In "The Great Titanic," from northwestern Alabama, the passengers call out to God in the first verse: "People began to scream and cry, / Saying 'Lord, am I going to die?'" Following the chorus (which includes the famous camp song line "It was sad when that great ship went down"), the lyrics speak directly to class discrimination. The rich refuse to ride with the poor, "So they put the poor below, / They were the first to go." God then demonstrates his power by destroying the unsinkable ship and killing 1,600 people who "didn't know that the time had come." A Texas version of the ballad, "God Moves on the Water," asserts that even though "the peoples had to run and pray," the archetypal first-cabin passenger went down unredeemed:

> Well, that Jacob Nash was a millionaire,
> Lawd, he had plenty of money to spare;
> When the great *Titanic* was sinkin' down,
> Well, he could not pay his fare.

With its doleful vocal, often accompanied by a wailing slide guitar, "God Moves on the Water" conveys genuine sorrow; lyrically, however, judgment and justice are the guiding themes. Jacob Nash—John Jacob Astor in some versions—was carrying too much baggage to get into heaven.[18]

The central concern in more secular African-American interpretations of the disaster was whether there were any blacks on board the ship. (There were not, in fact; but for blacks as well as whites, the meaning of the *Titanic*'s loss resided in myth and legend.) While the conventional narrative had made heroism a matter of racial exclusiveness, black writers demanded inclusion even in disaster and tried to broaden the chivalric honor roll. The "whole world" was quite properly "lauding the men on the ship for their heroism in their 'Women and children first' martyrdom," said the *St. Paul Appeal,* but "we can claim a few of the heroes [too]." Though the "daily press has made no special mention of him, we know he was there, and that he died like the other men. And we shed tears to his memory as well as to the men of other nationalities who died with him." Like suffragists and reformers, middle-class blacks accepted the Christian-chivalric myth only to expand and purge it of its racist connotations. The silence of the dailies on this heroic presence came as no surprise; white newspapers rarely reported on blacks except as criminals, which prompted one black paper to comment wryly about the coverage of the disaster: "There may have been a negro in the sinking of the great steamship *Titanic* off the Newfoundland coast last week, but the newspapers have not as yet discovered the fact. It is rather remarkable that there could be so great a tragedy without a negro somewhere concealed or exposed in it." When the apocryphal story surfaced of a black stoker who was "shot because he was about to stab a wireless operator," it conformed to the pattern in which blacks were either absent as heroes or present as villains in narratives of tragedy or disaster. As the *Philadelphia Tribune* sarcastically observed, "We thought it would be strange if there were no coloured persons aboard the fated ship. Of course, he had to be made to appear in the light of a dastard."[19]

In more subversive ways, absence and presence formed the basis of the two most remarkable black folk versions of the disaster: Huddie Ledbetter's blues ballad "Titanic" and the various *Titanic* toasts. Boasting about being nowhere near the scene of a disaster was a tradition of sorts in black folk songs. A lyric transcribed in Mississippi in 1909 asks, "O where were you when the steamer when down, Captain?" and answers, "I was with my honey in the heart of town." After 1912, in places as far apart as Mt. Airy, North Carolina, and central Alabama, the *Titanic* replaced the riverboat:

> O, what were you singing
> When the Titanic went down?
> Sitting on a mule's back,
> Singing "Alabama Bound."

But Leadbelly's song, which he began performing with Blind Lemon Jefferson in Dallas in 1912, names the absent person and specifies the reason for his absence: the heavyweight champion Jack Johnson and racism. "Jack Johnson want to get on board, / Captain said, 'I ain't haulin' no coal.'" While the lyrics do not say that the *Titanic* went down *because* the captain denied Johnson passage, they revel in the irony that discrimination saved the black hero from death. The exclusion of Johnson, as Lawrence Levine has noted, makes the disaster "an all-white affair" and thus a source of "pleasure" and relief rather than grief and loss. The song ends with rejoicing: "When he heard about that mighty shock, / Might o' seen a man doin' the Eagle Rock." In one version, Leadbelly not only describes a celebration, he demands it. "Black man oughta shout for joy, / Never lost a girl or either a boy."[20]

The precise origins of the *Titanic* toasts are uncertain; some were collected in Louisiana and Mississippi in the 1930s, others in such diverse locations as Texas, Missouri, and New York in the 1960s, but there is evidence that they date back closer to the time of the disaster itself. Toasts were a "social genre"; they were narrative poems performed in all kinds of settings. In the adventures of Shine, the protagonist in the *Titanic* toasts, the themes of presence and absence merge; Shine is on board when the ship hits the iceberg but long gone by the time it sinks. His story, through all its retellings and variations, manages to subvert nearly every feature of the conventional narrative. A worker from "down below," Shine is the first person to alert the captain to the magnitude of the accident. His reward for vigilance is a rebuke: "Go on back and start stackin' sacks, / we got nine pumps to keep the water back." After another attempt at warning the captain and another rebuke, Shine refuses to obey the order to return below deck. "Your shittin' is good and your shittin' is fine," he tells the captain, "but there's one time you white folks ain't gonna shit on Shine." (In some versions, Shine responds derisively to the captain's faith in the *Titanic*'s alleged unsinkability: "I don't like chicken and I don't like ham— / And I don't believe your pumps is worth a damn!"; "Captain, captain, can't you see, / this ain't no time to bullshit me"; "Well, that seems damned funny, it may be damned fine, / but I'm gonna try to save this black ass of mine.") Realism and common sense reside in the black laborer, not in the white officer. The captain is a martinet—complacent and ignorant—a far cry from the newspaper hero who went down telling his crew to "Be British!" A "thousand millionaires" stare as Shine jumps ship and begins to swim. All they do is watch; Shine, not Butt or Astor, is the visible actor.

In the toasts, the white heroes of the conventional narrative are passive and impotent, and their women appeal to Shine to save them. The disaster, however, destroys the facade of Victorian respectability and all illusions of strong white manhood and pure white womanhood. First-cabin women, whether a "rich man's daughter" or the "Captain's daughter," need Shine rather than the "protection" of their husbands and fathers; they explicitly offer him sexual favors for his help, but he refuses. He also refuses money. The captain, realizing his earlier mistake, pleads, "Shine, Shine, save poor me, / I'll make you richer than old John D."

But Shine knows that money is worthless in these circumstances: "Shine turned around and took another notion, / say 'Captain, your money's counterfeit in this big-assed ocean.'" Shine's code is anything but chivalric. He understands that the first-cabin passengers would do nothing to save him, and he cuts through the hypocrisy of their sudden kindness and generosity by demanding that they live out their selfishness to the end. "A nickle is a nickle, a dime is a dime, / get your motherfucken ass over the side and swim like mine."

In this Darwinian struggle, Shine is clearly superior; he has both the physical strength and the cunning to survive. He skillfully evades a shark attack and swims until he arrives safely in America. When he is present at the disaster, Shine is heroic: strong, shrewd, courageous, willing to resist white authority and its bribes. Once he is on shore, he celebrates his triumph and his absence by going to a whorehouse and getting drunk.[21]

The presence of the *Titanic* in African-American folk songs and toasts indicates both the depth of its resonance and the diversity of its meanings. It also suggests something about cultural categories. For many years, folklorists tried to preserve a rigid distinction between folk culture and popular culture. Folk expression was supposed to be local, organic, participatory, and pure, while popular culture was national, standardized, commercialized, and inauthentic.[22] Yet the *Titanic* disaster was a national—in fact, international—event that entered "folk" consciousness, directly or indirectly, through the standardized media of a modern industrial society. However obscure the origins of the *Titanic* folk songs and toasts may be, one thing is certain: they did not grow organically out of the pure southern soil. In this case, oral culture was both a product of and response to print culture. All news of the disaster came first through the wire services and commercial press. What various audiences—including "the folk"—did with that news is another story. The process at work in the African-American folk songs and toasts was the vernacular strategy of "signifyin(g)," defined by the critic Henry Louis Gates as "a metaphor for textual revision"—the playing of language games—often "aimed at demystifying a subject." As critical revisions, these texts wrought havoc upon the conventional narrative; some of them, defying the tone as well as the content of that narrative, even made the disaster into a joke. The sources, in other words, may have been standardized, but the responses were not. Some "consumers" of the conventional narrative became active producers of alternative narratives.[23]

ת

Socialists and other labor radicals constructed the most consistently subversive of all these counternarratives. They spoke directly to the silences in the conventional narrative, the class bias in its roll call of heroes, the conservative "lessons" it drew from the disaster. Only a few dissenting editorialists in the commercial press joined Charlotte Perkins Gilman in noting and criticizing the namelessness of the steerage victims and survivors. While Gilman viewed this as an unfortunate omission, others argued that class determined the *Titanic*'s status as news; it was a disaster only because rich, powerful people went down with the ship. "Had the Titanic been a mudscow with the same number of useful workingmen on board," the *Appeal to Reason* speculated, and had it "gone down while engaged in some useful social work[,] the whole country would not have gasped with horror, nor would all the capitalist papers have given pages for weeks to reciting the terrible details."[24] Consciousness of the *Titanic*, in other words, was the product of capitalism and its desire to legitimate itself. Anything that did not serve this purpose did not qualify as news and was excluded from consciousness.

Confronted with the myth of first-cabin heroism, socialists attempted to recast the disaster in terms that would undermine rather than bolster capitalism. Debunking was one strategy—asserting that "most of this 'hero' business is rubbish anyhow." A Socialist Labor party member played off the ambiguities of the conventional narrative, arguing that "the *Titanic* is disastrous enough without increasing its disastrousness" by sentimentalizing it; men who "calmly remained on board" on the assumption that the ship was unsinkable "were no heroes." Speaking to striking coal miners on the capitol steps in Charleston, West Virginia, the radical labor activist Mother Jones posed a series of questions meant to expose first-cabin heroism as a transparent fraud: "I have been reading of the *Titanic* when she went down. Did you read of her? The big guns wanted to save themselves, and the fellows that were guiding below took up a club and said we will save our people. And then the papers came out and said those millionaires tried to save the women. Oh, Lord, why don't they give up their millions if they want to save the women and children? Why do they rob them of home, why do they rob millions of women to fill the hell-holes of capitalism[?]"[25]

Jones's speech also provided an alternative version of events in which the "big guns" displayed their characteristic selfishness and the "fellows" from "below" acted heroically. Whether intentionally or not, her counternarrative inverted the well-circulated story of Major Butt with his iron bar beating back the crazed men from steerage. Here it was the millionaires who had to be kept at bay by workingmen trying to "save our people." While "the daily press has immortalized the multi-millionaires as men of heroic mould," remarked a writer for the radical Western Federation of Miners, it ignored "the common men who made up the crew of the *Titanic,* who with pistols in their hands kept back the patrician mob, who yearned to seek safety in the life boats." In this alternative scenario, the first-class men were the "mob," and Astor, begging to go with his wife, had to be waved back by the "heroic crew whose chivalry towards women and children in the hour of peril and death, will immortalize them as the bravest of the brave."[26]

This labor critique of the conventional *Titanic* narrative extended beyond the biases of the press into efforts to shape the historical memory of the disaster. At the intersection of socialism and feminism, the *Progressive Woman* condemned the Woman's Titanic Memorial Fund for trying to give permanent form to a distorted version of events:

> There is a movement on foot to build at Washington a monument to the heroes of the Titanic disaster. Said heroes are Messrs. Astor, Guggenheim, Butt, etc.—first cabin guests who "stood aside" to let first cabin women take the lifeboats in the wreck. It has developed that those who "stood aside" were unaware of the danger that threatened and are therefore less heroic than was at first supposed. However, there were men—stokers, engineers, etc.—who knew the exact situation they and the Titanic were in, who yet stood at their posts till the ship went down, never to come up again. These are the real heroes of the Titanic. If there is a monument raised for Titanic heroes, it should be to these unknown, unsung toilers in the hold of that unfortunate ship.[27]

A poem called "Fair Play" made the point more generally:

> A monument for millionaires
> A monument for snobs.
> No marble shaft for the men on the craft,
> Who simply did their jobs.[28]

In the radical counternarrative, heroism either transcended class or, as in this case, belonged exclusively to the proletariat. Class still determined conduct, but here ignorance and confusion described the "first cabin guests," while knowledge and fortitude characterized the workers.

Socialists joined in the widespread warnings about luxury and greed and in the chorus calling for reform, but they did so in their own, more radical terms. They did not qualify their critique with the theme of redemption, nor did they accept the progressive belief in the basic soundness of the system. One radical writer wondered whether, in their last moments, in the desperate knowledge that they would not be saved (or redeemed), the multimillionaires had thought of "the countless human beings whom they had wrecked and ruined in their mad gallop for wealth." Far from being heroic, the first-cabin men were implicated in their own fate. "So much space had to be given to the private promenades, golf links, swimming pools for the plutocrats aboard that there was no space left for life-boats when the crash came. Could misdirected ingenuity, perverted taste and mental and moral insanity go farther?"[29] The first-cabin men were both perpetrators and victims, murderers and murdered, in what Charles Edward Russell called the "true history" of the disaster. The *Daily People* wryly observed that while the capitalist contingent on board had at least been able to enjoy the ship's attractions in exchange for the danger of ocean travel, for the proletarian majority "the increased risk of drowning was thrown in for good measure" and nothing more.[30]

In the conventional narrative, the *Titanic* functions as a metaphor for the natural goodness of class, racial, ethnic, and gender hierarchies. The Left, too, treated the *Titanic* as a metaphor, with the difference that the disaster was capitalism. "The tragedy of the month, the sinking of the *Titanic*," said the *Ladies' Garment Worker*, "is typical of the constant tragedies which occur in our industrial life." Like the ship of state, the *Titanic* sailed with "proud boasts" and illusions. On the upper deck, "comfort and luxury . . . feasts, cards and gallantries" occupied the rich and beautiful. "Sounds of revelry" drowned out "the cry of the sick baby in the steerage," while "stokers far below in the stifling under-world" toiled and sweated. During the ship's final moments, the first-cabin men awakened "from their orgies of self-indulgence" and realized "their manhood obligations," but their redemption was hollow—"too late for this life." As a metaphor for class hierarchy, the *Titanic* "illustrated in herself and in her destruction" the "contempt for human life which under capitalism inspired and presided over her creation." The *Masses* grieved over "Our 'Titanic' Civilization" and asked:

> What in reality is one of these "floating palaces"? It embodies gross distinctions of comfort, of air supply, and of food; hateful class lines, the humiliating fencing off of decks and spaces on behalf of the few against the many; and more injurious still, inhuman conditions for most of the men who do the hard work: airless sleeping places, intolerably long hours, humiliations lavished on the toilers, and bodily and mental suffering inflicted upon some of them such as drives man by man to self-drowning, looking to find the cold depths of the ocean more hospitable than the treatment meted them by their fellow men.

Evidently a steamship is a true miniature of our present civilization. Evidently our commercial State is rightly called a "Ship." The two are indeed alike in irrationality.[31]

While the equation of the *Titanic* with capitalist society served as an indictment of the status quo, it also pointed hopefully toward the future. What confirmed the permanence of a certain vision of social order for conservatives represented the opposite to radicals. "Just as the *Titanic* went down in wreck and disaster so will capitalism which she so tragically typified also go down." Here, too, there would be casualities, "but it is to be hoped that when the crisis comes there may be life boats enough to carry humanity safely into the Socialist Republic."[32]

Paradoxically, visions of the classless future led some on the Left to embrace the myths that they tried elsewhere to debunk. The *Appeal to Reason* described the steerage passengers as "penned in like cattle" and kept back "with loaded revolvers" so that "the rich passengers" could "make sure of their escape," yet somehow rich and poor alike had done the "fine thing" of observing the rule of the sea, women and children first. Images of "rich man and poor man, millionaire and stoker" standing together as "equals and brothers, without a barrier between them, going down to death together" did not suggest, as they did in the conventional narrative, that the status quo was all brotherhood and harmony. But in a moment of crisis, they provided a glimpse of the classless future.[33] Catastrophe exposed the socialism at the core of every human being: the "realities" beneath the capitalist facade.

By laying bare human nature, the *Titanic* disaster demonstrated the viability of socialism. Critics who disparaged socialists for their utopianism—their naive disregard for the fundamental selfishness of human beings—needed only to be reminded of the disaster. "For we might rest our whole cause upon what happened that night on the *Titanic*," beamed Charles Edward Russell. To those who insisted that socialism required "a change in human nature," we "point to that night on the *Titanic* and say that for human nature so noble and good to be perverted and dragged in the mire and slimed in the filth and hardened in the fires of Capitalism is the most unspeakable of crimes and that the race had never better friends than those that are trying to rid the earth of such a monster."[34]

Emma Goldman made the same case in a different way. Undercutting the myth of noblesse oblige, she envisioned the workers dying "for those far removed from us by a cold and cruel social and material gulf—for those who by their very position must needs be our enemies—for those who, a few moments before the disaster probably never gave a thought to the toilers and pariahs of the ship." Self-sacrifice of this kind was "so wonderful a feat of human nature as to silence forever the ridiculous argument" that the classless society was unnatural and therefore impossible.[35]

In the context of the *Titanic* disaster, human nature proved remarkably malleable. Americans across the political and social spectrum seemed actually to agree that the disaster carried lessons about what was and was not natural—but their agreement stopped there. When it came to the content of those lessons—was woman suffrage natural? feminism? racial equality? socialism?—consensus evaporated. Despite its evocations of inviolability, permanence, and transcendence, human nature was dragged into the contest over the *Titanic's* meanings, where it provoked rather than resolved conflicts. As a social drama, the *Titanic* disaster produced a cacophony of voices rather than a chorus. Dissenting voices responded to the conventional narrative, revised it, and in some cases overturned it completely. The insistence that a certain "picture invariably presents itself" failed to convince those who well understood the meanings that such a picture conveyed. They preferred to draw their own.

It is tempting to make claims about the "cash value" of these counternarratives—to argue, for example, that they decisively altered power relations. They didn't. The purveyors of the conventional narrative did not, for the most part, even see or hear the counternarratives. But, as noted earlier, the significance of the *Titanic* does not reside in any changes it produced. It lies, instead, in the complex ways in which the disaster became a site of struggle. The conventional narrative tried to represent itself as common sense, to put itself beyond critical demystification, to treat the truths of the *Titanic* as self-evident, to allow for only one way of comprehending the event and its meanings. It would not even admit the possibility of dissent. At a time when abstractions such as "nation," "state," and "society" pervaded public discourse and concealed the demands of the aggrieved and the marginalized, the conventional narrative used similar rhetorical strategies.[36]

Yet the aggrieved and the marginalized *did* dissent. Their counternarratives quite consciously challenged the conventional narrative's pretense of a national consensus and, in doing so, resisted its attempts to render them invisible and to place existing power relations beyond contestation. They answered what was supposed to be unanswerable. If, in 1912, their responses were primarily for themselves, that does not diminish their importance. What is important is that they responded and that they left for posterity a record of their resistance.

From our perspective, this boils down to the crucial point that the *Titanic* disaster was historically, not intrinsically, meaningful. In a different way than those who constructed the conventional narrative, we like to think that the disaster's resonance is timeless—that it has to do with universal themes of humans against nature, hubris, false confidence, the mystery of the sea, hydrophobia, heroism, and cowardice.

But the *Titanic* seared itself into American memory not because it was timeless but because it was timely. Americans in 1912 made it speak to their concerns about contemporary politics and society, class and culture. Though many of them claimed to have found transhistorical truths in the disaster, such claims were themselves historically grounded in their own circumstances and ideological purposes. No more than any other event was the *Titanic* inherently memorable. Making rather than finding its significance, people worked and fought to shape how the disaster would, they hoped, be remembered.

NOTES

A different version of this essay appeared in Steven Biel, *Down with the Old Canoe: A Cultural History of the* Titanic *Disaster* (New York: W. W. Norton, 1996).

1. Walter Lord, *A Night to Remember* (New York: Henry Holt, 1955), 139; Wyn Craig Wade, *The Titanic: End of a Dream* (New York: Rawson, Wade, 1979), 296; Charles Pellegrino, *Her Name,* Titanic: *The Untold Story of the Sinking and Finding of the Unsinkable Ship* (New York: McGraw-Hill, 1988), 32. Richard Garrett has challenged the "end of an epoch" idea, arguing, "The only epoch it can take any credit for ending is that of gross negligence to do with matters concerning safety at sea" (*Atlantic Disaster: The* Titanic *and Other Victims of the North Atlantic* [London: Buchan and Enright, 1986], 253–54).

2. For a summary of the anthropological concept of social dramas, see Chandra Mukerji and Michael Schudson, "Introduction: Rethinking Popular Culture," in *Rethinking Popular Culture: Contemporary Perspectives in Cultural Studies,* ed. Chandra Mukerji and Michael Schudson (Berkeley: University of California Press, 1991), 23. See also Victor Turner, "Liminality and the Performative Genres," in *Rite, Drama, Festival, Spectacle: Rehearsals toward a Theory of Cultural Performance,* ed. John J. MacAloon (Philadelphia: Institute for the Study of Human Issues, 1984), 19–41.

3. Several recent studies of historical memory have shaped my own interpretive framework. John Bodnar, *Remaking America: Public Memory, Commemoration, and Patriotism in the Twentieth Century* (Princeton, N.J.: Princeton University Press, 1992); David Glassberg, *American Historical Pageantry: The Uses of Tradition in the Early Twentieth Century* (Chapel Hill: University of North Carolina Press, 1990);

220 / STEVEN BIEL

George Lipsitz, *Time Passages: Collective Memory and American Popular Culture* (Minneapolis: University of Minnesota Press, 1990); and David Thelen, ed., *Memory and American History* (Bloomington: Indiana University Press, 1990), make use of the concept of "struggles" or "contestations over meaning." In drawing the distinction between conventional and unconventional views of the *Titanic* disaster, I am guided by Bodnar's distinction between "official culture" and "vernacular culture" (see esp. 13–15), though I find these terms too limiting for my discussion.

4. See, for example, "Titanic Disaster Hits Home of the Entire Nation," *San Francisco Examiner*, Apr. 17, 1912, 2; "Heroic Acts on Titanic Never Surpassed in World's Annals," *Denver Post*, Apr. 17, 1912, 2; "Saved from Wreck," *Chicago Tribune*, Apr. 17, 1912, 1; "Waters of Atlantic Sound Requiem over Thousand Departed Souls," *Asheville Citizen*, Apr. 17, 1912, 1; and "Thousands Now Abandon All Hope for Loved Relatives on Titanic" *Charlotte Observer*, Apr. 17, 1912, 1.

5. Clark McAdams, "Enough Said," *St. Louis Post-Dispatch*, Apr. 22, 1912, 10. McAdams's poem is also printed in Ann E. Larabee, "The American Hero and His Mechanical Bride: Gender Myths of the Titanic Disaster," *American Studies* 31 (Spring 1990): 15–16.

6. *American Issues* (June 1912), quoted in Peter G. Filene, *Him/Her/Self: Sex Roles in Modern America*, 2d ed. (Baltimore: Johns Hopkins University Press, 1986), 81.

7. Rheta Childe Dorr, "'Women and Children First,'" *Woman's Journal*, May 4, 1912, 141.

8. Alice Stone Blackwell, "The Lesson of the Titanic," *Woman's Journal*, Apr. 27, 1912, 132.

9. Inez Milholland, quoted in "Women First Barbarous," *New York Tribune*, Apr. 19, 1912, 16. See also Larabee, "American Hero," 15–18.

10. Alice Stone Blackwell, "Suffrage and Life-Saving," *Woman's Journal*, Apr. 27, 1912, 132.

11. "Masculine Chivalry," *Progressive Woman*, May 1912, 8.

12. Agnes E. Ryan, "Lives against Lives," *Woman's Journal*, Apr. 27, 1912, 136; Blackwell, "Suffrage and Life-Saving," 132; Mary McDowell, "The New Chivalry and Industrial Life," *Life and Labor*, July 1913, 196, 198. McDowell's article was originally given as a speech at a WTUL meeting in St. Louis on June 2, 1912.

13. "Masculine Chivalry," 8; Anna Howard Shaw, quoted in "St. Louis Suffragists, Like Dr. Anna Shaw, Decry the 'Women First' Rule on Sea," *St. Louis Post-Dispatch*, Apr. 24, 1912, 10; Lida Stokes Adams, quoted in Margaret Hubbard Ayer, "The Titanic Disaster: Should Women Have Insisted on Men Having Equal Chance of Saving Themselves?" *Philadelphia Evening Bulletin*, Apr. 24, 1912, 7; Grace Guyton Kempter, letter to the editor, *Baltimore Sun*, Apr. 25, 1912, 6; Milholland, quoted in "Women First Barbarous," 16.

14. "A Woman," letter to the editor, *Baltimore Sun*, Apr. 22, 1912, 6; Kempter, letter to the editor, ibid., Apr. 25, 1912, 6; "Daughter of Eve," letter to the editor, ibid., May 1, 1912, 6; Emma Maddox Funck, letter to the editor, ibid., Apr. 26, 1912, 6.

15. The phrase was the title of an editorial in the *St. Louis Post-Dispatch*, May 4, 1912, 22.

16. "Titanic Disaster Hits Home," 2. Wade notes the black press's lack of attention to the disaster (*Titanic*, 294). The *Cleveland Gazette, Richmond Planet, Savannah Tribune, St. Paul Appeal,* and *Washington Bee* all printed some of the standard wire-service material.

17. Johnson, quoted in "Sermon on the Titanic Disaster," *Afro-American Ledger,* May 18, 1912, 2; "Belshazzar's Feast," *Richmond Planet,* Apr. 20, 1912, 4; "A Very Sad Affair with an Important Lesson," *Afro-American Ledger,* Apr. 20, 1912, 4.

18. Carl Sandburg, *The American Songbag* (New York: Harcourt, Brace, 1927), 254–56; Samuel B. Charters, *The Country Blues* (London: Michael Joseph, 1959), 62–63; Newman I. White, *American Negro Folk-Songs* (Cambridge, Mass.: Harvard University Press, 1928), 347–48; Harold Courlander, *Negro Folk Music, U.S.A.* (New York: Columbia University Press, 1963), 76–77; John A. Lomax and Alan Lomax, *Our Singing Country: A Second Volume of American Ballads and Folk Songs* (New York: Macmillan, 1941), 26–27.

19. Editorial, *St. Paul Appeal,* Apr. 20, 1912, 2; "Editorial Notes," *New York Age,* Apr. 25, 1912, 4; "Current Notes," *Savannah Tribune,* May 25, 1912, 3; editorial, *Philadelphia Tribune,* Apr. 27, 1912, 4.

20. White, *American Negro Folk-Songs,* 348–49; Charles Wolfe and Kip Lornell, *The Life and Legend of Leadbelly* (New York: HarperCollins, 1992), 44–45; Jerry Silverman, *Folk Blues* (New York: Macmillan, 1968), 149–50; Courlander, *Negro Folk Music,* 77–78; Lawrence W. Levine, *Black Culture and Black Consciousness: Afro-American Folk Thought from Slavery to Freedom* (New York: Oxford University Press, 1977), 258.

21. Bruce Jackson, "The *Titanic* Toast," *Veins of Humor,* ed. Harry Levin (Cambridge, Mass.: Harvard University Press, 1972), 205–23; Levine, *Black Culture,* 428–29.

22. Robert L. Dorman, *Revolt of the Provinces: The Regionalist Movement in America, 1920–1945* (Chapel Hill: University of North Carolina Press, 1993), esp. chaps. 3–4; Lawrence W. Levine, "The Folklore of Industrial Society: Popular Culture and Its Audiences," *American Historical Review* 97 (Dec. 1992): 1369–99, esp. 1376.

23. Henry Louis Gates Jr., *The Signifying Monkey: A Theory of African-American Literary Criticism* (New York: Oxford University Press, 1988), 88, 57, 52. In writing only about the content of the *Titanic* toasts, I am doing exactly what Gates warns against in his discussion of signifyin(g): ignoring its broader definition as "a game of language, independent of reaction to white racism or even to collective black wish-fulfillment vis-à-vis white racism" (70). My rationale is that I am writing a cultural history of the *Titanic* disaster, not a work of literary criticism or theory.

Gates shares an anecdote about a *Titanic* toast in his autobiography. In 1956, a teacher in a newly integrated West Virginia classroom asked the black students if they could recite any poetry. When one of Gates's classmates began to narrate Shine's exploits, the teacher, appalled, cut him off (Gates, *Colored People: A Memoir* [New York: Alfred A. Knopf, 1994], 92–93).

24. Charlotte Perkins Gilman, "Saving of Women in Disaster," *Forerunner,* May 1912, 140; "The Titanic Tragedy," *Appeal to Reason,* May 4, 1912, 4. A dissenting account, in the *Asheville Citizen,* observed that "the ever-present law of the submerged tenth decrees that no lists be made of steerage passengers, and, except in the households where death has laid its hand, the names of the Titanic's steerage passengers will never be known" ("The Loss of the Titanic," *Asheville Citizen,* Apr. 17, 1912, 4).

An African-American popular song made a similar point: "The rich folks with their millions had to go down, / Such as Astor, Mister Straub [*sic*] and Guggenheim, / The poor folks on the vessel were not mentioned, / We'll know them at the end of future time." William Jackson and Charles Wright, "The End of the Titanic in the Sea" (sheet music; Medina, N.Y.: Krompart Publishing, 1912). The sheet music is preserved in the collections of the American Folklife Center, Library of Congress.

25. Mother Jones, "Speech at a Public Meeting on the Steps of the Capitol, Charleston, West Virginia, 15 August 1912," in *The Speeches and Writings of Mother Jones*, ed. Edward M. Steel (Pittsburgh: University of Pittsburgh Press, 1988), 93–94.

26. "'There Are Others,'" *Miners Magazine*, May 2, 1912, 6; "Titanic Passengers in Steerage Brave," *New York Call*, Apr. 25, 1912, 2; "Titanic Tragedy," 4.

27. "Preventable Deaths of Workers," *Progressive Woman*, Sept. 1912, 2.

28. M. L. Clawson, "Fair Play," *Indianapolis World*, May 18, 1912, 1.

29. Editorial, *Miners Magazine*, May 9, 1912, 6; "Titanic Tragedy," 4; "Our 'Titanic' Civilization," *Masses*, June 1912, 3.

30. Charles Edward Russell, "Murdered for Capitalism," *Coming Nation*, Apr. 27, 1912, 3; "A Titanic Demonstration," *Daily People*, Apr. 18, 1912, 2.

31. "Lessons from the Titanic Disaster," *Ladies' Garment Worker*, May 1912, 14; "Titanic Tragedy," 4; "Our 'Titanic' Civilization," 3.

32. "Our 'Titanic' Civilization," 3; "News and Views," *Solidarity*, Apr. 27, 1912, 2; "Titanic Tragedy," 4.

33. "Titanic Tragedy," 4; Charles Edward Russell, "Realities," *Coming Nation*, May 4, 1912, 4.

34. Charles Edward Russell, "Human Nature," *Coming Nation*, May 4, 1912, 4.

35. Emma Goldman, quoted in "Suffrage Dealt Blow," *Denver Post*, Apr. 21, 1912, sec. 1, 8.

36. Daniel T. Rodgers, *Contested Truths: Keywords in American Politics since Independence* (New York: Basic Books, 1987), 172–73.

10 Building a Black Audience in the 1930s: Langston Hughes, Poetry Readings, and the Golden Stair Press

ELIZABETH DAVEY

"PEOPLE NEED POETRY"

Langston Hughes visited Bethune-Cookman College in Daytona Beach, Florida, on his way to and from travels in Cuba and Haiti in the summer of 1931. Mary McLeod Bethune, the president of Bethune-Cookman and a black educator who had founded her school for black women in 1904, welcomed him. She offered him meals and a guest room and invited him to read his poetry to the English classes at the college. At this moment in his career Hughes had published two books of poems and a novel. He had a growing national and international reputation as a poet, and his poetry was especially familiar to readers of the NAACP's magazine, the *Crisis*. But Hughes did not yet know how he would support himself as a writer during the depression. Bethune offered him an idea: he should travel through the South, reading his poems to inspire black students. "You must go all over the South with your poems," she told him. "People need poetry."[1]

By the time Hughes returned to New York, he had expanded Bethune's idea into a plan to develop a mass black audience for black literature. "I'd like to make a reading tour of the whole South in order to build up a sustaining Negro audience for my work and that of other Negro writers and artists," he wrote to Walter White, executive secretary of the NAACP (National Association for the Advancement of Colored People). Hughes recognized that developing a black public—as he termed it in his letter to White—for black writing was not simply a project of using the reading tour to promote sales of his books. Instead, he would use the tour to introduce black audiences to the possibilities of literature representing their own creativity, aspirations, and experiences. As Hughes explained to White, "I want to create an interest in racial expression through books."[2]

Because of this educational mission, assembling a traveling display about black literature and persuading his publisher, Alfred Knopf, to print an inexpensive edition of his first book of poems, *The Weary Blues*—to be sold at his readings for a dollar—were as important to his preparations as applying for a grant, buying a car, hiring a business manager/driver, and booking readings. But Hughes's most important preparation for the reading tour was the production of a pamphlet entitled *The Negro Mother and Other Dramatic Recitations*. The pamphlet was a collaboration with the white artist Prentiss Taylor; Hughes contributed six poems, while Taylor illustrated the pamphlet and managed its production.[3] At his readings, Hughes would sell the booklet for twenty-five cents; he would also sell illustrated broadsides of single poems for ten cents each. The Golden Stair Press, as they named their venture, attempted to bring Hughes's poetry within the financial reach of economically marginalized black Americans. It also gave Hughes, whose work had been constrained and sometimes manipulated by white patrons and publishers, a controlling interest in the publication and distribution of some of his poems.

In a promotional letter for the booklet, Hughes described the unavailability of the writing of the Harlem Renaissance to large black audiences. Most blacks, he said, could not afford to pay two dollars for a book of poems or a novel; and in any case, books produced by white publishers were largely advertised and sold to white readers. "Little or no effort is made to reach the great masses of the colored people," Hughes wrote.[4] To reach these "great masses," Hughes believed that new methods of distributing and circulating his poems had to be developed. His reading tour would present his poems to black and multiracial audiences across the South. But to reach an even larger audience, Hughes designed the inexpensive booklet to empower readers to present his poems publicly, by staging readings. In the promotional letter, Hughes described the need for poems "suitable for reading aloud, or for recitation in schools, churches, lodges, etc." The distinctly dramatic presentation of the poems of *The Negro Mother* suggests that Hughes thought that a mass black audience for black literature would be built through public readings, rather than private consumption of books. Even after his tour ended, by using *The Negro Mother* as a script, Hughes's readers could continue to nurture audiences in economically and educationally marginalized black communities.[5]

Hughes's construction of a black public in this promotional letter was informed by his involvement at the time with left and communist organizations and periodicals, such as the *New Masses*, and by his understanding of the importance of enlisting black middle-class readers in his project. In the fall of 1931, as he planned his tour and produced *The Negro Mother*, Hughes contributed to the communist campaign protesting the Scottsboro trials—the conviction of nine black teenagers charged with a gang rape in Scottsboro, Alabama—by publishing poems and a play protesting the verdicts in *Opportunity* and the *New Masses*.

Although his invocation of a black public as "the masses of the Negro people" suggests a public largely comprised of working-class blacks, in the promotional letter Hughes constructed the category of "the masses" in opposition to intellectuals. Reflecting upon the writing of the Harlem Renaissance of the 1920s—his own included—Hughes wrote, "I have felt that much of our poetry has been aimed at the heads of the high-brows, rather than at the hearts of the people." In his critique of intellectualism he attempted to appeal to the black press and black middle class, who had responded with outrage to many of the literary projects of the later Renaissance, including his own book of blues poems, *Fine Clothes to the Jew*. Promoting *The Negro Mother*, he wrote of these masses: "They have not cared for jazz, poetry or low-down novels—and one can't blame them much—since they usually know such things all too well in life." In this comment, he acknowledged the objections of critics writing in black newspapers and magazines to the experimentalism of projects such as his blues poetry. In effect, he presented himself to his critics as a reformed poet. The press responded to his pitch. The review of *The Negro Mother* in the *Amsterdam News*, for example, was titled "Converted at Last!" and reviewer Aubrey Bowser gloated, "Langston Hughes has taken a step in the right direction. His writings used to make colored readers steam with rage; now he is a convert to common sense."[6] Although Hughes's proletarian poetry during these same years showed an understanding of "the masses" predicated upon material conditions, the more populist construction of "the masses" in this letter reflects Hughes's need to appeal to and recruit the black middle class in order to reach those masses.

Audiences may have recognized Hughes's project within the tradition of the African-American sermon. As a touring black poet, Langston Hughes was a novelty; his presentations may have been understood by his audiences through their own experiences with traveling preachers. Though the texts of Hughes's poems were secular and generally did not resemble the style and substance of the sermon, the program of many of his poetry readings on the tour approximated a devotional service: he sometimes read from the pulpit in churches, and the musical interlude between the two segments of his reading was often performed by a local choir. Comparisons can also be made between the printing of the booklet of recitations and the distribution of texts of sermons, which were sometimes printed in pamphlets. Hortense Spillers supplies the example of J. W. E.

Bowen, a pastor whose official board passed a resolution in 1902 urging him to publish his sermons in pamphlet form for general reading.[7] The publication of a booklet of recitations resembled this use of the pamphlet to disseminate the text of an oral performance, the sermon. Hughes's desire to use oral performance and its replication to form a black audience also draws from this tradition. Spillers describes the importance of the sermon in fostering a sense of unity in black communities: "The sermons, preached across denominational and doctrinal differences, actually help create the sense of 'a people' forged from a background of divergent and originating African families."[8]

Hughes's reading tour and his inexpensive pamphlet were his attempt to forge an audience for black literature by preaching across (to borrow Spillers's language) tremendous differences in literacy. The 1930 U.S. census, the year before Hughes's tour, was the last to ask its respondents whether they could read and write; by 1940 the literacy rates were high enough that it was no longer considered a useful census question. Data from the 1930 census show that, though literacy was increasing among African Americans, significant illiteracy persisted: more than 16 percent could not read and write.[9] White and black illiteracy in the South was higher than the national average. Hughes would tour the states with the highest rates of illiteracy among blacks in the country—19.2 percent in Virginia, 20.6 percent in North Carolina, 23.2 percent in Mississippi, and over 26 percent in South Carolina and Alabama (compared with 2.5 percent in New York and 3.6 percent in Illinois).[10] As he read in churches, schools, and colleges in the segregated South, his audiences must have included older people who had not had access to basic schooling, as well as students in grade schools, high schools, and colleges.

Even among those with access to education there was a wide range of reading and writing skills. In 1940, the census began to record educational attainment—meaning the years of school completed. Nine years after Hughes's tour, the census reported that only 7.7 percent of nonwhites twenty-five years and older had finished high school, with 1.3 percent finishing college. In 1940 some 41.8 percent of nonwhites had attended school for less than five years.[11] Thus, Hughes's audiences must have included people who were illiterate, who had a few years of schooling and only basic reading and writing skills, young people in school who were learning to read and write, some people with high school educations, and some who were pursuing or had completed college educations.

The Great Depression placed economic constraints on the expansion of literacy among African Americans in the early twentieth century. Reading materials—especially magazines and books—became more costly and less plentiful. But in the twenty years prior to 1931, publications dedicated to black readerships had emerged, grown to large circulations, and diversified, demonstrating an expansion of literacy and literary interests among black Americans. Many major cities had black weekly newspapers: the *Pittsburgh Courier, Chicago Defender, New York Age, Amsterdam News, Philadelphia Tribune, California Eagle, Norfolk Journal and Guide, St. Louis Argus, Kansas City Call, Cleveland Call and Post, Baltimore Afro-American,* and *Atlanta World.* Several of these papers had national readerships; the *Defender* and the *Courier* were delivered throughout the country by Pullman porters and dining-car waiters and were distributed locally by newsboys, barbers, and shopkeepers.[12] Between 1910 and 1923 three national black magazines dedicated to politics and culture commenced publication: the *Crisis* in 1910, *Messenger* in 1917, and *Opportunity* in 1923. Of the three, *Crisis* had the largest circulation, reaching a peak of 95,000 in 1919.[13] Because *Crisis* and *Opportunity* published poems and short stories, book reviews and columns devoted to literary commentary, and advertisements for books, their subscribers could participate in the expansion of fiction and poetry written by black authors. *Crisis* sometimes offered books as a bonus with the purchase of subscriptions, enabling the subscriber to receive books that were not available in their communities.

The expansion of literary activities in black communities during these years also can be seen in the inception of several small literary magazines produced by black literary groups. In addition to the notorious *Fire!!* the decade saw the publication of *Stylus* by a literary society at Howard University, of the *Saturday Evening Quill* by the Boston Quill Club, and of *Black Opals* by a group in Philadelphia.[14] Alain Locke, who viewed the renaissance of black writing as centered in "the metropolis"—New York—described the activity of these groups as "the spread of beauty to the provinces."[15] While in the 1930s many African Americans struggled to acquire basic reading and writing skills, a growing number throughout the country were reading newspapers, magazines, and books; many read—and some produced—periodicals dedicated to fiction, essays, and poetry by black writers.

Hughes's tour and pamphlet *The Negro Mother* were both addressed to this simultaneous expansion of literary interests among African Americans and divergence of literacy skills within black communities. In planning his tour and distributing *The Negro Mother,* Hughes relied on black professionals and readers of national black newspapers and magazines to deliver his poetry to their communities. To schedule readings, he wrote to black colleges, junior colleges, and technical schools throughout the South. His desire to use the tour to bring black literature to the black masses was well publicized in advertisements and articles in *Crisis* and *Amsterdam News*. On October 28, 1931, for example, the *Amsterdam News* ran an article on the tour alongside a photo of Hughes signing a contract with his tour manager, Radcliffe Lewis. The release of *The Negro Mother* was also advertised in these same publications; the advertisement in the October 14, 1931, issue of the *Amsterdam News* announced: "A new book of poems full of aspiration, humor, and racial ideals in verse for public recitation." A full-page ad in *Crisis* offered a free copy of the booklet with a year's subscription to the magazine.[16] Hughes relied on a network of black readers, many dispersed in communities throughout the South (and the Midwest and West as well) but connected through publications, such as *Crisis,* to answer his call and to play an active role in promoting literacy and black literature in their communities.

They responded: "dear editor I me a reder of the Chris," wrote Mrs. Florence Duke of St. Louis to the Golden Stair Press in 1932, requesting several of the broadsides.[17] Her spelling errors remind us that the *Crisis* was read by and to people with a wide range of reading and writing competencies. Other letters sent to the press, letters that placed orders for or requested complimentary copies of *The Negro Mother* and broadsides, demonstrate that many of the readers of national black magazines and newspapers gladly took up the role of literacy and literary activism that Hughes offered. Librarians at the Glendale Public Library in California, the Minneapolis Public Library, and the Division of Negro Literature and History at the New York Public Library requested copies for their collections. Other readers requesting copies of *The Negro Mother* briefly described their intentions of circulating them within their communities. Letters sent to the Golden Stair Press suggest another order of literary groups in black communities in the early 1930s: in addition to the literary groups comprising black writers and editors that had formed in some major cities, in communities elsewhere in the nation, women's clubs and reading groups read together, discussed, and promoted literature. Mrs. B. J. Anderson, president of the Periclean Club of Birmingham, Alabama, wrote to request a copy of the booklet for an exhibit that would be part of a week devoted to promoting Negro literature and writers, and she suggested that after the exhibit the club would order copies for their circulating library. She explained: "The purpose of the venture is to encourage the Negro to greater aspiration in the field of literature; to acquaint the citizens of Birmingham with the achievements of Negroes in literature, and to increase interest in the same."[18] A handwritten note at the bottom of her typed letter added that the Periclean Club would be "presenting Langston Hughes during this week and would especially like to have the little pamphlet of his poems."[19]

Belle S. Roberts of Aberdeen, South Dakota, sent twenty-five cents and asked for any information on Hughes that would help her prepare a talk on Negro poetry and poets. "I will appreciate it very much as I want to tell my people," she wrote.[20] Hughes's reading tour and the inexpensive pamphlets made poetry available to black communities throughout the country, but it was readers within these communities—primarily women—who circulated the poems further, lending the booklet, lecturing on the poems and the poets, and reading the poems aloud.

RECITATIONS IN AMERICAN CULTURE

When Langston Hughes decided to write "recitations" to read and sell during his tour, he entered a tradition of reading poems aloud for education or entertainment—a tradition stretching back to the very origins of poetry but with a specific history of use within the United States. His pamphlet offered black audiences a version of the anthologies of poems, dramatic monologues, and famous speeches that were published in the United States for use in schools and for home entertainment—readers and "speakers" with such titles as *Introduction to the American Orator, The American Speaker, The United States Speaker, Uncle Herbert's Speaker and Autograph Album Verse,* and *The Ellen Terry Ladies' Reciter.* The anthologists who assembled readers for use in schools touted recitation variously as an important skill in itself, as training for public speaking, and as an avenue for the development of proper morality and behavior. In 1812, Increase Cooke described his project as a collaboration with parents and teachers "who think it of importance that the young be early taught to read and speak *properly* their native language, and at the same time, be trained to virtuous dispositions and affections, and established in correct principles of thinking and acting."[21] In their prefaces, Cooke and other nineteenth-century editors of recitations did not describe or announce the literary merit of their selections; instead, they offered poems that presented particular challenges to public speakers and that offered particular moral and historical lessons to their auditors. Anthologies such as *The American Speaker,* which aimed at providing schools with poems that would "inculcate wholesome sentiments," reprinted poems from magazines and published many anonymous ones. Of the signed poems in its pages, more were written by poets with names such as Miss Jemsbury, Mrs. Sigourney, and Mrs. E. T. Daniels than with names such as Byron, Bryant, and Longfellow.

Robert Wood Lynn, analyzing William Holmes McGuffey's *Readers,* which were widely used in America's schools in 1836–1920, argues that educators such as McGuffey used oration to form a particular public in Jacksonian America. The recitations contained in the readers preached a "patriotic piety" in an attempt to create a single public in a country increasingly divided by ethnic, racial, and religious differences.[22] The narratives of these recitations contributed to this end by reiterating particular histories in order to form a collective memory and by celebrating particular symbolic figures and acts. For example, the readings in McGuffey's elevated the Puritans to the status of "archetypal Americans"; they contributed to the elevation of George Washington to the status of mythic hero and "a symbol of the people and their steadfastness amidst hardships and crisis."[23] The form—the oration—was central to this project of creating a public, for McGuffey viewed the American orator as a kind of minister. Lynn observes, "Nearly all of the advanced *Reader*—its exercises in elocution, the rules of rhetoric, the prose and poetry—could be used in shaping the future celebrants of the American faith. In this respect 'McGuffey's' was more than a textbook or a literary collection of 'elegant extracts'; it was, in sum, a portable school for the new priests of the republic."[24] In Lynn's account, the mid-nineteenth-century recitation functioned to assert and form a white Protestant American public and to advocate behavior that would serve that public. Lynn observes that the formation of this public excluded black Americans, an exclusion shared by other "reciters" of the time. Even *The American Speaker,* published in New England on the eve of the Civil War, omits reference to African Americans and the institution of slavery.

Later in the nineteenth century, a number of publishers of popular self-help books, how-to manuals, and books of parlor entertainment published books of recitations, suggesting that the social function of recitation had shifted or expanded from moral, historical, and elocutionary instruction to home entertainment.[25] The advertisements for these collections touted their "humorous" and "comic" poems. Preeminent among these was the "dialect recitation," including (as the advertisements specified), the "french dialect," "Yankee dialect," and "Negro dialect." Excelsior Publishing House advertised a book entitled *Burdett's Negro Dialect Recitations and Humorous Readings* alongside *Burdett's Shakespearean Recitations and Readings.* During the late nineteenth century, popular public recitation of poetry seems to have been deeply entwined with racial mimicry and ventriloquism. This was the era of the tremendous popularity of Joel Chandler Harris and other white authors of "Negro dialect" stories. Michael North links this phenomenon with the concurrent rise of the standard language movement—exemplified by the compilation of the first *Oxford English Dictionary* during these years. North argues that as the ideal of a standard, correct English was asserted with increasing force (that functioned, he notes, as an impediment to social mobility), dialect was used by whites both to subscribe to an ideal of a correct usage and to violate its rules and demands in a socially acceptable way.[26] The pressures of an ideal, standardized language and the escapes provided by a ventriloquized dialect may have exerted themselves even more strongly in spoken performance. The popularity of these dialect recitations in local and domestic performances may lie in the fact that most whites could *not* speak "standard English"; dialect provided them with socially acceptable mispronunciations.

Dialect literature also reasserted antebellum representations of the South and of African Americans. The popularity of dialect literature coincided with the retrenchment of legalized racism in the post-Reconstruction South—the rise of Jim Crow laws, in particular. Southern white writers and performers of dialect monologues, such as Martha S. Gielow, a white Alabamian who performed "original monologues, character sketches, and cradle songs" in New York City and England, romanticized race relations in the antebellum South. In the preface to her book of "drawing room monologues," Gielow criticized the representations of blacks in northern minstrel shows, writing that "the quaint humor of their happy, simple natures has been turned into a wit they never possessed." Her poems and performances, she insisted, presented "a correct and natural dramatic impersonation of the old-time Mammy and Daddy, the devoted foster parents to the children of the South."[27] Her promotional leaflet, announcing her availability for "Recitals in Drawing-Rooms, Clubs, Churches, and Schools," suggests that the organization and form of Langston Hughes's tour may have followed the precedent of such white performers. By writing poems to be read aloud, calling them "recitations," and announcing his availability for readings in lodges, schools, and churches, Hughes entered a domain where black voices were often ventriloquized by whites, often to restore racist representations such as Gielow's figure of the "old-time Mammy."

This complicity of poetry readings and racial mimicry, and the appetite of white audiences for such performances, is best demonstrated by the outrageous popularity of Vachel Lindsay's poem "The Congo." Lindsay had walked to California early in his career, reciting his poetry in private homes and attempting to exchange a self-published booklet, *Rhymes to Be Traded for Bread,* for room and board. (In practice, his hosts usually made him do some manual labor as well.)[28] He eventually established himself as a nationally known poet, publishing in *Poetry* magazine and using his performances to generate publicity and book sales. Lindsay's most famous poem—and the most popular at his performances—was "The Congo," a poem that is driven by rhythms and sounds inspired by his own sense of African drumming and that describes a wild and primitive Africa lurking just below the surface of African-American culture.

Lindsay first performed "The Congo" in 1914. It soon became such a hit, with audiences demanding its performance, that in time he came to resent reading it.[29] It was Lindsay who "discovered" Langston Hughes and brought him to the attention of the white media, after Hughes, working as a bus boy at the Wardman Park Hotel in Washington, D.C., left poems next to Lindsay's plate as he dined. Lindsay included Hughes's poems in a reading he gave that evening, and the next morning the papers reported that—as Hughes recalls—"Vachel Lindsay had discovered a Negro bus boy poet!"[30] (As Arnold Rampersad notes, the discovered poet already had a book in press with Alfred Knopf!) Lindsay's travels, performances, and public image provided a precedent and model for Hughes, but it was a precedent located within a history of the performance of poetry as a performance by whites of "black" culture and language.

RECITATIONS AND A BLACK READING PUBLIC

Burdened as it was with a history of moral and historical instruction *and* racial ventriloquism, the seemingly simple task of writing popular recitations became a complicated project for the black author writing—and publishing—for black audiences. Hughes's sense of his audience's sophistication shows in the range of poems in his tour program: his early poems, blues poems, labor poems, and even poems that protested the injustice of the recent Scottsboro trials. He also read from his most famous, most innovative, and most recent work. But for the poems to be used, to be recited in the classroom, home, or church, Hughes thought that they had to comply with topical and formal conventions of recitations that teachers, drama directors, and other readers would recognize. The recitation would then provide a starting point for a larger engagement with literature.

Thus, in many ways the poems of *The Negro Mother* follow conventions of recitations that had been published in schoolbooks. These poems reiterate historical lessons—the service of black soldiers in World War I, the centuries of American slavery. Poems such as "The Big Timer" offered moral instruction: the speaker's boasting of the luxuries and vices of a life hustling in a city slides during the monologue into an uneasiness with his separation and isolation from "the folks, down yonder at home," his family and community.[31] Above all, the poems are inspirational, often urging the effort of climbing a staircase as a metaphor for racial advancement. "Oh my dark children," speaks "The Negro Mother," "may my dreams and my prayers / Impel you forever up the great stairs."[32] Hughes turned to this same metaphor when he named his project of publishing inexpensive booklets for a broad black audience. The Golden Stair Press offered metaphorical pathways—routes upward, roads from darkness to light—that faintly echoed the prescriptions for properly lived lives recited by schoolchildren from nineteenth-century readers.

The speakers of Hughes's poems could not advocate a morality rooted in a Protestant work ethic to listeners who were barred from education and equal employment. Hughes's recitations protest the limits placed on the individual as they urge the effort to move "up the great stairs." "Broke," which describes the odyssey of a man looking for work, provides a detailed account of unemployment *and* employment practices during the Great Depression—declining wages, increased hours, and racial discrimination. Such practices are exposed in the poem by "a dejected looking fellow shuffling along in an old suit and a battered hat," as Hughes described the speaker and his costume in the stage directions.[33] The poem provides a text for speaking out against working conditions as well as unemployment:

> Willing worker? Un-uh! Yes! What's that you say?
> De time is fourteen hours a day?
> Well er—er . . . how much does you pay?
> Six dollars a week? Whee-ooo! You sho pays well!
> You can take that job and go to —— I hope you choke,
> Even if I is broke.[34]

In "Broke," the humor of the disruption of the rhyme pattern relies on expectation of the rhyme's regularity (as well as the audience's anticipation of the taboo rhyme word). In *The Negro Mother,* Hughes's recitations most obviously follow their nineteenth-century predecessors in their use of rhyme; they regularly ring out in heroic couplets or ballad stanzas. Although the language of these poems is simple in both diction and rhyme patterns, Hughes's scripting—the layout of the text, illustrations, and directions for the performance at the head of each poem and running down the outer margin—would have produced musically and emotionally complex performances. Hughes specified musical accompaniments that drew from popular war songs, blues, jazz, and spirituals, "played," Hughes fancifully dictated, "by a piano or an orchestra." In "The Big Timer," the speaker's subtle self-questioning is scored into the accompaniment with music that shifts between loud jazz and the blues. Hughes used music to highlight changing moods, and sometimes he used music to underscore irony. For example, for the pamphlet's first poem, "The Colored Soldier," Hughes recommended that the World War I anthem "Over There" be played behind the former soldier's account of how his brother gave his life in France for a dream of democracy that had yet to be realized in the South.

The most complex transactions of protest and inspiration are made in the recitations' use of type characters. These speakers are "types" who speak as representatives of social positions rather than as real or invented individuals; the types are almost all identified in the titles: "The Colored Soldier," "The Big Timer," "The Negro Mother," and so forth. Walter Ong distinguishes between the use of "type" or "flat" characters in the narratives of primary orality (which he defines as "the orality of cultures untouched by literacy") and the "round" individuals that writing enables.[35] In oral narratives, type characters were used, Ong argues, to "manage" information beyond the narrative; he cites Odysseus, Brer Rabbit, and the spider Anansi as type characters that "manage a lore of cleverness."[36] Ong complicates this apparently simple distinction by arguing—as he does throughout his study *Orality and Literacy*—that features of orality and literacy interpenetrate. Though Hughes's recitations were *written* to be performed, they appeal to an oral mode of delineating character and manage information about different social positions inhabited by African Americans.

They also respond to the fact that African Americans were continually represented as "types" in white writing. Sterling A. Brown begins his 1933 essay "Negro Character as Seen by White Authors" with the statement "There are three types of Negroes," a framework he attributes to the white author Roark Bradford. But Brown then argues from his examination of writing by white authors that there are seven types of black characters.[37] Types had been used by whites in the United States to manage racist information about African Americans, producing what we more commonly and pejoratively term "stereotypes." The problem the use of types in his recitations presented Hughes lurks in the blurb Carl Van Vechten wrote for the pamphlet's promotional flyer, reprinted on the back of the pamphlet. Van

Vechten described the poems as "passionately lyrical presentations of widely known and well-beloved Negro characters." Indeed, his language echoes that used to preface white dialect stories and monologues, such as Gielow's introduction to her "Mammy's Reminiscences."

Hughes confronted the tension between type and stereotype directly in the recitation "The Black Clown." His directions specify that the speaker be dressed "in the white suit and hat of a clown," while Taylor's illustration depicts a black man juggling in a billowy, polka-dot clown suit, complete with the conical hat adorned by pompons. Hughes suggests, "Comic entrance like the clowns in the circus." The black clown was a popular stereotype in white culture; Brown identified this type in his essay as the "Comic Negro." The speaker places himself in the stereotype from the inception of the monologue:

> You laugh
> Because I'm poor and black and funny—
> Not the same as you—
> Because my mind is dull
> And dice instead of books will do
> For me to play with
> When the day is through.[38]

As the clown describes slavery, the disappointment following emancipation, and his continuing exclusion from schools and jobs, the musical accompaniment swings from "a gay and low-down blues" to "melancholy jazz" to spirituals. This is an inspirational poem that urges its audience to "Suffer and struggle / Work, pray, and fight." It is scripted as a performance of throwing off the stereotype, as the speaker throws off his clown suit and proclaims, "I was once a black clown, / But now— / I'm a man." In the brochure, Taylor illustrates this transformation, as the clown suit—split open—falls behind a man presenting himself in a three-piece suit. Together the text, illustrations, and directions script a performance that enacts the critical work of recognizing, historicizing, and dismantling a racist representation for a popular audience.

Hughes wrote Taylor from Memphis, "The Negro Mother poem has been making a great hit on my programs recently."[39] The poem's popularity on the tour suggests that women responded to its tribute to the historical struggle of black women and to its unadulterated inspirational message. The poem is written in stately couplets; spirituals were to be played to accompany the monologue. Without a "mood" track to indicate a changing tone, the speaker would recite the poem "with great dignity and strength and beauty in her face," as suggested by Hughes's directions. The poem mobilizes the conventions of educational recitations that sought to form a public—but it creates a black American public rather than a white Protestant American public. The rhetoric of freedom used to describe the voyage of the Pilgrims in nineteenth-century recitations is turned instead to the voyage of the black girl stolen from Africa: "I am the black girl who crossed the dark sea / Carrying in my body the seed of the Free." Hughes places that paradigmatic enslaved journey within a narrative of the struggle toward freedom; Taylor's illustration depicts her with her arm upraised, suggesting the Statue of Liberty. (This association is also made in the text of the poem, as the girl offers her experiences as a "torch for tomorrow.") Even more revisionary, when "The Negro Mother" tells her story of degradation, struggle, and survival, an anonymous black woman moves into a historical and mythical position previously occupied by the founding fathers.

Lynn argues that such reiterations of particular histories and celebrations of mythic predecessors who struggled and survived aspired to form a public in the nineteenth century. Certainly Hughes wanted to create a public, a black American public, and even more specifically, a black reading public that imagined itself through literary texts, through reading and listening to poetry. The "vocation" (Lynn's term) that the "Negro Mother" urges is specifically a literary vocation, as the monologue advocates reading:

Now, through my children, young and free
I realize the blessings denied to me.
I couldn't read then. I couldn't write.
I had nothing, back there in the night.[40]

She asks future generations to "Make of my past a road to the light / Out of the darkness, the ignorance, the night." Langston Hughes's "Negro Mother" told a story, a history, that probably was not told in books in the South in 1931. But her recitation also provided a voice for the literacy activist—the teacher, librarian, parent—urging others in the community to read as a way up "the great stairs."

The booklet's other recitations are all spoken by boys or men and use a persistently masculinist language; "The Negro Mother" is the sole poem in Hughes's booklet spoken by a female persona. Hughes may have imagined the ultimate performers of these recitations as male students, but in "The Negro Mother" he recognized (and played to) women's central role in education and in the development of a black reading public. "The Negro Mother" offered a monologue to the librarians, teachers, community leaders, and members of reading groups who would form and further the booklet's audience. It also recognized that it was largely women who would acquire the book and disseminate the poems in their communities. Indeed, women wrote most of the mail order requests for *The Negro Mother*. The book reclaims representation of black women in the South from the mammy of recitations such as Gielow's monologues—the surrogate mother of white southern children. In her place is an eloquent black woman who advocates education for all the children of her race.

After he had been on tour for a few weeks, Hughes urged Taylor to add another broadside to the series produced by the Golden Stair Press. He wanted copies of "Dark Youth of the U.S.A.," the booklet's final poem, to sell to schoolchildren. The poem's persona is a student; both the directions and the illustration at the head dictate that he should be carrying books. Even the poem's first lines demand this necessary prop: "Sturdy I stand, books in my hand— / Today's dark child, tomorrow's strong man." After Hughes had toured for a month, he sent ten dollars to Taylor to personally pay for a printing of the broadside. "If it can be printed by January 1st, I can try it out on the kids in Florida when the tours [*sic*] re-begins. I shall probably give most of them away, as I read to so many little youngsters who have no money, and who ask me for poems."[41] Two months later, Hughes reported to Taylor that he had indeed given most of them away. As he accounted for his sales, he wrote, "The only other thing is the Dark Youth Broadsides. Those I am using entirely as gifts to youngsters and teachers in little schools too poor to buy anything, as a rule."[42] These comments underscore his personal mission to leave some text behind—if not books or booklets, then at least a broadside—in each school he visited.

"The Dark Youth" is another recitation of African-American history and inspiration: "Long a part of the Union's heart— / Years ago at the nation's start / Attucks died," the student recites, attesting to the participation of black Americans in the founding days of the republic. Even more strongly than "The Negro Mother," the poem urges literacy and education:

To be wise and strong, then, studying long,
Seeking the knowledge that rights all wrong—
   That is my mission.
Lifting my race to its rightful place
Till beauty and pride fills each dark face
   Is my ambition.[43]

Each student who recited "Dark Youth of the U.S.A." took on the "mission" of advocating literacy and education as a path to a "rightful place" of full citizenship. The illustration at the foot of the poem shows a white student and a black student standing side by side, their hands clasped. They are standing behind a curtain, each pulling half of the curtain away with his outside hand. The image suggests both opening the curtain, revealing a new vision of interracial collaboration and equality, and closing it, signaling the end of a performance. As the final image in the booklet, it completes the invitation to use the booklet as a script, to present from it a series of performances that would mobilize the audiences of Hughes's public readings into a reading public.

"So Luxurious a Special Edition"

"In the tail piece, the slight resemblances to L.H. and P.T. are intentional," wrote Prentiss Taylor of the booklet's final illustration in 1967.[44] For Hughes and Taylor, the booklet closes with an image representing their collaboration and their friendship (and perhaps an erotic attraction). Their collaboration in the Golden Stair Press unfolded primarily through correspondence, as Hughes wrote to Taylor from points along the tour, and Taylor sent letters, booklets, and broadsides to Hughes to fulfill a demand for the booklet that exceeded their expectations. "Tour popping like firecrackers all Negro Mothers sold out please send twenty five copies with bill," Hughes cabled Taylor from Virginia after less than a week on tour.[45] The following day he sent a check to be put toward another printing and described the demand for the booklet: "The others have been sold out three days ago. Could have sold 50 or 100 more, I believe, at Hampton where there was a very large audience."[46] This demand continued through the duration of Hughes's tour, and the poet requested, and Taylor ordered and shipped, two additional printings of The Negro Mother. A passage from a letter sent by Hughes after three months on tour—he was in Memphis on his birthday—outlines his business sensibilities and the itinerary of the remainder of his tour: "We have on hand now only a hundred Mothers. They may last the week out, (Mississippi) but I must have some more at New Orleans. I can probably sell at least 500 more on tour, as I still have Tuskegee, Arkansas, Middle West, and Texas to do—and very likely California in late April & May.—if the latter another edition can probably be practically sold out. How many copies have you left in New York? If not many, I think it would be wise to start the 3rd edition going at once."[47] The three printings of The Negro Mother totaled 2,750 copies, with 200 copies each of five broadsides printed and sold.[48]

Around this time Taylor, who had been working on lithographs depicting the Scottsboro boys, proposed a booklet to Hughes that would collect these lithographs and Hughes's published writings about the trials. "That's a swell idea about the Scottsboro booklet," Hughes responded by postcard.[49] Hughes was concerned about how they would market and distribute this second booklet, but he supported the idea because he thought the booklet could contribute to publicity of the case and perhaps raise funds that they could donate to the defendants. In the months that followed, they passed drafts back and forth through the mail. In his letters, Hughes praised Taylor's lithographs but urged him to "try [to] put touch of terror in some one of the decorations."[50] When Taylor sent Hughes pages to autograph before the booklets were bound, Hughes answered, "I was certainly impressed, in fact, overwhelmed, by the size and beauty of the paper. I bow way down before so luxurious a special edition."[51] When he arrived in California, the final state on his tour, Hughes spoke at several mass meetings and political events. He had begun to realize that there was a large potential market for the Scottsboro booklet. He urged Taylor to speed its shipment, but the booklets arrived after the last major readings of the tour. Hughes then left the country, joining a group of African Americans on their way to Moscow to perform in a Soviet film; he left Taylor with the unsold copies.

Under Taylor's direction, the Golden Stair Press's second volume departed from the first not only in its explicit and provocative focus on a contemporary political event but also in its invitation to a different kind of consumption. While *The Negro Mother* was designed to empower people to stage their own poetry readings, the fine paper and dense lithographs of *Scottsboro Limited* made it more a book to be owned, collected, and privately consumed. This is one of the booklet's failures, for Hughes's poems in this volume, like the recitations of *The Negro Mother,* offer themselves as texts for public performance. *Scottsboro Limited* even includes the text of a one-act play, but in this format the poems and play are less recognizable as scripts. The poems in *Scottsboro Limited* are much more varied formally than the recitations in *The Negro Mother;* this variety provides texts that could be used to speak about the Scottsboro trials in a range of public contexts. The booklet's first poem, for example, is the allusive epigram "Justice," a poem that Hughes read often during the tour:

That Justice is a blind goddess
Is a thing to which we black are wise.
Her bandage hides two festering sores
That once perhaps were eyes.[52]

This revision of the familiar icon of justice provided audiences with a text that could be spoken in places and situations where it was dangerous to speak directly about the Scottsboro trials (as it was in many of the southern communities Hughes visited on his tour). It was a text that could also be rearticulated to allude to local injustices. The poem "Scottsboro," in contrast, topical and with short lines that could be shouted out, could be used at public events organized in support of the Scottsboro defendants. Taylor and Hughes ultimately blamed the failure of *Scottsboro Limited* on the booklet's politics and on the fact that Hughes was not able to sell it at public readings. But the booklet's appeal was also limited by the fact that it was produced and marketed as a book to be collected, rather than spoken from. *Scottsboro Limited* did not capitalize on the great innovation of the Golden Stair Press: its invitation to audiences to participate in and further the creation of a black audience for black literature.

NOTES

1. Langston Hughes, *I Wonder as I Wander* (New York: Rinehart, 1956), 41. Bethune accompanied Hughes and his friend Zell Ingram as they drove north from Daytona Beach to New York City; their journey gave Hughes a taste of how such a tour might be received. They were welcomed by Bethune's friends up the entire East Coast, and when they stopped at an academy in South Carolina the school ordered an impromptu assembly so the students could all hear Hughes read.

2. Hughes to White, Aug. 3, 1931, Rosenwald Papers, Fisk University Library, Nashville, Tenn.

3. Langston Hughes, *The Negro Mother and Other Dramatic Recitations* (New York: Golden Stair Press, 1931). Their mutual friend Carl Van Vechten witnessed the agreement between Hughes and Taylor and provided financial backing.

4. Hughes, "Promotion Letter," Oct. 13, 1931, in the Prentiss Taylor Papers, Archives of American Art, Washington, D.C. (hereinafter cited as PTP). I assume that this letter was sent to potential reviewers of *The Negro Mother*. Prentiss Taylor apparently typed copies of the letters he received from Hughes—sometimes adding commentary—before sending the originals to the Beinecke Library at Yale University. In this essay, references from Hughes's correspondence with Taylor are quoted from these annotated, duplicate letters held in the Archives of American Art.

5. This publishing project may have had some antecedents during the 1920s. Jean Wagner argues, "Communication between black poets and [black] people was never closer than during the decade after World War I. The poems made their ways among the masses, chiefly through the numerous black periodicals that provided them with an outlet." Wagner describes oral recitation as a significant mode of circulation of black poetry during the decade: poems were repeated by black ministers, orators, and working people. "In restaurant kitchens and barber shops, dishwashers and shoeshine boys passed poems from hand to hand and repeated them aloud." Wagner also describes Alain Locke's 1927 "brochure," *Four Negro Poets*—

which included poems by Jean Toomer, Countee Cullen, Langston Hughes, and Claude McKay—as an attempt to bring black poetry to a wider audience. See Jean Wagner, *Black Poets of the United States,* trans. Kenneth Douglas (Urbana: University of Illinois Press, 1973), 173–76.

6. Aubrey Bowser, "Converted at Last!" *Amsterdam News,* Jan. 13, 1932, 8.

7. See Hortense J. Spillers, "Moving on Down the Line: Variations on the African-American Sermon," in *The Bounds of Race: Perspectives on Hegemony and Resistance,* ed. Dominick LaCapra (Ithaca, N.Y.: Cornell University Press, 1991), 61–62.

8. Ibid., 49.

9. U.S. Department of Commerce, *Fifteenth Census of the United States, 1930,* vol. 2: *Population* (Washington, D.C.: Government Printing Office, 1933), 1223. The precision of these data has been questioned, largely because the census asked people to report their own illiteracy. Carl F. Kaestle concludes of these data: "At worst, census illiteracy statistics measure nothing more than people's willingness to admit illiteracy; at best, they indicate a minimal estimate of illiteracy." See Carl F. Kaestle, Helen Damon-Moore, Lawrence C. Stedman, Katherine Tinsley, and William Vance Trollinger Jr., *Literacy in the United States: Readers and Reading since 1880* (New Haven, Conn.: Yale University Press, 1991), 24.

10. *Fifteenth Census,* 1229.

11. John K. Folger and Charles B. Nam, *Education of the American Population* (Washington, D.C.: Government Printing Office, 1967), 145. Folger and Nam also discuss the limitations of these data, including the fact that they do not include education attained outside of public and private schools and colleges, such as job training, commercial courses, industrial training, and informal education; the variability of a "year of school"; and the unreliability of census subjects (134–35).

12. I have drawn this list of black newspapers and the description of their distribution from Walter C. Daniel, "Langston Hughes versus the Black Preachers in the *Pittsburgh Courier* in the 1930s," in *Critical Essays on Langston Hughes,* ed. Edward J. Mullen (Boston: G. K. Hall, 1986), 129.

13. Abby Arthur Johnson and Ronald Maberry Johnson, *Propaganda and Aesthetics: The Literary Politics of Afro-American Magazines in the Twentieth Century* (Amherst: University of Massachusetts Press, 1979), 35.

14. Johnson and Johnson's chapter, entitled "Black Renaissance: Little Magazines and Special Issues, 1916–1930" (ibid., 65–96), describes these short-lived little magazines.

15. Alain Locke, "1928: A Retrospective," *Opportunity,* Jan. 1929, 10.

16. Advertisement, *Crisis,* Nov. 1931, 363.

17. Duke to Golden Stair Press, 1932, PTP.

18. Anderson to Golden Stair Press, Jan. 12, 1932, PTP.

19. I suspect she means that the club was hosting one of the readings on Hughes's tour.

20. Roberts to Golden Stair Press, Mar. 18, 1932, PTP.

21. Increase Cooke, *Introduction to the American Orator* (New Haven, Conn.: Sidney's Press, 1812), n.p.

22. According to Robert Wood Lynn, 120 million copies of the readers were printed from 1836 to 1920; the series was the most widely used textbook in the common schools of the Midwest ("Civil Catechetics in Mid-Victorian America:

Some Notes about American Civil Religion, Past and Present," *Religious Education* 68 [1973]: 10, 12).

23. Ibid., 19.

24. Ibid., 23.

25. Excelsior Publishing House of New York advertised its series of books of recitations alongside books of etiquette and humor, games and calisthenics, foreign languages "at a glance," a gunsmith's manual, and other "Practical Trade Manuals." In the back pages of its books, Dick and Fitzgerald Publishers, also of New York, advertised a series of books of readings and recitals, dialogue books, amateur theatricals, cards and other games, books of humor, and self-help and self-improvement books such as *The Amateur Trapper and Trap Maker's Guide, Frank Converse's Complete Banjo Instructor without a Master,* and *The Art and Etiquette of Making Love.*

26. Michael North, *The Dialect of Modernism: Race. Language and Twentieth-Century Literature* (New York: Oxford University Press, 1994), 18, 23–24.

27. Martha S. Gielow, *Mammy's Reminiscences and Other Sketches* (New York: A. S. Barnes, 1898). The copy in Cornell University's Olin Library contains an autograph dated Dec. 16, 1899, and a copy of Mrs. Henry J. Gielow's announcement of her readiness to "receive engagements for recitals" attached to the inside cover. The book may well have been purchased by someone who attended one of Gielow's performances.

28. Don Cusic, *The Poet as Performer* (Lanham, Md.: University Press of America, 1991), 13–14.

29. Ibid., 17.

30. Hughes, *The Big Sea* (New York: Alfred A. Knopf, 1940), 212. Reporters visited Hughes at the hotel, interviewing and photographing him holding a tray of dirty dishes. He noted that the picture appeared in papers throughout the country and commented, "It was my first publicity break."

31. Hughes, *Negro Mother,* 14.

32. Ibid., 18.

33. Another economic reality of the depression, the fact that many unemployed or laid-off men were supported by working women, is dramatized at the close of the poem, when the speaker marries a working woman—not for love but for fried chicken.

34. Hughes, *Negro Mother,* 5.

35. Walter Ong, *Orality and Literacy: The Technologizing of the Word* (London: Routledge, 1982), 6, 151–55.

36. Ibid., 151.

37. Sterling A. Brown, "Negro Character as Seen by White Authors," *Journal of Negro Education* 11 (1933): 179–203. The seven types Brown describes are the contented slave, wretched freeman, comic Negro, brute Negro, tragic mulatto, local color Negro, and exotic primitive.

38. Hughes, *Negro Mother,* 8.

39. Hughes to Taylor, Feb. 1, 1932, PTP.

40. Hughes, *Negro Mother,* 17.

41. Hughes to Taylor, Dec. 16, 1931, PTP.

42. Ibid., Feb. 1, 1932, PTP.

43. Hughes, *Negro Mother,* 20.

44. Prentiss Taylor, ts., folder 9/16, PTP.

45. Hughes to Taylor, telegram, Nov. 8, 1931, PTP.

46. Ibid., Nov. 9, 1931, PTP.

47. Ibid., Feb. 1, 1932, PTP.

48. This figure comes from a handwritten tally under the heading "Golden Stair" in the Prentiss Taylor Papers. Typewritten notes from 1967 record the total of the three printings as 2,250 copies.

49. Hughes to Taylor, postcard, Feb. 13, 1932, PTP.

50. Ibid., telegram, Apr. 18, 1932, PTP.

51. Ibid., May 7, 1932, PTP.

52. Hughes, *Scottsboro Limited* (New York: Golden Stair Press, 1932), n.p.

Keeping the "Secret of Authorship": A Critical Look
at the 1912 Publication of James Weldon Johnson's
Autobiography of an Ex-Colored Man

JACQUELINE GOLDSBY

We often underestimate the importance of the first appearance of
James Weldon Johnson's *Autobiography of an Ex-Colored Man* because today's readers are most familiar with the 1927 edition. The 1912 version of
the book rarely receives specific critical due, no doubt because the later
imprint bears upon it the glamour of having been reissued by a major
publisher (Alfred A. Knopf) as a "classic" at the height of the Harlem Renaissance and because scholars now regard the 1927 edition as the standard form of the text.[1]

The era of the "roaring twenties" was not the era of the "mauve" 'teens;
that is, the world in which James Weldon Johnson made his literary debut was distinctly different from the one in which he presided over African America's culture of letters. By then Johnson's scope of influence had
broadened to, perhaps, its fullest range. For example, *The Book of American Negro Poetry* (1922) and *The Book of American Negro Spirituals* (1925),
survey collections compiled by Johnson for Harcourt, Brace and Viking
Press, respectively, had become standards in those fields. Though well
received upon its appearance in 1917, the more traditional settings of racial themes in *Fifty Years and Other Poems* seemed slight in comparison to
the innovative stylings of African-American sermons in *God's Trombones*
(1927). These triumphs not only distinguished Johnson in the literary field
but also enhanced his prestige as a formidable politician. His visibility as
executive secretary of the National Association for the Advancement of
Colored People (NAACP) reached its peak in the early to mid-1920s, partly because the zealous candor with which Johnson pursued the organization's agenda of political reform was tempered by the mannered restraint
that characterized his art.[2]

When *The Autobiography of an Ex-Colored Man* was published by Sher-

man, French, and Company in 1912, Johnson was an ambitious but strug-
gling musician-diplomat whose reputation as either a poet or novelist was
not yet secured and could not be developed freely, given the temper of the
times. For during those years African Americans were passing through "the
nadir," meaning that period of brutal political repression between the end
of Reconstruction and the outbreak of World War I. The gains achieved by
blacks following emancipation—the codification of national citizenship
and voting rights, participation in local, state, and federal government, and
unregulated movement throughout the public sphere—were systematically
dismantled through segregation, disfranchisement, and lynching.[3]

Though commonly practiced in the southern states, these acts crossed
regional borders in their literal form and through various media of writing. U.S. Supreme Court decisions such as *Plessy v. Ferguson* (1896) gave the
highest official sanction to individual states' curtailment of black civil
rights; academic treatises such as Frederick L. Hoffman's *Race Traits and
Tendencies of the American Negro* (1896) applied the philosophy of social
Darwinism and the emerging methodologies of statistics and sociology
to scientific inquiries confirming black degeneracy; and best-selling
fiction such as Joel Chandler Harris's *Uncle Remus Stories* (1881) and Thomas Dixon's *The Leopard's Spots* (1902) and *The Clansman* (1905) popularized
the myths of the alien and depraved nature of African-American moral
character, thus reinforcing the findings of legal jurists and social scientists
in the less assailable forms of fiction.[4]

While the "Negro problem" had not been solved by 1927, in 1912 the
issue was new enough that its effects wounded African Americans—literally and figuratively—on an unprecedented scale. Recalling his despair
over the election of Woodrow Wilson, a southern Democrat, to the White
House, Johnson lamented:

> Going back to the days of Reconstruction, the Negro in the South had al-
> ways felt, no matter what his local status might be, that he was a citizen of
> the United States. This feeling was manifest especially when such a Negro
> entered a federal building. There he felt that he was on some portion, at
> least of the ground of common citizenship; that he left most of the gall-
> ing humiliations on the outside. This, in reality, was only little more than
> a feeling; but, at that, it was worth something.[5]

Reading *The Autobiography of an Ex-Colored Man* in 1927, the visual artist Aaron Douglas sensed that Johnson was "such a Negro" who longed
to claim his national identity under the cultural aegis of the state. Douglas also recognized that, given the era in which he lived, Johnson labored

at his craft without such protection. Both men understood the irony of progress since, within fifteen years, each occupied a privileged seat in the cultural capital of New York: commissioned to design the dust jacket for the Knopf edition of the novel, Douglas wrote Johnson to thank him for the honor. Explaining why the book impressed him, Douglas exclaimed: "I am amazed at the gigantic effort which must have been necessary for the writing and publishing of the book at such an early date. The post-war Negro, blinded by the glare and almost sudden bursting of a new day, finds much difficulty in realizing the immense power and effort, which the pre-war Negro has made to prepare the country for what we now feel to be the 'Awakening.'"[6]

Indeed, Johnson himself was aware of the historical context of his authorship. Between 1922 and 1925, in an effort to solicit bids to revive his novel, Johnson circulated his last personal copies of the 1912 edition to such New York notables as Carl Van Doren, Carl Van Vechten, and Heywood Broun. To Broun, a columnist for the *New York World* and a member of the legendary Algonquin "round table," Johnson explained the novel's origins: "I published [this] book anonymously about fourteen years ago with a firm in Boston that went out of business during the war. I believe that the book was published out of time. Fourteen years ago there was little or no interest in the Negro. In fact, we had reached the deepest depths of apathy regarding him so far as the general public is concerned."[7]

What did it mean for an African-American author—a "pre-war Negro," to use Aaron Douglas's phrase—to write a book whose fate was to be "published out of time"? What incentives would sustain an artist when his audience showed "little or no interest" in his culture and voice? How would a black intellectual nurture his creative faculties in the face of the general public's "deepest depths of apathy"?

These are some of the questions that characterize the cultural moment when James Weldon Johnson first published *The Autobiography of an Ex-Colored Man* in 1912. It is important to frame them as such, because the appearance of the original edition of the novel and its subsequent reprintings are historically distinct events. Placing the novel in its original context allows readers to assess the complexity of Johnson's efforts to conceive a narrative form and to cultivate a reading public for what critics now consider the first modernist novel in the African-American canon. Ironically, however, such a historicist interpretation depends on readers' willingness to keep a "secret," for the significance of the 1912 edition of the book rests upon Johnson's clever—and, as we shall see, painful—handling of information about his authorship of the book.

To follow this line of argument, I will draw upon provisionally "secret" documents, namely, unpublished manuscript sources from Johnson's papers. Using those texts as my guide, I will first discuss how Johnson arrived at the topic for the novel, describe his tactics of composition, and outline his plans for marketing it to the reading public. Second, I will identify the changes made to the manuscript drafts of the novel, in order to interpret how Johnson's publicity strategies and textual revisions inform the trope of the "secret" that structures the novel as a whole. Finally, I will argue that these two points are linked by a third element. Johnson not only wanted his anonymously published novel to succeed in the literary marketplace; he also needed it—and used it—to rescue himself from a devastating political crisis. His unpublished diaries and correspondence reveal how the writing of the *Autobiography* was intimately linked to his struggles with the Taft and Wilson administrations to upgrade his diplomatic appointment in the U.S. consular service. The cloak of anonymity that Johnson draped over the writing and publicity campaign for the 1912 edition conceal a deeply wounding challenge to his personal authority, one that informed his desire for and pursuit of authorship and, so, points toward the novel's particular meaning for him in turn-of-the-century America.

❏

At the end of the nineteenth century, James Weldon Johnson was living in New York City and making a name for himself on the Broadway stage. Along with his brother Rosamond and singer-composer Bob Cole, Johnson penned the lyrics to such best-selling ballads as "Since You Went Away" (1900) and the Broadway smash hit, "Under the Bamboo Tree" (1902). But Johnson had begun to move away from writing musical verse when he enrolled in postgraduate courses at Columbia University. There, he met and studied with the renowned literary critic Brander Matthews, whose courses on realist drama and prose narrative sparked Johnson's intellectual interests in writing fiction. It was at this time and under Matthews's tutelage (1902–5) that Johnson conceived the project that would become *The Autobiography of an Ex-Colored Man*. Matthews read the first two chapters of the novel and gave Johnson encouraging feedback. The professor liked the title and commended his student for "writing about the thing he knew best."[8]

Between Matthews's inspiring support and his own enforced hiatuses from lyric writing, Johnson began to reconsider his vocation. He wanted to do "respectable" work, to join the professional classes available to college-educated black men at that time. Not that he wanted to be a schoolteacher or lawyer; Johnson abandoned those careers when he left his hometown of Jacksonville, Florida, for the cosmopolitan life of Manhattan. Clarity came in 1906, when an alluring political opportunity occurred. Charles W. Anderson, the political boss of New York State's black Republicans and a scout for the national power broker Booker T. Washington, approached Johnson with an offer. President Theodore Roosevelt had decided to hand out some spoils of office to African Americans, and the chancellor of the Tuskegee Institute recommended Johnson for a post in the U.S. consular service. Johnson promptly accepted his assignment to Venezuela because the job promised a kind of prestige he had been seeking but could not find through his success on Tin Pan Alley. In March of that year, Johnson packed his belongings—and his manuscript—and sailed for Puerto Cabello, Venezuela.[9]

Johnson resumed working in earnest on the *Autobiography* in this new setting and at his second consular commission a few years later, in Corinto, Nicaragua. In his published memoir, *Along This Way* (1933), Johnson recalled that the writing went smoothly once he settled into his post: "The story developed in my mind more rapidly than I had expected that it would; at times, outrunning my speed to get it down. The use of prose as a creative medium was new to me; its latitude, its flexibility, its comprehensiveness, the variety of approaches it afforded for surmounting technical difficulties gave me a feeling of exhilaration, exhilaration similar to that which goes with freedom of motion."[10] Notably, this public account contradicts the descriptions in his private correspondence of his writing process. In letters to family, friends, and colleagues, a different picture— a secret picture—of the author at work emerges.

␫

Neither Puerto Cabello nor Corinto compared to the cultural mecca of New York City. Johnson's writer's tools—typewriters and English-language books and periodicals—were scarce; intellectual comrades and diversions were few. Though Johnson enjoyed the dinner company of the Latin American elite, and while he regularly mingled with American commanders whose ships docked in Corinto's harbors, such gatherings did not match his private tutorials with Brander Matthews. In 1908 Johnson complained to his mentor: "I hardly think that I can gain anything more [by remaining abroad]. I feel my power to do better work than before, but I also feel the lack of incentive."[11] Johnson's wife, Grace Nail Johnson, became an earnest colleague: from their home base in New York City, she kept her husband's subscriptions up-to-date and served as a trusted confidante who was quick (her letters reveal) to critique Johnson's work. Still, the lack of immediate contact frustrated them both; thinking (and loving) through letter writing sometimes was not enough for the newlywed couple.[12]

The climate also worked against Johnson's creative advantage. In both Venezuela and Nicaragua the sweltering tropical heat all but withered his attention span; on a typical day, Johnson complained to his wife, the humid air demanded "the will power of madness to stick to work."[13] Then there were the duties of his job. Nighttime writing sessions were abbreviated when diplomatic dinner dates lasted late; and routine daytime tasks kept him away from his writing projects.[14] Most critically, during the years when Johnson completed the manuscript of the *Autobiography* (1908–11), Venezuelans quietly deposed their president, Cipriano Castro, while political factions in Nicaragua mobilized toward armed conflict. In Corinto, the political situation was especially tense. A brokered peace among the rival parties was tenuous by the time Johnson mailed the completed manuscript to his publisher in January 1912; by August and throughout the rest of the year, Nicaraguans were engaged in a civil war. As American consul in Corinto, Johnson was the primary civilian officer on site and therefore found himself at the center of a violent political storm.[15]

By his own admission—in private—these were hardly ideal circumstances in which to write a novel. In a letter to Brander Matthews, Johnson explained the toll the foreign settings took on his artistic faculties: "I have been hindered some by the condition of things here, between plague, fear of war and revolution, and the uncertainty of how long I should have to remain in Puerto Cabello, my mind has been far from being in a state for writing."[16]

Worried that he had lost his powers of concentration, Johnson sought guidance from his professor. In the same letter he confided that the novel's conclusion seemed problematic. The ending disturbed Johnson when he read it, for he feared it broke the structure and sense of the text as a whole: "Here is the M.S. of the last part of my book as I have re-written it. The job has been a fearful one. I feel that I have lost the spirit of the story, and I'm afraid that what I have just written is not up to the rest. I'm also afraid that I cannot write convincingly about love."[17] Johnson's tone suggests he is responding to Matthews's criticism of an earlier draft. To be sure, we lack Matthews's answer to Johnson's plea to confirm whether this was the case. Nevertheless, it seems fair to assume that the professor approved of the changes, because the "re-written" manuscript to which Johnson refers is the one that was ultimately printed by the publisher, Sherman, French, and Company.

⅃

Johnson's angst about the conclusion is telling and, critically, we can trace that concern through the draft manuscripts of the novel. Specifically, Johnson's revisions lead us to the book's final two chapters. There, the climactic lynching scene undergoes a remarkably self-conscious construction, and the actual conclusion of the novel gets revised altogether. The graphic markings of these changes in the manuscript draft not only reveal the aesthetic difficulties Johnson encountered as he crafted the end of the novel but also record his struggle to suppress the dark, terror-filled secret of his own life: his near-fatal encounter with a lynch mob in 1900.

As described in *Along This Way*, an angry posse of Florida's National Guardsmen almost murdered Johnson after hearing a report that he was seen taking a white woman into a secluded section of a local park in Jacksonville. (In fact, he was meeting with a light-complexioned black journalist who was writing about a catastrophic fire that had destroyed the town's African-American district.) For Johnson, the standoff with the mob robbed him of peace in his psychic life, traumatizing him for years afterward:

> For weeks and months the episode with all of its implications preyed upon my mind and disturbed me in my sleep. I would wake often in the nighttime, after living through again those few frightful seconds, exhausted by the nightmare of a struggle with a band of murderous, bloodthirsty men in khaki, with loaded rifles and fixed bayonets. It was not until twenty years after, through work I was then engaged in, that I was able to liberate myself completely from this horror complex.[18]

Johnson tried to work through his "horror complex" in the *Autobiography* by imagining a lynching as the climax of the plot. That this event gives rise to the narrator's epiphany—indeed, to conceive of the murderous encounter as an awakening—was not an easy task for Johnson, and we can see his pain take form on the page.

The margins of his legal pad are lined with bitter remarks about the inhumanity of lynching, commentary that shows how he struggled to attain a nondidactic tone in the final text and how he divided his personal self from the fictional persona he was trying to create. Even with the page spatially compartmentalized between the author's "true" self and his "real" character, Johnson's initial attempts at the passage are still disorganized. Entire lines are set down, stricken out, and rewritten with little regard for legibility in an apparent effort to keep the narrator's voice consistent with the ironic detachment and moral ambivalence that characterize the narrative prior to this moment. Johnson was deceiving both Brander Matthews and himself when he worried that he could not write "convincingly about love," for that was not the formal problem Johnson had to solve at the end of his book. Representing an act of hate as a meaningful experience was the narrative point he wanted to avoid but knew he must achieve.

The strain this scene levied on Johnson's imaginative reserves registers in the earliest draft of the novel's conclusion. There, he cannot decide what the consequences of the lynching scene should be. In that manuscript, the mulatto protagonist witnesses a lynching that so horrifies him he decides to flee the South, move to the North, and pass as a white man. He enrolls in a business college and becomes a successful real estate investor in New York. His charade is so effective that he woos and weds a white woman, hiding from her his true identity. However, in this version of the ending, with the narrator leading a successful but duplicitous life, the *Autobiography* fails to sustain the ironic detachment Johnson creates throughout the rest of the book. Allowing the narrator to escape the consequences of his actions—to have him marry and keep his identity secret from his wife—would have been to succumb to convention of the most sentimental sort.

This outcome is what creates the dilemma Johnson described to Matthews: What should be the logical relationship between the narrator's epiphany at the lynching and his subsequent actions? What lesson should the narrator—and the reader—draw from the knowledge of his secret? Johnson rewrote the ending to address these questions.

In the final draft manuscript, the narrator witnesses the lynching, moves North, passes as white, hits upon financial success, and meets the woman who is to become his wife. When he asks her to marry him, though, the narrator reveals his secret to her. At first, she recoils at the news and refuses his proposal. In time, she concedes her love for him and agrees to wed. As a kind of exchange (and, clearly, as a rite of penance), the narrator imposes a crippling stipulation upon himself: he chooses to live in silence, refusing to tell his wife's family or their friends and children the truth about his racial heritage. Upon bearing their second child, a son, the wife dies, leaving the narrator to raise his children alone. He forsakes adult romance, abandons his musical career, and wonders, in the end, if his denials have exacted too high a cost; whether, as Johnson wrote, he has "sold his birthright for a mess of pottage."

These revisions bring with them both a higher price and deeper narrative satisfaction: the narrator must confront and pay for his cowardice. His arrogance has been tempered, but his humility is difficult to bear, for the character and the reader alike understand that a true sense of completion must occur through his experience of punishment. However odd it may seem as a plan for narrative resolution, finishing the novel on this pessimistic note is precisely the place to end, because it allows Johnson to fulfill the promise made by the narrator at the story's outset: to "divulg[e] the great secret of my life" and, by so doing, to seek relief for the "vague feeling of unsatisfaction, of regret, almost remorse . . . of which I shall speak in the last paragraph of this account."[19]

◪

Thus, the revisions make the book a coherent whole, thematically and structurally. Still, it is not entirely clear from Johnson's manuscript files who prompted him to make these changes. Brander Matthews's response most likely played a significant role in the transition of the novel's conclusion. Such directives probably did not come from Johnson's publisher, however. Looking back on his contract with the book's publisher, Johnson accused Sherman, French, and Company of being "one of those quasi publishing companies who are in fact only job printers for authors."[20] True to Johnson's complaint, the firm seemed to handle the book with a laissez-faire approach. No one person at Sherman, French corresponded consistently with Johnson, suggesting either that the editors and staff offered little personalized attention to its authors, or that tasks were delegated without regard for roles or turf. The publisher's uneven level of involvement was most clearly reflected in its publicity campaign for the novel. Sherman, French printed an initial flyer for the book and then consistently retreated from incurring further expense to promote and market the book, even when the novel was clearly a critical success.

The firm kept close tabs on Johnson's complimentary copies, charging him for every book he requested. At the same time, the company was lax in capitalizing on the favorable press the book received. When Brander Matthews included the *Autobiography* in a review essay published in *Munsey's Magazine,* "American Character in Fiction" (Aug. 1913), Sherman, French printed a circular highlighting the relevant excerpt from the column. However, the company charged Johnson for the printing costs against his royalties, politely but firmly expressing its hope that sales triggered by the ad would clear out the remaining copies of the book. In 1914, Johnson prodded the firm to market the book toward a black audience and crafted a scheme with the *New York Age* to package sales of the novel with subscriptions to the newspaper. Sherman, French approved of the idea but in correspondence with Fred Moore the firm seemed lukewarm about following through on the project.[21]

In one sense, Johnson's choice of Sherman, French, and Company as the publisher of the *Autobiography* reflects the limited range of options available to black novelists in the early twentieth century. In those years, only Paul Laurence Dunbar and Charles Chesnutt managed to cross the color line segregating mainstream and African-American publishing firms; these authors' access to Houghton Mifflin and Dodd, Mead were truly exceptional. Most other African-American writers were bound by the rule that restricted circulation of their work to black publishing and reading circles.[22] In 1912, Johnson was a first-time black novelist whose manuscript was controversial because it broke with the traditional themes and narrative forms common to African-American fiction at that time. In comparison to Chesnutt's popular work, for example, Johnson's *Autobiography* lacked the buoyant raconteur Uncle Julius and the satirical wit of *The Conjure Woman* (1899). The alienated engagement of Johnson's protagonist with black folk culture avoided the trappings of nostalgia that shaped (and, ultimately, constricted) Dunbar's use of vernacular idioms in his art.

By the same token, what made Johnson's novel stand out against the work of Chesnutt or Dunbar also isolated it from the fiction published within black circles. The amoral outlook of the *Autobiography*—the narrator's solipsism, passivity, cowardice—made it a dubious contribution to the literature of racial uplift. The "ex-colored" man failed to measure up to the mixed race and "pure" black heroines and heroes of Frances Harper's *Iola Leroy* (1894), Pauline Hopkins's *Contending Forces* (1900), or Sutton Griggs's *Unfettered* (1902).[23] Evaluated from any angle, Johnson's novel posed a tremendous risk to any publishing firm except a "job printer for authors." Thus, despite his complaints in retrospect, a firm like Sherman, French, and Company offered the most viable option for the novel's publication.

Thus, the question becomes: Of the job printers available to him, why did Johnson choose Sherman, French, and Company? Why did he opt to place the manuscript with a firm run by whites rather than one operated by blacks? Johnson's currency as a novelist may have been untested, but his market value as a showman, politician, and poet was well known. As a Broadway lyricist, he conducted his business with a top music publisher in Manhattan, Edwin B. Marks and Company.[24] His political connections through Booker T. Washington gave him ready access to a nationally influential news weekly, the *New York Age,* and to Washington's own publisher, Doubleday, Page.[25] From his consular posts in Venezuela and Nicaragua, Johnson routed his early poetry to the *Century* magazine; he could have asked Richard Watson Gilder for advice on where to place the *Autobiography*. Brander Matthews also had connections Johnson could exploit; indeed, the critic probably recommended Sherman, French to Johnson. And there were other leads to follow. Black-owned firms, such as the press of R. L. Pendleton and the Murray Brothers Printing Company of Washington, D.C., handled fiction titles from time to time; Johnson could have submitted the manuscript to either of them but did not.[26]

Why? A special problem Johnson needed to guard against was the maintenance of his anonymity. His association with Sherman, French, and Company shielded his secret identity that much more fully. The spotlight of mainstream fame shone brightly on Johnson when he lived in New York City and wrote for the Broadway stage. After he accepted his consular service assignments, however, his prominence within those circles of recognition diminished. Within African America, though, Johnson's departure to Venezuela marked his arrival as a race man of merit. Indeed, his sojourn abroad increased his celebrity because it redeemed the success of his career in musical theater. The musician-turned-diplomat cut a handsome figure as a cultural hero, and the black press kept respectful watch over his performance at his posts in Venezuela and Nicaragua.[27] As the author of the "Negro National Anthem," Johnson could not submit a manuscript to a black publisher and expect that his anonymity would be maintained.

Johnson made mutual confidentiality a stipulation in his contract with Sherman, French not only because it was his right to do so but also because he knew the clause could be more easily respected by this white firm.[28] If Atlanta University's handling of the book was any indication, Johnson's secret would have lived a short life within black publishing circles. Johnson's alma mater operated a press that may very well have gambled on publishing the novel had Johnson made such a request. Instead, he arranged for Sherman, French to send the school a complimentary copy once the book was published. When the editor of the university's alumni bulletin recognized that the protagonist's journeys into rural Georgia were patterned after his own college experiences with Johnson, he quickly identified the anonymous author to the campus community. In the June 1912 edition of the *Crimson and Gray,* George A. Towns published his suspicions that Johnson was the author of the *Autobiography,* thus revealing Johnson's secret within this reading circle almost as soon as its members would have read the book.[29] Because publishing the book with a black firm may have undermined his strategy of concealment, Johnson's selection of a white job printer reproduced the effects of the conceit of secrecy: as an autobiography, it was entirely consistent that the protagonist would have selected a publisher that catered to unknown amateur authors and, further, that he would have done business with a white firm. Going to a black job printer would have signaled the "ex-colored man's" return to the world he had forsaken in order to pass for white.

◢

Given Johnson's professional network and range of options, it is rather duplicitous of him to imply that he was *forced* to choose Sherman, French as his publisher. It seems more accurate to say that Johnson actively selected the firm and that he did so with two related aims: to cultivate a diverse audience for the novel and to trade off of the firm's marginal status. As a job printer located in Boston, Sherman, French did not offer prestige, but it did broaden the potential public to which the book could be directed. The company's imprint would encourage white readers to consider the book because its titles were not usually associated with the unseemly "race question"; the author's affiliation with Sherman, French would legitimize the book's nonpartisan approach to a thorny and disquieting political problem.[30]

In this, Johnson evinced a shrewd business sense. By choosing Sherman, French he capitalized on a crucial development in the publishing world: the shift in power from the "gentleman publisher" to the "businessman publisher." Sherman, French represented an old tradition that was becoming functionally obsolete in the publishing industry by the early 1900s. Book making and book selling were no longer valued as craft labor performed by men of culture (and, usually, of leisure) who served art, not commerce; in the age of corporate capitalism, writing, reading, and publishing were viewed as commodities to be systematically exploited.[31]

Johnson understood this and played one sector of the industry against the other to further his own ambitions. On the one hand, he recognized that a significant part of the novel's marketability lay in its status as an autobiography and that his association with Sherman, French facilitated this claim. On the other hand, in order to sell the book, the fiction of "authenticity" had to be perpetuated for as long as possible and as assertively as possible. Still stationed in Nicaragua when the novel was released, Johnson relied on a select group to collaborate with him on this task. He drafted his entire family into his confidence and directed their efforts to promote this illusion on his behalf.

Grace Nail Johnson and her brother, John Edward Nail, headed up an informal publicity committee in the United States. Grace informed her husband that she planned "to suggest that the publisher send T[heodore] Roosevelt (as editor of *Outlook*) and also Dr. Felix Adler [copies of the book]—also to send us a copy of the *Hibbert Journal* (since it is a quarterly) containing a review of the book."[32] John Edward Nail and his father, John B. Nail, were to use their clout as wealthy real estate agents in Brooklyn and Manhattan to convince Brentano's to order copies of the book. Johnson also counted on the Nail family to spread word about the book within their circle of New York's black elite. "I know you will do all in your power to help give the book a start," Johnson told his father-in-law. "Talk it and write it to all of your friends and acquaintances," he suggested, but "without revealing your knowledge of the authorship." Johnson explained this caution: "There will be some of our mutual friends who will suspicion [*sic*] that I am the author; you need not deny it, only evade a direct answer, [and] that will all help to create interest and stir up curiosity."[33]

Johnson's family enjoyed a different social prominence in the black world of Jacksonville, Florida. Helen Johnson was a beloved retired schoolteacher at the all-black Stanton School, and the late James Johnson had been an esteemed minister and benevolent landlord in the community. Still, Johnson's mother had a role to play in drumming up support for the *Autobiography*. "Dear Boy," Helen Johnson wrote to her son, "I will do as you say concerning your book, and let a few read it, but enlighten no one as to the Author." Rosamond Johnson promised his brother that he would promote the book the best way he knew how; he would tempt theatrical producers into adapting the novel into a play.[34]

Johnson refused to be bound by Sherman, French's less-than-aggressive promotion of his book. He was full of his own publicity ideas, and he used his well-placed family to stimulate interest in and demand for the novel. His own success in musical theater primed Johnson to accept new protocols of cultural production. No stranger to the ways of commercial publishing, Johnson grasped what publisher Frank Doubleday observed about the art of selling books: "Each book is its own individual advertising problem. . . . The only thing about which you can be absolutely certain is that, if you have a reasonably good novel or history or nature book, there are people who will buy it. The problem is to reach and tell them about it, and to do this with as little waste of energy as possible."[35] Since Sherman, French, and Company was not predisposed to spend much energy cultivating the public's interest, it fell to Johnson to devise a marketing plan for the novel. Reluctant to claim the book was "a reasonably good novel"—he wanted critics to tell him that—he was quick to see how the novel's artistic ambitions also implied a way to sell the book. Writing to his wife Grace, Johnson explained:

> I wrote the book to be taken as a true story, and it is proven that I am suffi-cently a master of the technical art of writing to make it impossible for even so keen a critic as the one on the [*New York*] *Times* to say that the story is *not* true. . . . But in it all, the absolute secrecy of the authorship must be maintained. You can see the importance of this from the *Times* review; as soon as it is known that the author is a colored man who could not be the character in the book, interest in it will fall. There must always be in the reader's mind the thought that, at least, it may be true.[36]

Clearly, for Johnson in 1912, an important value of the book lay in its anonymity. He wanted readers to believe that the phenomenon of a ra-cially mixed man passing as white was one that was widespread and pos-sibly at play in any and every community (and, possibly, in any and ev-ery white family) throughout the country. As an "autobiography," the novel insists upon the realism of this point. Faced with such an "authen-tic" narrative, the reader must respond in one of two ways: paranoia or acceptance. Johnson described this effect to his publisher: "No one can read this book without feeling that he has been given new light on the complexities of this social problem; that he has had a glimpse behind the scenes of this race-drama which is here being enacted; that he has been taken upon an elevation and has caught a bird's eye view of the conflict which is being waged."[37]

White readers responded as Johnson hoped they would. All appreci-ated the cool, rational tone of the book; for such an explosive topic, the writer avoided divisive rhetoric and cant. Others enjoyed observing "the inner life of the Negro," as the *Albany Argus* put it. Scenes of gambling, of color-caste prejudice among blacks, of cakewalking, jazzing, preaching—and lynching—were provocative encounters that titillated white critics. Though some complained of the writer's narcissism and egotism, and while others thought that the novel duped readers into ignoring "the dangers of race amalgamation," most critics (with the predictable excep-tion of southern reviewers), appreciated the book and accepted the premise that the book was actually autobiographical. This pleased Johnson no end.

The issue of whether the novel was a "true" autobiography did not vex African-American critics in the same ways that the genre question con-cerned white critics, nor did African Americans find the narrator's status as a person of mixed race disturbing in and of itself. For example, the *Washington* [D.C.] *Bee* suggested that the autobiography would be "especially interesting . . . for the reason that the people of this city furnish some of the strong incidents of the story." The *Bee* cared less about the passing theme or the threat of miscegenation; its reviewer seemed relieved that the narrator married into the white upper class. Rather, the smart set of D.C. read the book as a social mirror reflecting the community's significance within the world of the black middle class back to itself.[38]

For some readers, however, the view of black community life presented by the ex-colored man was not so flattering. What distressed these readers was precisely what most piqued white readers' attention: the depictions of the "inner life of the Negro." Relating the text of Father John Brown's soul-stirring sermon, verbally diagramming the exuberant high steps of the cakewalk, or explaining the complicated rhythms and chords of ragtime piano were cultural habits that merited description; publicizing the genius of black folk culture might aid the cause of racial uplift. But delving into the dens of gambling and drinking, celebrating the shams of thieves and con artists, analyzing the bigoted attitudes of blacks toward one another—these were cultural secrets that ought not to have been exposed, especially to a white readership.

The *New York Age* and *Springfield* [Mass.] *Republican* leveled such a critique against the book. Compared to Booker T. Washington's *Up from Slavery*, the *Autobiography* lacked the "constructive" and "optimistic" outlook of the Tuskegee chancellor's doctrines of self-improvement. The book's "practical importance" lay in its value as a "warning account of the Negro underworld of the big city."[39] The *Chicago Defender* would not even grant the book such qualified merit. Indeed, the newspaper refused to review the book at all, most likely because its theme and plot outcome violated the *Defender's* code of reportorial ethics: "If [a story] is scandal, if it is a knock against the other fellow or if it is just one line that will hinder or discourage[,] it has no place in the newspapers published in the interest of the race." And in the case of *The Autobiography of an Ex-Colored Man*, the *Defender* adhered to its code.[40]

Johnson's novel uprooted the cultural grain that institutions such as the *Chicago Defender* sought to sow. The narrator's decision to renounce his black identity in order to lead his life as a white man no doubt shocked readers who wanted the novel to promote a more virtuous model of racial identity formation. Writing in Atlanta's *Southern Life* magazine, the journalist and independent publisher Charles Alexander lamented that the *Autobiography*'s outcome justified the idea that being "colored" was a shameful condition to be rejected at all costs. He had hoped that the book would stand as testimony to another point: "that the color of a man's skin is not a badge of inferiority; that it ought not furnish those of a different complexion with the excuse to hate, demean, and debar."[41]

Johnson enjoyed the controversy the novel sparked within black circles. He knew that he had given voice to difficult truths that would have otherwise remained buried by the morally rigorous dictates of racial uplift. To prolong the debate—and to stimulate sales of the book—Johnson kept up his charade when he returned to the United States from Nicaragua. Like the liminal figure of the ex-colored man, Johnson passed in and out of scenes where his book was the subject of discussion. At parties, he eavesdropped on conversations in which the novel was by turns praised and lambasted. He kept track of the rumors about the author's identity: many blacks had personal friends or acquaintances who passed for white; were any of those people the scribbling culprit? One man boldly stepped forward to capitalize on the confusion produced by the novel's anonymous source. At a social gathering the man asked Johnson's opinion about the rumors and then disclosed his "secret": he himself had written the book![42]

◢

However much he relished playing the role of a literary trickster in public, Johnson harbored his own "secrets" about the meaning of his authorship in his personal life. He was not a young man when he finished the *Autobiography*. At forty-one, he had high hopes for the novel's success. At his modest best, Johnson admitted that "the book makes a very presentable volume and doesn't read badly. I do hope it will have some success."[43] In a bolder moment he specified just what kind of "success" he hoped it would yield, declaring to his wealthy father-in-law: "I also hope that we pick up a few hundreds, or better, a few thousands on the book."[44]

The financial success of *The Autobiography of an Ex-Colored Man* would certainly have eased its cash-poor author of certain woes. His own middle-class background and his wife's upper-class inheritance impressed upon Johnson the importance of being both earnest and prosperous. But Johnson was a man of letters; money was not the main chance for him. If it were, he would have stayed in the United States, writing best-selling musical scores with his brother and Bob Cole. Material prosperity was not the only goal for Johnson; class and cultural status were.[45]

However, his quest for prestige as a nationally respected author was threatened during the writing of the novel. Over the course of his tenure in Nicaragua, Johnson became embroiled in a "race-drama" of his own that concluded with his dramatic departure from the consular service in 1913. The harm done to Johnson's self-esteem during this political conflict, evident in his letters and diaries from this period, suggests that his aspirations for personal authority were directly and painfully related to the publication of the *Autobiography*.

From the very start, Johnson's diplomatic appointment was politically charged, the result of power-brokering between President Theodore Roosevelt and Booker T. Washington, and between the president of Tuskegee Institute and his political rivals.[46] Not one to settle for favors, Johnson was determined to advance through the ranks of the diplomatic corps on his own merit.[47] Indeed, part of the reason he refused his family's pleas to leave Nicaragua was that he saw the opportunity offered him: if he could protect U.S. interests during a dangerous civil war, then he could be trusted with more responsibilities in other lands.[48]

Rising through the ranks of the consular service meant leaving Latin America, though, for authority and respect were granted only to those diplomats assigned to European posts. Johnson knew this, and he repeatedly asked to be transferred from Nicaragua to France. At each turn, he was denied.[49] Johnson harbored no illusions about these rejections; they were specific acts of discrimination against him because he was black. By 1910 President William H. Taft actively sought to cultivate the southern vote. To gain electoral ground in the Democrats' territory, Taft could not afford to support the promotions of African-American civil servants within the federal system, so the consular service rejected Johnson's requests. When Woodrow Wilson succeeded Taft two years later, neither Republicans nor blacks could hold rank positions in the new administration. As Johnson recalled in his memoir: "The South, it appeared, had taken the election of a Southern-born president, the first (to be elected) in sixty-four years, together with a Cabinet in which the proportion of Southern-born portfoilos was one-half, as a signal that the country had been turned over not only to the Democratic Party in general, but to the South in particular."[50]

Johnson's ambition could not be honored in this setting. He tried his hand at political deal-making but with no luck. The continual rebuffs and refusals wore down his confidence and self-esteem. "To say that I was bitterly disappointed would be putting it mildly," Johnson confided to his wife. "It [the denials] took the run out of me for a while."[51] Johnson was offered a slim carrot—a new assignment to the Azores—but this was not what he wanted. He wanted a portfolio in the heart of the empire and not a watchtower shift in its outposts. When Johnson presented his case to

William Jennings Bryan, the secretary of state flatly stated that, as a Republican in a Democratic administration, Johnson was lucky to have any berth at all. Johnson interpreted Byran's statement to mean more: "I left [him] with this clearly in mind," he recalled. "I was up against politics plus race prejudice." There was no way out of Corinto for Johnson. The only way he could recover from the humiliation of these refusals was to resign.[52]

To be forced to succumb to "circumstances over which [he had] no control"[53] must have frustrated Johnson deeply. For at the same time that he was writing his final drafts of the *Autobiography*, he was negotiating with political characters whose wills he could not change. Johnson may have experienced a "freedom of motion" while experimenting with the more flexible genre of prose fiction, but he also found his political ambitions restricted, mocked, and denied precisely because he dared to think that true talent transcended the bounds of color.[54]

Johnson's resignation from the consular service underscored the personal importance he attached to the 1912 publication of the *Autobiography*. Not only would a critically renowned novel mark Johnson's arrival as an intellectual of merit,[55] it would, perhaps, also sensitize the public to the "race problem" and lead to a peaceful resolution of this national crisis. If Booker T. Washington accomplished just that with his history-making speech at the Atlanta Cotton States Exposition in 1895, why could not a brilliant writer use his medium—in this case, the novel—to similar advantage? Diplomacy works in many ways.[56]

This may explain why Johnson deliberately circulated copies of the *Autobiography* to his colleagues and superiors in the consular service. Undoubtedly, he wanted to promote his book and counted these men as part of the buying public; they shopped at leading bookstores in New York, Washington, and San Francisco, and they assured Johnson that they would circulate the book within their circles.[57] But these were also consumers with political clout—Wilbur J. Carr was director of the consular service; the diplomat Charles E. Eberhardt, Custom House official Charles A. Stephens, and New York jurist Arthur R. Thompson were men with connections to Washington and the White House. Impressing these readers (and others like them) offered Johnson a particular satisfaction that differed in quality and degree from the praise he received from the liberal elite, black or white, of bourgeois Manhattan.

Of course, Johnson never acknowledged to these men that he had written the book; he simply recommended it to them as an interesting read. Carr, Eberhardt, Stephens, and Thompson suspected that Johnson had written the account, but their colleague neither refused nor denied their pleas "to know the author who modestly hides his identity," as one of them teased. Johnson's silence may have been in keeping with his directive to his family and close friends not to divulge "the secret of authorship," but it also allowed him a way to speak out against the Taft and Wilson administrations' employment policy. By refusing to grant his colleagues' requests to be promoted into the ranks of his confidence, Johnson issued his own rejection of the consular service's discriminatory protocol.[58] This certainly was the case with Wilbur Carr. When he learned of Johnson's resignation, he accepted the decision "with a great deal of regret." Johnson had enclosed a copy of Brander Matthews's review of the *Autobiography* with his resignation to Carr, who responded with obvious embarrassment: "It must be a great satisfaction to you to have such a high commendation from a man like [him]."[59] In the process of revealing his authorial identity to Carr, Johnson forced his superior to recognize his departure as the unfair effect of cruel policy.

⌐

"Brander Matthews writes me that he received the clippings you sent," Johnson wrote to his wife in 1912. "He says this is a poor time for any book, but adds that my book has the stuff in it to live through a political campaign."[60] As we have seen, various forces converged to define the public life of the 1912 edition of *The Autobiography of an Ex-Colored Man*.

Johnson's decision to let Sherman, French, and Company publish the novel both promoted and undermined the book's market value. On the one hand, choosing that firm lent credence to the book's autobiographical claims. Obscure and white-owned, Sherman, French shielded Johnson's anonymity to a degree that heightened the fiction that the novel's narrator was a "real" black man passing for white. By the same token, as an old-style "job printer for authors," the publisher was uninterested in converting the public's interest in the book into high-volume sales. Johnson's attempts to compensate for this limiting protocol indicate how new market conditions reinforced the racial barriers that blocked African-American authors from achieving uncontested status as national authors. The transformation of author-publisher relations worked at cross-purposes in this instance because the commercially minded Johnson needed but could not persuade the "gentlemanly" firm to take the financial risks necessary to make the book a lasting success. And yet, only a company like Sherman, French would accept Johnson's manuscript; a mainstream white publisher familiar with the work of Chesnutt, Dunbar, and Washington would reject it out of hand. As it turns out, then, the very features that made Sherman, French a strategic choice for Johnson also led to the book's going out of print by 1916.[61]

Black periodicals also played a contradictory role in the life of the novel's first edition. Johnson's desire for anonymous authorship precluded him from working with a black publisher. As a nationally renowned musician and politician, his name would have been too valuable a commodity for an African-American publishing house not to trade upon. Paradoxically, because he was so famous within black circles, Johnson had to sign on with a white firm in order to "keep the secret of authorship" secure.

Even so, for all of the political controversy and dialogue the novel sparked in black reading circles, it is unlikely that conventional outlets within black print culture would have sustained the book any longer than did Sherman, French. At the time the book was released, major black newspapers—the *New York Age, Chicago Defender,* and *Washington Bee,* for example—did not run regular book review columns, nor did the papers consistently advertise new books.[62] Compounding this problem, the national magazines that actively sponsored fiction writing and reading—Boston's *Colored American Magazine,* Atlanta's *Voice of the Negro,* and Philadelphia's *McGirt's*—had ceased publication altogether by 1912. Clearly, this weakened infrastructure hampered distribution of the book. Later in the decade, new venues emerged and took up the charge, as the *Autobiography* was serialized in Chicago's *Half Century Magazine* in 1919. In 1924, Johnson refused to issue serial rights to the *Pittsburgh Courier* because, he claimed, the novel had already been published by the black press twice.[63] Ironically, between his efforts to disclaim the novel as his own, and his subsequent decision to make the novel readily accessible to the black reading public, Johnson may have stemmed the book's sales.

The complications involved in finding the right publisher and venue for the book follow from a deeper problem with the novel. In 1912, the general reading public found *The Autobiography of an Ex-Colored Man* difficult to understand. Its theme, narrative style, and politics challenged the ideologies of "romantic racialism" (typified by the benign condescension of Thomas Nelson Page's plantation fiction and the explicit cruelty of Thomas Dixon's historical novels) and of African-American espousal of "racial uplift." The ambiguity and ambivalence that characterize the *Autobiography* perplexed white readers and set the black reading public on edge; neither audience knew how to respond to a novel that made an aesthetic virtue out of failure and dared to argue that the very idea of race was a social fiction.[64] Even the NAACP—whose integrationist platform and interracial membership was considered avant-garde in 1912—resisted embracing the novel's message. With a circulation of at least 9,000 readers nationwide, the *Crisis* had the potential to interpret the novel for the organization's member-subscribers and to promote sales of the book.[65] But the monthly magazine did not review the book until November 1912, and its late notice merely reiterated the publisher's promotional copy for the book. This angered Johnson, who suspected that professional jealousy may have been at work: the tempermental "Dr. Du Bois" probably was flexing his muscles against Johnson, whom the editor probably supposed was an ally of his archenemy, Booker T. Washington.[66] Du Bois's enmity toward Johnson eventually dissipated, however, and, once Johnson joined the national staff of the NAACP in 1916, their rivalry stimulated a productive alliance.

All of which is to say (as Brander Matthews tried to console Johnson), timing was key, and timing could resolve as many problems as it generated. "Secret" sources in Johnson's private papers strongly suggest that historical timing was, perhaps, the crucial factor determining the fate and meaning of the 1912 edition of *The Autobiography of an Ex-Colored Man*. For by the time of the 1927 Knopf edition, Johnson's anonymity was no longer—indeed, his name was prominently associated with the book. Nor was the question of whether or not the narrator's claims and experiences were "true"; its confirmed status as "fiction" kept such criticisms at bay. If anything, the novel's realism was measured by Johnson's accuracy in predicting the rise of black folk culture as a national art form. In other words, by 1927, the book's power as a statement of prophecy rather than as a narrative construct questioning the nature of testimony itself became the focal point of discussion. Consequently, the attendant issues of literary form were all but lost in the critical discussion of the book.

Recalling Johnson's artistic risks in introducing his novel to the reading public soon after the turn of the nineteenth century restores our appreciation of the primacy of literary form to his project. Nonetheless, these sources also reveal how deeply personal that narrative experiment was for Johnson. The novel's composition and success symbolized his need to rescue himself from the political humiliation he suffered during his final years in the consular service. Thus, the manuscript evidence chronicling the evolution of the novel allows us to distinguish more accurately between the autobiographical "I" of the text and Johnson's personal voice. For in the end—and unlike his protagonist—Johnson did not concede his ambition and self-respect for the outer trappings of success. Writing this novel in 1912, in such a highly "secretive" way, James Weldon Johnson not only launched his literary career, he saved his creative life.

NOTES

All manuscript sources cited in this essay are located in the James Weldon Johnson Memorial Collection of the Beinecke Rare Book and Manuscript Library at Yale University. Permission to quote from these materials was granted by the Yale Collection of American Literature, Beinecke Rare Book and Manuscript Library at Yale University, and by Ollie Sims Okala for the estate of James Weldon Johnson. This essay was made possible through the generous support of a Beinecke Summer Graduate Fellowship in 1994, and I thank the Beinecke Library's reference staff and curator Patricia C. Willis for their expert help. Beryl Satter, Jill G. Watts, Julia Ehrhardt, and C. Cybele Raver offered useful criticism of this work in its draft stages; my thanks to them for their support.

1. Knopf introduced the novel in the autumn of 1927 as part of its Blue Jade Library Series. The goal of this series was "to cover the field of semi-classic, semi-curious books . . . which for one reason or another have enjoyed great celebrity but little actual distribution." See Alfred A. Knopf, Borzoi Books Catalog in Scrapbook re: Autobiography of an Ex-Colored Man (1912). On the standardization of the 1927 edition, see the "Notes on the Text" in the most recent printings of the novel by Vintage (1989) and Penguin (1990).

2. In his biography of Johnson, Eugene Levy describes Johnson's political style as a combination of finesse and aggression, remarking that Johnson directed the NAACP's activities with an "iron fist" fitted into a "velvet glove" (*James Weldon Johnson: Black Leader, Black Voice* [Chicago: University of Chicago Press, 1973], esp. chaps. 8–12).

3. For important analyses of this period, see the following: C. Vann Woodward, *The Strange Career of Jim Crow*, 3d rev. ed. (New York: Oxford University Press, 1974); Rayford W. Logan, *The Betrayal of the Negro: From Rutherford B. Hayes to Woodrow Wilson* (New York: Collier's, 1964); August Meier, *Negro Thought in America, 1880–1915: Racial Ideologies in the Age of Booker T. Washington* (Ann Arbor: University of Michigan Press, 1968); Lawrence J. Friedman, *The White Savage: Racial Fantasies in the Postbellum South* (Englewood Cliffs, N.J.: Prentice-Hall, 1970); Joel Williamson, *The Crucible of Race: Black-White Relations in the American South since Emancipation* (New York: Oxford University Press, 1986); and W. Fitzhugh Brundage, *Lynching in the New South: Georgia and Virginia, 1880–1930* (Urbana: University of Illinois Press, 1993).

4. For a cogent discussion of literature's role in forging a national consensus on the "race question" following the Civil War, see Nina Silber, *The Romance of Reunion: Northerners and the South, 1865–1900* (Chapel Hill: University of North Carolina Press, 1993), esp. chap. 5.

5. Johnson, *Along This Way* (New York: Viking, 1935), 301.

6. Aaron Douglas to James Weldon Johnson (hereinafter JWJ), June 26, 1927, James Weldon Johnson Correspondence, Yale University, ser. 1, box 6, folder 132.

7. JWJ to Broun, May 2, 1924, ser. 1, box 4, folder 62.

8. Johnson reminisced about Matthews in his published memoir, *Along This Way*, 193. In *The End of American Innocence* (New York: Alfred A. Knopf, 1959), 63–64, Henry F. May described Matthews as "Columbia's specimen of the literary Grand Old Man" who combined "the gentleman's club and the most respectable Bohemia." Matthews mentored Johnson over the course of his career, consistently putting his resources at Johnson's disposal. For example, Matthews placed Johnson's poem "Fifty Years" in the *New York Times* (Jan. 1, 1913), from which point Johnson's career as a nationally renowned poet began. Matthews also wrote the introduction to Johnson's debut collection of verse, *Fifty Years and Other Poems* (1917). Johnson trusted Matthews so much that he directed his wife to appoint Matthews as executor of his literary estate. JWJ to Grace Nail Johnson (hereinafter GNJ), May 12, 1912, ser. 3, box 41, folder 21. For an interpretive account of Johnson and Matthews's relationship, see Lawrence J. Oliver, *Brander Matthews, Theodore Roosevelt, and the Politics of American Literature, 1880–1920* (Knoxville: University of Tennessee Press, 1992), chap. 2.

9. Between 1897 and 1915 Johnson cultivated a favorable but complex relationship with Washington. Johnson used Washington's resources as shrewdly as Washington traded on Johnson's evolving reputation. Charles Anderson recognized Johnson's appeal when he drafted the prosperous celebrity to join the Colored Republican Club as its treasurer in 1904 and then as president in 1905. Fred Moore appreciated the smooth intelligence of Johnson's wit when he offered him an editorial column at the Washington-owned *New York Age* in 1914. That Anderson and Moore acted on Washington's orders suggests that the politician-schoolteacher kept a sharp eye on Johnson's activities. See Levy, *James Weldon Johnson*, 99–102. For Johnson's reasons for wanting the consular post, see his *Along This Way*, 221–24.

10. Johnson, *Along This Way*, 238.

11. JWJ to Matthews, [c. 1908], ser. 1, box 13, folder 315.

12. During this period in Johnson's career, his wife fed his literary ambitions. Their correspondence shows her to be a frank, disciplined organizer who served effectively as Johnson's literary agent in New York. Johnson routed verse manuscripts to her which Grace then shopped around to poetry magazines. Grace forthrightly queried after Johnson's work and reminded him to stay focused on his literary projects. In an exemplary letter, Grace advised Johnson not to let the critical success of the *Autobiography* distract his attention from his work at hand: "Get your poems all corrected, so that you can send those off to Sherman, French & Co.— You haven't many more to do have you? . . . Don't start dramatizing the 'On Our Own' story—finish up what is already at hand. Wish I could help you in some way—if all works well we'll soon be together again. I'm sure our energies are being expended in trying to do the right thing honestly and to our best ability. So that must mean ultimate success." GNJ to JWJ, May 26, 1912, ser. 3, box 40, folder 4.

13. JWJ to GNJ, May 18, 1912, ser. 3, box 41, folder 21. Johnson also complained to his political sponsors about the living conditions in Latin America. See the following in Louis R. Harlan and Raymond W. Smock, eds., *The Booker T. Washington Papers*, 14 vols. (Urbana: University of Illinois Press, 1977): JWJ to Booker T. Washington (hereinafter BTW), Apr. 9, 1908, 9:494–95; and Charles W. Anderson to BTW, Nov. 30, 1910, 10:495–96.

14. This was especially the case in Corinto, where his duties increased considerably, given the traffic in American commerce and naval intelligence through the port city and because of the country's unstable political situation.

15. For Johnson's personal accounts of this turmoil, see *Along This Way,* chaps. 25–26; JWJ to GNJ, Aug. 17 and 31, 1912, ser. 3, box 40, folder 22; and JWJ Scrapbook, box 7, folder 2, "Nicaragua." Though the main theaters of battle were at the capital city of Managua and the east coast city of Bluefields, Corinto was a key port for the deployment of the U.S. Marines. Corinto was also the site where the rebel leader General Luis Mena surrendered to U.S. forces. For a concise summary of the event and the issues involved, see Lester H. Brune, *Chronological History of United States Foreign Relations: 1776 to January 20, 1981,* 3 vols. (New York: Garland, 1985), 1:511, and Karl Bermann, *Under the Big Stick: Nicaragua and the United States since 1848* (Boston: South End Press, 1986), chap. 9. On Venezuela, see Judith Ewell, *Venezuela: A Century of Change* (Stanford, Calif.: Stanford University Press, 1984), chap. 2.

16. JWJ to Matthews, [c. 1908], ser. 1, box 13, folder 315. Johnson's letter to Matthews produces some confusion in dating the composition of the *Autobiography.* In *Along This Way,* Johnson states that he began the novel in New York City and finished it in Venezuela; Nicaragua drops off his literary map, as far as the novel is concerned. However, the earliest draft manuscript of the novel (JWJ MSS+ 141) includes notations that are clearly written in Grace Nail Johnson's hand, suggesting that the timing may be different. In chapter 11, she practiced writing her name variously "Grace E. Nail," "Grace E. Johnson," and "Grace Nail Johnson"—apparently trying to decide whether to keep her maiden name or not. Johnson proposed to Grace while he was in New York in October 1909, when he was on a leave in between departing Venezuela for Nicaragua. The couple married in February 1910, and Grace accompanied Johnson to Corinto, where she stayed until the fall of 1911. What this suggests—since Grace's markings are found on the earliest draft of the novel—is that the book was not finished before Johnson left Venezuela for Nicaragua.

17. JWJ to Matthews, [c. 1908], ser. 1, box 13, folder 315.

18. Johnson, *Along This Way,* 170. For the entire account of the episode, see 166–70.

19. Johnson, *The Autobiography of an Ex-Colored Man* (New York: Vintage, 1989), 3.

20. JWJ to Carl Van Doren, Dec. 28, 1922, ser. 1, box 21, folder 493. It is a small irony to note that this same practice—sending unknown authors to small job printers—was one Johnson himself recommended to the many amateur writers who solicited his help after he became part of the mainstream literary establishment. In 1938, for example, Johnson advised the young Gwendolyn Brooks that her poems were not "sufficiently outstanding to interest first-rate publishers" and directed her to Valiant House—a second-rate firm, in Johnson's opinion. See JWJ to Brooks, Apr. 4, 1938, ser. 1, box 4, folder 59.

21. For an account of these dealings, see Johnson's correspondence with Sherman, French, and Company, ser. 1, box 18, folder 435.

22. On the relationship between black fiction writers and the publishing industry, see Dickson Bruce, *Black American Writing from the Nadir: The Evolution of a*

Literary Tradition (Baton Rouge: Louisiana State University Press, 1989); Arlene Elder, *The "Hindered Hand": Cultural Implications of Early African-American Fiction* (Westport, Conn.: Greenwood Press, 1978); and Richard H. Brodhead's discussion of Charles Chesnutt's career in *Cultures of Letters: Scenes of Reading and Writing in Nineteenth-Century America* (Chicago: University of Chicago Press, 1993), chap. 6.

23. For a useful critique of the limits of "uplift" ideology in African-American fiction at this time, see Kevin Gaines, "Assimilationist Minstrelsy as Racial Uplift Ideology: James D. Corrothers's Literary Quest for Black Leadership," *American Quarterly* 45 (Sept. 1993): 341–69.

24. Eugene Levy, "Ragtime and Race Pride: The Career of James Weldon Johnson," *Phylon* 1, no. 4 (Spring 1968): 368n. 23.

25. As evidence of Johnson's favored status within the Tuskegee ring, see Emmett J. Scott to JWJ, Aug. 3, 1915, ser. 1, box 17, folder 430, in which Scott advised Johnson of an investment opportunity in a motion picture company, offering to act as the go-between for Johnson should he want to pursue the lead.

26. For a list of black job printers during the period, see Donald Franklin Joyce, *Gatekeepers of Black Culture: Black-Owned Book Publishing in the United States, 1817–1981* (Westport, Conn.: Greenwood Press, 1983), 64–65.

27. For example, in its society column, the *New York Age* reported Johnson's leaves from the consular service, and both the *Washington* [D.C.] *Bee* and *Crisis* welcomed Johnson home upon his final return to the United States.

28. For this agreement, see JWJ to Sherman, French, Feb. 17, 1912, ser. 1, box 18, folder 435.

29. Towns to JWJ, July 1, 1912, ser. 1, box 20, folder 484, and the June 1912 issue of the *Crimson and Gray* in JWJ Scrapbook re: Autobiography of an Ex-Colored Man (1912). See also Miles M. Jackson, "Letters to a Friend: Correspondence from James Weldon Johnson to George A. Towns," *Phylon* 29, no. 2 (Summer 1968): 182–98.

30. Some of the titles published by Sherman, French include Winfield Scott Kerr, *John Sherman, His Life and Public Service* (1908); Frank Carleton, *Doan's U* (1909); A. Stuart Chisholm, *The Independence of Chile* (1911); and Edward Smyth Jones, *The Sylvan Cabin: Ode on the Birth of Lincoln and Other Verse* (1911).

31. My thanks to Julia Erhardt, who outlined this transformation for me. On this shift, see Susan Coultrap-McQuin, *Doing Literary Business: American Women Writers in the Nineteenth Century* (Chapel Hill: University of North Carolina Press, 1990), chap. 2. On the competitive features of the commercial approach, see James L. W. West, *American Authors and the Literary Marketplace since 1900* (Philadelphia: University of Pennsylvania Press, 1988).

32. GNJ to JWJ, May 26, 1912, ser. 3, box 40, folder 4. According to the historian John Tebbel, Roosevelt was notorious for issuing glowing reviews of the books he read. That Grace Nail Johnson understood the potential of Roosevelt's cooperation signals her astuteness as an observer of literary culture. On Roosevelt's generous critical spirit, see Tebbel, *Between Covers: The Rise and Transformation of Book Publishing in America* (New York: Oxford University Press, 1987), 176. On the personal connections between Johnson, Matthews, and Roosevelt, see Oliver, *Brander Matthews*, 47–49, 55–56.

33. JWJ to John E. Nail, May 26, 1912, ser. 3, box 42, folder 59. See also JWJ to GNJ, June 26, 1912, ser. 3, box 41, folder 22.

34. See John Rosamond Johnson (hereinafter JRJ) to JWJ, Apr. 27, 1912, ser. 3, box 40, folder 11. According to Johnson, his brother recommended a different title for the novel—"The Chameleon"—which Johnson rejected (*Along This Way*, 238). Rosamond also suggested that Johnson write a sequel to the *Autobiography*, "One Home," that would offer a more optimistic outlook for the reader—yet another revision of the novel's conclusion. "It should be a book on the order of 'One Way Out' depicting the happiness of life, its success, etc.," Rosamond explained. "Where there is but one home for the man—as well as the woman. . . . Everyone is happy—." JRJ to JWJ, n.d., ser. 3, box 40, folder 11.

35. Doubleday, quoted in Tebbel, *Between Covers*, 139–40.

36. JWJ to GNJ, June 26, 1912, ser. 3, box 41, folder 22.

37. JWJ to Sherman, French, Feb. 17, 1912, ser. 1, box 18, folder 435.

38. *Washington Bee*, Aug. 3, 1912, 6. The *Bee's* pecuniary opinion about the ex-colored man's marriage was shaped by its editorial position on interracial marriage. The paper argued that such unions could only be justified if the relationship advanced the class status of the black partner ("Inter-Marriages," Oct. 19, 1912, 4).

39. The *New York Age* reprinted the *Springfield Republican's* review in its editorial column on June 6, 1912.

40. Editorial, "Can You See the Point?," *Chicago Defender,* Jan. 6, 1912, 4.

41. Charles Alexander, "Autobiography of an Ex-Colored Man," *Southern Life,* Aug. 12, 1912, in JWJ Scrapbook re: Autobiography of an Ex-Colored Man (1912). See also the New York *Amsterdam News's* clipping in this collection (Dec. 26, 1912), which argues that the narrator's decision to "pass" does not signal his abandonment of the race.

42. For Johnson's account of his surveillance activities, see *Along This Way*, 239.

43. JWJ to GNJ, June 7, 1912, ser. 3, box 41, folder 22.

44. JWJ to John B. Nail, May 26, 1912, ser. 3, box 42, folder 59.

45. For one interpretation of this point, see Levy, "Ragtime and Race Pride."

46. See the following in Harlan and Smock, *Booker T. Washington Papers:* Charles W. Anderson (hereinafter CWA) to BTW, Jan. 12, 1906, 8:498; BTW to CWA, Mar. 8, 1906, 8:541; CWA to BTW, Mar. 12, 1906, 8:546–47; CWA to BTW, May 27, 1907, 9:274–77; CWA to BTW, Nov. 30, 1910, 10:495–96; and BTW to Ralph Waldo Tyler, Dec. 1, 1911, 11:379–80.

47. Johnson argues that Roosevelt's interest was not to promote black advancement on principle but to salvage his electoral viability with black voters following the disastrous race riot in Brownsville, Texas, in 1906 (*Along This Way*, 250–51). For secondary accounts of the riot, see Herbert Shapiro, *White Violence, Black Response: From Reconstruction to Montgomery* (Amherst: University of Massachusetts Press, 1988), 106. For Johnson's objections to political patronage, see JWJ to GNJ, Nov. 16, [1912], ser. 3, box 41, folder 23. See Levy's careful, book-length study of Johnson's political career for more on this point (*James Weldon Johnson*).

48. Johnson discusses this point in *Along This Way,* but in his correspondence with his wife and family he is more candid about his career prospects.

49. On Johnson's efforts and rejections, see Levy, *James Weldon Johnson*, 112–13, 116–17. Johnson's letters to Grace describe poignantly how much he counted on the promotion. He insisted that she study French and, at times, wrote to her in the language to test her progress. Clearly, he hoped that France would be a more suit-

able place to bring his bride, and her language skills would no doubt have been an aid to his work there. See, for example, JWJ to GNJ, May 8 and 18, 1912, ser. 3, box 41, folder 21.

50. Johnson, *Along This Way*, 300–301. See also Levy, *James Weldon Johnson*, 122–24. On Taft's and Wilson's discriminatory policies, see Meier, *Negro Thought in America*, 164–65; Williamson, *Crucible of Race*, 356–58; and Friedman, *White Savage*, 152–62. Rayford W. Logan, *The Betrayal of the Negro: From Rutherford B. Hayes to Woodrow Wilson* (London: Collier-Macmillan, 1965), examines this point.

51. JWJ to GWJ, Sept. 10, [1927], ser. 3, box 41, folder 23.

52. Johnson, *Along This Way*, 293. Johnson submitted his letter of resignation to Bryan on September 1, 1913. Johnson's correspondence to his wife illustrates the full depth of his humiliation. See his exchange in JWJ to GNJ, ser. 3, box 41, folders 22–23.

53. JWJ to Bryan, Sept. 1, 1913, ser. 1, box 4, folder 71. In response, Bryan did not even acknowledge Johnson's achievement in the Nicaraguan affair, as if to imply that Johnson performed his duties without distinction.

54. Johnson seems to have vented his frustrations in his personal diaries. Of the twelve notebooks contained in his manuscript files, Notebook 3 (JWJ MSS 367) stands out for its hostility and cynicism. It was probably written between 1909 and 1910–11 (though it contains one entry marked 1919). Johnson penned mean, embittered entries that simply have no comparison to the moods in his other notebooks. It is clear that he was injured, and in his writing he strikes back. His patience with whites had been exhausted, and he seems unable to entertain the possibility of civic social relations with them. As he noted to himself: "The open counterfeit [with] which some white people treat the better class of colored is the sincerest complement [*sic*] they could pay." In another, he complained: "Success anyhow is barely less than taking a mean advantage of your fellows." It is a significant coincidence that Notebook 3 is the one in which Johnson played out some draft ideas for *The Autobiography of an Ex-Colored Man*. This is also another indication that he did not complete the novel in Venezuela (see note 16).

55. Johnson speaks very tenderly about this aspiration when he describes his reaction to the *New York Times*'s review of the novel. See JWJ to GNJ, June 26, 1912, ser. 3, box 41, folder 22.

56. That this was Johnson's ambition for the novel can be easily inferred from his prospectus outline to Sherman, French. See JWJ to Sherman, French, Feb. 17, 1912, ser. 1, box 18, folder 435. Reviewers responded favorably to this goal as well; see the notices in JWJ Scrapbook re: Autobiography of an Ex-Colored Man (1912).

57. JWJ to GNJ, Sept. 11 and Nov. 16, [1912], ser. 3, box 41, folder 23. See also Wilbur J. Carr to JWJ, Oct. 8, 1912, ser. 1, box 5, folder 82; Charles E. Eberhardt to JWJ, Mar. 6, 1913, ser. 1, box 5, folder 101; Charles A. Stephens to JWJ, Sept. 24, 1912, ser. 1, box 5, folder 102; and Arthur R. Thompson to JWJ, Oct. 23, 1912, ser. 1, box 5, folder 102.

58. William E. Gibbs argues that Johnson's departure from the consular service freed him to conduct a public attack on Wilson's foreign policy. Indeed, Johnson did use his post as contributing editor to the *New York Age* (1914–23) to snipe at the racist underpinnings of Wilson's foreign policy in Latin America and the Caribbean. Significantly, Johnson's series of essays exposing the abuses committed dur-

ing the U.S. intervention in Haiti (1915–20) provided a wedge that Warren G. Harding needed in his challenge to Wilson in the 1920 presidential campaign. The articles ran in the *Nation* and helped to stir the anti-imperialist electorate to vote Republican. See Gibbs, "James Weldon Johnson: A Black Perspective on 'Big Stick' Diplomacy," *Diplomatic History* 8 (Fall 1984): 329–47.

59. Wilbur J. Carr to JWJ, Sept. 22, 1913, ser. 1, box 5, folder 82.

60. JWJ to GNJ, Aug. 31, 1912, ser. 3, box 41, folder 22.

61. By 1915 Sherman, French, and Company was eager to be rid of its supply of the novel. See Sherman, French to JWJ, Sept. 10, 1915, ser. 1, box 18, folder 435.

62. In my reading of periodical literature from this era, the cultural work of encouraging novel reading was shouldered by monthly journals, both secular and religious. Two outstanding examples of this are the *A.M.E. Church Review* and the NAACP's *Crisis* magazine.

63. In this letter, Johnson refused to issue serial rights to Calvin, who was editor of the *Pittsburgh Courier,* because he claimed the novel had already been published in the black press. The second serialization was not identified or located. Floyd J. Calvin to JWJ, Mar. 7, 1924, and JWJ to Calvin, Mar. 11, 1924, ser. 1, box 4, folder 79.

64. The divided reception accorded to the novel most likely informed Johnson's 1928 essay, "The Dilemma of the Negro Artist," in which he considered the rival demands that white and black audiences required from African-American artists (*American Mercury* 15 [Dec. 1928]: 477–81).

65. Walter C. Daniels claims this figure was the paid circulation rate (*Black Journals of the United States* [Westport, Conn.: Greenwood Press, 1982], 140).

66. JWJ to GNJ, Aug. 31, 1912, ser. 3, box 41, folder 22. There are two ways in which Du Bois may have known about Johnson's authorship. As a former professor at Atlanta University, Du Bois probably read the school's alumni bulletin and saw the June 1912 notice about the book. More simply, Du Bois may have felt threatened by a rival writer. Still enjoying the fame of *Souls of Black Folk* (1903), Du Bois had just released his first work of fiction, *The Quest of the Silver Fleece,* in October 1911. He unabashedly used the *Crisis* to promote the book, selecting illustrations from the novel to appear on the front cover and inside pages of the October 1911 issue. William Stanley Braithewaite was granted a page and a half to evaluate the novel. When compared to the slight treatment Johnson's novel received, it seems clear that Du Bois was acting out of self-interest.

CONTRIBUTORS

LYNNE M. ADRIAN is an associate professor of American studies at the University of Alabama. Her research includes a study of sex and gender in the ideology of Emma Goldman.

STEVEN BIEL teaches American studies courses at Brandeis University. He is the author of *Independent Intellectuals in the United States, 1910–1945* (1992) and *Down with the Old Canoe: A Cultural History of the* Titanic *Disaster* (1996).

JAMES P. DANKY, Newspapers and Periodicals Librarian, State Historical Society of Wisconsin, has published more than thirty reference works, bibliographies, and monographs on the radical press, women, and minorities, including *The German-American Radical Press: The Shaping of a Left Political Culture, 1850–1940* (1992, co-edited with Elliott Shore and Ken Fones-Wolf). Danky is also codirector of the Center for the History of Print Culture in Modern America and is working on a national bibliography of African-American newspapers and periodicals.

ELIZABETH DAVEY teaches in the Department of American Thought and Language at Michigan State University. Her research focuses on the publication, circulation, and influence of politically engaged poetries in the twentieth-century United States.

MICHAEL FULTZ is an associate professor in the Department of Educational Policy Studies at the University of Wisconsin, Madison, author of a number of journal articles, and a member of the editorial advisory board of the *Journal of Negro Education*. His research interests focus on African Americans and public education in America.

JACQUELINE GOLDSBY is an assistant professor of English at Cornell University. Her research focuses on representations of lynching in late nineteenth-century American literature.

NORMA FAY GREEN, director of the Graduate Journalism Program at Columbia College in Chicago, worked for twenty-five years in staff and management positions for newspapers, magazines, and book publishers in Michigan and Illinois. She teaches public affairs reporting, journalism history, and alternative press courses

273

and has published historical research on Chicago journalism, women journalists, the occupational imagery and mythology of journalism in popular culture, and network television coverage of terrorism.

VIOLET JOHNSON is an assistant professor in the Department of History at Agnes Scott College, Decatur, Georgia. Current research interests include Pan-Africanism and its reception in the United States.

ELIZABETH MCHENRY is an assistant professor of English at the University of Texas at Austin. She is completing a book on African-American literary societies and the culture of reading in the nineteenth- and early twentieth-century United States.

CHRISTINE PAWLEY is an assistant professor of information management at the College of St. Catherine, St. Paul, Minnesota. She is working on a study of the Wisconsin Traveling Library, 1920–50.

YUMEI SUN is a graduate student in American studies at the University of Maryland, College Park. Her dissertation research focuses on the role of the press in the Chinese diaspora.

RUDOLPH J. VECOLI has been a professor of history and director of the Immigration History Research Center at the University of Minnesota since 1967. Among his numerous publications are "Ethnicity and Immigration," in the *Encyclopedia of Twentieth-Century America* (1966), and "The Italian Diaspora," in the *Cambridge Survey of World Migration* (1995).

WAYNE A. WIEGAND is a professor in the School of Library and Information Studies at the University of Wisconsin, Madison, and codirector of the Center for the History of Print Culture in Modern America. He is author of *Irrepressible Reformer: A Biography of Melvil Dewey* (1996) and *Politics of an Emerging Profession: The American Library Association, 1876–1917* (1986).

Books in the History of Communication Series